Experimental Research Methods in Language Learning

OTHER TITLES IN THE RESEARCH METHODS IN LINGUISTICS SERIES

Quantitative Research in Linguistics, 2ⁿᵈ edition, Sebastian Rasinger
Research Methods in Applied Linguistics, edited by Brian Paltridge and Aek Phakiti
Research Methods in Interpreting, Sandra Hale and Jemina Napier
Research Methods in Linguistics, Lia Litosseliti

RESEARCH METHODS IN LINGUISTICS

Experimental Research Methods in Language Learning

AEK PHAKITI

BLOOMSBURY

LONDON • NEW DELHI • NEW YORK • SYDNEY

Bloomsbury Academic

An imprint of Bloomsbury Publishing Plc

50 Bedford Square	1385 Broadway
London	New York
WC1B 3DP	NY 10018
UK	USA

www.bloomsbury.com

Bloomsbury is a registered trade mark of Bloomsbury Publishing Plc

First published 2014

© Aek Phakiti, 2014

British Library Cataloguing-in-Publication Data

A catalogue record for this book is available from the British Library.

ISBN: HB: 978-1-4411-2587-3
PB: 978-1-4411-8911-0
ePDF: 978-1-4411-9793-1
ePub: 078 1 4411 2240 7

Library of Congress Cataloging-in-Publication Data

A catalog record for this book is available from the Library of Congress.

Typeset by Fakenham Prepress Solutions, Fakenham, Norfolk NR21 8NN
Printed and bound in India

CONTENTS

PREFACE

Language learning research is a growing discipline. Systematic and well-designed research is needed in order for this field of study to progress. The past few decades have seen a variety of new research paradigms and methodological approaches in language learning research, including quantitative research methods (e.g. survey research and experimental research), qualitative research methods (e.g. case study and ethnography) and mixed-methods research methods. This book focuses on a type of quantitative research (i.e. experimental research) that requires statistical analysis in order to make inferences and draw conclusions about language learning.

Why a new book focusing on experimental research?

Several published research books on language learning have covered the broad areas of quantitative, qualitative and/or mixed-methods research. Generally speaking, they provide a good coverage of the nature, principles, and methodology of language learning research. These books include Hatch and Farhady (1982), Seliger and Shohamy (1989), Nunan (1992), Brown and Rogers (2002), Mackey and Gass (2005), Dörnyei (2007), Nunan and Bailey (2009), and Paltridge and Phakiti (2010). Other books have focused on second language classroom research for language teachers (e.g. Chaudron 1988; McDonough & McDonough 1997; McKay 2006). In applied linguistics, some books are more about strategies for understanding research reports in language learning (e.g. Allison 2002; Perry 2005; Porte 2002, 2010). Porte (2010), for example, aims to help students and new researchers to critically read and appraise quantitative research papers in the field of second language learning. Allison (2002) provides a research approach to English language studies and discusses major issues in English language research, including a discussion of project, dissertation and thesis research and writing. Perry (2005) consists of two parts: approaches to research with examples taken from applied linguistics research and the components of a typical research article. There is, however, only limited guidance of how to go about conducting an experimental study.

Other research books devote themselves entirely to quantitative research methods (e.g. Brown 1988; Hatch & Lazaraton 1991). Brown (1988) explains the nature of second language quantitative research, particularly aiming at clarifying issues in statistics in second language research. Hatch and Lazaraton (1991) discuss the conceptual and statistical topics that are essential for good quantitative research. Mackey and Gass (2005) and Dörnyei (2007) provide some coverage of experimental research methods with examples taken from second language acquisition research. However, an in-depth discussion of more specific examples and the issues relevant to experimental research in language learning are needed for the reader to understand how experimental research can be implemented in a real-world research context. Since the general research methods books mentioned above aim to cover other types of research, such as non-experimental, survey research, case study and ethnography, they do not necessarily provide a full picture of what is actually involved in conducting experimental research.

Recently, there have been books dealing with specific types of research in language learning and use, such as survey research (Brown 2001b), research using case studies (Duff 2008), and research using discourse analysis (Paltridge 2006, 2012). To date, there has been no single-volume, comprehensive, yet accessible book on experimental research methods in language learning. One of the key goals of this book is to help students and researchers develop the ability to design an experimental study that can be carried out within the available time and using the resources available in a given context.

An experimental research methods book especially written for language learning research is needed, given the importance of specific examples and cases to research areas unique to the field of language learning. It can be argued that people can make sense of experimental research only when they see how it is actually applied in a real language learning research context. This book uses examples of experimental studies published in several major international journals, such as *Applied Linguistics, Language Learning, Language Teaching Research, Studies in Second Language Acquisition, TESOL Quarterly* and *The Modern Language Journal*. It discusses the underlying principles behind experimental research in language learning, including epistemological considerations and provide step-by-step guidelines of experimental research methodology. It illustrates the interrelatedness of the parts of the whole experimental research process.

Unlike most books, this book directly integrates applications of IBM® SPSS® (Statistical Package for Social Sciences) for statistical analyses with step-by-step instructions and data files for hands-on practice. The book forms a *gateway* into the often intimidating world of statistics for experimental research, and provides an opportunity for readers to ground their knowledge of statistics in a working knowledge of SPSS. It highlights the importance of a conceptual understanding of several statistical principles and the types of analysis necessary for successful experimental research, while minimizing the presentation of complex statistical formulas. The development of a working knowledge of SPSS will allow students to critically explore standard quantitative research and produce good research projects of their own. The book includes discussion on published studies and provides examples, guided questions and details of further suggested reading.

A distinctive feature of this book is its *companion website*, which houses online materials with up-to-date resources, lecture notes, data sets, and activities that cannot be made available in the print version. In particular, data files and samples will be provided that readers can analyze using SPSS in order for students to familiarize themselves with data analysis processes and gain insights into how to perform data analysis.

In summary, this book is introductory, yet in-depth in its treatment of the approaches to experimental research, and is comprehensive in the range of approaches it discusses. One important aim of the book is to make the subject of experimental research in language learning *accessible* and *meaningful* to readers without a background in this particular area. This book will also help readers develop their research literacy and their ability to not only critically evaluate, but also make use of the existing literature that utilizes experimental research as a means to understand a phenomenon of language learning.

Purpose and readership

Discussion on experimental research occurs in all the major journals and in many books in the area of language study and language learning. The intended audience for the book is third-year (or above) undergraduate and postgraduate students (e.g. Master of Arts [MA], Master of Education [Med], Master of Philosophy [MPhil], Doctor of Education [EdD], and Doctor of Philosophy [PhD]) in Applied Linguistics, TESOL (Teaching of English to Speakers of Other Languages) and Second Language Studies. The book is also suitable for experienced researchers wishing to expand their knowledge in experimental research in language learning. It is a comprehensive guide to conducting experimental research in the area of language learning.

Companion website of the book for instructors and students

A *companion website* hosted by the publisher is used to house online materials with up-to-date resources, lecture notes, data files, and useful activities that cannot be made available in the print version: http://www.bloomsbury.com/ experimental-research-methods-in-language-learning-9781441189110/

Errata
Despite my best attempts, some errors may appear in this book. An up-to-date list of corrections will be kept.

Comments/suggestions

The author would be grateful if you could send him your comments or suggestions so that he can improve this book in future editions and update the companion website. You can contact him at: aek.phakiti@sydney.edu. au or aek.phakiti@gmail.com

ACKNOWLEDGMENTS

I would first like to thank the following people who have been my academic mentors: Brian Lynch and Paul Gruba for their insightful knowledge about research methods and for their research supervision; Tim McNamara for his long-term dedication and inspiration to research and teaching; Brian Paltridge for his insight in language teaching research and for being such a great colleague at The University of Sydney; Carsten Roever for being such a good research adviser and friend; Jim Purpura for initially encouraging me to do a PhD degree, and for now being a wonderful colleague and friend; Janette Bobis for her academic and mentoring support; and Lourdes Ortega for her advice on several research issues.

I would also like to thank the many researchers and authors who have produced research methods books, chapters, and research publications that have helped me to deepen my understanding of the research issues and research methods involved in the field of language learning. Thanks go, in particular, to my colleagues and friends at The University of Sydney – Jack Richards, Marie Stevenson, Ken Cruickshank, Lindy Woodrow, Lesley Harbon and David Hirsh – for being there when I had some difficult questions to ask.

I am indebted to students who have taken the research methods unit at The University of Sydney. Many have read earlier drafts of this book, asked useful questions for clarification, and provided comments, helping me to refine my thinking. I particularly thank my research students, Robin Kyung Tae Kim, Tiefu Zhang, Rosmawati and Nick Zhi Bi, who were there for me when I needed them and who read so many drafts of my chapters.

I would like to thank Guy Middleton and Scott Molony, who worked very hard to read and help edit the book. I would next like to thank the many people at Bloomsbury for their assistance and particularly for being so patient with me and believing in me. Particular thanks go to Gurdeep Mattu, Andrew Wardell, Kim Storry and the many copy editors at Bloomsbury who worked with me to the completion of the book.

Finally, I would like to dedicate my work to my mum, who worked hard to bring up three children as a single mother; to my dad, who could not be here to see how far I have come; and to my two sisters, niece and nephew. Last but not least, I would like to thank Damir Jambrek, who has always been so understanding, caring and loving.

CHAPTER ONE

Introduction and Overview

Leading questions

1 What is research?
2 What do you think experimental researchers do in their research?
3 Do you think an experimental research design can provide an insight into language learning? Why or why not?

Introduction

This book aims to present a methodological framework of experimental research in language learning for people new to experimental research. This chapter introduces experimental research in language learning and the nature of academic and language learning research within applied linguistics. It aims to provide an overview of fundamental concepts of research in language learning in general (e.g. definitions of research, applied linguistics and language learning research). Such concepts are needed in an introductory chapter because they can be connected to associated concepts in experimental research introduced throughout this book. This chapter will also provide an overview of the contents of this book.

What is experimental research?

The first thing that comes to mind when you first hear or see the word "experiment" may be a scenario in which a group of scientists carefully examines subjects such as plants in a controlled environment. They, for instance, vary the amount of light and water available to their subjects, and measure changes in their subjects' growth before and after varying these conditions so that they can systematically compare the results of their analysis and decide which conditions yield the best outcome. Experimental research methods in language learning are similar to methods employed in this example. They, however, deal with language learners and aim to understand aspects of their learning. In language learning, for example, we would like to see whether a particular teaching strategy or activity could enhance students' learning performance. We may investigate whether a particular linguistic condition results in some form of difficulty in language acquisition among learners. Experimental research in language learning, unlike the botanical example above, does not usually occur in a scientific laboratory where all conditions are strictly controlled. In particular, learner participants are not locked up and can interact with the outside world. It is unrealistic for a language learning researcher to think that it is possible to control the influence of such interactions, and to do so is potentially unethical.

A glance at some experimental studies in language learning

Experimental research in language learning is usually conducted within a language classroom, which can be viewed as a real-life laboratory. Furthermore, unlike most natural science researchers, language learning researchers do not have complete control over all the variables that could influence experimental research outcomes. This is because human beings and the nature of learning and context are highly complex. Experimental research in language learning has a tradition of adopting the experimental principles and procedures used in human psychological research, which aims to understand what goes on in human minds, including those processes associated with learning, cognition, emotion and affect. Cognitive psychological research has influenced the way language learning research deals with language learners' psychology (Dörnyei 2005; Doughty & Long 2003). The approach to experimental research in this book is largely influenced by the way an experiment is considered and conducted in cognitive and psychological research generally, and in applied linguistics specifically.

Let us look at two sample studies in language learning that employed an experimental design.

Chen and Truscott (2010) examined the effects of repetition and first language (L1) lexicalization on incidental vocabulary learning using a posttest and delayed posttest experimental design. Seventy-two Taiwanese university students were *randomly assigned* into three groups (N = 24 per group). Each group received a different number of exposures to the target words. There were three phases of testing in this experiment: a reading comprehension task, an immediate posttest and a delayed posttest (two weeks later). It was found that the scores consistently increased with the number of input exposures.

Ammar and Spada (2006) investigated the effects of two corrective feedback techniques (recast and prompts) on students' language learning performance. The study focused on third-person possessive determiners (i.e. his and her). The study used a *quasi-experimental research design* because the study was conducted in three intact classes of English as a second language in Canada. The researchers used a pretest, immediate posttest and delayed posttest design to address the research aim. One class served as a *control group* for comparison purposes. There were 12 sessions (30–45 minutes each) over four weeks. There was one instruction session and 11 practice sessions, which included some semi-controlled and controlled practice. It was found that prompts were more effective than recasts.

According to these two examples, we can see that experimental studies compare research outcomes (e.g. learners' performance) according to the conditions that learners are exposed to. If an experimental study is conducted in an intact class, it is classified as *quasi-experimental*. This book will explore these types of research design.

Academic research

Research is a form of inquiry that involves questions and answers (Nunan 1992). We engage in some form of research activity on a daily basis, often without any formal recognition. For example, we may want to buy a new laptop, but we have some preferences and particular specifications we would like the laptop to have. We also have a limited budget. Perhaps with a computer-savvy friend, we then look up catalogs from different online stores. We eliminate many options as they are either beyond our budget or do not meet our specifications. We may end up with one laptop that is offered by two online stores (both of which we regard as trustworthy). Store A is more expensive, but offers an attractive deal including a free copy of Microsoft® Office® and anti-virus software. Store B is $300 cheaper than store A, but does not offer any special deal. We may look up how much it would cost to buy a Microsoft Office for Windows® license and anti-virus software only to discover that it costs about $300. We may then contact store A and inquire whether the store can offer a price matching the price offered by store B. Fortunately, store A accepts our proposal and we finally buy the laptop from store A and save $300. We have a bargain.

In this scenario, we have a goal to achieve, and a problem to solve (i.e. to buy the best laptop that suits our needs, within a limited budget). We collect information about prices, special deals, stores and their locations, and we eliminate choices and stores by means of comparison. Finally, we make an informed decision to buy a particular laptop. If we do not collect any information, we cannot be sure the price we pay is reasonable. Sometimes in academic research, we discover new significant findings that we did not anticipate. That would be a bargain as well. The processes involved in academic research are similar to those in this example.

Defining academic research

What is academic research? At the beginning of my first research methods class, I asked my students this question. While they came up with different ideas about its definition, some used the prefix re- (which means *again*) and *search* (which means to look for) to define academic research. They defined research as *searching again and again*. This seems to describe language learning research well – we want to make sure that our findings are replicable and generalizable to other groups of learners across different settings. Repetition and replication is likely to be necessary in many research areas, especially newly established ones. However, once the same issue/phenomenon (in different settings and groups of learners) is thoroughly understood by substantive previous research, we move on to new areas as new problems emerge and new methods become available. Hence *to search again and again* becomes a trivial activity.

Dörnyei (2007, p. 16) also notes that 'it's a waste of time … to … "reinvent the wheel" again and again.' Therefore we need to be careful not to research a topic that has already been well understood. In reality, however, it is difficult to know exactly when research has become substantive. This is due to the complexity of language learning, coupled with a lack of shared resources (e.g. limited access to academic journals or books) and different concepts of what constitutes language learning.

In this book, academic research is defined as *an intellectual act to discover new facts or knowledge by attempting to go beyond existing knowledge*. Academic researchers aim to improve existing knowledge by observing, collecting, and analyzing evidence. They make inferences and draw conclusions from the evidence. Research can lead to a cumulative body of knowledge that will ultimately improve ways of living and our understanding of the world (e.g. how to learn and teach languages successfully). In order to achieve these aims, researchers need to examine a topic or problem systematically. To succeed, academic research requires planned and organized actions for collecting and analyzing data in order to make appropriate inferences and warranted conclusions about the topic or problem under examination.

Primary and secondary academic research

On the one hand, *primary research* concerns first-hand data (referred to as *empirical data*) from research participants or documents to answer research questions. Empirical data can derive from tests, questionnaires, interviews, observations or publicly available documents. In language learning research, empirical data may derive from *natural data*, which include utterances language learners produce. *Secondary research*, on the other hand, does not require researchers to collect new empirical data. The most common types of secondary research are *library research* and a *review of the research literature*. Through secondary research, we can understand the body of cumulative knowledge and the recent developments of a theory.

Primary and secondary research studies are equally important for scientific knowledge about language learning. Primary research usually needs secondary research prior to the gathering of empirical data (e.g. in the form of a review of the literature). As mentioned earlier, we do not want our research to be trivial or to repeat mistakes made in previous studies. We also need to address research questions that are relevant and worth answering. Even in the case of new research areas, while there may have been no prior study of a particular topic, we still need to consider whether there have been other studies in the same locations and whether there are research methods available that are suitable for the aim of the research.

Applied linguistics and language learning research

Language is a tool used by humans to express their thoughts and emotions. It is a tool for social communication, and it plays a central cultural role. Applied linguistics is an interdisciplinary field of research inquiry that is mainly concerned with language use in social contexts. Hence, topics that deal with problems in human language use in society (e.g. language learning, language teaching, and language policy) are of interest and relevant to applied linguists. This field of inquiry emerged in the late 1950s when linguistic research had previously been narrowly focused on linguistic systems (Davies & Elder 2004). However, several real-world problems involving language and language use required more than an understanding of the language system itself. There was also a need for a better understanding of language use and socialization (see Davies & Elder 2004 for further discussion). Key areas of applied linguistics closely related to language education include language acquisition, learning and pedagogy, language testing and assessment, discourse and conversation analysis, and bilingualism and multilingualism. It is beyond the scope of this book to discuss in detail the different areas of language learning research. Macaro (2010) provides and discusses a comprehensive list of areas of research related to language learning. Lightbown and Spada (2013) also extensively cover topics in language learning.

In the applied linguistics literature, we see some discussion about the distinctions between first, second, third and foreign language learning (e.g. Macaro 2010; Ortega 2009). A first language (L1) is often referred to as the language that our parents and people in our society use in their daily conversations. A second language (L2) is generally referred to as a language second to the first language. English as a second language (ESL), for example, is discussed as English being learned and used by people whose first language is not English, but for whom English is the medium for daily communication (e.g. in the USA, UK, and Australia). English as a foreign language (EFL) is discussed as English being learned and used in a context in which the main language for communication is in learners' L1 (e.g. in China, Thailand, Brazil). You will notice that language learning can become complicated as people may learn more than two languages, and more and more people learn two or more languages simultaneously.

The distinction between second and foreign language learning can cause confusion in the field of second language acquisition (SLA), which is the sub-discipline of applied linguistics that aims to understand how people learn a second language and the factors that affect their language learning. SLA research not only examines second language learning, but also any foreign, third or fourth language learning. Due to the complexity of language learning, we see that the SLA literature often treats additional language and foreign language learning in the same second language acquisition framework. Of course, we know that learning a third language is not necessarily the same as learning a second language. A more solid theoretical framework for third or fourth language acquisition will eventually emerge as more research is conducted.

This book uses *language learning* as a broad umbrella term to cover these types of language learning. Furthermore, this book does not differentiate between language learning and language acquisition. There was an academic debate regarding the differences between acquisition and learning in the early years of SLA research (e.g. Krashen's hypotheses), but the issue has now been more or less resolved (Macaro 2010). Both terms refer to essentially the same thing and, therefore, can be used interchangeably. Furthermore, language learning and language use are inseparable because learners need to use their (limited) language knowledge in order to learn more, to improve and increase their proficiency, and to identify the mistakes they make through their interactions with other people.

The aims of language learning research

Generally speaking, language learning research aims to gain a better understanding of the nature of language learning in natural and instructed settings. It also aims to describe and explain individual and environmental factors that may affect the path, rate and success of language learning (see e.g. Ellis 2008; Gass & Mackey 2012; Lightbown & Spada 2013; Ortega 2009). Language learning research can yield not only advanced knowledge of how languages are learned, but also practical pedagogical implications for classroom practice, such as teaching methods and learning activities that can enhance or accelerate language learning rate or success. The objectives of language learning research include:

- exploring individual and environmental aspects associated with language learning or use

- describing characteristics of language learning phenomena

- explaining how language learning develops and why language development differs among different individuals

- predicting language learners' future learning behaviors, steps, performance or success

- testing or assessing language learning or use, as well as evaluating an effectiveness of a language instruction or program

- applying current knowledge or theory in classroom practice.

Any particular research study can have more than one of these aims. For example, a study that aims to describe a language learning phenomenon (e.g. the nature and use of test rehearsals and self-evaluation tasks among different proficiency levels) may yield practical classroom implications (e.g. how test rehearsals can be integrated in a normal classroom). Furthermore, research often leads to new directions of inquiry, as new findings are uncovered. It is, therefore, essential for a researcher to examine what previous research has achieved and what it has not. Researchers not only need to identify research gaps/needs, but they also need to avoid duplications of work and any theoretical or methodological errors/mistakes made in previous research. By examining the literature, we can identify and address new, important research questions.

Quantitative, qualitative, and mixed-methods research

The distinction between quantitative and qualitative research has been significant in academic research for several decades. In recent years, many researchers have adopted a mixed-methods approach. It is important to stress that quantitative, qualitative, and mixed methodologies are valuable for language learning research. Which method researchers choose depends not only on their preference for methods, but also on the suitability of the particular method to their research aims and questions.

Quantitative research seeks to determine a relationship between two or more variables. Quantitative research is primarily related to numerical data, measurement and statistical analysis. *Variables* may be categorical (e.g. gender and nationality) or continuous (e.g. numerical scores relating to language proficiency, test scores and motivational levels). The procedures of data collection and analysis are usually planned beforehand. Quantitative researchers exert some form of control over their research (e.g. by using standardized instruments and by controlling data collection procedures) in order to make accurate inferences about the variables under study and to generalize their findings to other contexts. Data analysis to answer research questions is mainly statistical. Examples of quantitative research strategies include experimental research, correlational research and individual differences research.

Qualitative research seeks to make sense of and understand the language learning and language use of an individual or a group of individuals in *natural*, as well as *classroom settings*. *Qualitative inquiry* is a generic term that appears in educational and applied linguistics research. It has been discussed in relation to naturalistic inquiry, ethnography, case studies and interpretive research, among others. These approaches use different research methods, but they share some characteristics typical of qualitative research. Qualitative researchers take the position that human behavior, such as learning and thinking, is bound to the context in which it occurs. They argue that social reality (i.e. culture, institutions and values) cannot be reduced in the same manner as physical reality. Qualitative researchers give importance to the uniqueness of the nature of language learning by an individual or group in a specific situation and context. This means that they do not primarily focus on generalizing their findings to other contexts. The ultimate goal of qualitative research is to portray the complex pattern of what is being studied in sufficient depth and detail in a particular context. Qualitative researchers do not seek control over their research setting and participants. Qualitative researchers usually take a *subjective stance*, which allows them to understand their research area meaningfully.

Mixed-methods research combines quantitative and qualitative methods in a single study (see Dörnyei 2007; Riazi & Candlin 2014). It has gained popularity in recent years. The *Journal of Mixed Methods Research* specifically aims to advance our knowledge of mixed-methods research across academic disciplines. In fact, a mixed-methods study is not simply about using qualitative methods in a quantitative study and vice versa (Dörnyei 2007). Researchers need to consider why two methods are needed and how they can complement each other to help them better understand a complex phenomenon such as language learning. The degree of success of mixed-methods research depends on the nature of the research topic; the level of advancement of theories underlying the topic; the need for qualitative and quantitative data; and researchers' perspectives about what constitutes a fact or truth.

Cross-sectional and longitudinal research

We can use a time factor to classify quantitative, qualitative, or mixed-methods research in language learning. *Cross-sectional research* refers to a situation in which researchers collect data from one or more cohorts (e.g. a person or group of people) at a single point in time. Researchers may ask participants to answer a questionnaire, take a test, or to be interviewed, usually just once or twice within a short time frame. Researchers then use the questionnaire, test, or interview data to examine or explore research issues. The *advantages* of cross-sectional research include:

1 A short period of time is spent on data collection;
2 There is good coverage of research aspects with a large sample size;
3 Systematic comparability of variables between different groups of participants; and
4 Generalization of findings to larger target populations.

Cross-sectional research can, therefore, be economical and feasible when researchers are faced with time and budget constraints. A *disadvantage* of cross-sectional research is that it does not allow inferences about causal-like relationships. This is because it does not examine what happens before and after data collection. As it is only a snapshot of information, it is not suitable for research that aims to understand individuals' development or changes over time. Correlational research and individual differences researchers often employ cross-sectional data collections (Dörnyei 2007).

Longitudinal research, by contrast, refers to a situation in which researchers collect the same aspects of information from the same participant(s) over a period of time. This method allows researchers to observe the *stability* of or *changes* in behavior, learning, abilities, and/or other cognitive and social development. The length of time that makes a study longitudinal is not clear-cut (Ortega & Iberri-Shea 2005). Some studies can take a few months to several years to collect longitudinal data. An *experimental study* that uses a pretest, a training intervention, a posttest and a delayed posttest may be considered to be approaching *longitudinal* if it lasts for a couple of months or one academic semester. This is because this period of time allows researchers to track changes in language learning or behavior. Longitudinal research can establish sequences of events as well. Ortega and Iberri-Shea (2005) discussed what constituted a longitudinal study and highlighted recent trends in longitudinal research in second language acquisition.

It should be noted that in ethnographic research, researchers who spend a long period of time collecting different pieces of information to answer different research questions are not necessarily conducting a longitudinal study in the strictest sense. While the data they collect may allow them to thoroughly understand the different perspectives of different groups of participants, the data are not necessarily *matchable* to allow an understanding of stability or changes. It is hence important to *distinguish* longitudinal research from *prolonged research* and *extensive data triangulation techniques over time* – the typical research characteristics of *case studies* and *ethnographies*. Longitudinal research requires *data matching* because it focuses on *the degree of development or change of an aspect over time* (e.g. due to age developments or situational/contextual circumstances; see Johnson & Christensen 2008).

In a longitudinal study, researchers are not necessarily present at a research site for several years. They can determine a number of month or year intervals before the same aspects of data can be collected from the same participant(s) again. A famous BBC program *Seven Up!*, which follows the same people every seven years for 40 years is a good example of a longitudinal study in which researchers are absent for seven years before they see the participants again. While it is easy to identify changes or developments in language learning, longitudinal research such as the *Seven Up!* program can face difficulties in explaining what causes or leads to a change or the developments observed. This is often the case when qualitative data, such as interviews or observations, is not collected. Longitudinal researchers are faced with several competing explanations for observed changes or developments. A key *drawback* of longitudinal research is that it can be expensive and requires a large amount of time and effort by researchers to complete. Dörnyei (2007) presents a good coverage of the cross-sectional and longitudinal research distinctions in applied linguistics research.

Reasoning and inferencing

Whether a study has a quantitative, qualitative, or mixed-methods design, researchers need to make inferences beyond their observations or data. *Reasoning* is defined as the act of drawing conclusions about a topic under study. There are two types of reasoning in research: deduction and induction. *Deductive reasoning* – often known as a theory-driven or top-down reasoning – is a process where we make use of pre-existing theories to guide our observation or to direct our attention to what to observe. When we analyze data, we link an *a priori* theory with our observed data. For example, a theory may suggest that successful language learners exhibit a greater degree of self-regulation than less successful ones. To test this, we collect data about the self-regulated behavior of learners exhibiting different levels of success. We then use data analysis to investigate the possible link between a high level of self-regulation and success in language learning. We aim to conclude whether or not the theory is supported by the data. Quantitative research typically starts with deductive reasoning.

Inductive reasoning – also known as a data-driven or bottom-up reasoning is a process by which we first observe language learners' behaviors or a particular phenomenon and then draw conclusions on the basis of those behaviors. Often this kind of reasoning is used for new research areas in which we do not have a pre-existing theory to guide us or we know very little about the topic under study. In an inductive process, we may observe that the majority of successful students, on the one hand, tend to set clear goals for their language learning, follow their goals by planning what to do step by step, and then monitor their progress toward achieving those goals. Less successful students, on the other hand, tend not to engage much in these activities. They often wait for their teachers to tell them what to do next. On the basis of these observed behaviors, we identify *common patterns* between successful and unsuccessful learners, and conclude that successful language learners are better self-regulated than less successful learners. Qualitative research typically starts with inductive reasoning.

It should be noted that both deduction and induction are based on *probabilistic reasoning* because we have to reason beyond the evidence. We should not strive for a *proof* of a truth or fact in language learning research because our reasoning can only be tentative based on what we can observe. Additionally, we have to distinguish theories from facts. Theories are merely *plausible explanations* of facts. Furthermore, a theory that is supported by empirical evidence today may no longer be legitimate tomorrow as new evidence is found by more rigorous research (e.g. Krashen's hypotheses; see Lightbown & Spada 2013; Ortega 2009). We should avoid using the words *prove* or *proven* in our research. In sum, research in language learning has more or less adopted *deductive–inductive reasoning*, because the exclusive use of one type of reasoning limits the advance of our knowledge about language learning. Furthermore, current research is usually informed by previous research, which requires us to relate our inferences to other research findings, even though our study may be the pioneer study.

Research vocabulary

While research terminology is introduced and explored throughout this book, and summarized in the glossary of key research terms in language learning, it is important to point out the following terms in the introductory chapter. We need consensus in regard to the meanings of specific research vocabulary items.

Science derives from a Latin word that means *knowledge*. Science is the approach to the discovery of knowledge through the use of empirical evidence. Scientific research involves studies in which knowledge is informed by *empirical evidence* collected and analyzed systematically and rigorously through an agreed-upon and acceptable method by researchers in the field. Unlike science, *pseudoscience* refers to a field of inquiry that claims that its findings are based on scientific evidence. The findings are, however, supported by inadequate, unscientific methods (e.g. through testimonial evidence by customers). In language learning, examples of pseudoscientific claims may be seen in the promotion of a language teaching program or textbook that guarantees a native-like proficiency and justifies this using testimonials from some former students, and in the promotion of a computer program that can grade students' speaking skills and give feedback in exactly the same way as human graders would do. Unless companies provide objective and substantive evidence from independent and credible researchers, and do not attempt to *suppress undesirable findings*, their findings will be doubtful and the research will be *pseudoscience*. People often have doubts about claims based on research projects funded by companies with a vested interest in the result.

Empiricism is the term used to describe the discovery of knowledge through the collection of data or evidence. We observe or experience a phenomenon in a real context or environment. Empiricism is different from intuition, personal beliefs or other kinds of knowledge that have been taken for granted for generations. Science strives to gather evidence that can be verified, falsified or disregarded if it is irrelevant, inaccurate, or useless.

Scientific knowledge is therefore accumulative knowledge derived from empirical data through the use of an appropriate research method, systematic data analysis, and empirical reasoning.

Research is the intellectual process of discovering new facts or improving knowledge. It can be achieved through the collection and analysis of data, together with an attempt to make inferences that transcend the data. The word research is a mass noun and takes a singular form. *Studies* can be used if we would like to count individual instances of research. Many students of English as a second language mistakenly use *many researches* when they mean *many studies*.

The term *data* is understood as information gained through observation by researchers to respond to a research question or hypothesis. In quantitative research, the word data is treated as *plural* because it is related to numbers (i.e. hard data), which can be counted and are derived from multiple sources. In quantitative research, researchers say, for example, 'the data *were* from ...; the data *were* analyzed' in their reports. Qualitative researchers prefer to say 'data is or was' because qualitative data is related to soft data, such as descriptions, words, documents, pictures, symbols or sounds (see Holliday 2007). It is not useful to debate in this book whether data should be plural or singular. Some people even go so far as to say that the singular form of data is *datum*, but the vast majority of qualitative researchers do not use this term. In this book, data will be treated as *plural* when it refers to quantitative data, but *singular* when it refers to qualitative data.

Participants are people who provide a source of data for research (e.g. those who respond to questionnaires, tests, interviews and observations). Some researchers use the term *subjects* instead of participants. In this book, participants will be the preferred term as people should have the choice to participate in a study as they see fit. Hence, they are not subjects. The term subjects is dehumanizing, while the term participants reflects a humanistic approach to social sciences research. The American Psychological Association (APA) recommends that researchers use participants.

Theory is a set of descriptions, explanations and/or predictions in relation to a particular topic (e.g. the relationships among various learning variables) that are not directly observable. Unlike concrete objects (e.g. a ruler, a building, a car), abstract aspects (e.g. happiness, motivation, anxiety) cannot be directly observed. The technical word for an abstract concept in research is *construct*. A theory is a useful propositional system of descriptions and explanations about things we do not understand well, which can guide us to pursue scientific knowledge by searching for empirical evidence. A theory can originate from a set of personal beliefs through personal observations. It can also be a result of human creativity or the application of problem-solving skills.

Constructs are used to refer to not only abstract aspects but also the focused topic of a study. We can make inferences about an abstract concept or a construct by observing people's behaviors or considering people's reported thoughts.

Hypotheses are statements about the nature of something that may predict some forms of behavior or thinking. Hypotheses are based on a theory, and the theory that postulates a particular set of hypotheses may be falsified or discontinued when a set of hypotheses is not supported by empirical data, or when its predictive power is no longer useful. A theory can be modified given new evidence and insight from various researchers and research sites. It should be noted that a theory that is agreed upon or accepted by researchers today may be rejected later as new conflicting evidence is found.

The characteristics of good researchers

There are some typical characteristics of good academic researchers that are worth mentioning in this chapter.

- Good researchers have a *genuine interest* in a research topic. A genuine interest is a key ingredient to sustain our effort to do research. It is thus important to spend some time searching for a topic that we are really interested in.

- Good researchers have and try to improve both *theoretical* and *methodological knowledge* appropriate for a particular research area and problem. When it comes to doing academic research, we have to study the existing knowledge of a research topic thoroughly (e.g. through a review of the literature) before collecting data to further such knowledge. We also need to know how to do research that is appropriate for a particular topic, as well as acceptable to other academics. Often, we learn more about research methods during the course of our research, as the need arises.

- Good researchers have *common sense*, *common research knowledge*, and *critical thinking skills*. Common sense is related to the ability to make sound judgments. It does not require specialized knowledge. Critical thinking is related to common sense. Critical thinking is the intellectual ability to rationalize, analyze and reflect on a situation or problem, and to use such information to guide our actions. Common research knowledge is a specialized form of common knowledge/sense that requires critical thinking skills. A lack of common sense and critical thinking will lead to poor research.

  For example, if a researcher would like to know about language learners' speaking ability but used a multiple-choice grammar test to make a claim about this, we may argue that this researcher lacks common sense and critical thinking skills. This researcher's findings or claims are not acceptable because people with common sense would know that learners need to speak or perform a speaking task in order to illustrate their speaking skills. Scores from a multiple-choice grammar test (though related to general linguistic skills) could not adequately and directly represent a person's speaking ability. Common sense and critical thinking skills, however, can improve as we do more study about research principles and conduct more empirical research. Common sense would direct us to theories related to speaking before we consider a measure of speaking ability. It is wise to learn some common or basic knowledge about how to conduct an experimental study because such knowledge will form part of our common sense and can be extended to the development of our critical thinking skills.

● Good researchers are *tolerant of ambiguity* and demonstrate *persistence*. As we do not know everything about the research topic and often learn about research as we go along, we will face countless examples of uncertainty and difficulty all the way through to the completion of a research project.

● Good researchers are *transparent* in explaining what they do step by step and act in a *socially and ethically responsible manner*. Transparency is important as it helps other people understand how we reach our conclusions. It helps them decide whether to believe our research results, and enables them to apply our findings and recommendations to their particular context and to the formulation of further research proposals. *Ethics* is also important because research is social. We have to follow the various codes of conduct for research and we have to carefully consider any adverse effects of our research on participants or society. In particular, we must take care to fully inform participants about our research project, obtain their consent to participate, maintain participants' anonymity, keep the data collected confidential and fully analyze the potential impact of our research on the field of study and on society at large.

● Good researchers have a strong *social research network*. While conducting a research study, we will have both good and bad times. Especially when we are having a bad time (e.g. unsure about how to interpret findings, lack of technical knowledge), we will need to seek help from others. When we have written a draft research report, we should seek opinions from other research professionals so that we can uncover any problems and inconsistencies, and further work can be done to eliminate them. A good research network can include research students, as well as researchers at a departmental and university level and other members of the academic community. It is important to attend conferences and seminars as these are an excellent way to gain exposure to new ideas and research methods, and to find ways to solve current problems.

Associations for applied linguistics

The following is a list of the key applied linguistics associations that have a strong interest in and support for research in language learning.

● *American Association for Applied Linguistics (AAAL)*: <http://www.aaal.org/>, viewed 11 July 2014

- *Applied Linguistics Association of Australia (ALAA)*:
  <http://www.alaa.org.au/>, viewed 11 July 2014

- *Applied Linguistics Association of New Zealand (ALANZ)*:
  <http://www.alanz.ac.nz/>, viewed 11 July 2014

- *British Association for Applied Linguistics (BAAL)*:
  <http://www.baal.org.uk/>, viewed 11 July 2014

- *Canadian Association for Applied Linguistics*:
  <http://www.aclacaal.org/>, viewed 11 July 2014

- *International Association of Applied Linguistics (AILA)*:
  <http://www.aila.info/en/>, viewed 11 July 2014

Peer-reviewed journals in language learning

The following journals publish a variety of research topics and approaches in language learning. They include numerous experimental studies in language learning and teaching:

Applied Linguistics; English for Specific Purposes; English Language Teaching Journal; International Review of Applied Linguistics; Language Learning; Language Teaching Research; Second Language Research; Studies in Second Language Acquisition; System; TESOL Quarterly and *The Modern Language Journal.*

Organization of the book

There are 16 chapters, including a bibliography, a glossary of key terms in language learning research, and an index. Each chapter will present an interconnected stage of experimental research, covering its essential features. At the end of each chapter, there will be exercises and discussion questions, followed by annotated suggestions for further reading.

Chapter 1 (*Introduction and Overview*) has presented key conceptual issues related to educational and language learning research, and experimental research in particular. **Chapter 2** (*Experimental Research Basics*) presents critical aspects and terminology related to experimental research in language learning (e.g. causal-like relationship claims, research questions and hypotheses, dependent and independent variables, and type of scales). **Chapter 3** (*Experimental Research Paradigms and Processes*) discusses research paradigms that influence experimental research and its processes. **Chapter 4** (*Experimental Research Designs*) presents and discusses the key types of experimental research designs in language learning.

Chapter 5 (*Validity in Experimental Research*) addresses types of research validity and issues related to the validity of experimental research. **Chapter 6** (*Ethical Considerations in Experimental Research*) addresses the importance of research ethics in experimental research in language learning. **Chapter 7** (*Quantitative Research Instruments and Techniques*) focuses on conceptual and practical considerations regarding instruments and data collection techniques for experimental research. **Chapter 8** (*A Hybrid Approach for Experimental Research*) discusses the importance of combining quantitative research instruments with qualitative data collection techniques. It presents qualitative data elicitation techniques and analyses (e.g. think-aloud protocols, interviews and observations).

Chapter 9 (*Descriptive Statistics*) explains stages in statistical analysis and descriptive statistics. It introduces the IBM® SPSS® Program by presenting basic functions, data preparation and data displays. It illustrates how to analyze descriptive statistics and create graphic displays. **Chapter 10** (*Inferential Statistics*) presents and discusses the inferential statistics required for experimental research (e.g. probability and probability values, research hypothesis, null hypothesis and alternative hypothesis, statistical significance, Type I and Type II errors, parametric versus non-parametric tests, practical significance, and effect sizes).

Chapter 11 (*Correlational Analysis*) presents several types of correlational analyses through the use of SPSS. **Chapter 12** (*Reliability and Reliability Analysis*) discusses the importance of reliability analysis for experimental research and the essential criteria for assessing the reliability of research instruments and interrater or intercoder reliability. It then illustrates how SPSS can be a useful tool to help researchers examine the reliability of their quantitative and qualitative data. **Chapter 13** (*Paired-samples and Independent-samples T-tests*) focuses on an application of *t*-tests for analyzing experimental research data.

Chapter 14 (*Analyses of Variance (ANOVAs)*) introduces three types of analysis of variance (ANOVA), including a one-way analysis of variance (ANOVA), an analysis of covariance (ANCOVA), and a repeated-measures ANOVA. **Chapter 15** (*Non-parametric Versions of T-tests and ANOVAs*) presents four non-parametric tests (Wilcoxon signed ranks test, Mann–Whitney U test; Kruskal–Wallis H test, and Friedman test). Finally, **Chapter 16** (*Experimental Research Proposals*) concludes this book by considering how to develop an experimental research proposal that takes into account the essential theoretical and methodological aspects.

Summary

Language learning researchers pursue knowledge about how languages are learned and how they can be effectively taught through observations, inferences and empirical research. They do not seek *absolute truth* about the nature of language learning, but a set of robust theories that are useful to describe and explain language learning phenomena. Language learning researchers have adopted research methods that allow them to systematically examine issues in language learning. Experimental research is the kind of research that has been employed to answer research questions in this field. In order to conduct experimental research appropriately, it is important to learn the basic principles and procedures of experimental research. This book aims to provide guidance on how experimental research can be conducted in language learning research.

Research exercise

To download exercises for this chapter visit: http://www.bloomsbury.com/experimental-research-methods-in-language-learning-9781441189110/

Discussion questions

1 To what extent do you agree or disagree with the statement "research is searching again and again." Why or why not?
2 In your view, why is it inadequate to explain language learning by simply understanding the linguistic system of a particular language?
3 A list of language learning research aims is provided in this chapter. Can quantitative, qualitative or mixed-methods research be adopted to address those aims? Which aims are more inclined toward a quantitative method, qualitative method or a mixed-methods approach?
4 Discuss the characteristics of good researchers presented in this chapter. Are there any other characteristics that should be added?
5 Reflection: What is the most important lesson you have learned from this chapter?

Further reading

Dörnyei, Z 2007, *Research methods in applied linguistics: quantitative, qualitative, and mixed methodologies*, Oxford University Press, Oxford.

This book provides a comprehensive discussion of research and the ways in which we pursue knowledge in applied linguistics. It discusses key issues in research, including types of research, validity, reliability, ethical considerations, research designs and data analysis. This book provides a good reference on how research in language learning can be carried out.

Johnson, B & Christensen, L 2008, *Educational research: quantitative, qualitative, and mixed approaches*, 3rd edn, Sage, Los Angeles.

Chapter 1 presents the importance and value of learning about educational research. It presents various kinds of research, including basic and applied research, and explains types of reasoning and basic assumptions of scientific methods.

Mackey, A & Gass, SM 2005, *Second language research: methodology and design*, Lawrence Erlbaum Associates, Mahwah, NJ.

This book provides a comprehensive treatment of research methods in second language research. It discusses issues related to data collection (e.g. common research instruments, validity, reliability and ethics), as well as methods in quantitative and qualitative research.

Mackey, A & Gass, SM (eds) 2012, *Research methods in second language acquisition: a practical guide*, Wiley-Blackwell, Malden, MA.

This edited volume addresses issues related to data types (such as how to use certain kinds of data to address research problems) and data analysis and methodology in second language acquisition research. The authors of this volume provide useful tips to deal with research strategically and proactively.

Paltridge, B & Phakiti, A (eds) in press, 2015, *Research methods in applied linguistics*, Bloomsbury, London & New York.

This is an edited volume of research methods in applied linguistics, focusing on issues related to language learning and teaching. This book is for beginning researchers in applied linguistics. It contains two main parts: research methods and approaches and research areas written by leading authors in the areas.

Walliman, N 2011, *Research methods: the basics*, Routledge, Oxon.

This book is a good starter for people new to academic research. It covers basic backgrounds for understanding research (e.g. research theory, ethics, main research methods and writing a proposal).

CHAPTER TWO

Experimental Research Basics

Leading questions

1 Do you believe in a cause–effect relationship in language learning? Why or why not?
2 What do you think are characteristics of an experimental research study?
3 What kind of research questions do you think experimental researchers ask?

Introduction

This chapter explores the basic concepts and issues that influence the way experimental research is typically conducted. Such basic concepts include causal-like relationship, independent versus dependent variables, research questions and hypotheses, scales and measurement in experimental research, and manipulation in experimental research. This chapter concludes with a presentation of research processes in an experimental study.

Experimental research in language learning

Numerous studies in language learning research published in peer-review journals (e.g. *Applied Linguistics, Language Learning, Language Teaching Research, Studies in Second Language Acquisition, TESOL Quarterly, The Modern Language Journal*, and so forth) aim to examine the subject of causation (e.g. the effects of corrective feedback on the acquisition of grammatical redundancies by Lyddon 2011; the effects of integrated language-based instruction in elementary ESL learning by Kim 2008; and the effect of teacher codeswitching with English-only explanations on the vocabulary acquisition of Chinese university students by Tian and Macaro 2012). In general, language learning researchers ask questions such as 'what are the reasons for some language learners to be more successful than others?' They are curious to know the potential effect of one variable on another.

If we want to examine the effect of motivation on language performance, care needs to be taken when designing and conducting research. We know that there are many factors contributing to language performance (e.g. differences in language proficiency, age, gender, anxiety and the amount of time spent on study). It can, therefore, be difficult for us to claim on the basis of our study that a high level of motivation results in better language performance.

However, if we can systematically control the influences of other potential contributing variables in which we are not interested, we may be in a better position to claim our research finding (e.g. that motivation leads to increased performance). Only in this way can our research findings become more valid. You will see throughout this book that in experimental research, researchers attempt to minimize the effects of unwanted *confounding* variables that can weaken the validity (or trustworthiness) of their research outcomes. It is therefore important that we know the *key methodological* criteria in experimental research.

Experimental research is a useful research methodology for those studies that aim to address a causal-like relationship. It allows researchers to strictly control the influence of factors that are not of interest by setting them constant across groups, but to vary the degree of a factor under study across groups of learners in order to understand a causal-like relationship. An experimental research design has been known to reside within a *quantitative research methodology* that is often adopted in language learning research. Experimental research is traditionally based on the *active theory of causation,* which attempts to identify those variables capable of human control and to manipulate them in order to achieve changes (see Cook & Shadish 1994).

This traditional way of thinking meant that an experiment was used to primarily describe causes, rather than to explain how and why they occurred (Cook & Shadish 1994). Experimental researchers today, however, counter that the original and strictest sense of the activity theory of causation is too simplistic to help make sense of numerous real-world language learning problems (Johnson & Christensen 2008). We know through several empirical studies in language learning that language learning is greatly influenced by several complex cognitive and social factors (see Ellis 2008; Ortega 2009). Experimental researchers usually aim to test whether their hypothesis is supported by empirical data, in a strictly controlled environment. Experimental research requires control over a situation to safeguard against threats to research validity, such as other variables that are not of interest, but which can influence research outcomes.

For example, we may aim to determine the types of feedback that best improve language learners' linguistic accuracy. To do this, we will *manipulate* different types of feedback variables that may enhance linguistic accuracy through the provision of different instructions to different groups of students, which include a control group to which no feedback is provided. We will then compare the linguistic accuracy of different groups of students receiving different types of feedback through the use of a *posttest* that measures levels of linguistic accuracy after the completion of the experiment. We may also compare posttest scores with pretest scores, which indicate levels of linguistic accuracy before the start of the experiment. Any statistically significant differences would allow us to determine the types of feedback that best facilitate linguistic accuracy.

However, several problems with the findings may arise if we do not control our experiment carefully. In order to enhance the validity of our findings, we carefully identify potential sources that co-exist with the target variable (here, feedback) before the experiment begins. These factors may include the extent of teachers' teaching experience, the materials used, the hour of the day of the classes, gender differences, pre-existing differences in language proficiency and measures of linguistics accuracy. These factors—known as *confounding* factors—need to be set *constant* across the groups of students. Confounding variables can be set constant by using the same teacher to give instruction, the same materials, and the same hour of the day for the classes. Additionally, standardized measures of linguistic accuracy should be used and there should be a gender balance between groups, if possible. Pre-existing language proficiency differences between comparison groups should also be avoided. If there is a pre-existing difference, an analysis that can take it into account should be used.

We have to *randomly* assign students into two or more groups so that each student has an equal chance of being placed in any one group. *Random assignment methods* can spread the effects of any confounding variable more evenly. Of course, we will also need to use reliable and valid measures of linguistic accuracy, and employ appropriate statistical analyses that yield answers to our research questions. It can be seen that there are many important considerations when we conduct an experiment. If we would like to be successful in conducting experimental research, we need to know what is involved in, and what is required for, this research strategy.

The key characteristics of experimental research

Experimental research should follow a *robust* research methodology that can help us investigate whether and the extent to which a certain factor (e.g. types of instructions, input or interactions) can facilitate or inhibit language learning. While language learning occurs in various settings (e.g. home and social events), the focus of this book is more on *instructed language learning*, rather than on *natural, informal language learning*. In a classroom we have more control over confounding variables, compared to natural settings. Furthermore, a classroom is one of the real-life situations of language learning, so it can be considered a real-life laboratory. In most language learning situations, even for first language learning, languages are formally taught in school, college or university. Instruction is an important method to help individuals learn languages and to improve their literacy levels more quickly than in a naturally exposed environment, which is highly dynamic and unpredictable.

The following sections will address the key characteristics or issues related to experimental research in language learning.

Causal or causal-like relationships

Experimental research in language learning allows researchers to vary a factor or factors, and to manipulate other factors by making them constant, and then to observe participants' behavior according to the variations made. Researchers can examine whether their hypothesis about a *causal-like* relationship is supported by empirical data. In this book, causal-like is used in place of causal, which is typically used in most quantitative methods. There are two reasons for this preference. First, we cannot have a direct proof that an experimental finding indicates a causal relationship. In most cases, we do not have direct access to what we are researching (e.g. direct observations of a research construct like motivation and language proficiency). We can only make inferences about it through the systematic observation of behavior that represent the target construct. Second, it is essential to be clear that statistical analysis in experimental research is not a method to discover causes. Instead, statistical methods can only test a theoretical relationship between one variable and another. Hence, what we come to understand is a causal-like effect rather than a causal effect.

Experimental research in language learning usually use terms, such as *the effects of*, *the effectiveness of*, *the influence of* and *the role of* to imply a causal-like relationship. Some researchers may not include such words in their titles. Here are examples of language learning research titles employing an experimental design:

- Baralt and Gurzynski-Weiss (2011): Comparing learners' state anxiety during task-based interaction in computer-mediated and face-to-face communication

- Gass, Mackey, Alverez-Torres and Fernández-Garcia (1999): The effects of task repetition on linguistic output

- Lee and Kalyuga (2011): Effectiveness of different Pinyin presentation formats in learning Chinese characters: A cognitive load perspective

- Park (2010): The influence of pretask instructions and pretask planning on focus on form during Korean EFL task-based interaction

- Rahimi (2013): Is training student reviewers worth its while? A study of how training influences the quality of students' feedback and writing

- Reinders (2009): Learner uptake and acquisition in three grammar-oriented production activities

- Sueyoshi and Hardison (2005): The role of gestures and facial cues in second language listening comprehension

- Takimoto (2006): The effects of explicit feedback on the development of pragmatic proficiency

- Vainio, Pajunen and Hyönä (2014): L1 and L2 word recognition in Finnish: Examining L1 effects on L2 processing of morphological complexity and morphophonological transparency

Research questions in experimental research

It is important to understand the nature of the research questions being asked in experimental research. If several empirical studies have come to an understanding that there is a relationship between certain types of feedback (e.g. explicit and implicit feedback) and language learners' writing performance (e.g. as measured by accuracy and fluency), then an experimental study can be set up to compare students' writing outcomes according to different types of feedback provided under the same conditions. Researchers may be able to answer the research question 'can feedback Type A (explicit) facilitate writing performance significantly better than feedback Type B (implicit)?' through the use of an experimental research design.

Ideally, the researchers will set all conditions in the environment constant for all comparison groups (discussed further below), except for the variable being tested. For example, Group 1 receives Type A feedback, while Group 2 receives Type B feedback; and Group 3 receives traditional writing instruction with unspecified feedback. Students' observed learning outcomes (e.g. writing scores from a pretest and a posttest) can be compared statistically both within and across groups.

The following are examples of experimental research questions:

- Do adult and child dyads respond differently to the amount of implicit negative feedback provided to NNSs [non-native English speakers] during task-based interaction? (Mackey, Oliver & Leeman 2003, p. 44)

- Does access to visual cues, such as gestures and lip movements, facilitate ESL students' listening comprehension? (Sueyoshi & Hardison 2005, p. 668)

- Does instruction in L2 phonetics improve learners' ability to produce L2 phones? (Kissling 2013, p. 725)

- Is there an effect of frequency of occurrence (1, 3, 5) on form recall of target lexical items when tested immediately after the learning session? (Peters 2014)

- To what extent is lexical focus-on-form beneficial during a focus on meaning activity (such as listening comprehension) in terms of students' receptive vocabulary learning? (Tian & Macaro 2012, p. 373)

As can be seen in the examples above, experimental researchers can ask a range of questions. Research questions in experimental research can be grouped into two types: theoretical questions, and practical or pedagogical questions. As pointed out in Chapter 1, research questions are used to frame our research focus and method to answer them. Theoretical questions are connected with *basic research*. On the one hand, basic research seeks empirical evidence that can inform a new theory, or refine and extend existing theories. Theoretical questions are, for example: *What is motivation in L2 learning?*; *How does it operate to direct language learners' behavior?*; *How is it related to other psychological processes?*; and *Why is it predictive of L2 learning success?* These research questions are directed toward a formulation of new theories or contesting pre-existing theories of L2 motivation.

Applied research, on the other hand, aims to address a practical/pedagogical problem in a particular setting. Some contexts of language learning present unique problems that require researchers/teachers to apply relevant theories or recommendations to real practice. Practical/pedagogical research questions are connected with applied research. For example, at a particular school, a majority of students experienced difficulty in grammatical accuracy in writing the description of an object. Despite several attempts to explicitly model how to construct a grammatically correct sentence, most students still failed to consistently produce acceptable sentences. Here, the practical questions may be: *How can teachers help students memorize a grammar rule?*; *Why do students forget grammar rules despite several repetitions and practices?*; and, *Can corrective feedback help students learn specific grammar rules sustainably?*. To answer these practical questions, researchers and teachers may examine theories associated with retention and corrective feedback in writing, for example. Examining pre-existing theories might allow them to gain insight into how they could apply those theories into practice successfully. Applied research conducted to address such questions may help provide a solution to the problems for a particular group of learners in a particular context. The solution, however, may not be generalizable or applicable to other learners in other contexts because applied research questions are often domain/situation-specific.

It should be noted that there is a *basic-applied research continuum* and most language learning research, particularly experimental research, is placed somewhere on this continuum. For example, an understanding of motivation in language learning can be applied in a language classroom by helping students to enjoy learning grammar rules. In pursuing a solution to help students to retain new grammar rules, researchers may find that motivation is a key variable to determine differences between learners who can retain more or fewer grammar rules for use.

Independent and dependent variables

In experimental research, we use the term *variable* when we consider an aspect or characteristic of something that can take different values or scores. The root of the word variable is the word *vary*. Age is an example of a variable because we know that the people around us span a wide range of ages. Other examples of variables include gender, first language, length of learning, intelligence, English language proficiency, motivation, anxiety and feedback. We research the nature of variables in language learning and examine how they are related to one another. Frequently, researchers use variables and constructs interchangeably. Constructs, however, are often discussed at a theoretical level and represent broader concepts than variables. Often, variables are discussed as observable behaviors or indicators of a particular construct.

In experimental research, we consider two types of variables: independent and dependent. An independent variable is a variable that exists freely, and is hypothesized to have an effect on other variables that are described as *dependent variables*. For example, if anxiety in test-taking is an independent variable, poor test performance can be considered a dependent variable. This is because a high or low level of anxiety can have an effect on how well students perform in a given test. We know that people are more anxious when a test is a high-stakes test (the results of which can influence the test-takers' lives by their effect on the success or otherwise of job and university applications) than when it is a low-stakes one (for which there are no consequences for failure).

Independent variables are factors that influence certain behaviors or psychological processes. We have learned from our discussion about types of feedback above that independent variables can be manipulated by experimental researchers. Here, researchers create different situations or conditions that students will be exposed to during the study. We need to have at least two levels of independent variables in experimental research, and this enables researchers to compare two different situations. In the example of feedback, we see that there are two levels of feedback: feedback Type A (explicit) and feedback Type B (implicit).

A *dependent variable* is a variable that changes as the independent variable being examined changes. In regard to feedback types, writing performance will be considered a dependent or outcome variable that is affected by the specific type of feedback employed. In experimental research, dependent variables are ones that researchers aim to measure through research instruments such as tests, questionnaires and observation schemes (see Chapter 5). Let us revisit the titles of some of the sample studies presented above and identify the independent variables (IVs) and dependent variables (DVs).

- Gass and Mackey (1999): The effects of task repetition [IV] on linguistic output [DV]

- Lee and Kalyuga (2011): Effectiveness of different Pinyin presentation formats [IVs] in learning Chinese characters [DV]: A cognitive load perspective

- Park (2010): The influence of pretask instructions [IVs] and pretask planning [IV] on focus on form [DV] during Korean EFL task-based interaction

Dichotomous and continuous variables

Experimental research is linked closely to *measurement* or *quantification* (the act of assigning values or scores to variables). It is important to discuss the different types of scales used earlier in this book to quantify variables (i.e. the magnitude of a variable). An understanding of measurement scales is critical for success in learning about experimental research. First, not all variables have the same mathematical properties, and different variables cannot be conceptualized or used in the same way in experimental research. The concept of measurement is an essential foundation to an understanding of how dependent and independent variables are quantified in experimental research.

We will start by discussing the two broad types of variables used in language learning research: *categorical* and *continuous* variables. Examples of categorical variables are gender, first language, nationality, country of origin, major field of study, teaching methods employed, and even the type of research being carried out. *Categorical variables* are used to group non-overlapping variables such as English proficiency levels (e.g. beginning, intermediate and advanced). A *dichotomous variable* is the simplest type of categorical variable because it has only two classes (e.g. biological male or female, pass or fail). In experimental research, categorical variables are often used as *independent variables* (variables that hypothetically result in differences in other variables). As in the example on the effect of feedback types on writing performance, experimental researchers can code Type A feedback as 1, Type B feedback as 2 and traditional class as 3. They then compare the writing performance of students across these codes.

Continuous variables can be arranged from lowest to highest. Age, length of residency, number of years learning a language and English language proficiency scores are examples of continuous variables. In experimental research, many continuous scores can be measured and treated as the outcomes of independent variables (e.g. language proficiency scores). As discussed above, *outcome variables* are known as *dependent variables*.

Measurement scales of variables

We now see that classifying variables as either categorical or continuous can lead to some difficulty in the achievement of precise measurements in experimental research. The question of the measurement of variables has received much attention, and the results are useful for empirical studies. The four-level scale system originally developed by Stevens (1946) is the most popular method for assigning scores to variables: *nominal, ordinal, interval* and *ratio* scales. It is important to understand these scales because we need to know which ones can be used for statistical procedures in experimental research.

Nominal scales use numbers to label or classify variables into categories. Variables that are measured using nominal scales are known as categorical variables (discussed above). For a gender variable, we may choose to use code 1 for males and 2 for females. For a first language variable, we may assign code 1 to English, 2 to French, 3 to Spanish and 4 to German, and so on. The purpose here is for identification purposes. The values from nominal scales thus do not have a mathematical property. For example, we cannot say that German is the best language just because it has the highest assigned code.

Ordinal scales are rank-order scales. They are used for ranking some quality or ability. For example, students may be ranked based on their grade point average (GPA). Ordinal scales allow us to compare the order of students' GPAs and make a decision on who should receive the best student award of the semester, for example. Ordinal scales do not indicate the degree of difference between the characteristics of one student and another. Students may be ranked 1 (highest), 2, 3, 4 and 5, etc., but we cannot deduce any significance from the fact that the student who is ranked number 1 has a score that has four scores higher than the student ranked number 5, for example. We can only say that the former is more successful academically than the latter. In experimental research, ordinal scales can be used as either dependent or independent variables, depending on the research questions being asked.

Interval scales have the features of both ordinal scales and equal distances or intervals. Examples of interval scales in language learning research include language test scores, personality scores and language aptitude scores. We know that students whose score in a writing test was 20 had a score that was 10 points higher than those who scored 10. However, we cannot say than those who scored 0 did not have any writing ability. That is, while we can compute interval scores for arithmetic and statistical purposes, there is an absence of a *true zero*, which does not permit us to make a *ratio* statement.

It should be noted that several educational and language learning variables (e.g. GPA, anxiety, learning strategy use, motivation and perceptions in language program effectiveness) have the characteristics of ordinal scales (or quasi-interval scales) rather than those of true interval scales. For example, in an evaluation statement about a language program (e.g. I am satisfied with the teaching of this unit), we cannot say that the distance between 1 (strongly disagree) and 2 (disagree) is the same as the distance between 4 (agree) and 5 (strongly agree). However, the measurement scales of these variables are commonly treated as if they were true interval scales, especially when a large sample size can be obtained. One may argue that when carefully constructed and designed, such quasi-interval variables can be treated by researchers as intervals and can be used for statistical tests. It is therefore essential that care is taken when using and interpreting statistics from this kind of data.

Ratio scales are measurements with all the properties of nominal, ordinal and interval scales and also possess a true zero. In physical measurements, for example, we know that weights, heights, and ages all have a true zero. In language learning, an example of this scale may be the number of times international students took the Test of English as a Foreign Language (TOEFL) before they were admitted into a university, or the number of questions students answer correctly in a listening test, compared to the number of questions they answer incorrectly. Nonetheless, as desirable in properties as ratio scales may be, educational and language researchers do not typically use these scales in their research. In experimental research, researchers typically use only the first three types of scales.

Constructs in experimental research revisited

The discussion of the types and measurement of variables so far is useful for conceptualizing a research construct. We can see that a construct can be as simple as one of the categorical variables discussed above (e.g. gender and age). However, psychological constructs in language learning research can be much more complex than these. If it is easy to examine a construct (e.g. age or height), we probably do not need to conduct research. Chapter 1 defined constructs as aspects or abstract concepts that researchers seek to understand. For example, we seek to understand abstract constructs such as intelligence, language proficiency, memory, language aptitude, motivation, self-regulation and anxiety. We know that these constructs cannot be seen directly or be easily measured. We need a sound theory to help us define and measure them.

As discussed in relation to deductive and inductive reasoning, what we can do to investigate an abstract construct is to systematically observe behaviors or performances (i.e. observable variables) that are hypothetically/theoretically linked to the construct. We then try to make inferences about the construct through statistical analysis. It is therefore critical for researchers to have a clear definition of an abstract construct of interest that other researchers would agree upon at the beginning of their research.

Typical questions often asked by students new to academic research are: *How do we find or know what constitutes a construct?*; and *how do we decide which variables to measure?* A simple answer to both these questions can be found by examining and studying relevant theories and previous research in those areas. This is a form of literature/library research that allows us to study how researchers/theorists in the field define a particular construct that we are interested in. By conducting a literature review, we also learn how other researchers have measured the construct by using research instruments or techniques to observe its linked behaviors and performances. We can use or adapt these existing research instruments for our own research purposes.

In research, there are two dimensions of a *construct* that we need to understand: constitutive constructs and operational constructs. A *constitutive construct* is one defined using the general definition of a term (e.g. motivation, self-regulation, language learning strategies and self-efficacy). For example, *motivation* can be described in general terms as a multifaceted psychological feature that acts as a driving force for individuals to achieve a desired goal. Motivation comprises a number of more general, trait-like features (enduring over time) and more situation-specific, state-like (fluctuating and unstable) components that direct and energize individuals' learning behaviors (see e.g. Dörnyei 2005). Such a definition of motivation gives us the general meaning of this construct. However, it is not precise enough for the purposes of research. An *operational construct definition* is essential for an empirical study as it allows other people to know exactly what researchers mean by a particular construct in a particular study.

In regard to motivation, Woodrow (2010) outlines how various researchers have defined and operationalized motivation according to various perspectives (e.g. Gardner's socio-educational model of language learning, self-determination theory, the process model of motivation and goal orientation theory). We see that within each of these perspectives, researchers can operationalize the construct definitions of various components of motivation differently. For example, within the self-determination theory, motivation is classified into intrinsic motivation (generated by individuals themselves) and extrinsic motivation (motivation generated by external factors, e.g. promise of rewards, threats of punishment). A researcher may be more specific in how they define intrinsic and extrinsic motivation in their study.

It is therefore important for an experimental researcher to carefully consider the operational construct definition for their research. In research reports, we often see how researchers operationalize their construct by stating, for example: For the purpose of this study, X is defined as .... Based on such an explicit statement, other researchers may be able to extend the findings of the study to their context of interest and can replicate the study. An operational construct is pivotal because it allows researchers to precisely vary the construct and measure its outcome in their research. It means that, through an operational definition, researchers can measure an abstract construct and connect behaviors with the construct more realistically. In an experimental study, Eckerth and Tavakoli (2012, p. 234) operationalized 'exposure frequency' as follows:

> The first independent variable, 'exposure frequency,' refers to the textual characteristics of the reading texts, and was operationalized on two levels, representing the frequency of the target words in the text. Each of the reading texts contained 10 target words. Five of these words occurred once in the texts (1-OC) and five occurred five times (5-OC). The two levels of exposure frequency were used to find out whether more frequent exposure to a word, 5-OC compared with 1-OC, would have an impact on the learning and retention of the word.

In experimental research, we often come across the use of the terms *variables, factors*, and *constructs*. Often researchers use the terms *constructs, variables*, and *factors* interchangeably. Variables are typically used to refer to items or questions that elicit a behavior underlined by a construct or factor of interest. It is crucial that a construct for one experimental study should not be so broad as to be impossible to investigate thoroughly. A construct such as language learning/acquisition is clearly too ambitious for any study. We should avoid examining too many constructs in a single study because there will be many limitations associated with each construct that will make it difficult to draw a reasonable inference or conclusion. This is simply because psychological constructs in language learning are multidimensional and complex.

Manipulation and control in experimental research

We have come across one aspect of *manipulation* in experimental research when we discussed how experimental researchers manipulate independent variables. When experimental researchers control variables or factors (e.g. by varying them) in a study, we can say that they manipulate them. Manipulation of independent variables in experimental research is necessary because it helps researchers control confounding variables (discussed above), as well as to systematically vary the independent variable of interest. However, it is *unethical* and *unacceptable* to *manipulate research participants* into engaging in activities that they do not wish to engage in. Participants should be well informed about the research procedures prior to their agreement or consent to take part in the research project. Participants must not be forced to take part in experimental research.

Manipulation in experimental research takes place when researchers vary a factor of interest with the intention of testing its effect (e.g. feedback Type A versus feedback Type B). Ahmadian and Tavakoli (2011, p. 43), for example, varied online planning and task repetition as independent variables under the following four conditions: (1) careful online planning without task repetition; (2) time-pressured online planning with task repetition; (3) careful online planning with task repetition; and (4) time-pressured online planning without task repetition.

Manipulation can also take place when researchers hold several conditions for two or more groups of comparisons *constant*, to avoid the potential confounding effects of their factors that can interfere with the experimental factor being examined. For example, Sagarra and Abbuhl (2013, pp. 200–1) controlled potential confounding variables as follows:

> To ensure that a lack of vocabulary knowledge did not affect the results, only learners who achieved 80% accuracy on the vocabulary test were eligible to participate in the study. Similarly, to control for previous knowledge of the target structure, only learners who scored at or below 25% accuracy on the grammar test were allowed to participate (because Spanish has four gender-number combinations, 25% was the minimum cutoff). Participants were randomly assigned to one of the seven groups depending on how many learners met the requirements to be included in the study later on.

Experimental researchers need to have a high level of confidence in the observed effect of the independent factor under investigation, so we need to make sure that the target independent variable of interest is *the only factor* that leads to observed changes of learning (significantly higher scores) or behaviors (e.g. attitude, perceptions about learning, motivation, reduced anxiety). We can only draw a valid conclusion if we are confident that no other factors have contributed to the observed changes. Let us consider the following example to illustrate the effect of a *confounding* variable on an experimental research outcome.

Suppose that we are interested in the effect of the number of hours spent improving the vocabulary ranges of EFL (English as a foreign language) high school students in Thailand. The first group is given an *extensive course* on vocabulary in the morning for 1.5 hours per day (Monday, Wednesday and Friday) for five weeks (a total of 15 hours), taught by a teacher with ten years' teaching experience. The second group is given an *intensive course* on vocabulary in the afternoon for 1.5 hours per day (Monday through Friday) for two weeks (total of 15 hours), taught by a different teacher with just two years' teaching experience. At the beginning of the study, students in both groups take a vocabulary pretest and at the end of the course, they take a vocabulary posttest. Both groups take the same tests. A statistical comparison between the vocabulary posttest scores of the two groups indicates that the first group significantly outperforms the second group. The researcher concludes that extensive teaching of vocabulary is more effective than intensive teaching of vocabulary. What are the major problems in regard to the conclusion drawn by this experimenter?

Clearly we see that the *primary independent variable of interest* is the intensity of hours for teaching vocabulary (extensive versus intensive). Nonetheless, the two comparisons have two other conditions that differ: the teacher and the time of day at which teaching takes place. It might well be argued that people learn better in the morning, and that experienced teachers are more effective and use better teaching strategies than those with less experience. In this experimental scenario, we can say that the time of day and teachers' teaching experiences are confounded with the number of hours of teaching vocabulary. We can control these two confounding variables by having the class taught at the same time of day by the same teacher (who should not be biased against any form of intensity).

It is preferable that the researcher is not the same person as the teacher, as there is the potential of bias during the instruction (e.g. the researchers believe that an extensive course is better than an intensive course, so they make more effort during the extensive course). There are circumstances in which it is unavoidable that a researcher is the teacher in a study. In such a case, the researchers need to consider measures to prevent their bias influencing the results of the study. The potential problem of researcher expectancy needs to be explicitly acknowledged in the research report. For example, Takimoto (2008) who was also the instructor in the study noted that: 'In behavioral research, researcher expectancy can be a problem when the researcher teaches experimental groups. For the present study, the researcher followed the instructional guidelines, which rigidly controlled for the effect with the double-blind technique after the data were collected to minimize any researcher expectancy effect during the treatments' (p. 382).

In addition to these confounding variables, there may be other factors that can contribute to the findings. For example, we do not know whether the first group of students initially had a higher degree of language ability, a better attitude toward language learning or higher motivation than the second group had. We also do not know whether the first group comprised of only girls (or a majority of girls) while the second group might have been mainly boys. We do not know the kind of teaching methods that the two teachers used in the classroom. It is therefore essential that in experimental research, two teaching situations be equal in every aspect except the one that the researchers are interested in. This is essential because researchers need to be able to rule out other plausible rival explanations of the research outcomes. Other feasible explanations are rival arguments against an experimental research finding.

As discussed earlier, the technical terms for unwanted factors that may interfere with the primary independent variable are labeled *confounding* variables. For the purpose of this book, we will not distinguish confounding variables from extraneous variables, which are confounding variables held constant across comparison groups. Without control, these variables will interfere with the independent variable being tested in an experimental study. The terms *confounding variable* and *extraneous variable* are often used interchangeably by researchers. We can control confounding variables by making sure that these potential variables are *equal and constant* for both experimental and control groups at the outset of the study.

It is important to remember that we must control any foreseen confounding variables in experimental research. One strategy to do this is to examine the literature in the relevant area as thoroughly as possible. Previous researchers are likely to have considered them in their research. A lack of control over confounding variables means that their effects may mix with the independent variable of interest to affect learners' measured performance or observed behaviors. Confounding variables are *threats* to the validity of experimental research.

Summary

Experimental research design considers the potential influences of confounding variables that may interfere or interact with a variable of interest to affect the research outcome. Researchers aim to minimize the influence of potential confounding variables by, for example, making several variables constant across the different conditions being examined (e.g. ability levels, time of treatment, materials, teachers) and randomly assigning participants into different groups (the participants to be placed in different comparison groups by chance). The next chapter will present and discuss experimental research paradigms and key features of experimental research processes.

Research exercise

To download exercises for this chapter visit: http://www.bloomsbury.com/ experimental-research-methods-in-language-learning-9781441189110/

Discussion questions

1 What are the ways in which experimental researchers can produce evidence of causality in language learning?

2 Discuss this research question: 'Does accuracy in the use of two functions of the English article system improve over a 10-month period as a result of WCF [written corrective feedback]?' (Bitchener & Knoch 2008, p. 200). What did these researchers aim to find out? What were the independent and dependent variables? Was this question a basic or applied question? Why do you think so?

3 Can you think of a situation in which you can do an experimental study? Think of a situation in which you can have control over your research. What would be the potential confounding variables that can influence your findings?

4 What is random assignment? Why is it essential for a true experimental study?

5 Reflection: What is the most important lesson you have learned from this chapter?

Further reading

Blom, E & Unsworth, S (eds) 2010, *Experimental methods in language acquisition*, John Benjamins, Amsterdam.

This edited volume provides various specific experimental methods and procedures for examining language acquisition.

Field, A & Hole, G 2003, *How to design and report experiments*, Sage, Los Angeles.

This book provides useful guidelines on how experimental research can be conducted appropriately in applied psychological and educational research. It discusses different methods of doing experimental research, presents ways in which data can be analyzed to answer research questions, and how to write up a research report.

Gass, S 2010, 'Experimental research', in B Paltridge & A Phakiti (eds), *Continuum companion to research methods in applied linguistics*, Continuum, London.

This chapter provides an overview of experimental research in language learning. It discusses the underlying assumptions of the experimental methodology, the specifics of experimental research, validity and reliability, ethical considerations, and a sample study focusing on research methodology.

Goodwin, CJ 2010, *Research in psychology: methods and design*, 6th edn, John Wiley & Sons, New York.

Chapter 5 discusses the essential features of experimental research including types of variables in experimental research, validity and threats to the internal validity of an experimental study.

CHAPTER THREE

Experimental Research Paradigms and Processes

Leading questions

1 Have you ever heard of the term 'research paradigm'? Do you know what it is about?
2 What are key criteria you have in mind when you read a research article?
3 What are typical steps researchers take to complete their experimental study?

Introduction

This chapter explores some philosophical concepts that influence the way experimental research is typically conducted through the notions of research paradigms. A research paradigm suggests a set of beliefs and methodological principles that researchers in a particular field hold similarly. This chapter also presents an overview of essential research processes in an experimental study.

Research paradigms in experimental research

Let us step back and reflect on how we have discussed research, including experimental research. When looking at ways of thinking about research and trying to understand the differences between quantitative and qualitative research, did you ask yourself *why* researchers collect and analyze data in a particular manner? In experimental research, why do researchers attempt to control or manipulate the research setting? In a case of ethnographic study, why do researchers make the choice of taking a research setting as it exists? These questions are related to research paradigms. A discussion of the research paradigms associated with experimental research is therefore particularly significant and relevant to the issues of validity, reliability and ethics in experimental research.

Although many researchers do not make an explicit statement of their research paradigm (e.g. I am a positivist; we are constructivists), it is important for students learning about research methods to realize that how researchers carry out their research is largely influenced by their paradigm of choice. Guba and Lincoln (2005) define a research paradigm as a set of related beliefs/assumptions that underlie an approach to research and its relationship to the world. A paradigm is related to how researchers see the world, what they believe constitutes knowledge about the world, and how this knowledge can be attained.

In order to help you understand what a research paradigm is and how it plays a critical role in experimental research, this chapter will discuss and compare three research paradigms: the positivist, postpositivist, and constructivist paradigms. While there are many other paradigms (see Guba & Lincoln 2005), at this stage these three paradigms are adequate to help you understand their place of experimental research in language learning.

Ontology, epistemology and methodology

There are three aspects that we consider when we attempt to understand a research paradigm. They are the ontological (what is reality?), epistemological (what is our relationship to reality?) and methodological aspects (how do we get to understand reality?) (Guba & Lincoln 2005).

First, at an *ontological* level, we ask: *what is reality?* How do we know what we think we know is real? In experimental research, for example, how do we know that the effect of an independent variable (e.g. feedback) on a dependent variable (e.g. writing proficiency) truly exists? Second, at an *epistemological* level, we seek to establish the relationship between ourselves as human beings and what we aim to know (e.g. research constructs and their causal-like relationships). We ask: *do we need to be objective and try to separate ourselves from the issue we try to understand?* or *do we permit subjective judgments to influence the issue we try to understand?* In experimental research, we stress the importance of being objective in our research. We know that our personal bias toward an issue of interest can result in serious problems when researching. We also strive for research measures that are highly reliable (i.e. consistent) so that the effect of errors of measurement on our inferences is minimized.

Third, at a *methodological* level, we ask: *how do we go about our pursuit of knowledge?* This level is related to the research methods we employ to understand reality. We ask: *how do we collect data that are suitable for our research questions?* and *how do we analyze them?* In experimental research, for example, we ask: *how can we best manipulate the independent variable of interest?*, *how can we identify and make potential confounding variables constant across comparison groups?* and *why do we randomize the selection of participants when assigning them into groups?*

There is a close hierarchical relation between ontology, epistemology, and methodology that underlies the way in which a particular person goes about conducting research. We now discuss the positivist paradigm from which experimental research originated.

The positivist paradigm

The *positivist paradigm* (or positivism) takes a *realist* perspective, which believes that the object of an inquiry really exists *out there* in the world. In language learning, for example, the positivists would assert that there are objects, such as language learning motivation, self-regulation and interlanguage inside each language learner's mind. In experimental research, they would also believe that a causal relationship between two variables can exist and that such a relationship can be investigated objectively through independent measures.

Ontologically, the positivists therefore argue that reality is governed by immutable laws and mechanisms essentially independent of by whom, when and how it is being examined. For self-regulation research, a researcher postulates that there is a cognitive mechanism that governs individuals' self-regulated behaviors, such as goal setting, planning, monitoring, and evaluation of their language use and learning. Such a cognitive mechanism may involve memory (working and long-term) and human information processing. The assumption that something exists is usually described through theory that should be robust enough to be generalizable across individuals and contexts.

Epistemologically, the positivists take an *objectivist stance* toward an inquiry. This means that they try to completely remove their influence from the research setting, so that they can make an accurate correspondence between their observations and the reality they aim to understand. For example, if they were to judge the level of English language proficiency of a group of language learners as accurately and fairly as possible, they would ask the learners to take a well-developed, standardized test, such as TOEFL (Test of English as a Foreign Language) and IELTS (International English Language Testing System), rather than ask students to subjectively evaluate their own proficiency levels. In an experimental study, the researchers should not be the teachers who provide a specific treatment to learners because the researchers are likely to favor one condition over another and therefore invest more effort in making a particular treatment work (see e.g. Takimoto 2008). This would make it difficult to replicate the findings or generalize the findings to other learners or settings.

In a language program evaluation, a well-trained evaluator not involved in the program or institute may be assigned to evaluate a program so that judgments are not influenced by a conflict of interest. The evaluator is likely to be sitting quietly at the back of the classroom and using a well-developed observation scheme and objectively interview teachers, students and administrators. When we conduct an experimental study, we have to be careful about *conflicts of interest* (i.e. an unfair gain of a person or group of people when their particular role can favor an outcome). Since experimental research strives for evidence of a causal-like relationship, researchers have to make sure that they are not a subjective factor influencing the research outcome.

Methodologically, the positivists carry out their research by controlling variables and manipulating the research setting. Variables are controlled by, for example, defining an operationalized construct, developing a systematic measure of the construct, piloting it prior to its actual use, and standardizing data collection procedures, etc. In terms of manipulation, they attempt to keep confounding variables constant and vary conditions in order to test for the differential effects of the independent variable of interest. On the basis of what we have discussed so far, it appears that experimental research is largely underpinned by the positivist paradigm. Nonetheless, it is unlikely that any experimenters today would describe themselves as pure positivists.

The postpositivist paradigm

The postpositivist paradigm (or postpositivism) is regarded as a *modified positivism*. The postpositivists take similar stances to those of the positivists. However, some of their stances have been modified to distinguish ideology from reality when conducting research. At an ontological level, unlike the positivists, the postpositivists maintain that, although the object of their inquiry exists outside and independent of their minds, they can never perceive it with total accuracy. This position is known as the *critical realist ontology* (Guba & Lincoln 2005). The reason for this imperfect perception is that no single research instrument or analysis is perfect. There is no perfect experimental research, but researchers can get better and better in the conduct of their research. The use of the term *causal-like relationships* instead of *causal relationships* suggests that it is difficult to make claims about causality given the limitations of our research designs.

Epistemologically, the postpositivists assume that objectivity is nearly impossible to achieve in research. They, however, retain the notion of objectivity as an ideology to regulate their research. While the truth or fact remains *objective* in the sense that it does not depend on their attempts to know it, the postpositivists argue that it is more or less a *regulative* idea. This modified positivistic position stresses that researchers can never entirely know the truth even though truth is absolute. They can, however, *approximate* it and can get closer and closer to it with better and better theories. In relation to language learning research, for example, it is not easy to verify the truthfulness of a theory formulated by researchers on the basis of simply focusing on accumulating *confirmatory evidence* that supports the theory/hypothesis. Researchers must also attempt to disprove it by attempting to gather any negative or disconfirming evidence. The postpositivists argue that there is no theory that is exempt from being criticized by means of objective, logical instruments. This principle follows the idea of the so-called *objectivity of science*, which should inform the objectivity of the critical method used.

However, it is important to note that while we try to be as objective as possible, we have to admit that objectivity in the social sciences and language learning research is more difficult to achieve than in the natural sciences. This is mainly because research deals with human beings. It is also rare that social scientists, including language learning researchers, can free themselves from the value system of their own social class/setting. This revised conception of objectivity and the nature of truth results in what they call a *modified objectivist perspective*.

Methodologically, the postpositivists modify the positivists' position by encouraging the use of *multiple strategies* for gathering and analyzing data (including qualitative data) within an experimental or quasi-experimental framework. Multiple strategies will allow them to gain a more complete set of empirical evidence. Experimental studies in language learning today adopt a *hybrid approach* (see Chapter 8) to collect and analyze both quantitative and qualitative data to address real-world practice. However, unlike the constructivist paradigm (discussed below), the data collection and analysis are still carried out and treated within the critical realist ontology. While the qualitative and quantitative data and analysis may be imperfect reflections of reality, it is believed that that reality exists independently of their attempts to know about it. The best way to find out about it, they would argue, is to maintain as much objectivity as possible. Qualitative data, for example, needs to be coded systematically by more than one coder. *Inter-coder reliability* estimates should be calculated and must be within a set reliability criterion in order to reflect the level of agreement between coders on what they discover.

The constructivist paradigm

Unlike the positivist and postpositivist paradigms, the constructivist paradigm does not share the realist or critical realist perspective. On the contrary, it takes the *relativist stance* that realities are multiple and exist in people's minds. Ontologically, therefore, there are multiple realities out there that are constructed by individual observers. It is important to note that *multiple realities* at the level of what there is to know (ontological) is different from the *multiple strategies* for gathering and analyzing data that the postpositivists embrace (Lynch 2003).

Epistemologically, the constructivist paradigm takes the *subjectivist position* that attempts to know things or find a reality are inherently and unavoidably subjective. Reality is therefore dependent upon, rather than independent of, research inquiry. This means that facts cannot be established as aspects of knowledge that are independent of human values. At the methodological level, the constructivist paradigm adopts a non-experimental, non-manipulative set of research procedures. Such have been referred to as ethnographic, dialogic and hermeneutic. Ethnographic studies employ a range of techniques associated with *prolonged fieldwork*, such as participant observations and in-depth interviews. Dialogic approaches are methods that allow an interaction with participants in the research setting. The constructivists argue that a dialog is essential as it encourages the participants to develop an understanding of what is being researched in their own terms. The term hermeneutic describes a research process in which the researcher forms interpretations or constructions, based on how close they can get to the data through observation notes and interview recordings, etc. This initiates a potentially never-ending cycle of interpreting these constructions, and refining and forming new constructions.

The choice of research paradigm does not predetermine the choice of research methods. We may believe that social phenomena are objective realities that exist independently of individuals' subjective frames of reference, but we can still choose to use various different qualitative methods, such as interviews and observations to investigate such phenomena. Researchers ascribing to the constructivist paradigm can similarly make use of frequency counts and other quantitative methods, such as questionnaires and tests associated with the positivistic or postpositivist paradigm.

In summary, no single research paradigm should be adopted to the exclusion of others because researchers need to know what works best and is appropriate to address their research purposes and questions within a topic domain, and the context of their research, including participants and social settings. In experimental research in language learning, we have to deal with research activities that have an impact on other people's lives or society. Furthermore, we often deal with topics related to linguistic knowledge, psychological processes, learner characteristics and factors that may affect their learning. When examining any of these topics, we are required to consider issues related to the explanation of what an abstract construct of interest is, how to measure it, and how it may be related to language learning. We are also likely to deal with a number of learners or individuals in order to identify an underlying trait or universal principle. It appears that the postpositivist paradigm is closely in line with the practice of today's experimental research.

In contrast, some topics such as the culture, values, or traditions associated with a particular context can be more appropriately examined through a constructivist perspective (e.g. by using case study or an ethnographic study). Unlike language tests or questionnaires, which are instruments in quantitative research, researchers themselves are in fact the research instruments. They must have good social skills that help them elicit data and hence need to be trusted by the members of the target community. Being objective and keeping a distance from the participants in this research context will neither work nor yield anything insightful. Clearly, research participants can reveal their information more honestly when they trust the researchers. Subjectivity is therefore necessary to pursue this kind of knowledge. It should also be noted that different researchers bring with them different background knowledge and experience into the research setting. They may see and interpret the same phenomenon differently. Some quantitative researchers, such as experimenters, may see this as a validity problem. However, since the aim of ethnographic research, for example, is to portray the setting and participants as they are, researchers in this field do not attempt to generalize their findings to other participants or contexts in the way that experimental researchers do. Qualitative researchers need to have different ways to validate their research findings. Strategies to enhance qualitative validity or trustworthiness include thick descriptions, member-check processes and debriefing (see Burns 2010; Casanave 2010; Starfield 2010).

The paradigm discussion has raised some major issues for language learning researchers (see Guba & Lincoln 2005). All researchers should articulate the philosophical basis for their research inquiry and regardless of the research paradigm they adopt, they need to be clear about what they will accept as legitimate evidence. We will next discuss processes in experimental research that are somewhat inherent to the postpositivist paradigm.

Experimental research processes

Prior to a discussion of experimental research design in the next chapter, it is useful to discuss key experimental research processes. When conducting academic research, it is vital to follow processes and procedures that can promote research success. Experimental research is no exception. Figure 3.1 presents the key stages of research processes. It is important to note that while research processes may appear sequential in Figure 3.1, in practice they are *iterative* (i.e. going back and forth). In Figure 3.1, solid double-headed arrows are used between each process in the case when issues are closely related. The dashed double-headed arrows are used to address

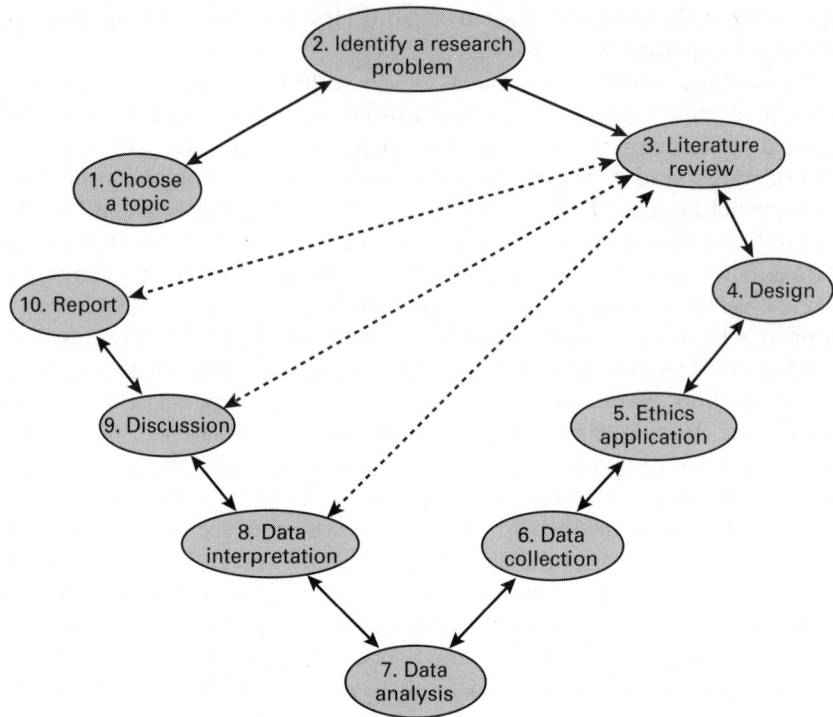

FIGURE 3.1   *A typical experimental research process*

the importance of making sense of the data in relation to the literature in the final processes. We will use Tian and Macaro's (2012) experimental research to illustrate some relevant issues.

Choosing a topic

In order to choose an appropriate research topic, it is necessary to read widely in a specific field of study. It is important to find a topic that we are really *interested* in as we will have to deal with it for a lengthy period of time. However, we need to check also that a topic is an *important* one and will be of interest to other scholars in the field. When we consider a topic, it is essential to evaluate beforehand whether it has already been well researched, and is *researchable* and *feasible* within a given time frame and using available resources (Paltridge & Starfield 2007). We should also have a sense of whether it will yield *new findings* or provide a *robust evidence-based solution* to a problem. Tian and Macaro's (2012, p. 367) research title 'Comparing the effect of teacher codeswitching with English-only explanations on the vocabulary acquisition of Chinese university students: A lexical focus-on-form study' was likely to yield new useful research findings.

Identifying a research problem

Research problems, of which there may be many within a specific research topic, need to be chosen carefully, so that the scope of the study is *manageable*. To properly choose a research problem, we need to conduct a *comprehensive review* of the relevant literature. Sometimes we may think we have found a good research topic and believe that it has not been studied before, which may not be the case. An up-to-date review of the literature and expert advice can be useful to find out whether the topic is suitable. To choose a good topic, we need to identify an important gap (i.e. a research problem) in the literature. Tian and Macaro (2012, p. 367) stated their research problem as follows:

> To date there has been research on teacher beliefs about first language (L1) use, its functions and its distribution in the interaction, but little on its effect on aspects of learning. Previous research on intentional vocabulary teaching has shown it to be effective, but whether the lexical information provided to learners is more effective in L1 or L2 has been under-researched and, moreover, has only been investigated in a reading comprehension context.

Doing a literature review

The relevant literature usually refers to existing theories and hypotheses, as well as previous empirical research relevant to the topic and problem. We can find the literature through academic books, research journals, databases, and conference presentations. A good review of the literature is critical because it allows us to gain a better understanding of the research problem. It helps us avoid *unintentional replication* of previous studies and gain insights into both theory and methodology. It is the knowledge of relevant research that helps us identify the *frontiers* of research aims, problems, questions and/or hypotheses. A review of the literature allows us to put our initial research questions into perspective. In other words, if we cannot link our topic and research problem with existing knowledge, we are unlikely to make a contribution to the field. One of Tian and Macaro's (2012, p. 368) key research aims was 'to explore the relative benefits of intentional vocabulary learning versus incidental vocabulary learning in a focus-on-form context (Long 1991).' At the end of their literature review, Tian and Macaro (2012, p. 373) asked three research questions:

1   To what extent is lexical focus-on-form beneficial during a focus on meaning activity (such as listening comprehension) in terms of students' receptive vocabulary learning?

2   Is students' receptive vocabulary learning better facilitated by a teacher's use of codeswitching or by providing L2-only information?

3   Do lower proficiency students benefit more than higher proficiency students from teacher codeswitching? In other words, is level of proficiency a covariate of the potential gains made from either condition?

Designing an experimental study

After reviewing the literature, we should have a good understanding of how to design a study to address the problem. We should have an idea of whether it would be properly addressed through quantitative (numbers), qualitative (words/descriptions) or mixed-methods research. A piece of experimental research is typically a *quantitative* one, which can combine some qualitative data (i.e. mixed-methods). It is important to be aware of our ability to learn about a particular research method (e.g. quantitative or qualitative). Beginning researchers or research students need to learn about the research method required to appropriately address a research problem. It is at this time that they need to study a particular research method very deeply so that they know what is involved, its strengths and weaknesses, and how to analyze the data necessary to answer the research questions. It is better to study research methods beforehand, rather than to spend a lot of time, effort and resources collecting data, only to realize that the data do not yield answers to the research questions being asked. Designing an experimental study involves *planning* how and when to conduct the research. We need to consider research instruments and data elicitation techniques, a research setting, research participants and length of a data collection period. Based on the implications from their literature review, Tian and Macaro (2012, p. 373) stated that:

> We used an experimental design with randomization to learning conditions in "extracted" (i.e. non-intact) classes, and with pretests, posttests and delayed tests. We controlled for teacher effect by having a single teacher (one of the authors) teach all conditions and we controlled for activity type by centring the vocabulary teaching episodes around one task type (listening comprehension).

Considering ethics

Ethical considerations are part of the research design stage. It is important to present this as a distinct sub-stage, so that their importance is not ignored or overlooked. In experimental research in language learning, we need human participants to provide data to answer research questions. We need to consider whether there will be any *physical* or *psychological* harm to our research participants. Other ethical considerations include the need to obtain participants' or their guardians' consents. Participants need to know what is involved in being part of the research. Participation in any study should be on a *voluntary* basis. Participants should be free to withdraw from participating and to withdraw their data for research use at any time. We should consider the issues of *privacy* and *anonymity* to protect the participants' rights and their *confidentiality*. The data should not be used for any other purpose beyond that of our initial research. It is common nowadays that research projects dealing with human participants be approved at an institutional level prior to any data collection. This is essential because there can be legal implications if a study is misconducted.

Although Tian and Macaro (2012) did not state much about ethical considerations, it can be implied that they had carefully considered research ethics as they stated that 'toward the end of September all students had the research project explained to them, and received an informed consent letter. Subsequently, 117 students agreed to participate' (p. 373).

Collecting data

The first stage of execution of the research stage is the collection of data. In experimental research, this involves setting up an experimental site (e.g. an experimental laboratory), which allows us some control of *independent* and *dependent* variables. There is a wide range of instruments to gather data related to the research problems. Quantitative instruments include language tests, questionnaires, ratings and observation lists. It is important to note that unlike qualitative research, many quantitative studies need a pilot study (including, for example, a mini trial of data collection, an execution of the procedures of an experimental treatment, and a testing of the research instruments to be used for *reliability*). In many cases, a series of experimental studies is expected because the first study is typically used to inform the following one. As a research student, it can be risky to propose a highly complex experimental study, because you are likely to make mistakes due to a lack of experience. It is better to set up a few small-scale studies, and to learn about the processes and limitations involved as you progress through them. Thus through an iterative process, our studies should improve over time. Tian and Macaro (2012) provided a detailed discussion of how the participants were allocated into experimental and control groups, how the instructional intervention and test materials were designed and considered to address the research problems, aims and research questions. They summarized their research procedure as follows (p. 375):

> After establishing the baseline tests, the vocabulary pretest was administered. One week later the instructional intervention began, and this lasted for 6 weeks. Two weeks after the end of the instructional intervention and last posttest a delayed test was carried out; the study was carried out over a period of 9 weeks. For a diagrammatic explanation of the study procedure, see Appendix 2.

Analyzing data

Once experimental data have been collected, we will begin to think more concretely about data analysis. All the obtained data need to be checked for completeness prior to a preliminary data analysis. Quantitative data are usually in the form of numbers. Researchers typically employ various statistical tests to answer their research questions. A statistical test is determined by the nature of the research question being asked. If, for example, we are investigating a potential linear relationship, a type of correlational analysis may be adopted. In experimental research, we are most likely to examine the differences between groups of learners exposed to different learning or task conditions. The need for an appropriate statistical test of our data will depend on whether our data are *parametric* or *non-parametric* (see Chapter 10). It is important to note that prior to any statistical analysis, we have to go through various *meticulous steps* in preparing the data for analysis. Such steps include data entry to a statistical program, data cleaning, checking for outliers, making sure that the statistical assumptions for a particular test have been met by the data and checking for the reliability of the research instruments. Tian and Macaro (2012) provided detailed information on their statistical analyses to answer each of the research questions. They use a repeated-measures ANOVA (analysis of variance) to compare changes within learner groups, and an ANCOVA (analysis of covariance) to compare differences between experimental groups.

Interpreting data

In experimental research, it is important to attempt to go *beyond statistical significance,* which merely assesses the chance that we are wrong in our findings. We also need to assess the *practical significance* of our findings. In particular, we need to take into account the influence of the sample size. Practical significance is related to whether the detected relationship is meaningful according to the underlying theory and the context of the study. It allows us to understand better the extent of the effect of an independent variable on a dependent variable, beyond simple statistical significance. In qualitative research, we usually present and discuss our interpretations and explanations of the findings in narrative form. We try to make sense of the data by asking what it tells us about the research problem. For example, Tian and Macaro (2012, p. 378), through the use of ANCOVA, found 'a significant group effect on posttest scores after controlling the effect of pretest scores, $F(1,64) = 9.178$, $p = 0.01^*$, $\eta_p^2 = 0.13$. A small effect size was obtained.' The researchers also used tables to report statistical findings because they made it easy to compare statistical values.

Discussing findings

Regardless of whether a study is carried out using quantitative, qualitative or mixed-methods, we must attempt to relate our research findings to the relevant theories and previous studies we have addressed in the review of the literature. This stage is connected closely with the *interpretation stage*, as well as the writing stage. We ask what our findings mean in light of the underlying theories and the issues addressed by previous researchers. When we discuss our findings, we can explain what the findings mean, and then compare or contrast them with those in previous research. It is therefore important to revisit the literature on the topic and, when appropriate, to update it. In this stage, we need to articulate why our findings are similar to or different from previous research findings, as well as how and to what extent they support the theories we aim to advance.

Tian and Macaro (2012, p. 381) pointed out that 'the results suggest that Lexical Focus-on-Form, during (or at least closely associated with) a comprehension activity, is beneficial for vocabulary acquisition. The two treatment groups made significant gains over the control group in the long term.' The researchers also discussed their research findings in relation to previous studies. For example, 'our findings supported the claim made by Ellis *et al.* (2011), who reported that teachers and students could navigate in and out of focusing on aspects of the code while still keeping the overall orientation of the message intact' (p. 382).

Writing up a report

Clearly we do not wait until the end of the research project to begin writing up the research report. As can be seen in Figure 3.1, the report should cover all stages of the research. It is strategically advisable to write continuously from the beginning of a research study to the end. However, the writing stage here may refer to the stage in which we aim to put all the different pieces of information together, making it more coherent for us to evaluate our study internally before we present it to other people. A research report may be in the form of a thesis or dissertation, or a research article, depending on the reason why we are doing the study in the first place. We should examine whether our original research rationale has remained the same or whether it has changed. It is important to make sure that we state actual research procedures, report and discuss the findings. At the end of the report, we should provide a discussion of potential research limitations and implications for future research. Tian and Macaro (2012, p. 383) discussed their research limitations in terms of potential differences between their experimental conditions and what happens in a normal classroom context.

A research report should be in a form *intelligible* to the target readership. This stage is close to the finishing line, at which point we will celebrate our achievement and share what we have contributed to existing knowledge.

Summary

We have discussed how experimental research is influenced by the paradigm adopted by the researcher. Paradigms are discussed at an ontological (i.e. truth), epistemological (i.e. the relationship between researchers and truth) and methodological (methods for establishing truth) level. While we cannot discuss all the issues related to research paradigms comprehensively in this chapter, such a discussion is important for an understanding of the philosophy behind experimental research. This chapter has also discussed experimental research processes. The next chapter will present and discuss experimental research designs for language learning research and ethical considerations.

Research exercise

To download exercises for this chapter visit: http://www.bloomsbury.com/experimental-research-methods-in-language-learning-9781441189110/

Discussion questions

1 Do you find it useful to distinguish the positivist, from the postpositivist and the constructivist? Why or why not?
2 Which difficult concepts about research paradigms have you encountered so far?
3 What are important aspects of a good review of the research literature?
4 In your view, which experimental stage(s) is the most critical to good experimental research?

5 Reflection: What is the most important lesson you have learned from this chapter?

Further reading

Guba, EG & Lincoln, YS 2005, 'Paradigmatic controversies, contradictions, and emerging confluences', in NK Denzin & YS Lincoln (eds), *The Sage handbook of qualitative research*, 3rd edn, Sage, Thousand Oaks.

This influential chapter identifies and treats research paradigms comprehensively (e.g. positivism, postpositivism, constructivism, critical-theory and participatory). It discusses major issues confronting research paradigms.

LeCompte, MD & Schensul, J 2010, *Designing and conducting ethnographic research: an introduction*, AltaMira Press, Plymouth, UK.

Chapter 3 provides a comparative and accessible synthesis of multiple research perspectives including the positivist, critical, interpretive, ecological, and social network paradigms.

CHAPTER FOUR

Experimental Research Designs

Leading questions

1 What is a research design?
2 Can you think of an example of a weak experimental study? What makes it weak?
3 Can you think of an example of a strong experimental study? What makes it strong?

Introduction

This chapter presents several types of experimental research design for language learning research, for example, pre-experimental, single-case, true experimental, and quasi-experimental design. Several examples of language learning research that adopt certain experimental designs are illustrated. We conclude this chapter by pointing out the limitations of experimental research.

Types of experimental research design

In previous chapters, we have already mentioned experimental research and some designs that have been used in language learning research. A research design is a *systematic outline* of the plans, stages and strategies involved in each of the experimental research processes. There are at least four major experimental research designs: *pre-experimental, single-case, randomized experimental* and *quasi-experimental designs*. This section will discuss the characteristics of these major types of design, but we will restrict our attention to designs that have been used in language learning research. Experimental researchers often combine the good features of one design with those of another to address a particular research problem or question.

The key distinction between these experimental research designs is *the extent to which a design deals with the threats to the internal validity of the study. Internal validity* is defined as *how well an experimental study can lead to a causal-like conclusion about the influence of the independent variable on the dependent variable.* Whether or not the conclusion can be trusted depends on the extent to which other confounding variables (e.g. maturation, attrition and instrument effects) influence the research findings. That is, the more confounding variables interfere, the worse the internal validity of the study.

Pre-experimental designs

As the name of the design suggests, this is a preliminary form of a more complex experimental design, such as a randomized design. This design is labeled as *pre-experimental* because it is not robust enough to draw conclusions about a causal-like relationship or a treatment effect. Pre-experimental designs are more exploratory than confirmatory in regard to making inferences about the relationship between an independent variable and a dependent variable. There is *no randomization* in a pre-experiment. Usually pre-experimental research is carried out in an *intact* or existing class. Pre-experimental designs are therefore weak versions of the quasi-experimental designs discussed below. There are many other variables that could play a role in influencing any findings based on a pre-experiment because many variables that are not controlled by the researcher. These variables may include a natural course of cognitive development or maturation in the participants, and specific events that may happen during the pre-experiment.

The three most common pre-experimental designs are: a *one-group posttest-only design*, a *one-group pretest-posttest design*, and a *posttest-only with non-equivalent groups*.

One-group posttest-only design

In the *one-group posttest-only* design, there is no measure of participants' dependent variable of interest (e.g. grammatical and vocabulary knowledge). Figure 4.1 presents a diagram of a one-group posttest-only design.

After an experimental treatment, participants are given a posttest and the scores are checked. If high-test scores are achieved, on the basis of the design, it is difficult to assume that they resulted from the treatment alone

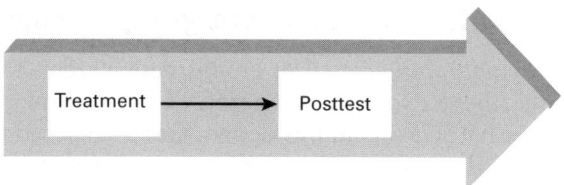

FIGURE 4.1   *A diagram of a one-group posttest-only design*

because there is *no comparison* of test scores with scores achieved before the treatment, and there are no comparison group scores to compare the posttest scores to. Student learning may naturally improve as they move on with lessons. The teacher's experience or attitude may play a role in influencing student learning.

One-group pretest-posttest design

The *one-group pretest-posttest* design is an improvement on the above design. There is only one group of participants who will be exposed to a treatment. Participants are tested before and after the treatment. In some way, this design is similar to action research where a teacher researcher aims to improve student learning by implementing some activities believed to help address a problem (see Burns 2010 for action research). Figure 4.2 presents a diagram of the one-group pretest-posttest design.

Their pretest and posttest scores will be compared to evaluate whether there is a significant gain. Researchers may use the paired-samples *t*-test (a parametric test) or Wilcoxon signed ranks test (a non-parametric version of the paired-samples *t*-test) to compare the group means (see Chapters 13 and 15). Researchers may assume that other independent variables such as pre-existing ability, attitudes and motivation, are constant among the participants. However, as we have discussed in the previous chapters, several independent variables can interact with the target independent variables, thereby interfering with measures of the target dependent variable.

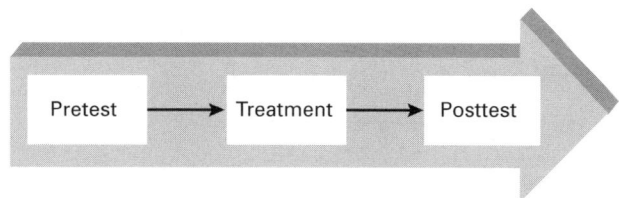

FIGURE 4.2   *A diagram of a one-group pretest-posttest design*

Posttest-only with non-equivalent groups design

The *posttest-only with non-equivalent groups* design seems to address the limitations of the above two designs in terms of comparison groups. There are two groups of participants in this design. One is exposed to an experimental treatment, whereas the other receives no treatment. In this design, there is no evidence to suggest that both groups are equivalent. At the end of the treatment period, both groups of students take a posttest and their test scores are compared. Figure 4.3 presents a diagram of the *posttest-only with non-equivalent groups* design.

Researchers use the independent-samples *t*-test (a parametric test) or the Mann-Whitney U test (a non-parametric version of the independent-samples *t*-test) to compare the means. If the experimental group outperformed the control group, the researchers may conclude that the treatment is effective. However, although it appears sufficient to make such a claim, problems lie in the fact that other threats are unknown (e.g. pre-existing ability or personal attributes between the two groups, maturation, and instrument effects). *Randomization* (discussed in further detail below) can help eliminate several threats to the internal validity of the study.

A pre-experimental design is the *weakest experimental design* since it does not have a *random assignment* of research participants, a *control group* that allows comparisons of a dependent variable, and effective strategies to control *confounding variables*. A pre-experimental design is *not recommended as a design for a main study* of an experimental research in language learning. This is merely because it does not allow appropriate inferences about a causal-like relationship between the independent and dependent variables. Nonetheless, pre-experimental design is *useful* for researchers to try out some developed treatment procedures and test instruments, and evaluate how they work in an experimental environment before commencing the main study. It is therefore *highly recommended* as a *pilot study* because researchers can begin to understand what works and what

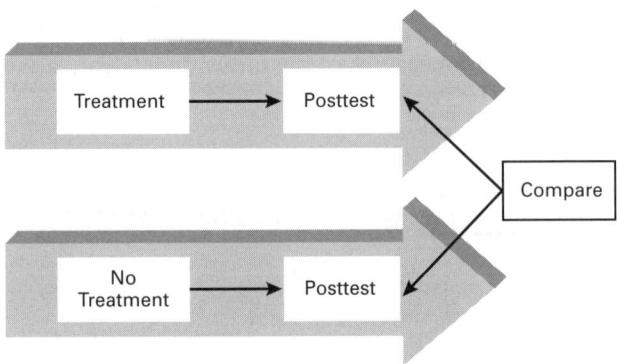

FIGURE 4.3   *A diagram of a posttest-only with non-equivalent groups design*

does not in their research design. Through a pilot study process, researchers will also realize any unforeseen threats to their research validity.

Single-case designs

The *single-case experimental design* is an experiment that has a sample size of *one* participant. Hence, there is *no comparison* group or *random assignment*. First, it is important to note that research on an individual or a small group of individuals has had its place in language learning or applied linguistics. In qualitative research, there are the so-called *case studies*, which allow researchers to explore and observe an individual's language learning without intervening. *A case study*, nevertheless, *should not be confused with a single-case design*. A case study does not typically aim to find out about causal-like effects through an explicit intervention like a single-case design. A single-case design aims to *examine whether an intervention is effective for a particular individual in terms of improvements in learning or behaviors*. Hence, similar to the randomized experiment and quasi-experiment designs, it exerts control over some independent variables by manipulating them.

In applied psychological, clinical or educational research, there are cases of individuals that need special considerations. Consequently, it can often be difficult to apply the findings of an experimental study to a specific individual. In language learning, there can be, for example, severely learning-disabled learners, learners with a lack of concentration or a high level of anxiety, and gifted learners. We may aim to test whether an intervention used in a *group experimental study* (e.g. true and quasi-experiments) is applicable to a certain individual. The nature of the single-case design is *dynamic*, since it is able to respond to an individual. It allows researchers to modify the nature of an intervention and search for an alternative intervention that is effective via objective measurements.

A single-case design is simply an extension of the quasi-experimental, one-group *time-series* design (Johnson & Christensen 2008). One popular type of a single-case design is the *withdrawal design*, which begins by measuring the target behavior of an individual (e.g. degree of disruptive behavior, concentration level and retention of linguistic knowledge in the classroom) over a period of time. This phase is important because it is used to establish a *baseline*, which serves as a *control period* for comparisons with the effects of the treatment. A baseline should be *stable* in order to serve as a standard for comparisons. In the next phase, the researcher introduces a *treatment* that is hypothesized to improve the learner's behavior. This treatment is given for a period of time, and the individual's target behavior is observed. The treatment stops when there is *ample evidence* that the intervention has had an effect on the target behavior or learning. In the final phase, the *treatment is withdrawn* and the behavior is observed

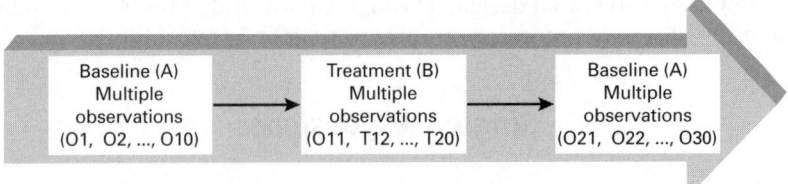

FIGURE 4.4   *A diagram of a withdrawal single-case design procedure (ABA Design)*

again over a period of time. It is expected that the behavior will *revert back* to its original state (i.e. return to the baseline condition). *Reverting back to the original baseline state is used to demonstrate the effectiveness of the treatment.* Figure 4.4 presents a diagram of a withdrawal single-case design procedure. A single-case design typically presents *graphic displays* and tables with a high level of detail of how the study is carried out. This is essential for transparency and replication by other researchers.

To briefly illustrate a graphic display of a single-case design, let us look at the following research scenario. Somchai, a Thai student who had trouble with reading comprehension, seemed to lack monitoring comprehension skills. To help Somchai improve his reading, an intervention that promoted monitoring comprehension through various activities and explicit instruction was implemented. The researcher asked Somchai to read texts and discuss how he engaged in self-monitoring.

The following was the data collection procedure and treatment. In the initial phase (establishing the baseline phase), his regular teacher and the researcher rated the quality of his comprehension monitoring across tasks. They assigned an average score for his monitoring skill. This phase lasted ten days. The inter-rater reliability estimate between the teacher and researcher was high ($r = 0.93$). Any disagreements were discussed and resolved. After the period of ten days, the researcher felt confident enough that these observations could form a *baseline* for comparison after the treatment. In the following ten days, an explicit intervention was implemented. The intervention was carried out by his regular teacher, who was trained by the researcher on how to provide instructions and carry out tasks. Somchai was engaged in activities on how to self-monitor during reading tasks and how to assess any reading difficulties he experienced. The teacher also provided explicit feedback on his reading performance and instructed him on how to improve his reading and self-monitoring. The teacher and researcher observed his comprehension reading and his verbal reports on how he monitored his reading comprehension. Both the teacher and researcher independently rated his self-monitoring during reading comprehension. After the period of ten days, the teacher and researcher then withdrew the

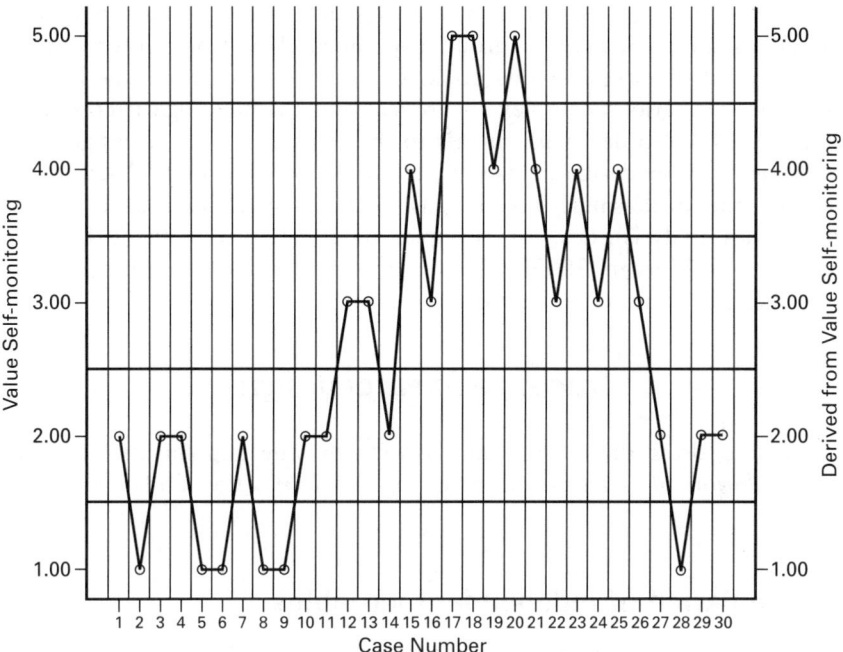

FIGURE 4.5 *A diagram of Somchai's self-monitoring during reading*

intervention, but continued to ask Somchai to carry out reading tasks and to report his thoughts. This withdrawal period lasted another ten days. Figure 4.5 presents a diagram of Somchai's self-monitoring during reading.

In this diagram, we can see that his comprehension monitoring improved during the intervention and started to decline after the intervention was withdrawn. The researcher concluded that the intervention was effective in helping Somchai improve his comprehension monitoring.

It is important to note that *ethics* should always be taken into account in all kinds of experimental research designs. A single-case design is no exception. For example, we need to ask ourselves whether it is ethical to return the participant to the original, undesirable behavioral state to prove that our treatment works. In the case of Somchai, the teacher should continue to implement the intervention method after the experiment was completed. This design has not been studied in language learning research as much as true and quasi-experimental designs. An example of a study that applied a single-case design is Kim (2008), who applied the logic of a single-case design to examine two different instructional approaches to improve the oral English skills of two learners. When Kim established a baseline for each learner, the data gathering techniques relied on the use of pretests and posttests.

It is to be hoped that experimental researchers will adopt this type of design as an alternative to group experimental designs. Unfortunately, it is beyond the scope of this book to cover single-case designs because they involve various complex theoretical and methodological considerations (e.g. how to deal with threats to the research validity), designs (e.g. multiple-baseline designs, changing-criterion designs, multiple-treatment designs and quasi-single-case designs) and statistical approaches (e.g. a time-series analysis). See, for example, Gast (2010), Kazdin (2011), and Morgan and Morgan (2009), who treat this type of design comprehensively in clinical, behavioral, and applied settings.

True experimental designs

We first address three important aspects of true experimental designs: *Manipulation of independent variables*, *randomization* and *comparison groups*.

Manipulation of independent variables

As discussed in Chapter 2, an experimental study assumes that an independent variable causes changes in a dependent variable. As we will see in the designs discussed below, researchers manipulate independent variables in order to test their hypotheses. There are three common methods researchers have used to manipulate an independent variable (Johnson & Christensen 2008). The first is known as the *presence or absence technique*, the second is the *amount technique*, and the third is the *type technique*. When the *presence or absence technique* is employed, the experimental group will receive a treatment, whereas the control group will not receive the treatment. In a real-life situation, a control group may be a class taught using a traditional or regular method. For example, Rahimi (2013) examined whether training student reviewers can help them assist their peers through providing high-quality feedback. There were two groups (i.e. a trained group and an untrained group).

When the *amount technique* is employed, experimental groups receive different amounts of the independent variable of interest. For example, Al-Homoud and Schmitt (2009) compared the effects of extensive (as a treatment group) and intensive (as a control group) reading approaches on Saudi Arabian students' vocabulary knowledge and reading fluency. Serrano (2010) also compared the effects of extensive instruction (over 7 months) and intensive instruction (over 4.5 weeks) on students' language learning.

When the *type technique* is employed, researchers divide the independent variable into types. For example, Ahmadian (2012) manipulated *online planning* into three types: pressure online planning, unguided careful online planning and guided careful online planning. Takimoto (2008) varied three experimental conditions (i.e. deductive instruction, inductive instruction with problem-solving tasks and inductive instruction with structured input tasks), and had a control group. Sagarra and Abbuhl (2013) varied four types of automated feedback for different groups of learners (i.e. no feedback, utterance rejection, recasts and enhanced recasts).

Randomization

It is important that we understand the difference between *random assignment* and *random selection or sampling. Random selection,* on the one hand, is a typical procedure in survey research that aims to generate a representative sample of a population group. However, random selection also applies in experimental research where there is a larger *population* that is difficult to recruit and include in an experimental study (e.g. due to their willingness or availability to participate). In random sampling, each member of the population has an equal chance of being selected as part of the sample. A representative sample will have characteristics similar to those of the target population, and therefore can represent the population.

Random assignment, on the other hand, is a technique used to place research participants into groups (e.g. experimental or control groups) in experimental research on the basis of chance. In other words, random assignment occurs after random sampling, although random assignment can be done without random sampling (e.g. when all members of the target population are present). Random assignment is important to minimize *the potential effect of confounding variables on the results of the study.* Furthermore, random assignment is an objective procedure to reduce the *subjective selection* of participants by the researcher. Subjective selection of participants might affect the research outcomes, rendering them hard to replicate by other researchers. Participants should have an equal chance of being placed in either group.

Random assignment is a *requirement for true experimental research* design (thereby also known as *randomized experimental designs*) because it enhances the internal validity of the study. Comparison groups (further noted below) need to be equivalent, or similar, in all possible aspects at the beginning of the research. If their characteristics are highly comparable, when we test the effect of an independent variable of interest on a dependent variable after the treatment period, we will have a high level of confidence that a statistical difference between the two groups can be attributed to the independent variable. Nonetheless, it is important to note that random assignment *does not necessarily guarantee* that we can control all extraneous variables because random assignment is still based on chance in the distribution of participants.

It is important to note that in true experimental design, random assignment is related to the task of assigning participants into groups. When researchers randomly assign experimental conditions or tasks to groups of participants, it does not make the study a true experimental study. The study should be considered a *quasi-experimental study*. For example, Hulstijn and Laufer (2001) randomly assigned their experimental tasks (i.e. reading comprehension with marginal glosses, reading comprehension plus 'fill in,' and writing composition and incorporating the target words) to six intact classes (pp. 547–8). Bitchener and Knoch (2008), who examined the extent to which different written correction feedback options helped students improve the accuracy in their use of the referential indefinite article 'a' and referential definite article 'the,' randomly assigned the four intact classes to one of the four treatment groups (p. 419). Adams, Nuevo and Egi (2011), who investigated how learners provided each other with different types of feedback and how they promoted learning of the English past tense and locatives, randomized the order of different treatment tasks to assign to participants. The researchers also randomly assigned classes (not participants) to the control (N = 32) and experimental groups (N = 39). Goo (2012), who evaluated the effectiveness of recasts over metalinguistic feedback on the learning of the English that-trace filter, randomly assigned six participating intact classes to one of the three conditions: 'recasts, metalinguistic feedback, and control' (p. 454). We will examine available methods for random assignment later in this chapter.

Comparison groups

Unlike the pre-experimental research, true experimental research uses random assignment and comparison groups. It is important to understand the rationale behind having comparison groups in experimental research. Having two equivalent groups with different conditions for the purpose of comparison is a basic element of experimental research. In regard to an independent variable of interest, after examining the literature thoroughly, experimental researchers will start to develop a hypothesis about the effect of the independent variable on a dependent variable, such as language learning success, linguistic accuracy, fluency and learning behaviors (e.g. improved self-regulation, higher motivation and less anxiety).

For example, a hypothesis could be *Pair interactions will lead to a better use of communication strategies in speaking.* Hence, it may be argued that those who are engaged in a pair interaction activity will be different to those who are not, in terms of their development of communication strategies and their success in using them in speaking. It is important to note here that researchers' hypotheses are *alternative hypotheses* in statistical testing.

In order to achieve this objective, researchers need *at least two groups* of participants that are exposed to the two different conditions. The group that receives the treatment (i.e. interaction activity) is called the *experimental group*. The group that does not receive the treatment is called the *control group*. Both the experimental and control groups are called *comparison groups*. We have learned about the potential influence of confounding variables that can co-affect the research outcome together with the target independent variable (i.e. interaction activity). Researchers need to make sure, for example, that the learners in both groups are *similar* in all aspects, except the treatment condition. In the example mentioned above, a measure of effective communication strategy use is applied to both the experimental and control groups at the end of the research program. Their communication strategy scores will then be statistically compared to examine whether the effect of the treatment makes a significant difference in terms of learners' communication strategy use.

For example, prior to the experimental study, Li (2013) administered a standardized proficiency test to the three groups of students and used a one-way ANOVA to test whether the three groups significantly differed in their test scores. Li (2013, p. 639) obtained a non-statistical significance between the three groups ($F(2, 75) = 0.15$, $p = 0.86$). Had a pre-existing difference been detected, it would have been more difficult to conclude whether the posttest differences were the results of the experiment or the pre-existing difference.

There can be more than two experimental groups, but there must be at least one control group in true experimental designs. A control group can be as simple as a group of learners in a *traditional classroom* setting, and an experimental group can be one to which researchers provide a different teaching method that is hypothesized to help students learn more success-fully. We now introduce some common forms of experimental design.

Posttest-only control-group designs

Figure 4.6 presents a diagram of a posttest-only control-group design. Participants are *randomly* assigned to an experimental group and a control group. Participants who are in the experimental group will receive a condition in which the independent variable is manipulated. However,

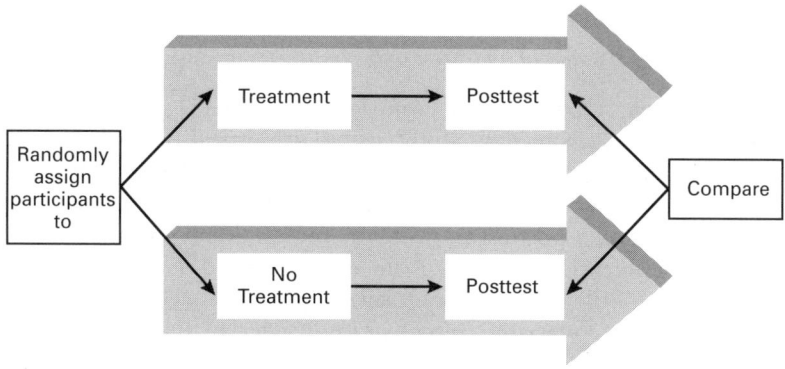

FIGURE 4.6   *A diagram of a posttest-only control-group design*

all other aspects are treated the same way for both groups. At the end of the experimental period, both groups take a posttest, which measures the dependent variable of interest. The scores of both groups are then statistically compared (e.g. independent-samples *t*-test, Mann-Whitney U test, one-way ANOVA or Kruskal-Wallis test) to examine whether the independent variable results in differences in the dependent variable between the two groups.

Ary, Jacobs, Razavieh and Sorensen (2006) recommended that there should be at least 30 participants in each group so that randomization has a strong likelihood of yielding equivalent comparison groups at the outset of the experiment. There can be an extension to this design. First, researchers can have more than two treatment groups for the purpose of comparison. For example, if researchers employ a type technique to manipulate the independent variable, there can be more than one experimental group. Second, researchers can add a delayed posttest into this design. Figure 4.7 is an example of this extension.

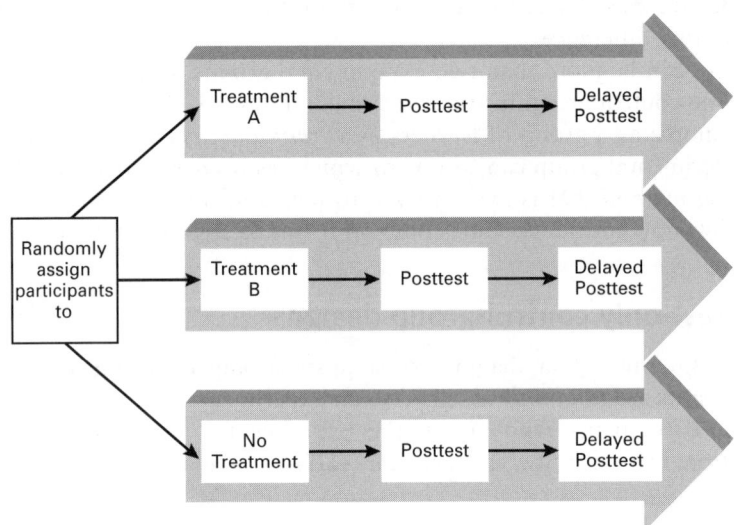

FIGURE 4.7 *A diagram of a posttest-only control-group design*

Van Gelderen, Oostdam and van Schooten (2011) provide a good example of an experimental study using a posttest-only design. The researchers aimed to gather evidence of the influence of lexical fluency in foreign language writing among grades 10 and 11 Dutch students. The researchers adopted a posttest-only design and randomly assigned students into two experimental groups (i.e. fluency training [N = 43] and topic knowledge [N = 40]). The baseline control group (N = 34) was added at a later stage. Two covariates (receptive knowledge of English vocabulary and metacognitive knowledge of writing and reading) were examined for differences through ANOVA. It was found that there was a statistically significant difference in the receptive knowledge of vocabulary, but not in metacognitive knowledge. The two experimental groups received a series of writing lessons. While the lexical group was additionally trained in the productive use of English words and collocations, the other group received extra training on topic knowledge. To control the experimental groups, participants' regular teachers were replaced by instructed teachers who had been trained on how to deliver experimental lessons (in this case a series of seven writing lessons that lasted 50 minutes each). The baseline control group did not receive the experimental instruction. The participants in the control group took the vocabulary and metacognitive knowledge tests and the posttests (comprising six writing assignments). We will highlight some of their findings as follows.

In regard to lexical fluency, it was found that the two covariates did not have a significant effect. These two covariates were not included in the subsequent analysis. A one-way ANOVA indicated a statistical significance between the two groups (i.e. $F[1, 25] = 54.22$, $p < 0.001$, partial eta squared = 0.68, large effect size; see p. 300 of their article; also see Chapter 14 for explanations of this statistic). The researchers also compared the speed and accuracy of students' writing between the two experimental groups (see pp. 301–2 for their considerations), and found that the students in the lexical condition were on average 1,130 milliseconds faster with their first keystrokes than the topic knowledge group. The difference was statistically significant (at $p < 0.001$, partial eta squared = 0.55). Finally, the researchers found that while the two experimental groups were found to be statistically different in some aspects, both outperformed the baseline control group.

Pretest-posttest control-group designs

The pretest-posttest control-group design is frequently adopted in language learning research. Figure 4.8 presents a diagram of a pretest-posttest control-group design.

In this design, participants are first randomly assigned to one of the three conditions, which include a control condition. Note that the simplest design for this type is to have one experimental and one control group. Second, they are pretested on the dependent variable. Typically on the basis of the pretest, the researcher will perform a statistical analysis to examine whether there is a pre-existing difference between the experimental group and the control group. Third, the experimental groups receive the experimental treatments, while the control group may receive a typical condition such as what is normally practised in the classroom. At the end of the treatment period, participants in both groups are tested on the dependent variable. Their scores are then statistically compared by means of the independent-samples t-test, Mann-Whitney U test, one-way ANOVA or Kruskal–Wallis test.

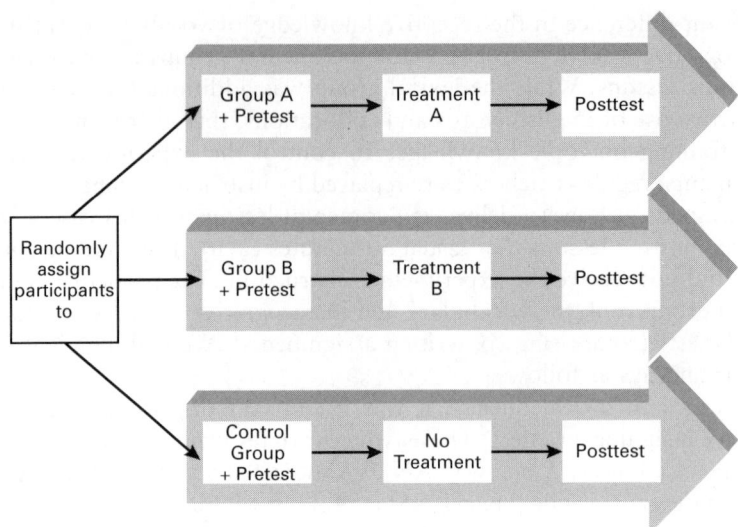

FIGURE 4.8   *A diagram of a pretest-posttest control-group design*

It is important to note that this design is prone to the *interactive effect* of the pretest and the experimental treatment. That is, the posttest scores might have increased because of the fact that the participants had taken the same test before in the pretesting stage. It is therefore strongly recommended that two parallel test forms be used. A *Solomon three-group design* aims to address the problems associated with having the same test for the pretest and posttest. In the Solomon three-group design, a treatment group that does not take a pretest is added (Solomon 1949).

As with the posttest-only control-group design, this design can be extended to include more than two treatment groups and more than one posttest (e.g. a delayed posttest). The pretest-posttest control-group design can control rival hypotheses that result from *history* (e.g. a specific event happening during the course of the experiment) and *maturation* (e.g. people growing older and thinking differently on account of it) effects. This is because the changes would occur to both the experiment and control groups in equal measure.

Takimoto (2008) examined the effects of deductive and inductive teaching approaches on the learning of pragmatic competence. The researcher randomly assigned participants into one of the four groups (i.e. three treatment groups [one receiving deductive instruction (N = 15), a second receiving inductive instruction with problem-solving task (N = 15), and a third receiving inductive instruction with structured input tasks (N = 15)], and one control group (N = 15) that did not receive any of the three treatments). Each teaching session (which occurred bi-weekly for two weeks) lasted 40 minutes and during the session, the instructor, who was also the researcher, gave all directions in Japanese. A pretest, posttest and delayed posttest were administered (see pp. 375–8 in the author's article). A one-way ANOVA showed no statistically significant differences among the four groups in their pretest scores. It was found that the three treatment groups had significant gains in both the posttest and delayed posttest scores for the discourse completion test and role-play test. Some differential gains were found in the listening test among the experimental groups. There were statistically significant differences between the experimental groups and the control groups across the posttest and delayed posttest.

Randomized matched subject, pretest–posttest control-group design

This design follows the methodological principles of the pretest–posttest control-group design above (see also Ary *et al.* 2006). However, participants are first matched in terms of their ability or personal attributes. It is assumed that there is a correlation between the matching variable and the dependent variable of interest. If two groups are needed, then a pair is matched and then randomly split between the experimental and control group. If three groups are needed, three participants are matched and then randomly split between the two experimental groups and the control groups, and so on. We discuss this matching technique later in this chapter. This design is effective in making sure that people of similar abilities (e.g. proficiency levels) are equally distributed across the groups, so that there is no difference between the groups at the beginning of the experiment. This design may not need a pretest because matching has already determined equal groups. There are three key difficulties in this design. First, there is normally more than one independent variable that is presumably correlated with the dependent variable, so researchers need to justify why a particular matching variable is chosen. Second, the matching of all participants needs to be complete before they can be randomly assigned into groups.

The study by Tian and Macaro (2012) used a version of the group matching technique in their experimental study. The researchers examined the effect of teacher codeswitching with English-only explanations on vocabulary learning. The researchers employed a stratified random allocation of students into the three conditions (i.e. two experimental groups and one control group). The 117 participants were first stratified into four proficiency levels (i.e. level 1 = 30; level 2 = 29; level 3 = 29; and level 4 = 29) and then randomly assigned into the three groups. This stratified and randomized technique made sure that all comparison groups had a comparable distribution of students with different proficiency levels. Prior to the experimental treatments, through the use of a one-way ANOVA, the researchers found no statistical differences among the three groups in the combined test scores, vocabulary pretest, listening comprehension test, and general proficiency test. The instruction lasted six weeks and a posttest and delayed posttest were used to measure changes. Among other statistical analyses, for example, the researchers employed ANCOVA using the pretest scores as the covariate when they examined the differences in the delayed posttest. The researchers found a statistically significant group difference (i.e. $F[1,95] = 28.07$, $p < 0.001$, partial eta squared = 0.23, small effect size, p. 378).

Repeated-measures design

The repeated-measures design allows the same participant to be exposed to more than one treatment condition. After each treatment, each participant takes a posttest, so that performance is measured under each condition. Figure 4.9 presents a diagram of a repeated-measures design. The test scores of each participant across the three conditions are compared to one another. In other words, each participant is their own control. For example, when two treatments are used in a repeated-measures design, a paired-samples t-test can be used. A within-group ANOVA can be used when there are more than two treatment conditions.

In this design, researchers do not need to be concerned with unequal initial differences between groups because all participants are exposed to all experimental conditions. Given this, fewer participants are needed than in other designs. However, this design is not without limitations. In particular, findings are limited in terms of the unknown effect of the sequencing of experimental conditions, which can co-influence the dependent variable. That is, the formerly exposed treatment condition may interact with the

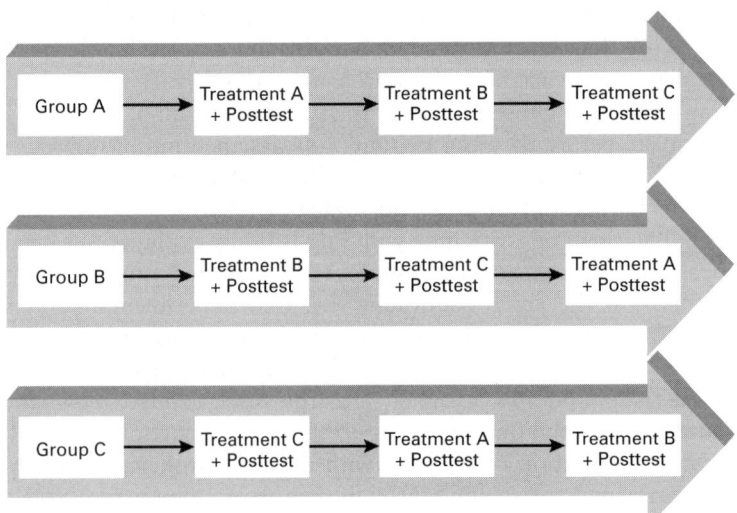

FIGURE 4.9   *A diagram of a repeated-measures design*

following treatment condition, which could in turn co-confound the subsequent posttest scores. This is known as the *carryover effect* (Ary *et al.* 2006) or the *sequencing effect* (Johnson & Christensen 2008). This limitation makes this design less popular than the pretest-posttest control-group design and the factorial design (discussed next).

Factorial designs

A 2×2 (two by two) factorial design is an example of a factorial design that takes into account different levels of two or more independent variables that may together play a role in affecting the dependent variable of interest. Instead of trying to control a confounding variable in an experimental study, researchers factor it into a research design so that they can determine their simultaneous effects. This design can examine both the independent and interaction effects on the dependent variable. This factorial design is usually applied with the pretest-posttest control-group design or the posttest-only control-group design discussed above.

For example, there may be two treatment conditions (e.g. explicit feedback and recast conditions). Researchers suspect that these conditions may have different effects on learning outcomes according to language learners' language proficiency levels (e.g. high- and low-ability levels). They then factor the language proficiency levels into their design, whereby the high-ability learners are randomly assigned to the explicit feedback and recast group, and the low-ability learners are assigned in the same way. All learners take a pretest, receive the treatment and then take a posttest. Figure 4.10 presents a diagram of this 2×2 factorial design. The two independent variable combination is located as a *cell*. In this design, there are four cells.

In language learning research, several studies employ a factorial design because researchers would like to consider different levels of factors that interact with one another. For example, Abbuhl (2012) employed a 2 (instruction: yes/no) × 2 (proficiency: higher/lower) × 2 (genre type: A/B) factorial design to examine the effect of explicit instruction on non-native speakers of English ability to use two signals of authorial presence (e.g. first person pronouns) while writing. Stafford, Bowden and Sanz (2011) used a 3 (time: AoT, AoA, and LoR) x 4 (treatment: +GE+EF, –GE+EF, +GE–EF, and

Language Ability (IV2)	Feedback Method (IV1)	
	Explicit Feedback	**Recast**
High randomly assigned →	High #1	High #2
Low randomly assigned →	Low #1	Low #2

FIGURE 4.10   *A diagram of the 2×2 factorial design*

–GE–EF groups) to investigate the extent to which pre-practice grammar explanations influence initial learning of Latin morphosyntax among Spanish–English bilinguals (AoT = current age in years; AoA = age of arrival in the US; LoR = length of residence; ±GE = provision (+) or not (–) of pre-practice grammar explanation during treatment; and ±EF = provision (+) or not (–) of metalinguistic feedback during treatment.

Quasi-experimental designs

Quasi-experimental research is classified under experimental research because it aims to examine causal-like effects. The term *quasi* is Latin for *almost*. We consider doing quasi-experimental research when we cannot achieve complete control over potential confounding variables that can be *threats to the internal validity* of the study. As discussed above, a true experimental research design randomly assigns participants into groups. However, we *cannot* do random assignments in quasi-experimental research. There are numerous real-life situations in language learning where random assignment is impossible. For example, there are intact classes that cannot be rearranged since the governing institution may have a policy to put students doing the same academic majors together in one class. Another situation may be that it is not ethical or practical to mix disadvantaged learners with high-ability learners. Yet another would be that girls and boys in some cultures may not study in the same classroom. It is therefore not possible to reassign them randomly.

Since random assignment cannot be done in quasi-experimental research, it is important to recognize that several potential threats from existing confounding variables (e.g. the characteristics of learners, disciplinary-specific knowledge, time of day, and teachers) are *present*. These threats make it difficult to make valid causal-like inferences because this can be achieved only when there are no other rival explanations (i.e. other plausible alternative explanations of the same finding). Yet quasi-experimental research can still yield some useful insights into a causal-like relationship. Usually such findings are treated as *suggestive* and prompt a more sophisticated randomized experimental research design. In this section, we will discuss three quasi-experimental designs.

Pretest-Posttest non-randomized control-group designs

This design is widely used in language learning research because in real-life language classrooms, it is not easy to reshuffle students randomly. Figure 4.11 presents a pretest-posttest non-randomized control-group design.

This design is similar to the randomized pretest-posttest design in Figure 4.8, except that it is non-randomized on participants (the dash line suggests non-randomized assignments). As noted earlier about random assignment,

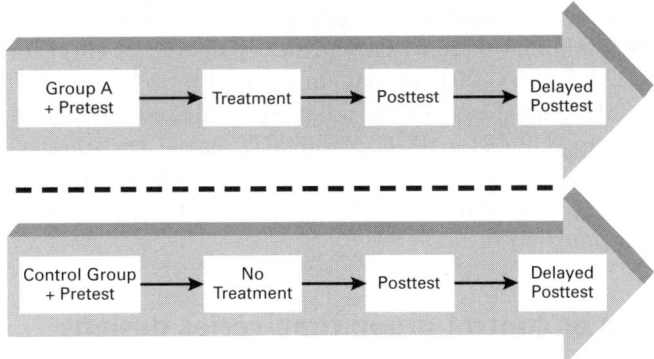

FIGURE 4.11 *A pretest-posttest non-randomized control-group design*

in a quasi-experimental design, researchers may randomize experimental conditions (e.g. types of treatment or task conditions) for intact classes. This method may help enhance the research validity, but it does not make this design a true experimental design. For example, if there are two treatment conditions and we randomly assign them to the two classes, each condition has a 50 percent chance of being implemented. While it may sound good in a report that researchers somewhat randomized some allocation, this hardly helps to eliminate threats to the research validity.

It is important to note that we can have more than two comparison groups and can add as many delayed posttests to suit a particular research purpose. We do not need to have a delayed posttest if we are not interested in a prolonged effect. This quasi-experimental design is quite robust, although there are several existing threats to the internal validity of the design (see Chapter 5). It is recommended that researchers test whether there is a pre-existing difference between comparison groups on the basis of the pretest. If there is a pre-existing difference, an ANCOVA (analysis of covariance) that uses the pretest scores as the covariate is highly recommended.

Zyzik (2011) investigated the effects of lexical knowledge and pedagogical sequencing on Spanish idiom learning through the use of a pretest-posttest non-randomized control-group design. There were two experimental groups, a thematic group (N = 21) and a verb group (N = 25), and a control group (N = 19). The experimental instruction, which was conducted by the researcher, lasted ten weeks. The control group was not explicitly taught Spanish idioms. All participants took three tests before and after the experiment: a vocabulary test, a written production test and a multiple-choice recognition test. The pretest and posttest were the same in each area. On the basis of a univariate ANOVA (analysis of variance), Zyzik (2011, p. 423) found a significant main group effect for the multiple-choice recognition test and the written production test. A 3×2 (i.e. three participant groups × two time effects) repeated-measures ANOVA was used to examine participants' improvement over time on the recognition task. It was found that there was a statistically significant effect for the time ($F[1,62] = 220.5$, $p < 0.001$, partial eta squared $= 0.78$), group ($F[2,62] = 24.3$, $p < 0.001$, partial eta squared $=$ not reported) and interaction between time and group ($F[2,62] = 38.1$, $p < 0.001$, partial eta squared $= 0.52$). The study suggested that prior lexical knowledge had some significantly supportive effect on Spanish idiom learning, although it had a limited impact on production tasks.

One-group or control-group time-series designs

We encountered this type of design when we discussed the single-case design built on the principles of the one-group time-series designs of quasi-experimental research. A time-series design is used for intact classes in which participants are periodically measured on a dependent variable multiple times before and after an experimental treatment is introduced. Figure 4.12 presents an example of a one-group time-series design. Unlike the pretest-posttest one-group in pre-experimental designs, this time series design allows researchers to observe consistency in terms of changes in the dependent variable over time before and after the treatment. This design cannot control the history effect because it does not have a control group. Therefore, when researchers add a control group, this time-series design is called a control group time-series design. If the control group is non-equivalent, it can be difficult to rule out a rival explanation of a pre-existing difference.

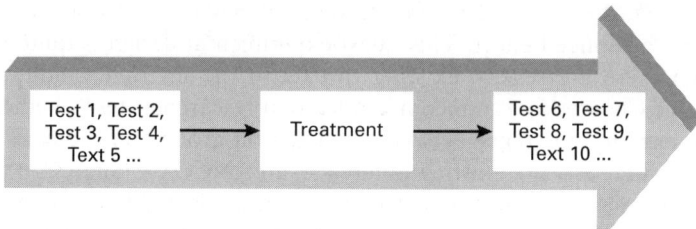

FIGURE 4.12   *An example of a one-group time-series design*

Laufer and Rozovski-Roitblat (2011) examined the extent to which long-term retention of new words was influenced by two factors (task type and the number of word occurrences in the teaching materials) and the interaction of the two factors. To achieve this aim, the researchers used a one-group time-series design in which all participants (final N = 20) were exposed to the six conditions built into the modified textbook (i.e. (a) 2–3 times T+F [text + focus-on-form], (b) 2–3 times T+Fs [text + focus-on-forms], (c) 4–5 times T+F, (d) 4–5 times T+Fs, (e) 6–7 times T+F, and (f) 6–7 times T+Fs) over a period of 13 weeks (52 academic hours). There were 30 different words assigned to the T+F conditions and another 30 different words were assigned to the T+Fs conditions. The participants took unannounced tests (recall and recognition) of the 60 target words. The tests were scored dichotomously (i.e. 1 or 0). The researchers used a multivariate (3×2) ANOVA for passive recall to examine the effect of task, number of encounters and their interaction. Laufer and Rozovski-Roitblat (2011, p. 403) found 'the main effect for the task type ($F[1,19]$ = 24.43, p < 0.0001), the number of encounters ($F[2, 38]$ = 13.24, p < 0.0001) and an interaction between them ($F[2, 38]$ = 9.34, p < 0.001). No interaction effect was found in the passive recognition ($F[2, 38]$ = 3.03, p < 0.06, n.s.), but one was found for the main effect for the task type ($F[1,19]$ = 103.02, p < 0.0001), and the number of encounters ($F[2,38]$) = 9.72, p = 0.0004).'

Methods for random assignment in experimental research

This section introduces three common random assignment techniques in experimental research (which we discussed above) in further detail.

The coin-toss technique

A simple idea for a random assignment technique is *coin tossing*, in which heads or tails is assigned to each participant, which allows their placement to happen with a 50–50 chance. This method may not present any problems if the sample size in our study is large. It is also useful when we pair participants, for example, according to their ability and assign them into one of the two comparison groups. However, given that sample sizes in language learning research are rarely large, coin tossing as a technique to assign participants into groups can result in some distribution problems. This is simply because we may end up having unequal numbers of participants for each group or, in a worst-case scenario, we have no participants being placed in one of the groups.

For example, if there are 30 participants to be placed into experimental and control groups (we hope to have 15 participants per group), we will flip a coin by assigning heads to the experimental group and tails to the control groups. Using a binomial distribution, the probability of achieving a 15–15 split is just 0.14 (i.e. 14 percent). We will most likely end up repeating the coin-toss procedure again and again until we get equal numbers. It may be thought that once 15 participants have been assigned to one or other group that we can stop tossing the coin and assign the remaining unassigned participants to the other group. However, this is not permissible as the random assignment process will not have been completed.

The block-randomized technique

In order to guarantee that an equal number of participants are assigned to each group, we can use a procedure called *block randomization* (Goodwin 2010). This randomization technique can ensure that each group will have a participant randomly assigned to it in a sequential manner. Thus equal numbers in each group can be achieved so long as the sample size is divisible by the number of groups. While we can use a table of random numbers for this, we can conveniently use a computer program to generate a sequence of conditions to meet the requirements of block randomization. According to Larson-Hall (2010, p. 29), we can instruct Microsoft® Excel® to create random numbers for us by typing '=RANDBETWEEN(1,100).' The numbers in the brackets can be adjusted according to the number of participants we have.

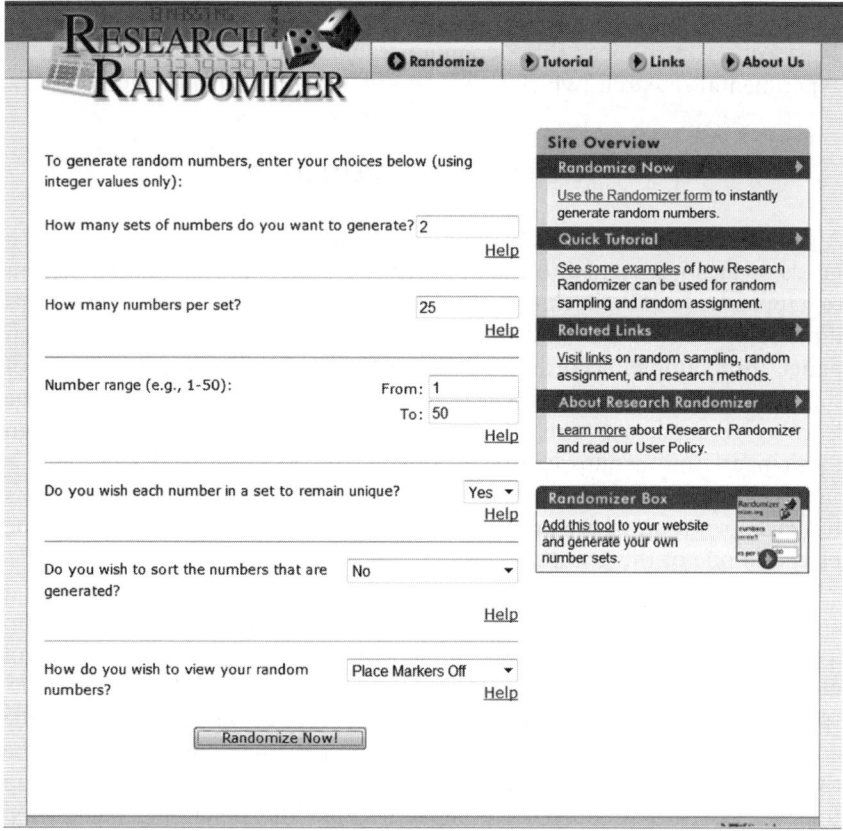

FIGURE 4.13   *An example of conducting a random assignment through the randomizer (Urbaniak & Plous, 1997–2014)*

There are a few websites that provide an online randomization program. These include:

- <www.randomizer.org>, viewed 11 July 2014

- <http://www1.assumption.edu/users/avadum/applets/RandAssign/ GroupGen.html>, viewed 11 July 2014

- <http://www.graphpad.com/quickcalcs/randomize1.cfm>, viewed 11 July 2014

When using these web-based randomization tools (Urbaniak & Plous 1997–2014), it is important that we assign an identity (ID) code to each participant using *integers* (e.g. 1, 2, 3, etc.). Figure 4.13 illustrates the random assignment process through *Randomizer*. This online tool is

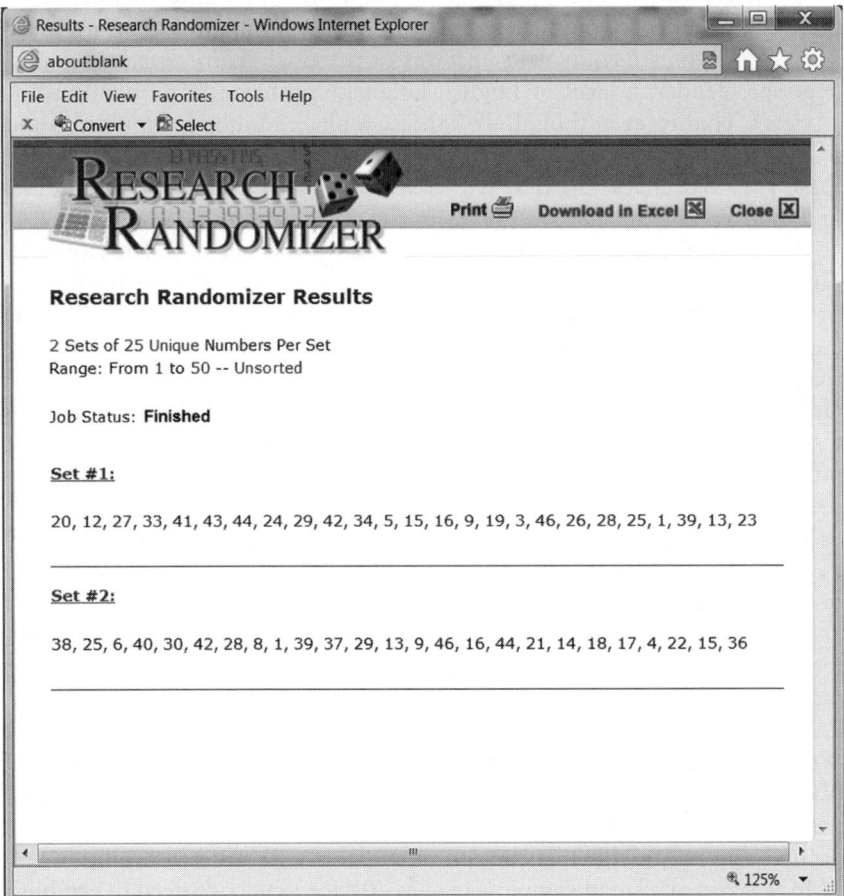

FIGURE 4.14 *An example of the creation of randomly assigned groups through the randomizer (Urbaniak & Plous, 1997–2014)*

easy to use, and it also provides quick tutorials on how to use it. In this example, there are two sets of numbers we aim to generate (N = 25 each). There are 50 participants. Figure 4.14 shows a randomized outcome. As this is a randomized procedure, if we run it again, we will have two new randomized sets of participants.

The matching technique

It is also important to know that experimental research in language learning needs to take into account the fact that learners are unique individuals. We know that individual differences in variables can affect language learning (see e.g. Lightbown & Spada 2013), and this needs to be factored into the research method adopted. An *equal number* of learners per assigned group *does not guarantee* that the groups are equivalent. In other words, while there can be an equal number of participants per group, this does not mean that the groups are equivalent in terms of personal characteristics or traits (e.g. age, gender, a level of English language proficiency, motivation and anxiety). That is, even though we can use a block randomization technique to assign groups, we may still end up having two groups *unequivalent* in these personal characteristics, which will then affect the research findings and their validity.

For example, a large proportion of high proficiency students may be randomly assigned to the experimental group, while a large proportion of low proficiency students are assigned into the control group. We may conclude that the treatment works when in fact it does not. A technique that can be used to prevent this, particularly when the sample size is not large, is called a *matching technique*. Typically researchers ask participants to take a language test or answer a questionnaire so that they can use the information gained to decide on a matching variable. Researchers may also seek to obtain some additional information about the participants, such as GPA and English proficiency test scores. This information is practical as participants do not need to be asked to do a pre-determined test or questionnaire.

There are two kinds of matching technique that we can use for experimental research: group matching and pair matching. A *group matching technique* allows us to place participants who have a similar trait (e.g. English language proficiency levels) together into different group clusters. We then randomly place each group cluster (e.g. high-ability) into one of two or more different comparison groups (using the block randomized technique above). By doing this, we can make sure that each comparison group has a reasonable distribution of students with different abilities.

In the case of a small sample size (e.g. 20), for which we need to establish two comparison groups, a *pair matching technique* can be used. First, we can pair participants, for example, according to their similar test score and then randomly assign each element of the pair into a different comparison group. We can use a coin-toss technique to assign each element of the pair into a different group. Matching techniques will at least give us confidence that high-, medium-, or low-ability students are evenly assigned into the two or more comparison groups. In addition, knowing participants' ability level at the outset allows us to compare the gains of a specific ability group through a comparison of pretest and posttest scores. In research reports, researchers should explicitly inform readers of their random assignment technique because readers need to see how participants have been assigned into groups.

There are a few examples of studies adopting some matching procedures (e.g. Tian & Macaro 2012 discussed above). Another unique example of matching is in the study conducted by Mackey, Oliver and Leeman (2003), who examined the effects of interlocutor types on the provision and incorporation of feedback in task-based interaction. The researchers randomly assigned each age group (i.e. children [8–12 years old], and adult) to form 12 NS-NNS dyads and 12 NNS-NNS dyads (NS = native speakers of English; NNS = non-native speakers of English). It is important to note that the researchers also used a *matching strategy* in their study since each pair was gender matched and the study had equal numbers of male and female dyads.

There should be strong reasons for the choice of the matching variable used in any experimental study. Usually, the justification for the choice of a matching variable is that it can have a *predictive effect* on the experimental outcome (e.g. based on previous research findings). This technique can, however, be difficult in practical terms as only one matching variable can be adopted (e.g. English language proficiency, motivation or learning style). A critical review of previous research and how other researchers chose their matching technique may help us to decide on a particular variable to match.

Limitations of experimental research

We have discussed several types of experimental research designs that can be used for language learning research. We have seen some strengths and weaknesses of particular research designs. Regardless of what design we adopt for an experimental study, there remain two general limitations of experimental research that we should be aware of and they are as follows:

- *Limitations due to language learners*: Language learning is highly complex and multidimensional. We deal with language learners as research participants who vary in their background characteristics, psychological traits and social settings. Most of the time, we need to deal with many variables that interact with one another. Many social situations in which an experimental study takes place are not necessarily stable and clearly defined. An experimental research design is therefore not the only method that can help us understand the nature of language learning.

● *Limitations due to researchers*: Researchers are also human beings. Although researchers can attempt to be as objective as possible, it can still be difficult to be fully objective in their observation. It is, therefore, important for experimental researchers to be aware that they are contributors to error (intentionally or not) in research. Any findings can never be perceived as absolute.

Summary

The experimental research design that we choose to use is critical to the validity of our research findings, conclusions and the recommendations we make. This chapter has presented a range of experimental research designs along with some examples of studies in language learning. There are a lot more complex designs, but they have not been presented due to the introductory nature of this book. We have mentioned some inferential statistical tests such as the *t*-test, and ANOVA in this chapter. They will be explained in more detail later in the book. The next chapter will discuss important issues relevant to the validity of experimental research.

Research exercise

To download exercises for this chapter visit: http://www.bloomsbury.com/experimental-research-methods-in-language-learning-9781441189110/

Discussion questions

1 Experimental research requires control over a situation in which research validity must be safeguarded. Why is it important to control variables in experimental research?

2 We have discussed three typical experimental techniques to manipulate an independent variable of interest (i.e. the *presence or absence technique*, the *amount technique* and the *type technique*). Which experimental designs discussed so far apply any of these techniques?

3 Can you think of a situation in which you can use a single-case design? Are you interested to know further about this design?

4 A pretest-posttest control-group design is a strong experimental design often applied for language learning research. What are strong components of this design? What are limitations of this design?

5 What is the most important lesson you have learned from this chapter?

Further reading

Field, A & Hole, G 2003, *How to design and report experiments*, Sage, Los Angeles.

Chapter 3 first addresses the three aims of research, which include reliability, validity and importance. It then discusses and presents various experimental research designs and concludes with a discussion of ethical considerations in an experimental study.

Goodwin, CJ 2010, *Research in psychology: methods and design*, 6th edn, Wiley, Hoboken, NJ.

Chapter 7 presents several basic experimental research designs for testing the effect of one independent variable. Chapter 8 covers experimental research designs that involve two or more independent variables. Both chapters explain several designs clearly and provide examples of psychological studies to illustrate the designs.

Johnson, B & Christensen, L 2008, *Educational research: quantitative, qualitative, and mixed approaches*, 3rd edn, Sage, Los Angeles.

Chapter 11 comprehensively introduces various experimental research designs, key assumptions and potential threats to the internal validity of each study. Chapter 12 addresses quasi-experimental and single-case designs. The authors also compare and contrast experimental, quasi-experimental and single-case designs.

CHAPTER FIVE

Validity in Experimental Research

Leading questions

1 'A measure is not valid if it is not reliable'. Why do you think this can be the case?
2 In academic research, why do you think we need to pay attention to research validity?
3 Do you know various types of research validity? If so, what are they?

Introduction

This chapter discusses in detail what we mean by research validity in experimental research. A good understanding of validity and potential threats to research validity is critical for good experimental research. We first define the notion of validity and discuss it in relation to the internal and external validity of an experimental study.

Validity in experimental research

The research paradigm adopted for a particular piece of research typically plays a crucial role in the discussion of research validity at an ontological, epistemological and methodological level. Language learning researchers need to make sure that their research is well considered in terms of: (1) theory; (2) methodology; and (3) ethics. In experimental research, we need to ask ourselves whether our study has followed required methodological procedures and whether we have properly collected and analyzed the data according to acceptable standards.

Validity and reliability

When we consider research validity, we will inevitably mention research reliability. *Validity*, on the one hand, is related to the *accuracy*, *correctness* and *legitimacy* of the measurements and observations made during data collection, and the soundness of the inferences made on the basis of the data collected. In other words, we ask whether our research findings are based on trusted data and analysis. *Reliability*, on the other hand, is often related to the issue of the *consistency* of research instruments, observations, or measurements of a construct. Reliability is closely related to validity in the sense that an experimental study cannot be valid if it uses unreliable data to analyze and answer the research questions.

For example, a reading test can be reliable in measuring students' reading performance consistently. That is, the score of each student is roughly the same no matter when we give it. This test can therefore be valid if we use its score to infer students' reading proficiency. However, the same reading test scores cannot be valid if we use them to infer how well the students can write, although reading and writing are strongly related to each other. Another example of reliable, but invalid, data would be those obtained when a judge consistently gives low scores to high-ability students, but gives high scores to low-ability students. In this case, the manner of assigning test scores is consistent, and therefore reliable, but the scores cannot be assumed to be valid because they do not reflect students' actual abilities.

Like validity, we usually consider issues of reliability in relation to the research instruments being used and the research results. The *reliability of instruments*, on the one hand, is concerned with the *degree to which the results of a questionnaire, test or other measuring instruments are consistent*. That is, we need concrete and strong evidence that the data (e.g. scores) derived from an instrument would be the same if the instrument were administered repeatedly. In quantitative research, we use reliability estimates, such as *Cronbach's alpha and Kuder–Richardson 20 (KR20)* estimates, to determine whether an instrument is reliable (see Chapter 12). The *reliability of the research result of a study*, on the other hand, is concerned with the degree to which the research result (e.g. the difference between experiment and control groups) is likely to reappear if the study could be *replicated* under the same conditions. To assess the reliability of research results, statistical analysis is used to answer research questions or address the research hypothesis. We often discuss the reliability of the result in terms of the validity of the research used to obtain it (e.g. statistical validity, concurrent or criterion-related validity, discussed below).

As can be seen, validity is concerned with the relevant theoretical basis of a piece of research and the soundness of inferences made on the basis of the data used (reliable or not). It is therefore important to remember that reliability is a *prerequisite* for research validity, but it is not a *sufficient* condition for validity. Research validity, nevertheless, is not necessarily *directly observed* because to assess it requires a wide range of critical considerations (e.g. relevant theories, research aims, the method adopted, the accuracy of the data, and the soundness of the inferences made). We also need *common sense* to determine whether an aspect of a study is reasonable. Reliability, in contrast, can be examined more directly from data through various statistical analyses and measures. Reliability estimates, for example, can be obtained in numerical form with clear acceptability guidelines. This chapter aims to discuss various concepts of validity in experimental research. Once we have explored research validity extensively, it will be easier for us to deal with research reliability.

Defining validity

It is not easy to draw up a precise definition of validity as it is multifaceted. From the postpositivist point of view, the simplest definition of validity for experimental research is *the extent to which research findings, inferences and interpretations are accurate, reasonable and supported by empirical data*. In experimental research, for example, we would like to have a high level of confidence that an inferred causal-like relationship derived from our study is as accurate as possible. An empirical study should be *legitimate* in terms of its chosen conceptual framework, research design, and data collection, analysis and interpretation.

It is impossible, however, to have one definition of validity that addresses all the issues in research processes. Research methodologists present a range of validity types that need to be considered by quantitative researchers. These include *internal* and *external validity*, *construct validity*, and *statistical validity*. Once we understand each of the validity types, we can begin to establish the validity framework for experimental research and prevent several kinds of threats that can co-influence findings. The best way to tackle research validity is to start from a broader level of validity (e.g. internal and external validity), and then move to more specific levels of validity (e.g. construct validity, content validity and statistical validity). Like reliability, it is important to realize that there is a distinction between the *validity of the study as a whole* and the *validity of the research instruments and procedures*. The former largely relies on the latter.

Broader concepts of validity

When we consider whether an experimental study is valid, the first thing we do is to ask whether a causal-like relationship found or not found is *plausible* and supported by the empirical evidence. Empirical evidence should be credible in terms of how it is obtained. For example, researchers conducting an experimental study on corrective feedback ask *does corrective feedback (i.e. explicit or implicit) result in improved writing skills?* This fundamental type of validity is known as *internal validity,* which is closely related to what is considered and done during research processes. *External validity*, on the other hand, is related to a generalization of the study to other participants and settings. Experimental researchers ask: *to what extent could the inferred causal-like relationship be generalized to other persons, settings, and times?*

Internal validity

Internal validity is the *most fundamental type* of research validity because it is concerned with the logic of the causal-like relationship between the independent and dependent variables under examination. It is related to the extent to which other confounding variables influence the research outcomes. The less confounding variables' interference, the better the internal validity of the study. Confounding variables are threats to the internal validity of an experiment and are one of the key reasons why there is a need to control the research setting and potential confounding variables. Internal validity is therefore a *prerequisite of external validity*. That is, experimental research findings cannot be generalized to other populations, settings, times or treatments if they are not internally valid.

In order to better understand what we mean by internal validity, we need to outline and discuss potential threats (i.e. interfering influences) to the internal validity of an experimental study. Threats are other possible independent influences beyond those identified by the experimenter that can have an effect on an outcome or dependent variable. Threats to internal validity may be numerous. However, for experimental research, there are two major groups of threats that need to be considered: (1) threats related to research participants; and (2) threats related to research instruments and procedures. Generally speaking, threats to the internal validity of an experimental study are closely related to *errors in rejecting* or *accepting a null hypothesis* (thereby resulting in an incorrect conclusion about the causal-like relationship). If we can eliminate these threats, we will have higher confidence in the observed causal-like relationship due to the experimental treatment. Figure 5.1 provides a diagram of threats to the internal validity of experimental research. Each is discussed below.

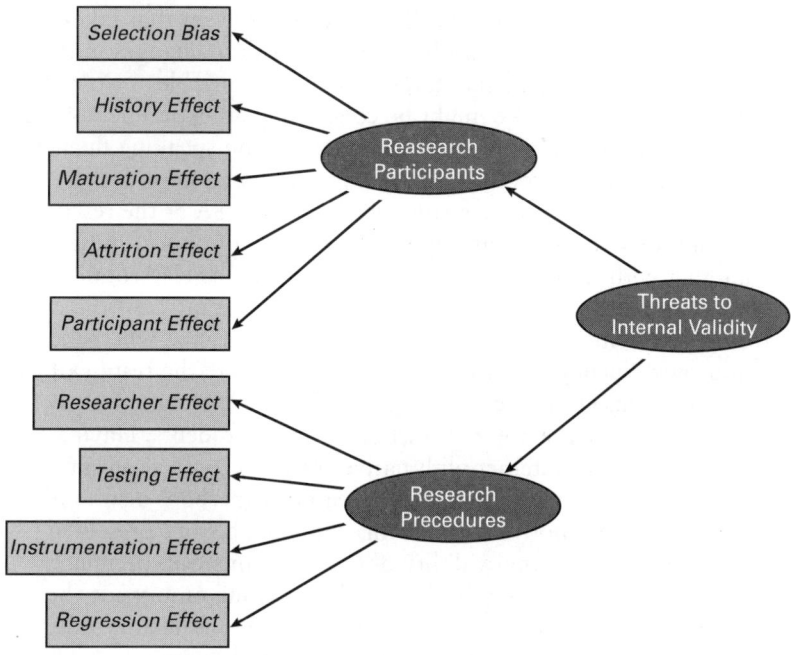

FIGURE 5.1   *Threats to internal validity of an experimental study*

Threats relevant to research participants

●   *Selection bias*: This threat is particularly influential to the internal validity of an experimental study when there are major pre-existing differences between the treatment and control groups. This threat is, therefore, associated with the characteristics of the research participants (e.g. age, gender, intelligence, language proficiency, motivation and anxiety). Experimental researchers need to consider this type of threat at the outset of the experimental study. We need to make sure that learners with these characteristics are distributed equally between comparison groups. If participants in the experimental group, for example, have a higher English proficiency level or are more motivated than those in the control group, it is most likely that the participants in the experimental group will outperform those in the control group, regardless of the treatment. A selection bias effect is likely to be present in a *quasi-experiment* using intact groups from fixed classes where researchers cannot do random sampling or exert control over the classroom environment. We discuss how to prevent this threat in Chapter 4.

●   *The history effect*: It is crucial to note that what we mean by history here has nothing to do with the past (i.e. literal history). In fact, this threat is related to a specific situation or event that takes place during an experimental study. This can result in changes in the experimental outcome (i.e. target dependent variables). Consider the following scenario. We might be conducting an experimental study on the effect of peer task-based interactions on speaking fluency and accuracy. However, during the experimental period, there was a large group of exchange students from the USA at the research setting. Our research participants had plenty of opportunities to interact with these exchange students outside the classroom (e.g. taking them to tourist places, shops and restaurants). At the end of the experiment, it would be difficult to determine whether improved fluency and accuracy in speaking were the results of the peer task-based interaction treatment. The results would likely be confounded by the presence of the exchange students. Having ample opportunities to interact with native speakers could result in better fluency and accuracy without the treatment (perhaps also in higher confidence and motivation). In this example, history presented a threat to the internal validity of the experiment. Experimental researchers need to be mindful of what is going on outside their experimental studies. They need to document any history threats in order to better understand and justify research outcomes.

- *The maturation effect*: This threat is mainly associated with biological, cognitive or psychological developments that occur naturally within the participants of the experimental study. That is, as participants get older, they become more mature and wiser as they begin to understand how the world around them works. A maturation effect is more pronounced when we conduct an experiment with young children, than with adults, or when we conduct an experiment extensively over a long period of time. Consequently, when the target dependent variable is measured after an experimental treatment, there could be a significant gain in the dependent variable. We cannot be certain that this change was merely the consequence of the treatment. Maturation is a threat to the internal validity of a study because we can mistakenly infer that the experimental treatment works.

- *The attrition effect*: This effect is also known as the *mortality effect*. This threat is present when there is an imbalance in the loss of participants across comparison groups. For example, if lower-ability students in the control group gradually drop out, the average of a posttest score could be much higher than it would otherwise be. When this posttest score is compared with that of the experimental group out of which high-ability students dropped, there might be no statistically significant difference between the two groups. Due to this effect, it is difficult to conclude that the experimental treatment did not work. The attrition effect is likely to happen when an experimental study is longitudinal in nature, since research participants can drop out over time.

- *The participant effect*: There are four well-known participant effects. The *Hawthorne effect* is related to the fact that experimental participants change their behavior due to the mere fact of the experiment taking place, rather than the specific treatment of the experiment. This could lead to results that favor the treatment. The Hawthorne effect is named after the plant of the Western Electric Company in Hawthorne, Illinois, where the researcher found that the level of light intensity increased or decreased workers' productivity. However, the researcher realized that the attention given to the participants and their knowledge that they were taking part in the experiment played an important role in increasing their productivity. In other words, the experimental participants were aware of what the researchers were after and consequently reacted positively. This is often the case in experimental research because ethically, participants need to be informed about the aim of the study and voluntarily agree to take part in the study.

The *placebo effect* is related to the fact that experimental participants believe that they are receiving a special treatment that can help them improve their current condition (e.g. language learning difficulties). They report that they feel instantly much better or learn much more effectively after the treatment or training (regardless of the true experimental effect). In medical research, a *placebo* is a neutral substance (e.g. glucose tablets) that is given to participants to make them believe that they are receiving the actual experimental medicine. The researchers give all participants (experiment and control groups) a substance that appears to be the same, so that attitudes on receiving the treatment do not vary among participants. In language learning research, of course, our participants will not be given a substance to take as in medical research. Rather, what our participants will receive may be a particular teaching method or learning activities/tasks that they perceive to be different from other classes. Their attitudes may work in favor of, or against the experiment.

The *John Henry effect* occurs when participants in the control group invest more effort in their learning to compete with those in the experimental group. They want to do as well as, or better than, those in the experimental group. The researchers may find that there is no difference between the two groups or may even find that the control group outperforms the experimental group, leading to the conclusion that the experimental treatment is not effective. The same may apply to other teachers who are in other traditional or control classes and feel threatened by the idea that they may not be effective teachers. They invest more effort in their teaching, resulting in their students' higher learning performance.

- The *demoralized effect* is related to how students in the control group feel that they are not being treated fairly because an experimental treatment could have helped improve their learning, had they been placed in the experimental group. They feel demoralized and unenthusiastic, and consequently do not invest any effort in their learning. The researchers observe a significant gain in performance in the experimental group but not in the control group. They conclude that the treatment works to improve learning. The demoralized effect is of special ethical research concern. Usually researchers will inform the participants in the control group that when the study is completed, they will provide extra sessions for the control group in regard to the treatment or activities given to the experimental group. Thus, those in the control group can receive benefits to their learning, and thereby not feel left out or that they are being treated disadvantageously from the beginning of the study.

- *The diffusion effect*: This effect is related to situations in which the participants in an experimental group share the details of the special treatment with those in the control group. This effect may occur, for example, when we are conducting an experiment on an innovative method to help language students memorize words effectively. If the students in the experimental group discuss and share this method with their peers in the control group, who in turn adopt the method without our knowledge, then at the end of the experiment, we may find little difference in the students' ability to memorize new words between the two groups. We may then incorrectly conclude that this innovative method is ineffective and cannot be recommended for further use. To prevent this effect, it is essential that researchers inform the participants in the experimental group not to share with the participants of the control group the details of the special treatment.

Threats relevant to research instruments/procedures:

- *The experimenter/researcher effect*: This effect is related to the unintentional influence of the experimenters on the research outcome. For example, a personal bias toward a particular treatment or an expectation of the research outcome may be transmitted to the research participants. If researchers prefer one treatment to another, they are likely to be enthusiastic about it and therefore invest more effort during the experiment without necessarily being aware of what they are doing. A researcher who has a neutral attitude toward the special treatment may have different findings. In the case of a subjective evaluation, such as speaking and writing, participants may receive higher marks because the researcher knows they are in the experimental group. A solution to this threat, while not entirely guaranteed, is not to have the researchers involved in the teaching of both the experimental and control groups. The instructors should not have any *personal gain* in teaching both groups and need to be informed and consistently reminded to be neutral in both groups. However, as a research student, you may not have enough financial support to employ someone to teach for you in your experimental research. Furthermore, as a student researcher, you may aim to have a sense of what a treatment is like and how it works. This aim requires first-hand experience. In such a situation, it is therefore very important that you try to be as objective as possible during your teaching. Perhaps your research supervisor or adviser can be asked to monitor your teaching or discuss your actions with you from time to time. Nonetheless, you need to address this threat as a limitation of your study and discuss whether it was present and in what way you tried to minimize its influence.

- *The testing effect*: This effect typically occurs when researchers use the identical pretest and posttest (e.g. Liu, Wang, Pefetti, Brubaker, Wu & MacWhinney 2011; Satar & Özdener 2008). Participants may do better in the posttest because they remember the answers to some of the questions, or are familiar with the test questions, tasks or content of the pretest. This may mean that their improvement in their test performance may not be because of the experimental treatment. To minimize this effect, researchers should use parallel test forms (i.e. tests that measure the same constructs with similar test questions or tasks, but based on new texts or questions). For example, Ammar and Spada (2006, p. 554), control for the test–re-test effect by using 'three different sets of pictures, each comprised of six pictures, for each testing sessions (i.e. pretest, immediate posttest, and delayed posttest). However, care was taken to keep some pictures constant to allow for the effects of the treatment over time to show.' To produce *parallel test forms*, researchers need to develop test specifications. An example of parallel test forms includes several international tests such as IELTS and TOEFL.

In regard to other psychological measures, such as motivational strategy, language learning strategy, attitude and language anxiety questionnaires, participants may be triggered to consider issues presented in the questionnaire items at later stages. When the same questionnaire (e.g. a language anxiety questionnaire) is administered at the end of the experimental study, participants may report lower levels of language anxiety because they have realized that anxiety is negative to their learning and try to reduce it, despite the treatment.

- *The instrumentation effect*: This threat is related to the testing effect. While researchers may attempt to avoid the testing effect, which is related to the use of the same instrument for both the pretest and posttest, the change of the instrument for measuring the dependent variable can influence the research outcome. If you use parallel tests for a pretest and posttest, they must be truly parallel. The instrumentation effect is apparent when the pretest and posttest are different in terms of formats, tasks and difficulty levels. If multiple-choice reading questions are used in a pretest, but short-answer questions are used in a posttest, it is difficult to be certain that an increase or decrease in test performance is an outcome of the treatment.

  Furthermore, when a dependent variable is assessed by means of observations (e.g. classroom observation schemes), the instrumentation effect can exist. This is merely because the observations are based on subjective judgment and human observers are known to be prone to inconsistency in judgment due to tiredness, boredom or other factors. This can also be a problem when the observer in the pre-experimental period and post-experimental period is not the same. One way to minimize the instrumentation effect in relation to observation is to use *two observers*, rather than one. If a video recording is possible, it is highly recommended because then the two observers can discuss the discrepancies in their observations using the video recording. Along with a moderator, training is also essential to improve consistency and accuracy during an observation.

- *The novelty effect*: This effect is somewhat similar to the placebo effect discussed above. However, the novelty effect is related to the innovative look of a treatment or method that may *excite* learners, thereby causing them to be enthusiastic about the treatment. For example, we may be interested in the impact of Facebook on reading comprehension and writing. The method may be different from the other methods the participants have experienced, and they may perceive it to be effective to their reading and writing, when in fact it is not. In other situations, a new method may also cause *anxiety* in participants due to the unfamiliarity of the activities or tasks. For example, participants may feel stressed if there are an unusually large number of steps required to accomplish a language task. The novelty effect is a threat to both the internal and external validity of the experiment.

● *The statistical regression effect*: This effect is often observed when participants with *extreme scores* (e.g. the highest or lowest) in the pretest achieve scores in the posttest that are closer to the mean score (i.e. the average group score). On the one hand, if a student is among the lowest scorers in the pretest, then they are more likely to have a higher score than a much lower score after the treatment. On the other hand, if a student is among the highest scorers, then that student is likely to either stay at the same level or have a lower score after the treatment. This phenomenon is known as *regression toward the mean*. In order to prevent this effect, researchers need to identify the participants with the extreme scores and employ a matching technique to distribute these participants across the experimental and control groups equally. The regression effect can interact with the so-called *ceiling effect*. That is, when some learners are at the advanced level, they may not have much room for improvement. On the other hand, some learners at the beginner level will have much more room for improvement. Therefore, regardless of the treatment, the ceiling effect can play a role in affecting the dependent variable. Finally, the statistical regression effect can be present when unreliable measures are used in an experimental study. Good experimental researchers always check the reliability of their instruments.

External validity

As presented earlier, external validity is associated with generalizability of the inferences made on the basis of an experimental finding to *other learners* (with similar characteristics) and *other settings* (see Figure 5.2)

For example, we ask whether the same result (e.g. that explicit corrective feedback enhances students' writing quality) can be observed in other student participants, in other similar settings and at other times? External validity is often of concern because we would like to assess whether the study can be useful for other people. This is often related to the *importance* of the problem being addressed by an empirical study. External validity is a key to research funding because if a study could only be generalized to

FIGURE 5.2 *External validity of an experimental study*

a particular learner group within a particular setting and time, it would be unlikely that funding could be secured for the study to take place at all. After all, experimental researchers need to ask whether their study can improve other people's lives (e.g. by improving language learning). It is ambitious, however, for any experimental study to satisfy all external validity requirements. Addressing the external validity of an experimental study is in fact more difficult than addressing that of the internal validity. First and foremost, an experimental study does not have external validity if it does not have internal validity. In other words, a badly designed experimental study cannot be generalized. We will discuss some critical issues related to generalization to (1) other learners and (2) other settings.

Generalization to other learners

Ideally, experimenters have control over the choice of participants in their study, whose characteristics will ideally fit the research purpose. If there are more available suitable participants than can be accommodated, then random sampling should be used to make the selection. Random sampling is a method for choosing participants that are representative of the target learner population. Nonetheless, as in other kinds of research, success in experimental research depends on *accessibility* to participants. Inferences are, therefore, largely affected by the sample of participants in the study. We also rely on volunteers, so we often have participants whose characteristics differ from other learners (e.g. they may be more motivated, more confident and more willing to improve their learning). In order to have a high level of confidence in generalizing our findings, we need to provide evidence that the characteristics of the sample in our study are similar or identical to those of the target population. Studies should therefore include a detailed description of the relevant characteristics of the participants so that generalizations to groups of similar learners can be confidently made.

Generalization to other settings

We ask: *to what extent are the findings applicable to other contexts or settings?* Recall that experimental research requires a strict control of the variables under examination. We need to eliminate confounding variables that can influence the effect of the target independent variable on the dependent variable. In a real-life situation (e.g. a typical language classroom), however, many things can be only loosely controlled. To generalize, we need to consider the characteristics of the experimental setting and the context to which a result is to be generalized. Therefore, we need to ask: *to what degree is the experimental condition representative of that in other settings?* For others to generalize our research findings to other settings, researchers need to provide detailed information of the research setting (e.g. size of the school, college or university, cultural backgrounds, access to resources such as library and technology, etc.), research conditions and the research procedures of our experimental study.

In summary, the most important threats to the external validity of an experimental study are the problems of its internal validity. Careful attention should be paid to a range of threats to the internal validity. This, however, will not be enough. We also need to consider the associated validity types in each of the stages in experimental research.

Specific aspects of validity

This section discusses six common types of validity: construct, content, criterion-related, statistical, predictive and face validity.

Construct validity

In Chapters 1 and 2, we introduced the construct as an abstract concept that we aim to understand (e.g. English language proficiency, motivation, strategy use). Such an abstract idea cannot usually be directly observed but must be inferred from, for example, systematic analyses of measured responses to test tasks and reported behaviors provided in questionnaire responses. Construct definitions need to be critically examined during the *literature review stage* because past and current researchers can have different perspectives toward the same construct. We need to evaluate whether we agree or disagree with what other theorists or researchers say about the construct of interest. We also need to propose clearly how to define a construct theoretically and operationalize it in our research. Basically a construct definition that is supported by several empirical studies by various researchers is likely to be more valid than a construct newly introduced with little empirical support. Generally speaking, construct validity is the *degree to which the construct of interest is validly defined, measured and inferred.*

There are two levels of construct validity in experimental research: (1) the construct validity of research instruments; and (2) the construct validity of experimental studies. They are interrelated. That is, if a research instrument lacks construct validity, we will find it difficult to argue for the construct validity of the study. The *construct validity of a research instrument* (e.g. language tests, questionnaires and observation schemes) concerns the extent to which an instrument measures what it is intended to measure. Consider the following example. Research participants are asked the extent to which they agree with the following statement: *I am anxious when I take a test.* On the surface, it seems that this item captures test anxiety. If a researcher includes this item in a questionnaire for measuring students' motivation and claims that the responses indicate students' motivation, there will be a theoretical problem with the construct validity of the questionnaire. In other words, this item does not appear to connect with the theoretical *construct definition* of motivation.

When we conduct a review of the relevant literature, we need to examine how other researchers operationalize their research constructs and devise research instruments to measure them. We need to check whether the rationale behind the choice of research instruments is viable and credible.

In contrast, the *construct validity of research* concerns the question of whether the inferred causal-like results support the theory behind the research. To test this, we need to examine the extent to which the causal-like results are supported by the participants, treatment conditions, setting and inferential statistical tests being used. Researchers need to describe how participants are chosen and randomly assigned into groups, for example. In terms of the treatment conditions, they need to describe and explain the nature of the special treatments for the experimental group and how they differ from those of the control group. In terms of statistical analysis, researchers need to provide empirical evidence that the test(s) being used to infer a causal-like relationship is (are) appropriate.

In summary, construct validity is not easily assessed. However, it is central to the entire process of an experimental study. What we need to do when we conduct an experimental study is to comprehensively review how a construct has been defined and explained by theories and other researchers. If there are no adequate explanations of the construct of interest, we are at risk of making a faulty inference. Adequate explanations can lead to good research instruments. Additionally, we need to outline clearly what we do when we manipulate or control the independent variable, and provide the rationale behind why it is done that way.

Content validity

Content validity is related to the construct validity of a measurement. It is related to how a construct of interest is transformed into something measurable, yet representative of the construct. Content validity can be defined as *the extent to which sample behaviors or abilities are relevant to, and representative of, the construct being defined.* For example, if we are interested in making an inference about students' ability to identify main ideas in academic reading texts, we need to ask them to read a variety of academic texts and summarize the main idea of each text. Because there are many texts out there and we cannot use them all for this purpose, we need to use samples of texts so that we can infer students' ability to identify main ideas. In this case, the extent to which the chosen texts, questions and reading tasks are representative of existing texts and tasks is related to content validity.

For psychological measures (e.g. motivation, self-regulation, anxiety), we consider whether we have relevant items representing the construct or sub-constructs, and whether we have sufficient items. The more items we use, the better the chance that we have an adequate representative of the construct. Accordingly, when we consider the content validity of our research instrument, we ask if the samples of the construct are *relevant* to the operational definition (e.g. are they related to the target descriptions of the construct?) We also ask if the target construct is *under-represented* (e.g. have we included enough texts, tasks or items to represent what we aim to measure). To enhance the content validity of a research instrument, we can pilot it with sample students for some preliminary analysis or content analysis. We can ask experts or experienced researchers to examine our test or questionnaire.

Criterion-related validity

This kind of validity is related to construct validity in the sense that an instrument should have a strong relationship with other instruments that measure the same or similar construct. In a language test, we may find a moderate relationship between reading and writing scores. This is because there are some shared language abilities that are useful for both reading and writing, such as grammatical ability and vocabulary. However, if an instrument is claimed to measure general English language proficiency, a strong correlation between such an instrument and other instruments (e.g. TOEFL and IELTS tests) is to be expected. Simply put, there should be a high correlation between scores achieved in the test used as the research instrument, and those achieved in a test such as TOEFL for the criterion-related validity of our instrument to be established. In regard to the result of the study, criterion-related validity can be confirmed if the research result (e.g. causal-like relationship) is similar to, or in line with, previous studies conducted with the same aim. This can be achieved through a comparison of studies via a review of the literature, a meta-analysis (see Ortega 2010; Oswald & Plonsky 2010), or replicated studies (see Abbuhl 2012; Porte 2010).

Statistical validity

Because we make inferences about an experimental study via the use of statistics (e.g. to compare the performance of two or more groups exposed to different treatments), we have to make sure that we have performed sound statistical analyses leading to the inferences and conclusions. Statistical validity is closely associated with what we discussed as internal validity. We evaluate whether an observed causal-like relationship between the independent and dependent variables is most likely to exist. Researchers establish their empirical inferences via the use of the probability that something is likely to occur (on the scale of 0 to 100 percent). In statistical tests, such as correlations and *t*-tests, researchers typically set a *probability value* to be less than 0.05 before they can reject a null hypothesis (e.g. that there is no relationship between two variables; that there is no difference between two groups with different treatments). They also have to work to guard against errors in rejecting a null hypothesis when they should accept it (Type I error), as well as in accepting a null hypothesis when they should reject it (Type II error). Apart from such considerations, researchers need to make sure that they use an appropriate statistical test to yield a required inference and that they have met the statistical assumptions of such a test.

Predictive validity

At an instrumental level, predictive validity is related to the level of predictability of current test scores, or reported behaviors to future scores, or behaviors. For example, language proficiency tests, such as the IELTS and TOEFL tests, are used to predict whether or not international students whose first language is not English can be successful in language use at an English-medium university. Similarly, if we use a questionnaire to measure students' levels of general anxiety, we should be able to have a sense of the level of anxiety of these students in the future.

At the level of the result of the study, predictive validity is somewhat related to the external validity of the study. That is, we ask how much the causal-like result can be extended beyond this specific study to other participants with similar characteristics or other settings. We usually address predictive validity issues during the data analysis and interpretation of research results.

Face validity

Face validity is not validity in the sense in which the term has been used so far. It is related to the appearance of a research instrument being used or an experiment being conducted. For example, a speaking test has face validity when test-takers are asked to speak and interact with other people. An experimental study has face validity when it has both control and experimental groups, and uses a random assignment method. Nonetheless, while an instrument may appear to measure what it claims to measure or a study appears to look like an experimental study, we cannot be sure that they are valid on the basis of their appearance. For example, in a speaking test, we need to examine how it is based on a sound theory of speaking (e.g. construct of speaking ability), communicative speaking tasks and speaking test techniques. That is, we need to see how construct and content validity, etc. have been considered and addressed. In the same way, in an experimental study, we need to see how relevant and appropriate theories are used to inform a hypothesis about a causal-like relationship, and to define dependent and independent variables. We need to see how participants are sampled and randomly assigned. We also need to see how well a treatment is provided (e.g. activities, length of treatment). In other words, it is not enough to see that a study must look like an experimental study. We need to consider a whole range of validity types and criteria to argue for the validity of the whole study.

Summary

In an experimental study, it is essential that we carefully and reflectively consider a range of validity types and threats that can limit our ability to infer a causal-like relationship. In this chapter, we have discussed the validity of experimental research in terms of internal and external validity. Additionally, specific types of validity (e.g. construct validity, content validity and statistical validity) have been discussed. A number of threats to experimental research validity and how such threats can be prevented are considered. The next chapter will consider ethical issues and practice in experimental research.

Research exercise

To download exercises for this chapter visit: http://www.bloomsbury.com/ experimental-research-methods-in-language-learning-9781441189110/

Discussion questions

1 In your view, why is it difficult to separate reliability from validity?
2 Which one do you think more important for an experimental study: internal validity versus external validity? Why?
3 We have discussed various kinds of threats to experimental research validity (e.g. selection bias, maturation effect, attrition effect, and testing effect). What kinds of threats do you think are the most serious threats to experimental research validity? Why do you think so?
4 If you had to choose only *one* of the following types of validity for your study (namely construct validity, predictive validity or statistical validity), which one would you choose? Explain your reasons.
5 Reflection: What is the most important lesson you have learned from this chapter?

Further reading

Dörnyei, Z 2007, *Research methods in applied linguistics*, Oxford University Press, Oxford.

Chapter 3 discusses issues related to validity criteria for both quantitative and qualitative research. It also discusses relevant issues of reliability and ethical considerations.

Mackey, A & Gass, SM 2005, *Second language research: methodology and design*, Lawrence Erlbaum Associates, Mahwah, NJ.

Chapter 4 begins with the topic of research hypotheses and types of variables in quantitative research. It then discusses various kinds of validity and reliability.

CHAPTER SIX

Ethical Considerations in Experimental Research

Leading questions

1 What do you think can be an impact of a study on research participants?
2 What do you think are research ethics?
3 Why do we need to think about ethics when we conduct research?

Introduction

This chapter addresses the importance of research ethics in experimental research in language learning. It discusses essential principles of ethical research conducts by all researchers dealing with human participants. Issues such as participant consent, anonymity and confidentiality are presented. Finally, it discusses experimental researchers' key responsibilities and obligations to their research participants and profession.

Ethical considerations in experimental research

As experimental research aims to improve knowledge about language learning and advance education, we need language learners to participate in experimental studies. Researchers will need to access some personal information about participants (e.g. age, gender and contact information), as well as their thoughts, attitudes, beliefs, details of specific past experiences, and language performance. As a result, researchers need to follow some ethical protocols to safeguard their research participants in terms of confidentiality and their right to privacy. Participants need to voluntarily agree with researchers to take part in a study. They have the right to know what is involved and what they will be doing in the study. They must not be forced to participate. Researchers need to consider any potential risks (e.g. physical and psychological harm) that could affect research participants during the experimental study. Researchers must attempt to eliminate these risks. Furthermore, experimental research has the potential to reveal some individual characteristics, which could also have a consequence on participants. For example, it may be found that Michael cheated in an examination (this is not good for Michael as it will embarrass him and the people around him may lose respect for him or begin bullying him) and that Liza has a bad memory (which could affect Liza's employment prospects if this information is publically available). Because what happens during and after an experimental study can have an impact on particular individuals in a social context, researchers need to consider and respect individuals' right to privacy.

Ethical considerations should not be restricted to research participants. They are also related to researchers' *professional integrity*. The public needs to *respect* research professionals as legitimate so researchers should take care not to behave in a manner that could damage their credentials. Researchers are responsible for what they do in their research to society at large. Ethical considerations in experimental research, therefore, reflect the relationship between research and society. A well-designed and groundbreaking experimental study will not be accepted by society if it is conducted unethically.

In the past few decades, research organizations, such as the *American Psychological Association (APA)*, *American Educational Research Association (AERA)*, *British Association for Applied Linguistics* and *Applied Linguistics Association of Australia* have developed and implemented ethical research guidelines and codes of ethical conduct that regulate research employing human participants. These are designed to encourage respect for participants' rights, especially their privacy, and to promote integrity among researchers, highlighting researchers' responsibilities toward the public when they publish their research findings. We will highlight some of these ethical guidelines below.

The APA code of ethical conducts

The American Psychological Association (APA 2010) provides a code of ethical conduct that includes five general principles and 89 standards, which are clustered into ten general categories (see Goodwin 2010). The five general principles are:

- *Beneficence and non-malfeasance*: Experimental researchers should be aware of the benefits research participants will gain from being part of the study, and the physical and/or psychological dangers, which require prevention. Researchers are required to do their best to safeguard the welfare and rights of the researcher participants.

- *Fidelity and responsibility*: Experimental researchers should establish trust with their participants and should be aware of their professional responsibilities to not only their participants, but also the public. Such responsibilities include avoidance of *conflicts of interest*, which can result in manipulating research participants' right to participate (e.g. perceived *coercion* in their volunteering) or research outcomes, which may favor researchers' personal interests.

- *Integrity*: Experimental researchers should seek to promote research accuracy, honesty, and truthfulness of scientific knowledge and educational advancement. Experimental researchers avoid deceiving research participants about the research aim and procedures. However, if *deception* is necessary to maximize research benefits (e.g. knowing the exact aim of the study may change participants' natural or true behaviors or thoughts) and care has been taken in terms of physical and psychological harm to research participants, it may be ethically justifiable.

- *Justice*: Experimental researchers should be aware of the issues related to bias, fairness and justice in their research. Experimental researchers should be aware of their professional limitations and expertise in the field.

- *Respect for people's rights and dignity*: Experimental researchers should respect individual participants' right to privacy, confidentiality and welfare. Experimental researchers should respect individual participants' language, cultural and religious backgrounds.

The AERA ethical standards

The AERA (2004) provides similar standards to those of the APA code of ethics (see Ary *et al.* 2006), which include participants' or their guardians' right to:

- knowledge of the likely risk and potential consequences from being involved in a study.

- *confidentiality*, whereby information will not be disclosed to the public without participants' or their guardians' permission. Confidentiality includes not revealing participants' actual names or the institute to which they belong, nor the research site and location where a study is conducted.

- researchers' honesty about the research aim and processes. Deception is to be avoided but may be practised only when needed for scientific purposes with justification.

- a withdrawal from the study at any time as well as a withdrawal of any data provided earlier in the study.

It is beyond the scope of this chapter to cover all the guidelines and recommendations. More can be found out about these guidelines on these institutions' websites:

- *APA* <http://www.apa.org/ethics/code/principles.pdf>, viewed 21 February 2014

- *AERA* <http://www.aera.net/AboutAERA/AERARulesPolicies/ CodeofEthics/tabid/10200/Default.aspx>, viewed 21 February 2014

- *BAAL* <http://www.baal.org.uk/dox/goodpractice_full.pdf>, viewed 21 February 2014

- *ALAA* <http://www.alaa.org.au/files/alaas_statement_of_good_ practice.pdf>, viewed 21 February 2014.

Informed consent, anonymity, and confidentiality

There are three key principles that experimental researchers need to carefully consider and implement before, during and after recruiting research participants.

Informed consent

Prior to seeking informed consent, researchers need to consider and plan how to recruit research participants. Researchers typically know the target population of the study. The recruiting of participants may be done via notice boards, through lecturers or professors, emails or internet sites. Once researchers have arranged a meeting with potential participants or their guardians to discuss the study, they need to provide more detailed information about what will be involved for the participants. It is important to note that research participants may include non-students, such as teachers. This is particularly the case in experimental research to be conducted in intact classes. Thus *responsible teachers need to agree to take part in the study and sign the consent form as well.*

Not all participants are able to give their consent (e.g. children under a certain age), in which case parents or legal guardians need to give their consent on their behalf. Informed consent involves several processes. In particular, participants or their guardians need to be informed of all the potential risks and benefits of the study both in written and oral form.

Typically, researchers will prepare the participant information statements about the study and the consent form to give to potential research participants. When necessary, a *translation into another language* may be needed in order to avoid language barriers and establish trust from participants. Research assistants or someone who can speak participants' or their guardians' native language may also be required for the question-and-answer sessions.

Researchers are required to have a *debriefing session* at which they meet participants or their guardians and explain elements of the research project, such as its aims and the research procedures to be used. A question-and-answer component should be included. Researchers may be able to have a research assistant provide this debriefing session. There are two important issues to note here. The first is the issue of *deception.* While researchers need to inform their participants about their general research aims, with good justification, specific aims based on a particular hypothesis of the study may not be revealed because such a revelation may change the nature of the findings. Some researchers may say that if they reveal the specific hypothesis of the study to potential participants (i.e. exactly what they would like to find out), the effect could be detrimental. Fewer people may agree to take part in the study, and those who do take part may change their natural behavior or focus their attention on a particular aspect because they know what is being examined (i.e. reactivity effects). The issues of deception have been discussed widely in experimental research (Field & Hole, 2003). In general, *deception should be avoided.* The best strategy to deal with deception is to discuss it openly with experienced researchers, experts and the research ethics committee of your institute before commencing a study.

The second is the issue of *coercion.* Researchers need to be clear on how they plan to prevent or minimize coercion, and be honest in the case of any coercion actually occurring. This issue is related to researchers' potential conflicts of interest. In particular, there is the danger of coercion when students who are enrolled in the researcher's class refuse to take part in the study. Researchers need to be fair to these students and must not abuse them by undermining their academic performance or grades, or treat them harshly, unkindly or unfairly merely because they have refused to take part in the proposed study.

Following the debriefing, potential research participants or their guardians should receive the information statements and the consent form to read. They can then sign or not sign the consent form and return it to the researchers.

Anonymity

The issue of anonymity can be either a simple or complex one. On the one hand, anonymity (i.e. unidentifiability) promotes participants to be truthful in expressing their thoughts and attitudes, thereby resulting in higher research validity. Anonymity is particularly vital for valid survey research. On the other hand, complete anonymity (i.e. even the researchers do not know who the participants are) is difficult to achieve in experimental research because researchers need to be able to scrutinize participants' data (e.g. for pretest-posttest or between-groups comparisons). Experimental researchers are also likely to spend some period of time with participants. Anonymity, however, can be achieved to the extent that the researchers are the only ones who know the identities of the participants and that researchers promise not to reveal participants' identities to the public. This is related to the confidentiality issue discussed below.

Confidentiality

Confidentiality can be achieved through the use of pseudonyms (unreal names) to refer to research participants and the name of the research site (e.g. school, college, university or company). Pseudonyms are important because research participants should not be traceable. This is particularly critical when, for example, there are not many students or staff in a known institute. This level of anonymity is closely linked to confidentiality. Confidentiality goes beyond the issues of knowing or revealing participants' identities. It is linked to the concept of participants' privacy of personal information. Confidentiality involves ethical considerations that do not allow people who are not the researchers in the study to have access or partial access to the data for use in other purposes. Researchers may be asked whether the data they have collected can be used in another study to be conducted by other researchers. However, by granting other people access to the data, *the anonymity and confidentiality protocols will be breached.* Confidentiality is also related to the fact that researchers should not share the data in the public domain. Typically the data must be stored in a safe or locked cabinet or in a secure storeroom for a minimum of seven years (depending on an institute's mandate) before they are destroyed. Access to archival data that are to be stored in an online database needs to be restricted. Personal information should be removed and identity numbers should be assigned to each of the participants. Finally, it is important to note that confidentiality may be governed by state or federal government laws. Researchers are obliged to check the legal system in this regard.

Examples of the participant information statements and consent form

There is no one standard format for the participant information statements and consent form, and each institute will expect certain information to be included. However, it is useful to have some examples so that the issues related to ethical considerations and practice in experimental research become clearer for people new to academic research. Figures 6.1 and 6.2 are examples of the participant information statements and consent form of an experimental study, respectively.

Institute Letterhead

Researcher Address and Contact Information

STUDENT PARTICIPANT INFORMATION STATEMENT

Strategic Reading Strategy Instruction

(1) What is the study about?

You are invited to participate in a study that evaluates the usefulness of a reading strategy instruction program that is designed to help English as a second language (ESL) learners improve their reading comprehension, self-regulation of their reading as well as their reading strategy use to enhance comprehension accuracy.

(2) Who is carrying out the study?

The study is being conducted by Mr XXX and will form the basis for the degree of Doctor of Philosophy at XXX University under the supervision of Professor XXX in the Faculty of XXX.

(3) What does the study involve?

You are invited to participate in a study that involves a reading strategy instruction which lasts 8 weeks (3 hours per week). During the 8 weeks of this reading strategy instruction program, you will learn about reading strategies that will help you improve your reading skills. These strategies are integrated in a range of reading tasks and activities. You will attend the class twice a week, each of which lasts 1.5 hours.

During the reading strategy instruction program, you will be asked to complete questionnaires and take reading tests as follows:

The **Background Questionnaire** will ask about your demographic information (e.g., gender, and number of years since you have learned English).

The **Reading Strategy Questionnaire** will ask you about the strategies you currently employ when you read English texts or complete reading tasks.

The **Metacognitive Awareness of Reading Questionnaire** will ask you about your knowledge of your reading and strategy use.

Before and after the reading strategy instruction, you will be asked to take a **reading comprehension test** (total of 2 tests). The tests are used to indicate the level of your reading performance and improvement over the course of 8 weeks.

You may be asked to take part in an **individual interview** or a **group interview**. We would like to gain an understanding of your experience in and attitude towards this strategy instruction. The interviews may involve audio recordings. The interviews will take place immediately following a class and will be arranged with participants beforehand. During the individual interviews, participants will be asked to respond to questions about which reading strategies they normally use, and why and how they use them. In the interviews, participants will be asked about the reading strategy lessons, what is useful and what is not useful for them. Participants may be asked about their experiences in and perception of the reading strategy instruction. The interviews will last about 30 minutes each.

(4) How much time will the study take?

This is an 8-week reading strategy training program in which you will meet twice a week for 1.5 hours each. During this reading strategy training program, you will read several English texts and answer comprehension questions about them. Your teacher will teach you reading strategies and provide specific feedback on your reading performance. These teaching activities can help you improve your reading comprehension, accuracy, and fluency throughout the 8-week period of teaching.

During the 8 weeks of training, you will be asked to complete reading strategy questionnaires and if you agree, you will be interviewed because we would like to know how you have improved your reading comprehension and whether this training has benefited your learning. You will take two reading comprehension tests. All of these activities, except for the interviews, will be completed in classroom time.

FIGURE 6.1   *An example of a participant information sheet*

(5) Are there any risks involved in this project?

This study involves zero physical risk because this research has been carefully designed to minimize any risks to students. There will not be consequences in failing this program. You will receive a lot of useful feedback and tips to improve your reading skills. However, it is possible that you may feel self-conscious about being audio-recorded in interviews. However, this is a normal response. We will do our best to make sure that you are comfortable in the interview.

You may also be concerned about being identified in any material that is published. In relation to confidentiality, all responses will remain anonymous.

(6) Can I withdraw from the study?

Being in this study is completely voluntary. You are not under any obligation to consent, and if you do consent, you can withdraw from the study at any time without affecting your relationship with us or your university.

For example, you may ask us to stop the interview at any time if you do not wish to continue. The audio recording will be erased and the information provided will not be included in the study.

(7) Will anyone else know the results?

All aspects of the study, including your information and results, will be strictly confidential and only the researchers will have access to the data.

The study will be reported as a PhD thesis. It may be submitted for publication, but all individual participants will not be identifiable in all reports.

(8) Will the study benefit me?

This whole process is expected to benefit you by helping you to enhance your awareness of reading strategy use. It is hoped that the data collected can help you raise your awareness of your reading processes and strategy use. You will receive feedback on your reading performance as well as on how you process reading texts. The lessons can help you become aware of your strengths and weaknesses in reading comprehension. If your particular reading problems are identified, you will be guided, so that you can improve your reading skills.

Upon the completion of this instruction, you will receive a certificate of participation along with a report of your reading performance.

(9) Can I tell other people about the study?

You are welcome to tell other people about the study and your participation.

(10) What if I require further information about the study or my involvement in it?

When you have read this information, Mr XXX will discuss it with you further and answer any questions you may have. If you would like to know more at any stage, please feel free to contact Professor XXX at XXX University. You may contact Professor XXX about more information on the study at +61 2 XXXX XXXX or email XXXX@XXX.edu.au.

(11) What if I have a complaint or any concerns?

Any person with concerns or complaints about the conduct of a research study can contact The Manager, Human Ethics Administration, XXX University on +61 2 XXXX XXXX (Telephone); +61 2 XXXX XXXX (Facsimile) or ro.humanethics@XXX.edu.au (Email).

This information sheet is for you to keep. Thank you.

FIGURE 6.1   *An example of a participant information sheet* (continued)

PARTICIPANT CONSENT FORM

I, ...[PRINT NAME], hereby consent to participate in the research project "**Strategic Reading Strategy Instruction**"

In giving my consent I acknowledge that:

1. The procedures required for the project and the time involved have been explained to me. I acknowledge that I will attend the reading strategy instruction for a period of 8 weeks, complete questionnaires, and take a reading comprehension test at the beginning and the end of the strategy instruction program. I may or may not take part in individual or group interviews. All questions I have about the project have been answered to my satisfaction.

2. I have read the Participant Information Statement and have been given the opportunity to discuss the information and my involvement in the project with the researcher/s.

3. I understand that being in this study is completely voluntary – I am not under any obligation to consent.

4. I understand that my involvement is strictly confidential. I understand that the results of this study may be published. I have been informed that no information about me will be used in any way that is identifiable.

5. I understand that I can withdraw from the study at any time, without affecting my relationship with the researcher, the XXX University, or my current university.

6. I consent to:

    - Attend the reading strategy instruction program for 8 weeks   YES ☐   NO ☐
    - Take two English reading comprehension tests   YES ☐   NO ☐
    - Complete background and reading strategy use questionnaires   YES ☐   NO ☐
    - Participate in individual interviews with audio-recording if invited YES ☐   NO ☐
    - Participate in group interviews with audio-recording if invited   YES ☐   NO ☐
    - Receive feedback   YES ☐   NO ☐

If you answered YES to the "Receive feedback" question, please provide your contact details below..

Address: _____

Email: _____

....
Signature

....
Please PRINT name

....
Date

FIGURE 6.2   *An example of a consent form*

Institutional research ethics approval

While being a professional academic researcher requires both qualifications and knowledge of research and ethical research practice, experimental researchers cannot conduct research in any manner they please. Despite the fact that researchers understand participants' rights and their own obligations, they still need to submit their research ethics application forms to the relevant institutional research ethics review committees. Sometimes researchers are required to submit an ethics application to their research institute. If another institute is involved in the study, another ethical application will need to be submitted to the research ethics committee of that institute. The key reason for this is that the other institute's institutional obligations must be considered and safeguarded. For example, in case something goes wrong in an experimental study and the public, research participants or their guardians take legal action against the researchers or their institute, researchers should be confident that they have done everything in their power to minimize the risk to themselves and their institute.

An *institutional ethics committee* is made up of several academics from various departments or schools and legal experts of the institute who will review an ethics application including a research proposal. *Their mission is to safeguard research participants, researchers and the institute(s)*. Research ethics application guidelines and considerations can vary from one institute to another so we need to be aware of possible variations. *Data collection must not take place prior to the research ethics committee's approval*. Once a research ethics application has been approved, we can begin the experimental study and collect the data according to what has been approved. Any modification to a study, such as change in a research instrument or treatment needs to be formally submitted to the committee for further approval. Usually a research project is given approval for a certain period of time (e.g. for three years). A progress report or request for ethics renewal may be required. A completed report of the study is usually required when the study is completed.

Experimental researchers' key responsibilities and obligations

Experimental researchers' key responsibilities and obligations can be summarized as follows.

Responsibilities and obligation to research participants

- Provide adequate information to research participants. This includes information regarding the aim of the study, what they will do when they take part in the study, their right to withdraw from the study, how their identities will be kept secret and how their confidentiality and privacy are to be safeguarded. Obtain a written consent from them prior to commencing an experimental study.

● Consider all potential physical and psychological harm that may occur in an experimental study and constantly monitor them throughout the study. In language learning, some researchers may, for example, aim to examine the effect of anxiety on language learning and expose learners to extreme anxiety, which may result in their psychological damage.

● Reward their cooperation and efforts to take part in the study. Rewards may be financial, but may also include the provision of feedback or information on what happened in the research. Those participating in a control group should receive the treatments or instructions provided in the treatment groups, particularly when they are effective in promoting learning. In other words, if an experimental treatment is effective for the experimental group, researchers are obliged to offer the treatment to participants in the control group at the end of the data collection period.

Responsibilities and obligations to the profession

● Plan an experimental study carefully. This involves a comprehensive review of the literature for both theoretical and methodological considerations. The study is likely to yield knowledge to the field and offer insights or new solutions to existing problems. All researchers are obliged to select the most appropriate research method and techniques that serve the purposes of the proposed study.

● Do not abuse any colleagues or research students by asking them to collect the data for the study they are not involved in without an appropriate reward. If they help you collect the data voluntarily, you need to do the same for them.

● Always submit an ethics application to the institute's research ethics committee for approval. An institute has a much larger network and obligation than an individual researcher. If something goes wrong in a study that has not been approved by the ethics committee, not only will the institute's reputation be damaged, but you may also be faced with legal action. This means you may lose your job or credibility as a trustworthy researcher.

● Write your research report (e.g. as a research article, a thesis or dissertation) clearly and honestly. You need to interpret your research results and conduct your data analysis carefully.

At the same time, you should guard against any temptation to over-interpret or generalize beyond what the data and results can support. When the data do not support your original hypothesis, it is important to be honest about your findings. Do not consciously or subconsciously modify data or interpretations so that they support your personal or original views.

Summary

In this chapter, we have discussed the importance of ethical considerations when carrying out an experimental study. Any research design we choose will not be accepted by society if researchers are being unethical about their research. Ethical considerations are vital ingredients of any good experimental study. The next chapter will discuss quantitative research instruments and data elicitation techniques for experimental research.

Research exercise

To download exercises for this chapter visit: http://www.bloomsbury.com/ experimental-research-methods-in-language-learning-9781441189110/

Discussion questions

1 How would you describe ethics in research?
2 Why are ethical considerations for human participants important in experimental research?
3 What should you do to make sure that your experimental research is ethical?
4 Do you consider *deception* good or bad in experimental research? Why or why not?
5 Reflection: What is the most important lesson you have learned from this chapter?

Further reading

De Costa, P in press, 2015, 'Ethics and applied linguistics research', in B Paltridge & A Phakiti (eds), *Research methods in applied linguistics*, Bloomsbury, London.

This chapter stresses the importance of ethical considerations before, during and after the data have been collected.

Dörnyei, Z 2007, *Research methods in applied linguistics*, Oxford University Press, Oxford.

Chapter 3 discusses issues related to validity criteria for both quantitative and qualitative research. It also discusses relevant issues of reliability and ethical considerations.

Goodwin, CJ 2010, *Research in psychology: methods and design*, 6th edn, John Wiley & Sons, Hoboken, NJ.

Chapter 2 presents key ethical guidelines for research with humans. Several examples are discussed to illustrate examples of unethical research.

CHAPTER SEVEN

Quantitative Research Instruments and Techniques

Leading questions

1 Can you give an example of a research instrument and describe a situation in which it is used?
2 If you designed an experimental study, what kind of research instruments would you adopt?
3 Why do you think an understanding of advantages and disadvantages of a particular research instrument or data elicitation technique is important?

Introduction

This chapter aims to explore research instruments and data elicitation techniques. It is important that we use research instruments or data elicitation techniques that can yield reliable, valid and useful data. In experimental research, we use an instrument or technique that can capture observable behaviors, knowledge, psychological processes or language performance as accurately as possible. This chapter considers quantitative research instruments (e.g. language tests, questionnaires and quantitative observations). We will consider the fundamental concepts behind the development and use of quantitative research instruments and data elicitation techniques.

The nature of research data

One of the key aims in experimental research is to find out whether one independent variable (e.g. feedback) can lead to change, improvement or degradation in another variable (e.g. writing ability). We can achieve this aim by systematically comparing two or more situations in which the independent variable (e.g. the feedback types on academic writing) is manipulated to vary. For example, a first group receives explicit feedback, while a second group receives implicit feedback. A third group may not receive any form of feedback. Data are needed to answer a research question or hypothesis. In the example given, we need to measure students' academic writing performance (as the outcome). When we consider what data we need, we have to understand the connections between research constructs, research data, measurement and data analysis.

Empirical data are often referred to as raw data and are those unprocessed data gathered in the course of our study (e.g. participants' learning, thinking, processes and performances). The data need to be categorized, sorted, filtered and analyzed so that they can be used to systematically answer research questions. Quantitative data are data to which we can assign values or numbers. Age, height and length of time are examples of quantitative data. As we noted in earlier chapters, language learning research often deals with abstract concepts that cannot be directly observed. Abstract concepts are labeled research constructs (e.g. self-regulation, motivation and language proficiency). While we can, for example, examine students' pieces of writing, it is not easy to judge their quality. However, we can examine and use writing theories to create criteria for good writing (e.g. content, organization and language use). Such criteria may help us make a reasonable inference about students' writing ability.

When we deal with a psychological construct, we can ask learners to rate, for example, a level of happiness using a scale from 1 (not at all happy) to 5 (very happy). Several psychological constructs (e.g. motivation, anxiety, self-efficacy, cognitive knowledge and language ability) are quantifiable. Experimental research typically uses instruments such as tests, elicitation tasks, inventories, questionnaires and rating scales to obtain data. Some qualitative techniques, such as think-aloud protocols, stimulated recalls and interviews, can also produce quantitative data by means of quantitative coding and frequency counts.

Experimental research in language learning incorporates the use of pretests and posttests into research design. The reason for the need for pretests and posttests is that we aim to find out whether any changes occur after an experimental treatment or whether there is an initial existing difference between the experimental and control groups. We also need to compare the performance of the treatment group with that of the control group. In experimental research, we can use a range of standardized quantitative measures as pretests and posttests. They can be any instruments, not just language tests (e.g. questionnaires, rating scales), that we use before and after a treatment or an intervention.

Examples of research instruments in experimental research

Quantitative instruments are associated with numbers and concepts of measurement. *Measurement* refers to the act of assigning values to something. Because we have already discussed issues surrounding measurement and types of scales in Chapter 2, we will not discuss them here. It is important to note that many quantitative instruments make use of scales (e.g. nominal, ordinal and interval) to measure a target construct. In many circumstances in language learning research, quantitative data can offer us more information than words (e.g. the ranks of students in a class, test scores and GPA). They allow us to approximate how well a person can do something based on some given standard and to compare one person's performance with that of others. Nonetheless, quantitative data alone will not be enough for experimental research. We need appropriate statistical techniques to help us analyze the numbers. We need to know what kind of quantitative data each instrument can produce so that we can use an appropriate statistical tool to answer a particular research question.

Figure 7.1 presents examples of the experimental research instruments and data elicitation techniques. Several experimental studies in language learning use them for pretests, posttests and delayed posttests.

Quantitative research instruments and techniques

Commonly used quantitative instruments and data elicitation techniques are presented as follows.

Language tests and assessments

Tests and assessments are commonly used in experimental research, particularly when the research deals with learning and cognition. Assessment is a broader concept than tests as it includes both tests and non-tests (e.g. self-assessment and portfolio assessment). A test is typically used in a strictly controlled and standardized manner. Generally speaking, a test can tell us how well a person has learned something, knows something or can do

Study	Title	Sample Research Questions	Research Instruments/ Elicitation Techniques
Gass and Mackey (1999) in *Language Learning*	The Effects of Task Repetition on Linguistic Output	RQ1: Does task repetition yield more sophisticated language use? (p.554)	Holistic Measure (magnitude estimation) between Times 1 and 3, and Times 1 and 4; Analysis of Morphosyntax between Times 1 and 3, and Times 1 and 4; and Analysis of lexical sophistication between Times 1 and 4
Kang (2010) in *The Modern Language Journal*	Negative Evidence and Its Explicitness and Positioning in the Learning of Korean as a Heritage Language	RQ1: Does negative evidence contribute to the improvement of learner knowledge of a target form in the context of learning Korean as a heritage language at the postsecondary school (p.587)	Background Questionnaire; Grammaticality Judgment and Correction; Picture Description; Story Sequencing; Spot the Difference
Marsden and Chen (2011) in *Language Learning*	The Role of Structured Input Activities in Processing Instruction and the Kinds of Knowledge They Promote	RQ1: Do affective activities, either alone or following inferential activities, have an impact on learning the –ed past test inflection? (p.1066)	Timed Grammaticality Judgement Test (GJT); Self-Report following the GJT (i.e., written questionnaire); Written Gap-filling Test; Oral Tests; Self-Report following the Oral Tests (i.e., brief structured interviews); and Attitude Questionnaire
Sheen (2010) in *Studies in Second Language Acquisition*	Differential Effects of Oral and Written Corrective Feedback in the ESL Classroom	RQ1: Is there any difference in the effect of oral recasts and direct written correction on the acquisition of English articles? (p.211)	Speeded Dictation Test; Writing Test; Error Correction Test; and Exit Questionnaire
Takimoto (2006) in *Language Teaching Research*	The Effects of Explicit Feedback on the Development of Pragmatic Proficiency	RQ1: Does instruction involving a structured input task promote Japanese learners' pragmatic proficiency? (p.398)	Two Input-based Tests (i.e., Listening Test and Acceptability Judgement Test); and Two Output-based Tests (i.e., Open-ended Discourse Completion Test and Role-play Test)

FIGURE 7.1   *Examples of experimental research instruments and data elicitation techniques*

something. In language learning research, tests and assessments are needed because, for example, we need to:

● assess students' language ability/proficiency

● discover how successful students have been in achieving the objectives of a course of study

● provide feedback to learners so that they know the status of their learning and how to move forward

● evaluate the effectiveness of teaching or an experimental program.

Language proficiency tests

A language proficiency test is based on a theoretical model of language proficiency (see e.g. Bachman & Palmer 2010). It can assess students' knowledge of and ability to use a language in general without reference to a curriculum or syllabus. It can usually rank students in relation to one another. One of the main considerations in constructing a proficiency test is *discrimination* among different ability levels. This can be achieved by using a mixture of easy, medium, difficult and very difficult items/tasks. Test discrimination is essential because it will make it possible to distinguish between students at different levels. If the test only consisted of easy items, it would be difficult to distinguish a medium-ability student from a high-ability student. Language proficiency tests usually measure four language skills (i.e. reading, listening, writing, and speaking). Some tests may include a direct assessment of vocabulary and grammatical ability.

There are many English language proficiency tests that can be considered for an experimental study, including TOEFL, TOEIC (Test of English for International Communication), IELTS and OET (Occupational English Test—a specific purpose test). The key strength of using proficiency tests in experimental research is that they are professionally developed and are strongly related to theories of language proficiency. They are also internationally recognized. One limitation of this type of test for experimental research is that it may not be suitable for some groups of students (e.g. low-ability students) or for a specific research focus (e.g. a proficiency test may not measure what we intend to examine in a study). It can also be expensive for a research project to adopt a commercial proficiency test. However, there are usually retired proficiency tests that researchers may consider for use without payment being required.

Achievement tests

An achievement test is associated with the language curriculum or syllabus for a course that students are undertaking. It can assess what students have learned and rank them in terms of their level of mastery of the subject. Discrimination among different students may or may not be important for achievement tests. For example, if a well-defined body of knowledge is tested (e.g. a set of words or grammar rules), discrimination is not a major concern. We are only interested in how much each student knows. However, if a more abstract construct is tested (e.g. the ability to identify main ideas and guess the meaning of a word from its context), discrimination is important because only by including items of different levels of difficulty can different levels of knowledge among the students be distinguished.

Achievement tests can be *standardized* or *teacher-made*. Experimental research that is conducted in a language classroom can use achievement tests as pretests and posttests. A key advantage of using an achievement test is that it is related to the context of teaching and learning (i.e. it is syllabus-relevant) and can be seen as authentic (i.e. with strong language content from the lessons taught). However, achievement tests are often poorly developed, and lack a clear and justifiable rationale for testing something in a certain way. Several achievement tests do not have *test specifications* or clear underlying constructs. Furthermore, the lack of a theoretical construct of language ability in an achievement test makes it difficult to make a substantive claim about test scores and generalize research findings.

Researcher-made tests

In experimental studies in the language classroom, achievement tests may not be suitable for use because the study may have a focus on a particular skill or ability that cannot be measured using available achievement or proficiency tests. Researchers can develop a suitable test by consulting existing theories about a topic of interest, as well as by reviewing and examining what other researchers who have conducted a similar study have used. By examining existing researcher-made tests, researchers can learn not only about the types of tests that have been used, but also about some of the weaknesses of those tests. In some situations, researchers can adopt an existing researcher-made test or adapt some parts of such a test for use.

One of the key advantages of using a researcher-made test is that the test can be designed to elicit the specific ability we are interested in. As such, it will produce data that can be used to answer a specific research question. Note that it is important that a pilot study is carried out before the main study is undertaken. A pilot study is conducted to make sure that an instrument is appropriate and feasible for use. One of the key drawbacks of researcher-made tests is that they are time-consuming and costly to develop. To develop a suitable test, a good understanding of principles in language testing and assessment is required. Supervisors of postgraduate students are usually able to give advice on this matter.

Performance assessments

A performance assessment aims to measure what students can do (e.g. speak and write), rather than what they know (e.g. grammar, vocabulary and pragmatic knowledge). A performance assessment often takes the form of a *direct* assessment in which students are assessed by carrying out an activity that requires them to use a particular target language skill. For example, instead of taking a multiple-choice test identifying correct sentences, students are asked to write an essay so that their writing ability can be judged against established criteria. Performance assessment is also known as authentic assessment because students are using the target language communicatively (see McNamara 1996 for a comprehensive discussion on issues related to performance assessment). Figure 7.2 presents an example of a performance assessment task in writing. This is an example of an *integrated test task* that requires test-takers to use more than one language skill (e.g. reading comprehension before writing).

ENG333 (Advanced English Writing I)

Student ID: _____   Name: _____   Date: _____

Directions: Read the following paragraph about research findings on the impact of social media on students' academic performance. Write an essay (approximately 300 words) in response to the research findings. For example, do you agree or disagree with the research findings? What are your strategies to not spend too much time on social media? Give reasons and examples to support your point of view. Write your essay on the provided answer sheet. You have 50 minutes to complete your essay.

"A new study released by researchers at The University of Sydney suggests a negative connection between social media use and poor academic performance. The study examined not only traditional social media outlets, such as Facebook and Twitter, but also social technology such as texting and [instant] messengers. 1000 participants took part in the study (500 males and 500 females, ages between 18 and 20 years). The study found that female participants spent 8 hours a day on average, whereas male students spent on average 5 hours, using some form of social media. There was a statistically significant difference between males and females in the reported number of hours spent using social media. The study also found that social networking, watching movies, and TV were the factors most negatively associated with academic performance among the study participants."

FIGURE 7.2   *An example of a performance assessment task*

Two scoring methods are typically used in performance assessment. The first is *holistic* (or *impressionistic*) *scoring*, which allows raters to indicate an overall impression of students' performance using a single score. The second is *analytical scoring*, which is based on various specified criteria. In writing, such criteria are, for example, *fulfilment of the test task, communicative command of the target language, organization of discourse*, and *linguistic errors* (see Weigle 2004). In speaking, the scoring criteria include *accuracy* (e.g. intelligible pronunciation; grammatical/lexical accuracy), *appropriateness* (e.g. appropriate to function and to context), *range* (e.g. wide range of language), *flexibility* (e.g. ability to take turns; adaptability to new topics/changes of direction), and *size* (e.g. ability to make lengthy and complex contributions; ability to expand and develop ideas independently; see Luoma 2004). Brown (2012) provides a comprehensive treatment of rubrics in language assessment. See also the American Council on the Teaching of Foreign Languages (ACTFL) Proficiency Guidelines for examples of performance assessment rubrics.

Performance assessments, however, have some disadvantages that need to be considered carefully. First, they are subjective assessments because two trained raters can assign a different score to the same performance (further discussed below). Second, they are expensive because two raters are needed and they are time-consuming to produce, compared to other test methods, such as multiple-choice and short-answer questions. Finally, there are factors that influence people's performance that have little to do with the abilities we would like to measure. For example, success in writing depends not only on linguistic skills (e.g. vocabulary, grammar), but also on personal characteristics (e.g. intelligence, experience, motivation, anxiety and interest) and the characteristics of performance tasks and conditions (e.g. topic, task difficulty levels, time constraints and scoring methods; see

Bachman & Palmer 2010). Unless we define writing ability broadly, it is difficult to infer students' target ability from performance assessments.

Self-assessment

This type of assessment is driven by an interest in involving learners in all phases of assessment (see Oscarson 2014). It is assumed that since students know about their learning, they should be able to report on the extent to which they can or cannot do something well. Self-assessment of language ability typically uses *can-do* statements (e.g. I can carry on a daily conversation with a stranger; I can identify the main ideas in texts) and employ rating scales such as 1 (Strongly disagree), 2 (Disagree), 3 (Neutral), 4 (Agree) or 5 (Strongly agree); see questionnaires below). See also the *Common European Framework of Reference for Languages: Learning, Teaching, Assessment* (<http://www.coe.int/t/dg4/linguistic/source/framework_en.pdf>, viewed February 24, 2014). Figure 7.3 presents an example of a self-assessment in reading comprehension.

While this form of assessment is useful for formative assessment purposes (e.g. to check student learning progress and to provide feedback), there has been skepticism in regard to this form of subjective assessment, largely due to learners' inability to provide accurate judgments of their achievement, ability or proficiency (see Ross 1998). In a high-stakes situation (in which

Self-assessment in Reading Comprehension

Student ID: _____   Name: _____   Date: _____

Directions: Rate the following statements about your reading abilities. Use the following scales to rate your abilities (i.e., how much they are true of you.)

1	2	3	4	5
Not at all true of me	Not true of me	Unsure	True of me	Very true of me

No	Aspects	1	2	3	4	5
1.	I can scan and skim text for general and specific information.					
2.	I can skim text to evaluate information.					
3.	I can identify the main ideas and the purpose of a passage.					
4.	I can guess meanings of unknown words from context clues.					
5.	I can identify phrases or word equivalence.					
6.	I can predict topics of passages and the content of a passage from an introductory paragraph.					
7.	I can recognize abbreviations of words.					
8.	I can make decisions about appropriate information.					
9.	I can discriminate between more and less important ideas.					
10.	I can distinguish facts from opinions.					
11.	I can analyze reference words.					
12.	I can draw inferences from content.					
13.	I can identify the title of a text and the appropriate heading.					
14.	I can recall word meanings.					
15.	I can summarize the content of a given text.					

FIGURE 7.3   *An example of a self-assessment in reading comprehension*

tests have consequences for students, e.g. the tests may be pass/fail), students may overrate their ability. On the other hand, in low-stakes situations, students can be harsh on themselves in terms of what they can do. This type of assessment can be highly subjective. In experimental research, if researchers aim to determine an objective impact of a treatment, self-assessment should be *avoided* as the main instrument. A more objective instrument (e.g. a language test) should be adopted. Self-assessment can, however, be useful to complement a study when it is used to examine students' perceived processes of learning.

Peer evaluation

Peer evaluation is driven by an interest in nurturing students' peer mentoring and supportive environment (e.g. to develop co-operative learning). When students know what is expected of them in their learning, they should be able to judge not only themselves, but also their peers, because students interact with one another in the classroom. In an oral presentation task, for example, students can rate their peers' performance in terms of organization, content, clarity of presentation and non-verbal communication. They can provide some written feedback of how their peers can improve their presentations. Figure 7.4 presents a peer-evaluation form that is used for evaluating students' group presentation.

Like self-assessment, peer evaluation is useful for formative assessment and encourages the development of evaluative processes. Unlike self-assessment, when peer evaluation does not contribute to grades, students have a tendency to be kind to their peers in their assessments. However, when peer evaluation involves group competition, students can be harsh on other groups.

Portfolio assessment

Because most tests, such as proficiency and achievement tests, are restricted to one time and involve highly pressured performance judgments, students' results in these tests may be inadequate for decision-making. Portfolio assessment is related to a collection of language performance samples of students over time. This method allows us to obtain a developing picture of students' learning achievements since students will be less stressed than in a test. While portfolio assessment can be appealing, however, it is difficult to use to determine the gains from an experimental study. It is important to note that a portfolio is not a test and in fact, scoring a portfolio can be much harder than scoring a test. There is the issue of *fairness* in portfolio assessment because there are other factors that can determine students' portfolio performance. For example, higher-income parents are likely to provide more expensive materials or better technology to their children

ENG422 (Oral Communication in English I)

Group presentation

Group No: _____   Topic: _____ Date: _____

1	2	3	4	5
Strongly disagree	Disagree	Neutral	Agree	Strongly agree

No	Aspects	1	2	3	4	5
1.	The presentation covered the assigned tasks and was interesting, comprehensible and useful.					
2.	The main issues relating to the topic were discussed appropriately.					
3.	The presentation reflected a good understanding of the subject matter, and an appropriate depth of treatment of the subject matter.					
4.	The presentation reflected an awareness of the topic being presented.					
5.	The presentation reflected evidence of original/critical thinking and analysis.					
6.	The presentation reflects a good collaborative effort of all the group members.					
7.	The Powerpoint Presentation was well-structured, easy to follow, and engaging.					
8.	Presenters completed their presentation effectively within the given time.					
9.	Questions/comments were appropriately and clearly answered or addressed.					
10.	The handout for the audience was useful.					

Score (out of 20): _____
Comments/recommendations:

_____
_____
_____
_____
_____
_____

FIGURE 7.4   *An example of a peer-evaluation form*

than lower-income parents. There is a lack of evidence as to the authorship of the work assessed because it can be done outside the classroom. Nonetheless, like self- and peer assessment, portfolio assessment can be useful for examining processes and factors during an experimental study.

Key considerations in using language tests and assessments

There are some issues worth considering in regard to language tests and assessments. We shall examine objective and subjective tests, skills-based tests and assessments, test specifications, test techniques, test scores, pretests and posttests, and the ceiling and floor effects.

Objective versus subjective tests

When we consider a test in an experimental study, we will encounter two methods of scoring: objective and subjective scoring. An *objective test* is a test that has answer keys we can use to mark students' responses to questions. This is objective because an answer is either correct or incorrect, and a human scorer does not need to make their own judgment. Objective tests are reliable because they produce consistent scoring. *Subjective tests*, on the other hand, require a human scorer to make a judgment on students' performance. Subjective tests include tests that require learners to complete a task by speaking or writing, for example. Although a set of criteria or rubrics of specified abilities, along with a rating scale (e.g. 1 = very poor to 5 = very good) can be used, scorers' personal characteristics, opinions or attitudes toward a particular language use can influence their judgment, and thereby the test scores that they assign. As a result, different judges may assign a different score to the same piece of writing, for example. In subjective tests, we need to train scorers and use two raters to judge the same performance. We need to report on an interrater reliability estimate (see Chapter 12).

Skill-based tests and assessments

It is beyond the scope of this chapter to cover what is involved in the assessment of a language skill (e.g. speaking, see Luoma 2004; writing, see Weigle 2004; listening, see Buck 2001; reading, see Alderson 2000; grammar, see Purpura 2004; and vocabulary, see Read 2000). Each skill requires a careful theoretical and methodological consideration of a language skill construct, assessment methods (e.g. test techniques, tasks and scoring methods) and interpretations of test scores.

Test techniques

There is a wide range of test techniques that can be used to test students' language skills. Techniques are methods for stimulating and engaging students to perform a task so that their ability or performance can be elicited and assessed. Test techniques range from *selected-response* techniques (e.g. multiple-choice, true/false and ordering) to *constructed-response* techniques (e.g. *limited-production* tasks, such as those involving short answers, information transfer, cloze test, gap-filling, dictation and sentence completion; and *extended-production* tasks, such as essays, reports, role-play and interviews). Figure 7.5 provides an example of selected response and limited production tasks.

A good test combines various test techniques because there are strengths and weaknesses in any particular test technique. The language testing books suggested above present these techniques associated with particular language skills. In language learning research, there are other examples of elicitation tasks utilizing these techniques (e.g. picture descriptions, story completion tasks; see Gass & Mackey 2007 for a comprehensive treatment).

Examples of Common Limited Response Test Techniques

Technique	Example	Advantages	Disadvantages
Multiple-choice questions: Ask test-takers to choose an answer from multiple options.	Platinum is harder than copper and is almost as pliable _____. A. gold B. than gold C. as gold D. gold is	Complete grader reliability; grading is simple, rapid; cost effective; difficulty levels can be estimated in advance via pre-testing; clear instructions about what to do	Some flaw in questions affect performance; effects of guessing; expensive to develop; time-consuming and demanding for satisfactory items; answering multiple-choice items is an unreal task.
Short answer questions: Ask test-takers to provide a short answer to a question.	*Text to read* The main purpose of the passage is to _____. The passage mainly discusses _____. In what city was Joe "King" Oliver's band based? _____	More confident for students' performance; a wide number of questions can be set based on predictions of responses; assess complicated skills (e.g., inferencing and main ideas; more real life language use in English for academic purposes	Involves test takers writing (not the intended construct); need to establish a range of possible acceptable responses
Cloze: Ask test-takers to complete a space that completes the sentence meaningfully and appropriately. Every n^{th} word (e.g., 6th, 7th) is deleted.	A bird's territory could be small or large. Some species of birds claim only their nest and the area right around it, while others claim a far larger territory. Gulls and penguins, for example, (1)_____ in huge colonies, but even (2)_____ the biggest colonies, each male (3)_____ his mate have small territories (4)_____ their own immediately around their (5)_____ .	Easy to construct and easily scored; high degree of internal consistency; accepted as a measure of reading as it involves multiple reading skills (e.g., inferencing and referencing).	Deleted words may be irrelevant to knowledge tested; need time to complete; difficult to score when various test takers produce various possible answers; need to train graders for consistency; unreal tasks
Selective gap-filling: Same as Cloze, but items selected for deletion based on what is known about language, about difficulty in text, and the way language works in a particular text.	Males defend their territory chiefly against other males of the same species. In (1)_____ cases, a warning call or threatening pose may (2)_____ all the defense needed, but (3)_____ other cases, intruders may refuse to leave peacefully.	Can determine where deletions are to be made and to focus on those items; easy for iterations to maintain the required number of items	Similar to Cloze; testing more restrictive reading skills where only single words are deleted; need to decide how to deal with misspelling when answers are correct.
Information transfer: Ask test-taker to label a diagram, complete a chart or number; a sequence of events		Suitable for testing an understanding of processes, classification and narrative sequences; realistic task for various situations	Good care is needed for non-verbal tasks; dangerous for cultural, cognitive and educational bias; tasks can be very complicated (students can spend too much time working out the problem)
Dichotomous items: Ask test-takers to indicate whether a statement is true or false.	Read this information from a language school brochure: Write T (true) or F (false) ____ You will receive more information before you leave. ____ The best way to get from Sydney to Canberra is by train. ____ The school will pay for a taxi from the bus station to your host family.	Easy to construct; scoring accuracy and economic; easy to amend; assessing comprehension of factual information from text.	Problems with guessing (50-50% chance); less discriminating; requires absolute true/false answers

FIGURE 7.5   *An example of selected-response and limited-production tasks*

The importance of test specifications

It is essential to develop a test specification for your pretests and posttests or other tests to be used in your experimental study. Figure 7.6 presents the key components of a test specification. Figure 7.7 presents an example of a

Overall test specifications

Components of test/assessment	Descriptions of components, examples
Title of test/assessment	Clear, precise title
Purposes of the assessment	e.g., formative/summative; Proficiency/achievement/diagnostic/screening/placement/ pre-test/post-test
Decisions to be made	Achievement/selection/research; high- or low-stakes
Abilities/knowledge/skills to be assessed	Definitions of the language abilities, knowledge, skills or constructs to be assessed and inferred from the test performance
Weighting of the assessment	Proportion of the assessment score that contributes to the overall grade or achievement
Test length	Number of test sections, number of ta ofs, texts, word limits; specification of the word limit for each task
Student time allowance	The period of time allotted for students to complete the assessment tasks
Students' characteristics	Number of students, year of study, age, nationalities, level of education prior to enrollment, academic discipline; undergraduate/postgraduate; amount of learning prior to the assessment
Format of the assessment	e.g., multiple-choice, gap-filling, cloze, information transfer, closed-book exam, open-book exam; take-home exams, essays, report, assignments
Rationale for the choice of test format	Why test formats are chosen; how validity, reliability, fairness and practicality are addressed
Medium/Channel	e.g., paper and pencil; computer-based; Word processing; hard-copy or online submission
Nature of the assessment tasks	Descriptions of what is involved in this assessment; expected responses
Assessment instructions/directions	What to do and how to complete the assessment task; time allotted; examples of instructions
General criteria for students	Objective or subjective assessment; assessment criteria/expectations for students; holistic or analytic scoring method for writing and speaking
Methods of grading	e.g., objective or subjective judgment; computer scorer/ teachers/external assessors
Scoring rubric/criteria for teachers/assessors	e.g., grading schemes; criteria for grading; holistic or analytic; scorer training/discussion
Amount of time to grade	Recommended amount to spend grading per task (if applicable)
Validation considerations	e.g., how test tasks correspond to the course objectives; assessment reliability; rater training; ethical considerations
Attached documents	e.g., unit outline, time frame, lessons

FIGURE 7.6   *Key components of a test specification*

test specification for a reading test. Test specifications can be developed for an entire test, as well as for a specific test section.

See Bachman and Palmer (2010), Carr (2011), and Davidson and Lynch (2002) for extensive discussion and examples of test specifications.

What makes up a test score?

It is important to note that an observed test score (e.g. from a pretest and posttest) is not necessarily a true reflection of students' ability or performance. In classical test theory, an observed test score is the result of the combination of an underlying ability of interest, test-method facets (e.g. test

Test Specifications for a Reading Section

Test-takers: Undergraduate and postgraduate ESL students currently admitted into a university program.

Time allocation: 1 hour

General Description:

This is a reading proficiency test which measures students' ability to comprehend English text. The purpose of this test is for English as a second language (ESL) student after admission to a university. The following are the list of reading constructs in this test:

a. Scanning for information;
b. Scanning to sequence the information of the text;
c. Skimming for information;
d. Skimming to evaluate information;
e. Skimming for the main point of a text;
f. Guessing meanings of unknown words from context;
g. Identifying phrases or word equivalence;
h. Transferring information from a text to a grid;
i. Matching key words with definitions;
j. Drawing inferences from content;
k. Identifying the title of the text and the appropriate heading;
l. Identifying the main ideas or the purpose of a passage;
m. Identifying the topic of a passage;
n. Identifying specific information from text
o. Analyzing reference words

Prompt attributes:

Instruction: "**General Directions:** In this section you will read several passages. Each one is followed by several questions about it. Answer all the questions/tasks following a passage on the basis of what is stated or implied in that passage."

Requirements for the text: The topics to be selected in this section include topics related to academic reading. Texts used are composed of: (1) grammatical features (e.g., the relationship between the structure of sentences and the vocabulary used, such as sentence types and verb forms); (2) pragmatic features (e.g., the relationship between the intent of the writer, such as exposition and argument); and (3) discourse features (e.g., the relationship between the nature and the structure of the text as a whole, such as rhetorical properties (e.g., definition, description, classification, illustration, cause/effect, problem/solution and comparison/contrast) and textual organizations (e.g., prose).

This section will consist of 4 texts ranging from 450 words to 700 words. The texts and words will be a general/nontechnical in nature to tap into the students' academic reading ability. However, texts should not be overly simplified.

Description of the test items: Given the reading skills to be tested, it should be noted that some skills can only be assessed indirectly. For example, to recognize the main idea of a text, other skills identified above may be needed, not merely the skill of identifying main ideas. For ease of item writing, the following table of specifications should be used.

Skills tested	No. of items	Type of item per skills	Desired weighting
Main topics	4	Multiple choice (2); Matching (2)	4
Main ideas	4	Multiple choice (2); Matching (2)	4
Best title	3	Multiple choice	3
Writer's purposes	3	Multiple choice	3
Reference words	5	Multiple choice (2); Short answers (3)	5
Implied statements	5	Multiple choice (2); Matching (2); Short answer (1)	5
Vocabulary in context	5	Multiple choice (3); Short answer (2)	5
True/false statements	5	True/false (3); Multiple choice (2)	5
Specific details	6	Multiple choice (2); Short answers (2)	6
Total	40		40

FIGURE 7.7   *An example of a test specification for a reading test*

techniques, test tasks, time allowed and scoring), personal characteristics (e.g. age, gender, first language, experience and motivation), and a random error of measurement (e.g. due to room temperature, noise, well-being during test taking). An understanding of the influences of these factors on a

Guidelines for question writing

Question	Explanation	Example
Main idea, main topic and main purpose questions	These questions ask learners to identify an answer choice that correctly summarizes a main idea and subject of the whole passage or the author's purpose of writing the passage.	"What is the main idea of this passage?" "What is the writer's main purpose in writing this article?"
Factual questions	These questions ask learners to locate and identify answers to questions about specific information and details in the passage.	"According to the passage, where is **A** located?" "According to the passage, **A** ... " "Which is true about **A** according to the passage?"
Negative questions	These questions ask learners which of the answer choices is NOT discussed in the passage.	"Which in the passage is NOT true about ... ?" "According to the passage, the following are ..., EXCEPT ... "
Inference questions	These questions ask learners to draw conclusions based on information in the passage.	"The author implies which of the following is true?" "Which of the following can be inferred from the passage?"
Vocabulary-in-context questions	These questions ask learners to identify the meaning of a word or phrase as used in the passage.	"The word '...' (line 6) can be best replaced by ... "
Reference questions	These questions ask learners to identify the noun to which a pronoun or other expression refers.	"The word 'it' (line 7) refers to ... "

Correct answer and distracters for multiple-choice question: The following guideline can be used to write the correct answer and distractors.

    a. correct answer

    b. irrelevant possible answer

    c. partially correct answer, but incomplete

    d. key features of the answer are incorrect

Correct answer for short-answer tasks: Answers are supported in a given text. Answers should be no more than 3 words.

Correct answer for matching tasks: Answers are evident or directly implied in a given text.

Correct answer for true/false tasks: Answers are evident or directly implied in a given text.

Response attributes:

The students will read each text with questions about it. They will read the text and then study the questions. In multiple-choice tasks, they will select the correct answer from among the choices given in the test item. In short-answer tasks, they will write their short answers (no more than 3 words). In a matching task, they will match a pair that corresponds to each other correctly based on a given text. In true/false tasks, they will indicate whether a statement is true or false according to what is directly implied from a given text. The students then will provide their answers on the answer sheet.

FIGURE 7.7   *An example of a test specification for a reading test* (continued)

test score is critical to research validity and conclusions drawn on the basis of test scores and statistical comparisons.

The ceiling and floor effects

In Chapter 5, we discussed threats to the internal validity of a study. There are two important threats to the internal validity of an experimental study in relation to a pretest and posttest: the ceiling and floor effects (Johnson & Christensen 2008). The *ceiling effect* is related to a restriction of the upper end of the test score range. This effect is related to higher-ability students whose test performance may be underestimated because the test may be *too easy* for them (i.e. there will be many homogenously high scores) or the test does not allow them to demonstrate their ability to a sufficiently high level. In an experimental study in which two teaching methods are compared, it may be found that high-ability students' performance in the pretest and posttest associated with both methods are very similar, leading to the conclusion that neither method makes a difference for this group of learners. However, such a conclusion may be *erroneous,* since the test could be restrictive in terms of reflecting their actual ability.

In a similar vein, the *floor effect* is influenced by a restricted lower end of the test score range. The floor effect concerns lower ability students whose performance cannot be captured adequately, simply because the test is too difficult for them, resulting in homogenously low scores for these students. They may get all (or almost all) of the questions incorrect. In an experimental study in which two teaching methods are compared, it may be concluded that the two methods are equally (in)effective for this group of learners. Nonetheless, if a less difficult test had been used, the true ability of these students might have been better reflected in their scores, which would show more variability.

In summary, in an experimental study, it can be difficult to observe a significant change in the highest and lowest level students' performance when a test cannot adequately measure these students' abilities. This may be in spite of the fact that the intervention has had a beneficial effect on the students' language abilities.

Questionnaires and inventories

In this book, we do not distinguish questionnaires from inventories because both rely on individuals' self-reporting on issues that are descriptive of themselves. Questionnaires can collect quantitative or qualitative data or both, whereas inventories are usually quantitative instruments. Questionnaires are typically associated with survey research aiming to explore an issue with a large sample size, whereas scales and inventories are used in individual differences research for examining language learners' psychological attributes or traits (e.g. motivation, anxiety, personality, and cognitive and learning styles). Unlike language tests, there are no right or wrong answers in questionnaires. Experimental research in language learning also adopts the use of questionnaires to measure psychological constructs such as strategy use awareness, anxiety, self-efficacy and motivation, before, during and/or after a treatment.

One of the most predominant techniques of questionnaires is a Likert scale (named after Rensis Likert, who was the first to develop it), which is used to quantify a construct of interest. A Likert scale is a discrete response scale (ordinal-scale like) that research participants choose, for example, 1 (never), 2 (rarely), 3 (often), 4 (usually) or 5 (always). Participants read a series of items or statements and choose the scale that most closely reflects them. It is essential that several statement items are used to measure any one construct in a questionnaire. The key reason is that a construct can be highly complex and multidimensional, and therefore requires several items to capture its various facets. Furthermore, the use of many items can allow researchers to obtain enough data representing a target construct to identify measurement consistency.

Apart from the use of Likert scales, there are several other techniques that are suitable for questionnaires. These techniques include dichotomous items (e.g. yes/no), multiple-choice items, items that need to be ranked in order of importance, checklists, semantic differential items (which require a scale similar to a Likert scale) and open-ended questions. Questionnaires are useful and practical for research purposes in terms of their measurement precision and participants' familiarity with questionnaires. They can be administered quickly and economically with a large group of participants.

As in language test development, we need to consider issues related to the definition of a construct of interest, the taxonomies of a questionnaire (which are similar to test specifications) and measurement (e.g. use of scales in closed ended questions and constructed responses in open-ended questions). A *taxonomy*, similar to a test specification, specifies the kinds of variables and the amount of data (e.g. number of items) needed for quantitative analysis. It is important to have enough items to measure any one construct (see Oxford 2011 for examples of questionnaire taxonomies). Figure 7.8 presents an example of a questionnaire for examining reading difficulty.

There are different ways to arrive at a total score in Likert scale questionnaires. One way is to sum the weights of all the responses chosen by the correspondents. Another way is to compute a final score for each sub-construct by averaging the responses associated with that sub-construct. This method of calculating a score is preferable to the former weighting system because it can be interpreted within the scale descriptors being used. Of course, when a Likert scale questionnaire is used, descriptive statistics and reliability analyses are necessary.

Questionnaires may, however, be limited by respondent bias (e.g. *self-deception bias*—they think they can do something, but they cannot—and *prestige bias*—they provide answers that make them look good or feel better). There may be unmotivated or disinterested participants who may answer a questionnaire without reading the items or answer *neutral* or choose the middle scale throughout (this is especially true of Likert scale questionnaires). See Dörnyei with Taguchi (2010), Gilham (2007) and Phakiti (2014) for a comprehensive discussion of questionnaire development.

Online Reading Difficulty Questionnaire

This questionnaire is to be completed by English as a second language (ESL) international postgraduate students. This questionnaire investigates academic reading difficulty. It will take approximately 20 minutes to answer this questionnaire. Your identity and information from this survey will be absolutely confidential. Please contact Aek Phakiti (aek.phakiti@sydney.edu.au) if you have further questions or would like to know more about this survey. Thank you for your cooperation in completing this questionnaire.

1. **I consent to participating in this survey.**

    ○ Yes ⟵⟶ (Asking participant
    to consent)

    ○ No

2. **What year did you start your postgraduate degree?**

    [   ]

3. **What is your nationality?** ⟵⟶ (Background
    information)

    [   ]

4. **What is your age?**

    [   ]

5. **Your current overall IELTS score**

    ○ 5.5-6.0

    ○ 6.5 ⟵⟶ (Choose
    one option)

    ○ 7 or above

    ○ Not applicable

6. **Your current IELTS reading score**

    ○ 5.5-6.0

    ○ 6.5

    ○ 7 or above

    ○ Not applicable

7. **Please indicate (check) kinds of texts you read to study. You may have read them either with peers or on your own. You can check more than one box.**

    ☐ Journal articles

    ☐ Text books

    ☐ Book chapters

    ☐ Unit of study outlines

    ☐ Notices ⟵⟶ (Checklist)

    ☐ Emails

    ☐ Databases

    ☐ Lecture notes

    ☐ Technical reports/manuals

FIGURE 7.8   *An example of a questionnaire for examining reading difficulty*

☐ Others (please specify) [   ]

8. **Reading difficulty: Please indicate a degree of difficulties on the following aspects using the following scales. 1 = Not at all; 2 = A little; 3 = Moderate; 4 = Much; 5 = Very much; N/A = Not applicable in my case.**

When I read in order to learn and fulfill course requirements, I find it difficult to ...

	1	2	3	4	5	N/A
search for alternative sources of reading texts.	○	○	○	○	○	○
skim and scan in order to read more texts.	○	○	○	○	○	○
compare and contrast ideas.	○	○	○	○	○	○
determine the main idea or aspects of a passage.	○	○	○	○	○	○
analyze ideas and identify implications of the reading	○	○	○	○	○	○
remember major ideas for later or future use or reference.	○	○	○	○	○	○

(callout: 5-point, Likert scale, with not applicable)

9. **What specific difficulties or obstacles do you have in your academic reading?**

[   ]

(callout: Open-ended, exploratory item)

10. **Please comment on what you do/have done to overcome your reading difficulties.**

[   ]

11. **Would you be willing to participate in a follow-up interview about the questions or issues in this survey?**

○ Yes

○ No

(callout: Dichotomous item)

12. **If "yes", please provide your details below. Note: Even if you provide your name here, your survey responses will remain confidential.**

☐ Name [   ]

(callout: Fill in the blank)

☐ Email [   ]

☐ Contact number [   ]

(callout: A closing with thanks to participants)

Thank you for your cooperation.

FIGURE 7.8   *An example of a questionnaire for examining reading difficulty* (continued)

Rating scales

The principles behind the development and use of rating scales are similar to those that apply to the development and use of questionnaires. Rating scales are often used in self-assessment, peer evaluation and performance assessment. They can be affected by various types of error/bias and rater characteristics. The *linearity error* is related to the tendency of a rater to be generous when rating individuals' abilities. The *severity error* is associated with the tendency of a rater to be harsh on all individuals. Another key error in rating scales and in most Likert scale questionnaires is the *central tendency error,* which is related to a rater's tendency to avoid extreme rating scores (e.g. 1 or 5). As noted in regard to performance assessment, raters need comprehensive training, and moderation during their rating. Two raters are recommended to minimize the potential effect of such errors.

Intelligence, aptitude, and language aptitude tests

Aptitude is often viewed as *raw learning power* (Dörnyei 2005). That is, if we have a talent for a certain area, learning is easy for us, leading us to high ultimate attainment. Aptitude tests are useful as measures of individuals' general ability to do something. Aptitude is one of the human intelligence traits. Most aptitude tests aim to predict students' future learning success, which differentiates these tests from achievement tests.

Language learning aptitude tends to play a role in the rate of language learning development. Although it is not necessarily true for all high-aptitude learners, people with a higher language aptitude learn a new language more quickly than those with lower aptitude. Ortega (2009) gives examples of learners with exceptional language aptitude. In language learning, several language aptitude tests have been developed for the purpose of measuring individuals' potential for language learning success (see Doughty 2014 for a comprehensive review). Typically, a language aptitude test has various sections for measuring language aptitude constructs. It can be administered in a group or individually. For example, the *MLAT* (Modern Language Aptitude Test; Carroll & Sapon 1959) measures four aspects of language aptitude: *phonemic coding ability* (i.e. the ability to identify and memorize new sounds); *grammatical sensitivity* (i.e. the ability to understand the function of particular words in sentences); (3) *inductive language learning ability* (i.e. the ability to figure out grammatical rules from language samples); and *rote learning ability* (i.e. memory for new words). See <http://lltf.net/aptitude-tests/language-aptitude-tests/modern-language-aptitude-test-2/>, viewed 11 July 2014, for further information.

Other language aptitude tests include The *DLAB* (Defense Language Aptitude Battery (Peterson & Al-Haik 1976), which is similar to the MLAT, but is used for selection into the Defense Language Institute and is not available to the public. The *PLAB* (Pimsleur Language Aptitude Battery (Pimsleur 1966) is similar to MLAT but less auditory. The *CANAL-FT* (Cognitive Ability for Novelty in Acquisition of Language as Applied to Foreign Language Test (Grigorenko, Sternberg & Ehrman 2000) is based on the theory of psycholinguistic and acquisition processes. Recently,

Hi-LAB (High-Level Language Aptitude Battery; Doughty, Campbell, Bunting, Mislevy, Bowles & Koeth 2010) has been developed to predict the language learning attainment of adult language learners at advanced levels (see Linck *et al.* 2013). According to Doughty (2014), Hi-LAB assesses several aptitude constructs (e.g. memory, acuity, speed, primability, induction, pragmatic sensitivity, and fluency). Scores from each section can indicate the potential strengths and weaknesses of an individual.

In experimental research, given the purpose of an aptitude test, it may be infeasible or impractical to use an aptitude test as a pretest or posttest. Participants' available aptitude scores, however, are useful for an experimental research design because they allow us to control an aptitude variable, so that it is a constant independent variable that is not interacting with an independent variable of interest. It should be noted that administering an aptitude test can be costly and time-consuming due to its comprehensiveness—various multidimensional aspects of aptitude need to be tested (see Doughty 2014).

Quantitative observations

In language learning research, there can be a large discrepancy between what learners report via questionnaires about their thinking, beliefs and attitudes and their actual behaviors. Accordingly, direct observation is a data collection technique that can help researchers overcome such a discrepancy, by allowing them to observe learners' patterns of behavior in a specific context. Direct observation allows researchers to determine to what extent learners' habits or behaviors are present. In experimental research, systematic direct observation is usually carried out quantitatively by using an observation scheme, rating scales or checklists. As observers are the research instrument (i.e. the ones that record the data through observations), observers need to be as *objective* and *consistent* as possible in their observations (i.e. they need to be impartial). Researchers can tally frequencies of behaviors, activities or events within a specific time frame.

Quantitative observation involves standardized procedures surrounding the questions of not only who and what is to be observed, but also when, where, and how to observe. Standardized observation instruments, such as checklists or observation schemes, are often used in quantitative observation (see Gass & Mackey 2007, Chapter 8). In language learning research, COLT (Communicative Orientation of Language Teaching; Spada & Fröhlich 1995) and MOLT (Motivation Orientation in Language Teaching; Guilloteaux & Dörnyei 2008) have been used to observe the language classroom. Observation schemes, such as MOLT and COLT Part A, which use a comprehensive checklist technique (with more than 40 categories) and require minute-interval observations, could be difficult to use accurately and reliably without extensive training. That is, an observer needs to have a good understanding of the scheme components and practise using it comprehensively before the main data collection. The schemes are cognitively demanding, especially when a classroom is highly dynamic and several activities take place simultaneously, while at the same time observers need to keep track of what to observe within the scheme.

In experimental research, it is important to consider whether an existing observation scheme is suitable for the context of a study and whether researchers are competent enough to use it. An observation scheme or instrument should be developed on the basis of a specific research purpose and should be piloted prior to its actual use. Figure 7.9 presents an example of a classroom observation scheme.

Similar to rating scales, in order to be successful, extensive training for observers is essential. Ideally, two observers should be employed for consistency in observations and for verification purposes. A video recording should be used to help verify or revisit observations. If you are doing a doctoral degree, you may not have the budget to find another observer. You may verify your observation schemes by double-checking them using the video recordings. Some portion of the video recordings (e.g. 10 percent or 15 percent) may be double-coded by another observer so that an intercoder reliability estimate can be calculated.

A key threat to the usefulness of an observation technique is the *observer effect*. People (e.g. teachers, students) have a tendency to act differently when they are aware that they are being observed. They may change their behavior because of the presence of an external observer in the classroom. It is therefore important to make observations on multiple occasions. Typically the first three observation sessions should not be used for data analysis as the results can be misleading. Participants will be settled and act more naturally after a certain time. Moreover, observers will begin to have a sense of what the classroom is like during the first three sessions. It is important to note that observations can be *expensive* and *time-consuming*, so it is important to think strategically how many observations are needed and how to maximize quantitative observations in experimental research (e.g. only observe after certain activities take place; observe during a specific time, for example, 15 minutes at the beginning of the treatment).

Validity, reliability, practicality, fairness and ethics revisited

When we consider quantitative instruments and techniques, there are five key principles that need to be considered. The first is *validity*. An instrument is valid when it measures what it intends to measure and fulfills its purpose. That is, it must collect the data we require so that we can make well-founded inferences. The second is *reliability*. A measure is reliable

Classroom Observation Scheme

Visit No.: _____   Class observed: _____   Teacher: _____

Date: _____   Time: _____   Observer: _____

Aims: This observation scheme is to check how the teacher delivers and manages classroom activities that promote students' effective learning.

1	2	3	4	5	N/A
Strongly disagree	Disagree	Neutral	Agree	Strongly agree	Not applicable

No	Aspects	1	2	3	4	5	N/A
Teaching Organization							
1.	The teacher arrived at class on time.						
2.	The teacher made sure that the physical classroom was well-organized and in order.						
3.	The teacher checked students' attendance.						
4.	The teacher checked whether students brought books/materials to the class.						
5.	The teacher discussed students' homework.						
6.	The teacher presented the aim of the lesson clearly.						
7.	The teacher outlined what would be covered in the session clearly.						
8.	The teacher related the lesson to previous lessons.						
9.	The teacher summarized the key lesson points before finishing the class.						
Teaching and Learning Activities							
10.	The teacher explained an activity clearly.						
11.	The teacher explained content knowledge structurally with clear examples.						
12.	The teacher used teaching tools (e.g., audio devices, computer, whiteboard, handouts) effectively.						
13.	The teacher varied types of learning activities to individual work, group work, and whole class)						
14.	The teacher monitored students' learning engagement.						
15.	The teacher asked students questions to check students' understanding/learning.						
16.	The teacher listened to students' questions and responded appropriately.						
17.	The teacher used positive language (e.g., very good, well-done) to promote students' motivation.						
18.	The teacher respected students' opinions/reasons.						
19.	The teacher corrected students' errors/mistakes appropriately.						
20.	The teacher had a good control of how the class was run/managed.						
21.	The teacher managed the time well.						
22.	The teacher assigned and explained homework to students clearly before the end of the class.						
23	The teacher summarized key lesson points at the end of the class.						
Overall							
24.	The teaching and learning activities were interesting and engaging.						
25.	The classroom atmosphere was relaxing.						

What were the strengths of today's class?

_____
_____
_____

What were the weaknesses of today's class?

_____
_____
_____

Overall comments/or notes for any items above:

_____
_____
_____
_____

FIGURE 7.9   *Example of a classroom observation scheme*

when it can produce scores consistently. In a language test, for example, it can distinguish scores among high-, medium- and low-ability learners. Reliability is a necessary, but insufficient, condition for validity. The third is *practicality*. A measure is practical when it can be administered and scored in a reasonable amount of time and with a reasonable use of resources. Yet it can produce valid and reliable data. The fourth is *fairness*. A measure is fair when the participants know the purpose of the measurement and are treated fairly across groups of participants. A fair measure avoids bias (e.g. questions or test tasks are easier for one group of students than for another group, and raters are inconsistent in marking when they deal with certain topics). The fifth is *ethics*. A measure is ethical when it is not only fair, but also used appropriately, bearing in mind its potential consequences on an individual or a society.

Validation and a pilot study

Prior to the use of quantitative instruments and other data elicitations in the main study, it is essential to try them out with a group of participants similar in character to the target participants of our study. This phase of research is normally discussed as a pilot study or a validation study. *Validation* is related to the steps taken by the researcher to make sure that a measure to be used will likely be valid and that proper inferences can be made about the construct of interest based on the data. Validity evidence may include *content-related evidence* (e.g. the measure is in line with the theory adopted; experts agree on what the measure can capture), *internal structures* (e.g. reliability estimates) and *criterion-related evidence* (e.g. the measure correlates with other measures of a similar construct). The following are things we can do to validate our measure/instrument before using it in the main study.

Expert judgments: We ask experts (e.g. other researchers and your research supervisor) to check a research instrument and highlight foreseeable problems (e.g. clarity and techniques). Experts may provide oral feedback/comments on the instrument. They may identify questions or items that might not be related to what we aim to measure (i.e. construct-irrelevant variance). Some constructs may not be adequately measured (i.e. more items may be needed). Experts may comment on the practicality of the instrument as well. Information from the judgmental/expert analysis can result in the improvement of the research instruments to be used.

Analysis of cognitive processes: This validation strategy is highly recommended and practical as a pilot study. A small number of participants can be asked to provide verbal protocols of the measure (e.g. test tasks), which should show which mental processes are engaged by the test tasks. In a questionnaire, they can be asked whether they understand the statements and whether they have difficulty rating the items. Participants may indicate that the time allocation is too short to complete the questionnaire. All this verbal information will allow us to understand how participants interpret question-naire items. If this interpretation is different from what we intend to convey, then we can alter the questionnaire to make our intended meaning clearer.

Analysis of internal structures: If possible, we should pilot an instrument with a minimum of 25–30 people of similar characteristics to the research participants. We can check whether the data are normally distributed and whether the reliability estimate (e.g. Cronbach's alpha; KR20) is high enough (e.g. above 0.70 for questionnaires and rating scales and above 0.80 for language tests). In rating scales, we can check the level of agreement in percentages, correlations or even Cohen's kappa. This preliminary analysis will allow us to examine items that may appear problematic due to our chosen wording, which can then be improved, and in some cases, removed. If a sample size allows, we can conduct an exploratory factor analysis to examine an underlying factor of items. However, it may not always be feasible, especially when items/questions are based on a robust theory and especially when a small sample size is possible. What we can gain from this internal analysis is a level of confidence that the measure to be used is likely to be useful for our study. It also allows us to have a sense of what we can do with the data in the main study.

Analysis across different groups of participants: This validation process is related to the comparison of scores among participants with different characteristics. For example, in a proficiency test, the pilot test scores should reflect the differences between low-level, mid-level, and high-level learners. We can simply examine the mean score of each group and determine if they are reasonably different.

Comparative analysis with other external criteria: This validation process is related to the concurrent or criterion-related validity of a measure/instrument. In some situations, there may be other existing similar measures to the one we have developed. When we can ask participants in the pilot study to complete our instrument and other similar instruments, a correlation between the two instruments should be strong (e.g. 0.70). If we obtain a correlation of 0.70 or above, we have some evidence that our instrument is likely to be valid when used in an actual study. The assumption for this evidence is that, in the case of a language test, test-takers who do well on one test should also do well on the test being piloted, so long as the two tests are similar. This validation strategy may not be feasible in many pilot studies due to time constraints, access to participants and budget.

It is important to note that a pilot study or validation of a research instrument may indicate several problems in the research instrument. Nonetheless, with these findings we can attempt to address the problems by modifying or revising our instruments. A pilot study may not guarantee that our instrument will work in the main study, but it allows us to have some sense that our instrument will or will not work.

Summary

This chapter has explored a range of research instruments, such as tests, questionnaires, rating scales and quantitative observations. The topic of research instruments and technique is indeed complex and multidimensional. Some instruments (e.g. tests, and questionnaires) need to be written about at much greater length. It is important to note that there is *no perfect* research instrument. Each type of instrument has both strengths and weaknesses, so we should try to use a variety of instruments so that they complement one another. At the same time, we need a good understanding of what instrument is suitable and effective for a research purpose, question or hypothesis. The next chapter will present a hybrid approach to experimental research which combines both quantitative and qualitative data as multiple strategies to examine a phenomenon closely and critically.

Research exercise

To download exercises for this chapter visit: http://www.bloomsbury.com/experimental-research-methods-in-language-learning-9781441189110/

Discussion questions

1 What are common characteristics of quantitative research instruments?
2 If you would like to examine the effects of feedback on students' academic writing, what instruments would you choose? Explain your reasons.
3 Why is it important for experimental researchers to develop a test specification or questionnaire taxonomy for their research?
4 What would you gain if you piloted your research instruments before you conducted your experiment?
5 Reflection: What is the most important lesson you have learned from this chapter?

Further reading

Fulcher, G 2010, *Practical language testing*, Hodder Education, London.

This is a practical and accessible book in language testing and assessment. It covers a range of topics and issues in language testing (e.g. types, test developments, test analysis and use).

Mackey, A & Gass, SM 2005, *Second language research: methodology and design*, Lawrence Erlbaum Associates, Mahwah, NJ.

Chapter 3 presents a range of data collection methods, instruments and techniques in various areas of language learning research (e.g. processing research, interaction-based research).

Norris, J & Ortega, L 2003, 'Defining and measuring SLA', in CJ Doughty & MH Long (eds), *The handbook of second language acquisition*, Blackwell Publishing, Malden, MA.

This chapter addresses issues of measurement in SLA research. It discusses the connection between research constructs, data and measurement. Issues of the reliability of measurement are stressed.

CHAPTER EIGHT

A Hybrid Approach for Experimental Research

Leading questions

1 What do you think is a hybrid approach?
2 Do you think it is adequate to rely on only one type of data (e.g. either quantitative or qualitative data)? Why do you think so?
3 Do you think it is easier to analyze qualitative data than quantitative data?

Introduction

This chapter discusses the importance of combining quantitative research instruments with qualitative data collection techniques. It presents the concept of a *hybrid approach* to experimental research that arises from the influence of the mixed-methods approach for combining statistical methods with qualitative ones. The hybrid approach is related to a pragmatic approach of research methodology that experimental researchers avoid restricting themselves to using only a specific traditional method. Qualitative data elicitation techniques (e.g. think-aloud protocols, interviews and observations) are presented.

A hybrid approach to data collection

Experimental research is traditionally quantitative research because it is concerned with the measurement of outcomes (e.g. behavior or performance before and after treatment or teaching). However, more and more experimental research has moved toward a *hybrid approach* in which qualitative data is also collected together with quantitative data. A hybrid approach aims to combine the strengths of both the quantitative and qualitative method to gain a greater understanding of the influences of independent variables (e.g. instructions and environmental factors) on dependent variables (e.g. language learning and behaviors). Although this book mainly treats experimental research as quantitative research, it takes a *hybrid approach* by which qualitative data can be triangulated with quantitative data. This hybrid approach is essential because choosing to use just one approach (i.e. either quantitative or qualitative analysis) can be inadequate to advance our theoretical and practical knowledge about language learning. Both quantitative and qualitative methodologies can strengthen the quality of a research study because one can support and complement the other. The hybrid approach is linked to the notion of data triangulation—the collection of information from various sources using different methods in order to avoid the bias inherent in any one particular source or method. It should be noted that under the research paradigm dialog (see Chapter 3), triangulation remains at the level of methodology (i.e. how do we go about our pursuit of knowledge?). It is not so much at the ontological or epistemological levels.

A hybrid approach to experimental research therefore can adopt three common mixed-methods designs (see e.g. Nastasi, Hitchcock, Sarkar, Burkholder, Varjes & Jayasena 2007; Plano Clark & Creswell 2011; Tashakkori 2009). First, there are designs in which language learning researchers aim to use one method to *complement* another. Researchers may begin with a research question that can be answered through the use of inferential statistics. On the basis of their findings, they seek to collect qualitative evidence by means of individual and group interviews or observation. Researchers analyze the qualitative data to support or counterbalance their quantitative findings.

Second, there are designs in which researchers use one research approach as the *starting point* for another. For example, researchers may interview a group of language learners and on the basis of their qualitative data analysis, they develop a Likert scale questionnaire for a larger group of learners. Several research methodologists (e.g. Dörnyei 2007; Plano Clark & Creswell 2011) use *upper case* or *lower case* letters to highlight the weight or emphasis of methods being adopted in a sequential mixed-methods study (e.g. QUAN→qual; QUAL→quan; QUAN→QUAL).

Third, there are designs in which researchers ask a set of sequential research questions and use a quantitative method to answer a particular question, and a qualitative method to address others. For example, the question *what is the effect of intrinsic motivation and self-efficacy on willingness to communicate (WTC) in English?* could be answered via the use of an experimental study. The question *why are they so influential to WTC?* could be answered via qualitative analysis of selected individual interviews with high-, medium- and low-ability students who took part in the experimental phase.

It is important to note the distinction between *data triangulation* and *mixed-methods research*. Data triangulation is a technique by which different sources of information are collected to help researchers gain a deep understanding of a subject matter (e.g. a combination of interviews from various groups of participants, observations and documents on the same topic; a combination of various language tests, academic grades and various kinds of questionnaires to inform about participants' language proficiency levels).

Some experimental researchers have begun to incorporate qualitative data analysis in their studies. For example, Walters and Bozkurt (2009) investigated the effect of keeping vocabulary notebooks on vocabulary learning via a quasi-experimental research design (one experimental group and two control groups).They interviewed both the teachers and students in Turkish to find out about their attitudes toward the use of vocabulary notebooks. The researchers found a range of aspects related to the use of vocabulary notebooks (e.g. students' attitudes toward keeping vocabulary notebooks, their perceived differences between previous study methods and vocabulary notebooks, teacher's intentions to continue using the vocabulary notebooks in the classroom). Walters and Bozkurt (2009) provide authentic excerpts from the student and teacher interview data.

Mizumoto and Takeuchi (2009) examined the effectiveness of explicit instruction of vocabulary learning strategies through a pretest-posttest control-group design. They also gathered qualitative data (using study logs from the experiment group, and semi-structured interviews and follow-up interviews using a stimulated-recall technique) to 'clarify the causes of the findings obtained through the quantitative data sources' (i.e. questionnaires and vocabulary test, pp. 430–1). Through qualitative data analysis, the researchers found 'two reasons for the increased use of input-seeking, oral rehearsal, or association strategies' (p. 440). These reasons were students' realization of the effectiveness of the existing strategy repertoire and their attempts to use the strategies they believed to be useful. The researchers used excerpts from students' interviews to illustrate cases and examples.

Vandergrift and Tafaghodtari (2010) evaluated the effects of a metacognitive, process-based approach to teaching French as a second language listening through the use of a quasi-experimental design. The researchers asked students 'to comment on any changes in their MALQ [Metacognitive Awareness Listening Questionnaire] responses from the beginning, through the middle point, and the end of the study' (p. 484). The researchers also used several excerpts from the students' stimulated-recall protocols to identify changes and reasons.

Shintani, Ellis and Suzuki (2014) sought to examine the effects of two types of form-focused written feedback (i.e. direct corrective feedback [DCF] and metalinguistic explanation [ME]) on the accuracy of use of two grammatical structures (i.e. the indefinite article and the hypothetical conditional) by Japanese learners of English. The researchers randomly assigned research participants into five groups (ME, DCF, ME with revision, DCF with revision and the control group). This study not only examined the effects of the focused written feedback using statistical analyses, but also investigated how students not involved in the main study responded to the DCF and ME. The researchers used the interview data to infer that students in both groups reconstructed their writing more strategically.

As can be seen from these four studies, incorporation of qualitative data is useful and complements proceeding quantitative research findings. However, qualitative data, obtained from sources *other than interviews*, is needed in a *hybrid approach*. This chapter aims to promote more use of qualitative research techniques for experimental research.

Qualitative data in experimental research

It is important not to confuse *qualitative* with *quality*. Some people prematurely define qualitative data as data focusing on quality. In fact, quality is an evaluative judgment and hence quantitative or qualitative data can be judged in terms of their quality (e.g. is the data reliable and relevant?). Qualitative data is information that can be described in words, rather than numbers. For example, we can interview research participants. Interview responses can then be coded and categorized into patterns and themes. A picture, video or visual media is qualitative because we can describe the content in words. When we observe the activity in a language classroom, we can write down what is going on, the atmospheres, and teacher-student or student-student interactions. Such observations can be expressed in words. Unlike quantitative research, qualitative research generally uses data elicitation techniques, rather than instruments (e.g. think-aloud protocols, stimulated recalls, individual or group interviews, diaries, and spoken or written language). The primary focus in using qualitative data is to explore or describe a phenomenon or process, and explain or exemplify an issue or a case.

Having pointed out the differences between quantitative and qualitative data, it is important to note that such differences can be superficial. Whether or not data takes the quantitative or qualitative form largely depends on *what researchers do with them*. For example, researchers may adopt stimulated recall and individual interviews with research participants. Clearly, the data will be transcribed in words (which is qualitative), but instead of using the data to describe or explain an issue, they decide to code the interview transcripts using frequency counts of a target behavior (e.g. number of translations in a given task). Researchers make sure that two people code the same data similarly and calculate an intercoder reliability estimate. They then use frequency counts for each participant for the purpose of conducting a statistical analysis. In this example, we can see that the stimulated recall interviews are quantitative, rather than qualitative. The use of both quantitative and qualitative data is in keeping with the most common underlying research paradigm for experimental studies, which is postpositivism that recommends multiple strategies for data collection (see Chapter 3).

Naturalistic data

Naturalistic data is collected from observation of phenomena, which occur naturally without researchers' intervention and which are unaltered by the act of gathering. Much of the data collected by language learning researchers is not naturalistic, although at first glance it may appear that it is. For example, if we would like to know the nature of a language classroom and we visit the classroom to observe, what we see cannot be treated as 100 percent naturalistic data, despite that fact that we are merely observing. This is because participants may react unnaturally due to our presence. This is a reason why such observations are classified as qualitative, rather than naturalistic. The act of accessing naturalistic data can make it less and less naturalistic due to an observer effect. The observer may mitigate the observer effect by also being a participant in the activities of the classroom. Such participation will require certain ethical issues to be addressed, including the approval for such participation from the participants.

In language learning research, we may aim to gather data on a child's speech at different times over a period of months so that we can find patterns of words or utterances. This can be seen as naturalistic data if the data is collected in one of the child's usual environments. The issue here is related to the *sampling* of speeches or utterances because we cannot be there with the child 24 hours a day. A mother or a child carer may collect the data for us, but it will be quite demanding for them given their responsibility to take care of the child. It will also be quite expensive given the lengthy period of time required.

The most common and most accessible natural data may be gathered from authentic printed materials (e.g. archival data, newspapers, magazines, past students' assignments, and online social networks or blogs,). However, experimental research has not made much use of naturalistic data to answer research questions as it is difficult to treat the data systematically for statistical analysis.

Qualitative research techniques

This book cannot treat qualitative data collection techniques comprehensively due to the focus of the book on quantitative methods for experimental research. However, it is important to present some qualitative data collection techniques that are useful as part of a *multiple strategies approach* to gain a greater understanding of the research issue under investigation. It is important to note that the following qualitative techniques may be used in participants' L1, given that their focus is on content, rather than on their language ability. The use of L1 can enhance research validity because participants do not have a language barrier as they may have if the techniques are used in L2. This section includes think-aloud protocols, stimulated-recall and retrospective interviews, individual and group interviews, and qualitative observations. A brief discussion of qualitative data analysis is also included.

Think-aloud protocols

The think-aloud protocol technique is an introspective technique that allows researchers to have access to participants' online cognitive processing or thinking, particularly *higher-level thinking* (see Ericsson & Simon 1993; Sasaki 2014). This technique is useful for examining individual differences in cognitive processing. As the title suggests, participants are asked to *think out loud* or *verbalize their current thoughts* while they are carrying out a language task, such as reading and writing. Think-aloud protocols are limited in terms of the access they grant to participants' so-called *consciousness, awareness* or *attention*. These terms reside within the same *consciousness* realm. However, as cognitive processing is highly complex and involves unconscious processes as well, what researchers gain is only part of what may be going on. Think-aloud protocols can be limited because some people are not good at expressing themselves, or prefer not to express or share their thoughts. Extensive training for both *participants* (who need to fully verbalize their thoughts) and *researchers* (who need to be quiet, but prompt verbal responses when appropriate) is *essential* to enhance the quality of this verbal report technique.

Typically, researchers can analyze think-aloud data quantitatively (e.g. that data gained from participants answering *what* questions) or qualitatively (e.g. that data gained from participants answering *why* and *how* questions). In quantitative analysis, after transcriptions have been drawn up, researchers need to use coding schemes to code the data by segmenting them into units or frequency counts. Data are then analyzed statistically to answer research questions (e.g. using ANOVA). Furthermore, 10 to 15 percent of the transcripts may be randomly selected for analysis by a second coder. An intercoder reliability estimate needs to be calculated (e.g. Cohen's kappa or the Pearson correlation coefficient). Experimental research can use think-aloud techniques for qualitative analysis as well. Bowles (2010) comprehensively addresses issues and controversies associated with think-aloud protocols in second language research (e.g. reactivity for time and accuracy).

Stimulated recalls and retrospective interviews

Stimulated recalls and retrospective interviews are retrospective techniques that allow researchers to examine learners' cognitive processes, thoughts or feelings during task completion (see Gass & Mackey 2000). Retrospection is a post-event verbal report. Unlike the individual and group interviews discussed below, the focus of stimulated recalls and retrospective interviews is on language learners' cognitive activities or processes. Given the limited span of the human working memory, stimulated recalls and retrospective interviews should be carried out immediately after learners have completed language tasks or activities. These techniques are useful when researchers do not want to interrupt learners' naturally occurring processes during task completion (unlike the think-aloud method above). Participants may be provided with stimuli for the activities they have just finished to help them recall what happened and what they did. In retrospective interviews, they may be asked to explain their reasons for doing certain things. Another key limitation of retrospective interviews is that the participants might *re-construct their thoughts* as they were not aware of what was going on due to automaticity or unawareness of their thoughts. What they reported might not be what actually happened during task completion, but may just reflect their general tendency to do things in a certain manner. Stimulated recalls and retrospective interviews can be analyzed quantitatively through frequency counts based on data coding and statistical analysis. They are useful for exemplifying cases or examples from learners about certain cognitive processes.

Individual and group interviews

Interviews are useful data elicitation techniques for both quantitative and qualitative research. Individual interviews are *one-on-one interactions* between an interviewer and interviewee, whereas group interviews (as with a focus group) can be conducted with more interviewees at the same time (e.g. a group of five). Block (2000) and Talmy (2010) provide a practical review and tips for conducting qualitative interviews in language learning and applied linguistics research. Usually researchers employ *purposive sampling*, which identifies who to interview (e.g. learners with similar performance or psychological attributes). Interviews provide information that researchers cannot obtain through observations, and they can be used to verify past observations. In recent years, interviews have begun to be conducted via chat rooms or online video calls such as Skype. It is important to note that in speaking assessment, interviews are a type of students' performance assessment. The focus is on language ability. The interviews discussed here focus on participants' perspectives.

Quantitative interviews are those in which interview questions and responses have been prepared beforehand. They are similar to structured questionnaires but are carried out verbally. Quantitative interviews are therefore standardized and researchers aim to compare the answers obtained. In most cases, the responses are converted to numerical form for the purpose of quantitative analysis. Of interest to this section are *qualitative interviews,* which allow researchers to explore research issues in depth (e.g. attitudes, beliefs, opinions and perceptions). The data is *naturalistic* because the responses are produced by research participants. Qualitative interviews are typically audio-recorded and transcribed for analysis. Researchers typically adopt purposive sampling through the use of specified criteria (e.g. psychological characteristics, their proficiency or achievement levels, gender, and first language). In language learning research, three types of interview techniques are often used: structured, semi-structured and open-ended interviews.

Structured interviews strictly follow a set of questions that all participants will answer. As with quantitative interviews, all interviewees are asked the same questions, so that answers can be compared and common patterns across participants can be identified through frequency counts or statistical analysis. Unlike quantitative interviews, structured interviews are more open to responses by interviewees. That is, although researchers control what to ask, interviewees are free to answer them in any manner they see fit. Structured interviews are mechanistic, and someone who does not know the research area well but can be trained to carry out interviews can do this job. The researcher may aim to interview as many people as possible so that they can generalize the research issues under examination.

Semi-structured interviews are similar to structured interviews. However, they allow interviewers to ask *follow-up* questions (e.g. when participants say something intriguing or provide some unexpected responses). Regardless of the open nature of follow-up questions, interviewers still have to ask all the prepared interview questions so that the data collection is complete and organized chronologically. Like structured interviews, patterns can be identified and frequencies obtained through coding. When high interrater reliability estimates are obtained for two coders, the data can be used for statistical analysis. Semi-structured interviews are efficient when interviewers know the topic well, so it is usually researchers engaging in the research project who carry out this type of interview. Structured and semi-structured interviews that are carried out in a standardized manner may minimize interviewers' effects and bias.

Open-ended interviews are more exploratory than the above two types. Of course, researchers should have a topic that they aim to investigate, but are free to probe to find out more information about a particular aspect from interviewees. Open-ended interviews allow researchers to develop a theme of interest during the course of the interviews. Researchers can explore the uniqueness of an individual residing within a particular setting. Open-ended interviews can be conducted just one time or multiple times, depending on the research context. Case studies and ethnographies usually adopt this type of interviews. The data does not need to be coded for reliability before analysis can take place because the purpose is to discover or uncover an issue, or gain insight into individuals' perspectives. Researchers are likely to present the data through direct quotes or describe the data in such a way that readers have the freedom to develop their own interpretations. The open-ended interview technique can produce different and non-systematic information that can be difficult and time-consuming to extract. Usually experienced and well-established researchers adopt this technique as they know the topic very well and their existing reputation allows readers to trust how they interpret the data to reach their findings. Beginning researchers may not know what to do with the interview data and may not obtain useful data that fits their research aims.

All interviews are time-consuming and can be expensive. Like questionnaires, it is difficult to claim that participants tell the truth, or report their true feelings or perspectives. Researchers rely on participants' accounts. Good interviewers are good listeners and should avoid influencing interviewees' responses by imposing their own agenda or bias. Good interviewers have social skills, are good observers of non-verbal communication facets and can promptly react to responses effectively. For more information on interview techniques and analyses, see Dörnyei (2007), Gass and Mackey (2007), and Holliday (2007).

Qualitative observations

In qualitative observation researchers observe, record and describe what they see in a setting without having to tally frequencies of behaviors or check predetermined lists. Spada and Lyster (1997) conceptualize some of the issues associated with classroom observation. Qualitative observation focuses on forming a holistic picture of an issue. With the permission of participants to video-record activities or settings, observers do not need to write extensive notes. As with other forms of data collection, researchers need to obtain formal permission for the observations from participants. For example, in Ammar and Spada's (2006) study, the researchers noted that 'unfortunately, the participating teachers did not agree to any video-recording or audio-recording of the classrooms, and they were also unwilling to have observers in the classroom on a regular basis because of the potential disruption that it might cause' (p. 553).

Qualitative observers aim to obtain a complete description of behaviors, interactions, cultural norms, values, attitudes or social practice in a specific natural setting. They do not numerically summarize occurrences or durations of observed behaviors. Qualitative observations therefore rely on narratives or words. The observers may make brief notes during their observations, but later expand them as field notes. LeCompte, Preissle and Tesch (1993, p. 294) provided useful guidelines to help observers direct their qualitative observations (e.g. 'who is in the group?,' 'what are their characteristics?' and 'what is happening here?').

Unlike quantitative observations in which observers are *complete observers* (typically hidden from the group or sitting quietly at the back of the classroom or setting), qualitative observers typically adopt the role of *complete participants* (i.e. as members of the group), *participants as observers* (i.e. they do not initially belong to the group, but actively participate in the setting and become insiders), and *observers as participants* (i.e. they interact with other participants enough to establish rapport but do not really get involved in the behaviors and activities of the group being observed). The observer must decide what degree of participation will provide the most appropriate data.

Since the postpositivist research paradigm governs much of the principles in experimental research, and this paradigm endorses multiple data collection strategies, most experimental researchers would prefer to adopt qualitative observations in which they take the *complete observers* or *observers as participants* position. In principle, experimental researchers would be cautious about the impact of observers on the participants or classes being observed (because of the *observer effect and bias*, for example). Both can lead to an inaccurate picture of the group and its interactions during observations. Experimental researchers, however, need to establish an explicit mechanism to minimize the effect of observer expectations, which are likely to exist since they probably know their quantitative findings and look for qualitative data to complement them. Experimental researchers should nonetheless be open to unexpected findings and allow themselves to observe what is going on with an open mind.

Quantitative analysis of qualitative data

The variety and diversity of qualitative approaches means that there is *no single right way* to analyze qualitative data. The most appropriate way depends on the research field and the specific topic, as well as the research paradigm adopted by the researcher.

Qualitative data such as that obtained through think-aloud protocols, stimulated recall and interviews can take numerical values through systematic data coding, and therefore can be used as quantitative data. Gass, with Behney and Plonsky (2013) provided several examples of these data elicitation techniques. Foster, Tonkyn and Wigglesworth (2000) comprehensively present several principled methods and resources for dividing spoken data into units for oral data analysis and discuss the short-comings in their method. Such units include:

- *semantic units* (e.g. proposition, C-unit and idea unit)
- *intonational units* (e.g. tone unit, idea unit and utterance)
- *syntactic units* (e.g. sentence, idea unit, T-unit and C-unit)
- *analysis of speech unit* (e.g. independent clause/sub-clausal unit).

It is beyond the scope of this chapter to go into the details of how each unit is defined and can be implemented. There are several studies that have quantified qualitative data such as verbal reports. It is essential that inter-coder reliability estimates be computed when quantifying qualitative data (discussed in Chapter 8). For example, Mackey, Oliver and Leeman (2003) asked each dyad (e.g. a pair of native English speakers [NS] and non-native English speakers [NNS]) to carry out two tasks (i.e. one-way and two-way tasks) using a counterbalanced design. The participants' scripts were then transcribed. The researchers used the first 100 utterances in each task for transcriptions. The transcripts were coded, using descriptors such as targetlike or nontargetlike. Based on 25 percent of the data set, the inter-coder agreement was 96 percent. The researchers used a chi-square (χ^2) test to compare differences in the nature of feedback versus no feedback conditions in the case of nontargetlike utterances between NS-NNS and NNS-NNS adult and child dyads.

Qualitative analysis of qualitative data

There are a range of qualitative data analysis approaches that experimental researchers can consider using to address issues such as why and how participants do or do not behave in a certain manner during an experi-mental period (see e.g. Berge 2007; Dörnyei 2007; Duff 2008; Friedman 2012; Johnson & Christensen 2008; Punch 2005; Richards 2003 for options of how qualitative data analysis can be performed).

Typically qualitative data needs *systematic coding* so that researchers can focus on the data relevant to their research questions. Experimental researchers can add qualitative data derived from learners of different abilities or characteristics to their study. Content analysis can be adopted and comparisons can be achieved through systematic coding (see Punch 2005). Unlike statistical comparison, comparison in qualitative research is not automatic and is not determined by any probability value. Researchers need to identify abstract concepts and code them. At the first level of coding, it is by comparing different indicators in the data that researchers arrive at the more abstract concepts behind the empirical data.

Researchers can perform frequency counts and content analysis (see e.g. Galaczi 2014 who provides useful and clear explanations of content analysis and how it can be done). Frequency counts can help researchers identify the issues and characteristics shared by elements of a group of learners. According to Berge (2007, p. 303), content analysis is a 'careful, detailed and systematic examination and interpretation' of unstructured word-based data to explore the underlying meanings. Content analysis can therefore be applied to examine qualitative data, such as that obtained from individual interviews, stimulated-recalls, retrospective interviews and think-aloud protocols. According to Dörnyei (2007), content analysis should be performed via a procedure of transcribing the data, pre-coding and coding, growing ideas, and finally interpreting the data and drawing conclusions. Furthermore, *anecdotes* from the participants can be used to provide particular examples of cases relevant to quantitative findings, as well as *unique cases*.

Researchers may also adopt an *analytic induction method* (see e.g. Kelle 1995), which allows concepts to be developed inductively from the data. Such concepts are then raised to a higher level of abstraction and their interrelationships can then be traced out. The analytic induction method involves a series of alternating inductive and deductive steps, whereby data-driven inductive hypothesis generation is followed by deductive hypothesis examination for the purpose of verification. Hammersley and Atkinson's (2007) analytic induction framework can be useful for experimental research. First, an initial definition of the phenomenon of interest is formulated. Second, some cases of this phenomenon are investigated by documenting potential explanatory features. Third, on the basis of the data, a hypothetical explanation is framed to identify the common factors across the cases. If necessary, more cases are investigated to test the hypothesis.

Miles and Huberman's (1994) qualitative data analysis framework is one of the most useful frameworks for experimental research. Their analytical framework is directed at tracing out lawful and stable relationships among social phenomena. Miles and Huberman's approach to qualitative data analysis is *transcendental realism* with three main components: *data reduction*; *data display*, and *drawing and verifying conclusions*. Good qualitative analysis involves iterative displays of data. Qualitative data reduction occurs continually throughout the analysis process. Data reduction and display rest mainly on the operations of coding and memoing. For example, in the initial stages, data is reduced through editing, segmenting and summarizing. In the middle stages, researchers further reduce the data through systematic coding and memoing associated activities so that they can identify themes, clusters and patterns. Later, data reduction occurs through conceptualizing and explaining research findings. The second feature of Miles and Huberman's framework is data display, which helps to organize, compress and assemble information. Because qualitative data are typically *voluminous*, bulky and dispersed, displays are effective to help researchers to make sense of the data at all stages of the analysis. Researchers can display their data through the use of graphs, charts, networks and diagrams of different types. Finally, researchers can begin to draw and verify their conclusions. Conclusions are typically in the form of propositions and, once they are drawn, need to be verified.

Summary

According to the current trend in experimental research, we will see an increased adoption of a hybrid approach to systematic quantitative and qualitative data collection, and analyses. While the application of the hybrid approach may still be evolving and fine-tuning its way into experimental research, clearly it has a significant potential to allow not only experimental researchers, but also other kinds of researchers in language learning to gain greater insight into multidimensional factors that are part of language learning.

This chapter has discussed the hybrid approach to experimental research designs. There are some important limitations in combining various methods in one study (e.g. cost-effectiveness, time consumption and complexity of a particular methodology) that we need to consider as well. The next chapter will introduce descriptive statistics for analysing experimental data.

Research exercise

To download exercises for this chapter visit: http://www.bloomsbury.com/experimental-research-methods-in-language-learning-9781441189110/

Discussion questions

1 Think about an experimental study you have read. What was the research aim? If you could combine qualitative data into the study, what qualitative data technique would you choose? Why?
2 What do you think the characteristics of good qualitative researchers are?
3 If you design an experimental study in language learning, will you consider combining quantitative and qualitative research methods?

4 What do you think the potential problems or difficulties could be in combining quantitative and qualitative methods in one experimental study?

5 Reflection: What is the most important lesson you have learned from this chapter?

Further reading

Baralt, M (2012), 'Coding qualitative data', in A Mackey & SM Gass (eds), *Research methods in second language acquisition: a practical guide*, Wiley-Blackwell, Malden, MA.

This chapter presents how to code qualitative data using NVivo, which is a software program for helping researchers manage their qualitative data.

Chaudron, C 2003, 'Data collection in SLA research', in CJ Doughty & ML Long (eds), *The handbook of second language acquisition*, Blackwell Publishing, Malden, MA.

This chapter comprehensively discusses data collection procedures and methods in SLA research (e.g. naturalistic data, language production data collection techniques). Advantages and disadvantages of commonly used research instruments and techniques are addressed. Reliability and validity of research instruments and data collections are critically presented. This is a must-read chapter.

Flick, U 2014, *An introduction to qualitative research*, 5th edn, Sage, London.

This book is very accessible for beginning researchers who would like to explore how to design their research using qualitative research methods. It provides several qualitative techniques and data analysis.

Gass, SM & Mackey, A 2007, *Data elicitation for second and foreign language research*, 2nd edn, Lawrence Erlbaum Associates, Mahwah, NJ.

This book is devoted to describing and explaining measures and data collection techniques in various areas of second language research (e.g. psycholinguistics-based research, cognitive processing research, survey-based research).

Holliday, A 2007, *Doing and writing qualitative research*, 2nd edn, Sage, London.

This is one of the most comprehensive qualitative research books in applied linguistics. The author carefully treats issues in qualitative data, data collection techniques and data analysis. Numerous examples of qualitative data and analysis are presented.

Holliday A 2010, 'Analysing qualitative data', in B Paltridge & A Phakiti (eds), *Continuum companion to research methods in applied linguistics*, Continuum, London.

This chapter presents the underlying assumptions and methodology of qualitative data analysis in applied linguistic research. It discusses qualitative data techniques, instruments, validity and ethical considerations.

Punch, KF 2005, *Introduction to social research: quantitative and qualitative* approaches, Sage, London.

This book covers a wide range of quantitative and qualitative research methods. It discusses fundamental considerations in developing research instruments and using data collection techniques. Both quantitative and qualitative data analysis approaches are discussed with social research examples.

Riazi, M & Candlin, CN 2014, 'Mixed-methods research in language teaching and learning: Opportunities, issues and challenges, *Language Teaching*, vol. 47, no. 2, pp. 135–73.

This is a state-of-the-art article that addresses the nature and scope of mixed-methods research in language teaching and learning.

<http://www.antiochne.edu/clinical-psychology/qr/>, viewed 11 July 2014.

This is an online resource for qualitative research methods compiled by Susan Hawes, Antioch University New England.

CHAPTER NINE

Descriptive Statistics

Leading questions

1 Do you think statistics is difficult to understand? Will it be difficult to learn? Why do you think so?
2 What, do you know, is involved in performing a statistical analysis of experimental data?
3 Can you give an example of descriptive statistics? What does it tell us about language learners or research participants?

Introduction

This chapter will explore what we do when we have collected quantitative data. It first discusses the stages involved in statistical analysis. It is important to be aware of the overall process of statistical analysis in experimental research before considering some basic statistics. Following the discussion of the stages in statistical analysis, this chapter introduces descriptive statistics, which are useful for describing the characteristics of quantitative data. Inferential statistics, which will be discussed in Chapter 10, rely on descriptive statistics. Finally, this chapter introduces IBM® SPSS® that can be used to help us analyze descriptive statistics.

Stages in statistical analysis

Figure 9.1 presents nine sequential stages in performing statistical analysis. Despite the suggested sequence of analysis, researchers often move back and forth between stages because, for example, they may find problems

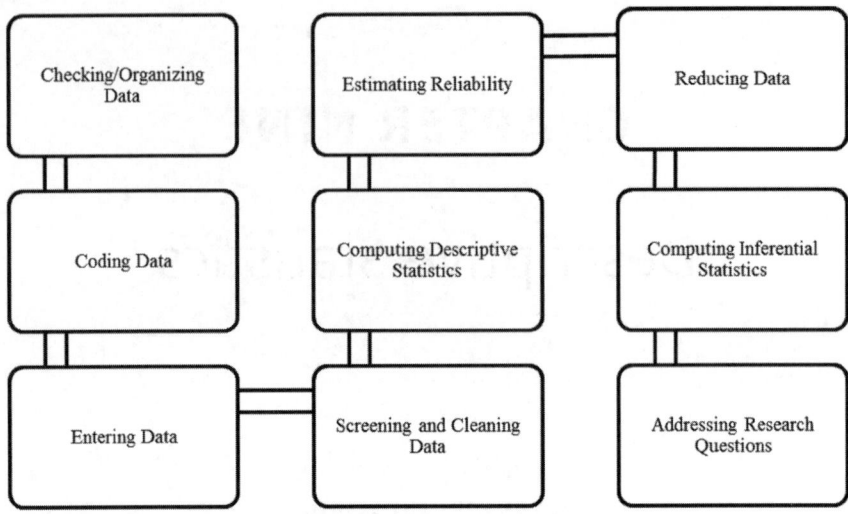

FIGURE 9.1   *Stages in statistical analysis*

with the earlier stages during a later current stage. Each stage will be discussed as follows.

Checking and organizing data

After we have collected quantitative data for addressing our research aims and questions, it is necessary that we check whether all participants' data are complete. For example, some participants may not have answered some questionnaire or test items. Incomplete data are missing data and we need to make a decision on how to deal with them. In a language test, missing data (e.g. lack of answers) will result in a zero score, but this might not mean that there was an absence of the ability being tested. Some qualitative data such as think-aloud protocols and interviews may be quantified for statistical analysis. We need to transcribe such data and organize them before we begin a quantification process (e.g. tally and frequency counts). We should double-check all data to be analyzed, and record what we have done in this stage. The best strategy to organize data is to assign an identity number (ID) to each participant. Various sets of data from each participant will be assigned the same ID for matching purposes. IDs are important because we may need to return to the raw data after we have been through various statistical analyses.

Coding data

Unlike assigning IDs to the data, coding data is related to the process of classifying or grouping data sets. In a sense, coding data is closely related to organizing data so that we know how to statistically analyze them meaningfully. We discussed in Chapter 2 the nature of quantitative data as described through scales (nominal, ordinal, interval and ratio). Coding the data according to these scales is what we do in this stage. To illustrate this, our data typically include *nominal data* (demographic information of participants, e.g. gender, language groups, achievement/proficiency groups, experimental/control groups). We need to code these data in a way that allows us to perform a group analysis to test our research hypothesis.

For example, males can be coded 1 and females can be coded 2. The experimental group can be coded 1 and the control group can be coded 2. Recall that a nominal scale does not have a mathematical property, which will allow us to judge whether one variable is higher or lower than another. We can perform frequency counts and percentages in nominal data. Nominal data can be used as independent variables for statistical analysis (e.g. to compare the mean scores between the experimental and control groups). Since experimental research requires researchers to *think ahead* about the measurement of research constructs, various ordinal and interval data (e.g. Likert scale data, test scores) are often already coded and ready as input for analysis. Some ordinal data such as achievement grades (e.g. A (Excellent) to F (Fail)) need to be coded (e.g. A → coded 5; F → coded 1).

Experimental researchers use a variety of tests in their studies. In most language tests or language task elicitations, how they score a test or measure needs to be clearly stated. For example, Sagarra and Abbuhl (2013, p. 204) stated that 'correct answers in the screening and testing activities received 1 point and incorrect answers 0 points. To receive 1 point on the written and oral posttests, learners had to produce the target adjectives with correct gender and number.' In performance assessment tasks that require subjective judgments, there should be two raters. Kissling (2013) used a production test, which asked participants to read aloud. Kissling (2013) used auditory and acoustic properties of Spanish sounds as the criteria for scoring as follows: English-like (1 point) to Spanish-like (3 points). A Spanish-speaking rater who was not involved in the study and was not aware of the research purpose rated the production data. The researcher 'independently rated a randomly selected 10 percent of the approximant and rhotic data' (p. 728). It was found that the interrater agreement on rating was 95 percent (Cronbach's alpha = 0.96). It should be noted that a high level of interrater reliability is crucial because, for example, in Kissling's study, the scores were rated by one assessor.

In experimental research, we may be able to code some qualitative data such as standardized think-aloud, performance assessment or interview data for quantitative data analysis. Such coding processes are not as straightforward as coding quantitative data. Coding systems need to be developed for systematic quantifications of the variables of interest. Researchers can, for example, tally for frequencies of occurrences and calculate a *t-unit* (i.e. shortest grammatically allowable sentences into which writing can be split or minimally terminable units, Hunt 1966) or an AS-unit (i.e. analysis of speech unit, see Foster, *et al.* 2000). Quantitative data derived from qualitative data are *often* analyzed using a *non-parametric test* (see Chapter 7). Some think-aloud protocols data may be analyzed using a parametric test. Unlike quantitative data, quantifying qualitative data remains largely subjective because people can vary in the way they interpret the meaning or content of the qualitative data. Typically, researchers are expected to report an interrater or intercoder reliability estimate in their report.

Entering data

This stage is related to entering data into a computer program (e.g. SPSS®, Microsoft® Excel®). Once the data have been coded and numerical values have been assigned to each participant, we can key them into a statistical software program. Later in the chapter, we will introduce the IBM® SPSS Program by presenting issues relevant to data entry including naming data files, defining variables for data recording and entering data into a designated file. While entering data, we will discover that there may be missing data, as well as potential outliers (e.g. extreme cases that can distort statistical results). As mentioned earlier, we need to find a strategy to deal with them. In some cases, we can code data as missing. In other cases, we may have to remove the participants who have too many data missing.

Screening and cleaning data

This stage is related to checking for accuracy in data entry accuracy. It is related to the use of descriptive statistics (discussed below). In order to check for incorrectly entered data, we can look for abnormal or impossible values in the data set (e.g. by looking at the minimum and maximum scores; by using visual diagrams such as histograms and pie charts). In a questionnaire, if a Likert scale ranges from 1 to 5, we may find a score of 11, which is an impossible value. This can be a result of an entry mistake and we should check the original data.

Computing descriptive statistics

This stage may overlap with the screening and cleaning data stage. Descriptive statistics provide basic information about the data (e.g. mean scores, minimum and maximum scores, standard deviations). It is essential to check the nature of descriptive statistics because it can largely determine whether we need to employ a *parametric test* for normally distributed data or a *non-parametric* test for non-normal distributed data. Descriptive statistics will be further discussed below.

Estimating data reliability

Experimental researchers need to check that the data to be analyzed are reliable and valid. The reliability of a research instrument is related to its consistency of measurement. The validity of a research instrument refers to the fact that the instrument actually measures what is intended to be measured. In experimental research, a reliability coefficient (e.g. Cronbach's alpha and KR20 coefficients) is used to indicate the level of reliability of a research instrument.

Reducing data

Data reduction is often necessary when there is a large set of test questions or questionnaire items from which the data derives. In a language test, it is impractical to enter students' scores for each question in a computer program. Without reducing the number of variables, we will experience difficulty in managing and analyzing the data. We often summarize the score for each test section (or sometimes for an overall test) for data entry and statistical analysis. This is a simple way to reduce the data. In a questionnaire (e.g. Likert scale), we often compute a score for each sub-scale we design (i.e. composite). For example, if items 1 to 5 aim to measure students' goal settings, we can combine the scores of items 1 to 5 by computing their average. This score can then be used to represent a variable called *goal settings*. This is also a simple method for reducing the data.

Nonetheless, there can be more complex issues regarding the data we deal with that may result in further data reduction. For example, when we analyze a test and find that some questions are not useful to elicit information about students' language ability, we need to make a decision whether to exclude those questions from the data set. When we perform a questionnaire reliability analysis, we may also find that some items significantly reduce the reliability estimate of a particular sub-scale (e.g. Cronbach's alpha may be found to be 0.60, but when calculated excluding item 1, a value of 0.80 is found), and we need to make a decision on whether to exclude those items from the data set. In quantitative question-naires, researchers often perform an exploratory factor analysis (EFA) to identify common factors. This analysis can result in fewer items being collected. EFA is used in exploratory research and requires a large sample size. In experimental research, sometimes EFAs are not practical or feasible due to the small sample size being used.

Computing inferential statistics

Inferential statistics are key statistical analyses that can yield answers to research questions. If we aim to find out differences between two comparison groups, we need to employ an inferential statistic that can inform the research findings. Statistics are probabilistic, and we would like to have a high level of confidence that our statistical inference is not based on chance. Inferential statistics involves testing hypotheses, examining effect sizes and so on.

Addressing research questions

This stage takes place simultaneously with the computing inferential statistics stage. When we analyze data using inferential statistics, such as a *t*-test, we consider whether the findings make sense, and how to report and discuss them. Answering the research questions during data analysis is critical because it helps facilitate the task of writing up the findings. In summary, it is important to be aware of the sequential stages involved in statistical analysis and to understand how they are linked. The guidelines of the stages discussed in this section can help us make sure that we achieve the objectives of the experimental study we set. The next section will introduce the key concepts of descriptive statistics.

Descriptive statistics

In order to learn about statistical analysis for experimental research, it is essential to begin with descriptive statistics and then move to inferential statistics. Descriptive statistics provide the basic characteristics of quantitative data (e.g. frequencies, average scores, most frequent scores). We use descriptive statistics as measures of quantitative data (e.g. measures of central tendency, measures of variability and measures of relative position). This section will explain such conceptual foundations of descriptive statistics. In this section, a calculator will be used to compute descriptive statistics, so that the logic of the basic mathematical computations for statistics can be seen.

Measures of central tendency

One way to define central tendency is the mean (i.e. sum of scores divided by the number of scores). We will also discuss the measures of central tendency known as the median and the mode.

The mean

The mean is the most widely used descriptive statistic in applied linguistics research (including experimental research and most qualitative research). The *mean* is simply the average of the data/scores. Table 9.1 presents a set of scores whose means can be computed using a basic calculator. Calculate the means and check whether you have the same as those in Table 9.1. Is the mean in data set 4 representative of the scores?

Table 9.1 Calculations of means

Set	Scores	Mean
1	4, 3, 5, 1, 6, 2, 5	26 ÷ 7 = 3.71
2	1, 2, 3, 4, 5, 6, 7, 8, 9, 10	55 ÷ 10 = 5.5
3	5, 8, 10, 13, 6, 5, 7, 10, 5, 12	81 ÷ 10 = 8.1
4	20, 25, 30, 35, 28, 26, 25, 32, 180	401 ÷ 9 = 44.56

The median

The median is the value that divides the data set exactly into two sets: half the scores are smaller than the median and half the scores are larger. In order to calculate the median, we need to re-arrange the data in ascending order. Table 9.2 presents the re-arranged data sets in Table 9.1.

Table 9.2 Calculations of Medians

Set	Scores	Median
1	1, 2, 3, **4**, 5, 5, 6	4
2	1, 2, 3, 4, **5**, **6**, 7, 8, 9, 10	(5+6) ÷ 2 = 5.5
3	5, 5, 5, 6, **7**, **8**, 10, 10, 12, 13	(7+8) ÷ 2 = 7.5
4	20, 25, 25, 26, **28**, 30, 32, 35, 180	28

As can be seen in Table 9.2, when there are two values that fall in the middle, we need to average them to compute the median. The median is particularly useful as a descriptor when the mean is distorted by extreme cases (known as *outliers*). Data set 4 has an outlier, which is 180. This value distorts the mean of the scores. By removing this value, the mean becomes 27.63, which better represents the data set.

The mode

The mode is the value that occurs most frequently in the data. Table 9.3 presents the identification of the modes, compared to the means and medians in Tables 9.1 and 9.2. There is no mode for Data Set 2. When a data set has a large sample size, there is a possibility that we have more than two modes. When the distribution has two modes, it is called *bimodal* and when it has more than two modes, it is called *multimodal*.

Table 9.3 Calculations of modes compared to means and median

Set	Scores	Mean	Median	Mode
1	1, 2, 3, 4, **5**, **5**, 6	3.71	4	5
2	1, 2, 3, 4, 5, 6, 7, 8, 9, 10	5.5	5.5	No mode
3	**5**, **5**, **5**, 6, 7, 8, 10, 10, 12, 13	8.1	7.5	5
4	20, **25**, **25**, 26, 28, 30, 32, 35, 180	44.56	28	25

The normal distribution

The *normal distribution* refers to the shape of the data distribution that is unimodal (one mode), symmetrical about the mean, and bell-shaped. When we work with a relatively small sample size as above, it is unlikely that we will have a normally distributed data set. When there is a small sample size, it is not useful to try to move beyond descriptive statistics (i.e. to a level of inferential statistics, which in many cases requires the normal distribution). Figure 9.2 presents an example of a normally distributed data set.

A common statistical assumption for most inferential statistics is the *normal distribution assumption*. In a reasonable sample size (e.g. 30 upwards), when the mean, median and mode have the *same value* or close to one another, the data set is likely to be normally distributed. In research reality, a perfect normal distribution is rare. It is hence wise to make use of *skewness* and *kurtosis* statistics. Of course, we do not need to worry how to compute these statistics, SPSS can do this for us in a mouse click (see the next section on how this can be done). *Skewness statistics* tell us

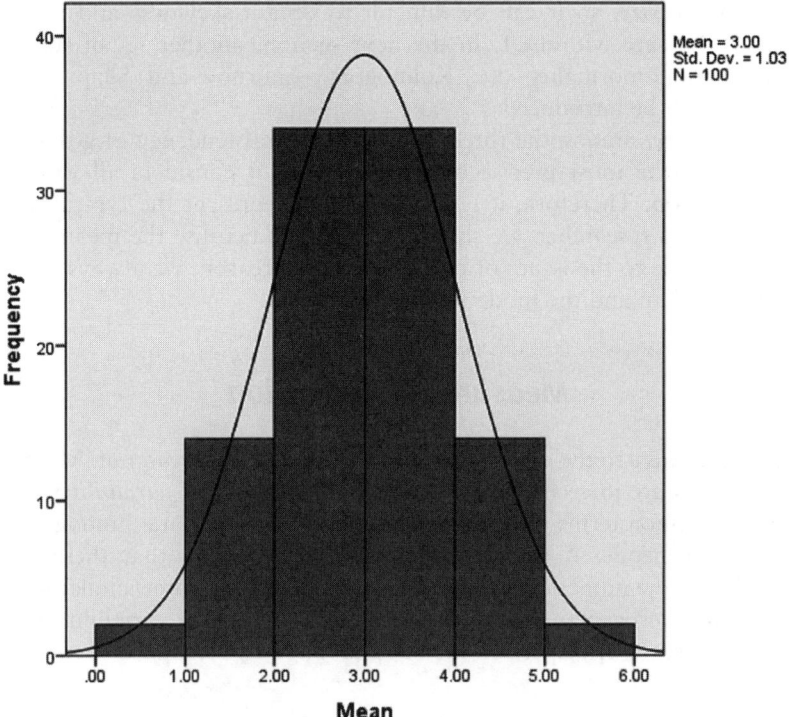

FIGURE 9.2   *Normal distribution*

the extent to which the data set is symmetrical. A data set is symmetrical if the skewness statistic is zero. A positive sign indicates that the median and mode have values smaller than the mean (i.e. the distribution moves toward the left), whereas a negative sign indicates that the mean has a smaller value than the median and mode (i.e. the distribution moves toward the right). In Figure 9.2, the skewness statistic is 0.00.

Kurtosis statistics shows the extent to which the shape of the distribution is *pointy*. A normally distributed data set has a kurtosis value of *zero*. A positive sign suggests that the distribution shape tends to be sharp, whereas a negative sign suggests that the distribution tends to be flat. In Figure 9.2, the kurtosis statistic is –0.20, suggesting that it was not very pointy.

In statistical analysis, a conservative rule of thumb is that the skewness and kurtosis statistics should be within a *±1 range*. Figure 9.2 is considered normally distributed because the skewness statistic is 0 and the kurtosis statistic is –0.20. A more relaxed rule of thumb is to allow the skewness and kurtosis statistics to be within a *±3 range*. As a quantitative researcher, I prefer the more conservative rule. However, it is handy to know the more relaxed rule because in experimental research we often deal with a small sample size, so it can be difficult to obtain skewness and kurtosis statistics that are within ±1. In the next section, another set of statistics for examining normality (i.e. Kolmogorov–Smirnov and Shapiro–Wilk statistics) will be introduced.

In summary, among the three indices of central tendency of a data set, the *mean* is the most precise measure because it considers all values in the calculation. Therefore, it is often used to represent the typical score. However, as a researcher, we should be cautious because the mean can be misleading due to the issues of outliers. For this reason, we always have to take the median and the mode into account.

Measures of dispersion

Dispersion refers to the extent to which the data set is spread out. Measures of dispersion are interchangeably known as *measures of variability*. There are two common terms we use to discuss dispersion of data: homogeneous and heterogeneous. A homogeneous data set suggests that there is no variability in the numerical values (i.e. everyone has the same/similar score), whereas a heterogeneous data set indicates that there is variability in the values. Measures of dispersion include the *range* and *standard deviation*.

The range

The range is easy to calculate. It is simply the difference between the highest and lowest scores in the data set. The range is only based on the two extreme scores in the data set. In Table 9.1, the ranges for data sets 1 to 4 are 5, 9, 7, and 160, respectively. The smaller the range, the more homogenous the data set is. In data set 4, the range is very large, but as discussed earlier, it is affected by the extreme score (i.e. 180). Accordingly, researchers do not often use the range because the score can give limited/partial information about the data. In the next section, we will look at the *interquartile range*, which marks the difference between the 25th percentile and 75th percentile. The interquartile range covers scores that are within the two middle quartiles.

The variance and standard deviation

The variance and standard deviation are commonly used measures of dispersion. The method for calculating the variance and standard deviation is not very complicated. Table 9.4 presents an example of how to calculate the variance and standard deviation of data set 1 in Table 9.1. It is important to note that the calculated variance and standard deviation here are slightly smaller than those computed by SPSS because we only use two decimal points in the calculation.

Table 9.4 Computing the variance and standard deviation (SD)

Scores	Score minus Mean	(Score minus Mean)^2
4	4 – 3.71 = 0.29	0.29 × 0.29 = 0.08
3	3 – 3.71 = –0.71	–0.71 × –0.71 = 0.50
5	5 – 3.71 = 1.29	1.29 × 1.29 = 1.66
1	1 – 3.71 = –2.71	–2.71 × –2.71 = 7.34
6	6 – 3.71 = 2.29	2.29 × 2.29 = 5.24
2	2 – 3.71 = –1.71	–1.71 × –1.71 = 2.92
5	5 – 3.71 = 1.29	1.29 × 1.29 = 1.66
Sum ($\sum$)		19.4
Variance		19.4 ÷ 7 = 2.77
SD		$\sqrt{2.77}$ = 1.66

The *variance* is defined as the average of the squared deviations from the mean. As can be seen in Table 9.4, each deviation score from the mean squared, the average of these is then calculated to give the variance. The standard deviation is then calculated by taking the square root of the variance. The standard deviation indicates how much, on average, the individual values differ from the mean. For example, as the mean is 3.71 and the standard deviation is 1.66, the score at 1SD is 5.37 (i.e. 3.71 +1.66) and the score at –1SD is 2.05 (i.e. 3.71 – 1.66).

The smaller the standard deviation, the more homogeneous the data set is. It should be noted that like the mean, the standard deviation is susceptible to extreme values (outliers). The variance and standard deviation are key ingredients of several inferential statistics such as ANOVA and ANCOVA.

In practice, it will be time-consuming to compute the variance and standard deviation of a large data set. As presented in the next section, SPSS can do this for us with ease. The example above is only to help illustrate the calculations.

The standard deviation and the normal distribution

We mentioned above that in a normally distributed data set, the mean, median and mode have the same value. It is also true that the normal distribution has approximately 68 percent of the scores falling within ±1 standard

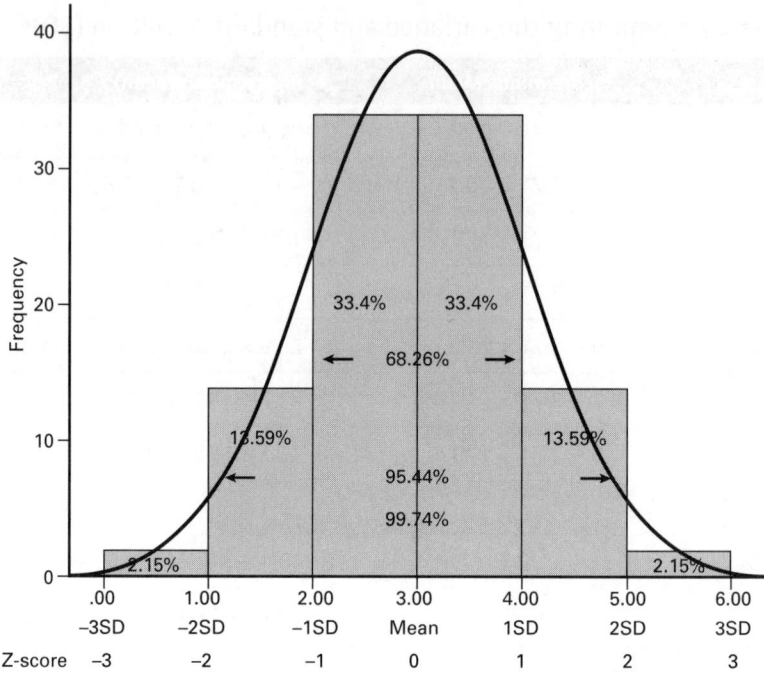

FIGURE 9.3   *Normal distribution with standard deviations and z-scores*

deviation from the mean. Figure 9.3 presents the normal distribution shape with standard deviations and z-scores (discussed further below).

We can approximate the percentages of data coverage within 1SD (68 percent), 2SD (95 percent), and 3SD (99.7 percent) when we have evidence that the data are normally distributed.

Measures of relative standing

In many situations, we will be interested to know how a learner's score is related to other learners' scores (i.e. relative standing). Typically we can achieve this using *percentile ranks* and *z-scores*.

Percentile ranks

The percentile rank is a statistic that tells us the percentage of scores in the distribution that are below a given score. For example, a score with a 40 percentile rank has 40 percent of scores below it. It is quite simple to calculate a percentile rank as follows: rank of a score ÷ [total number of scores +1].

To illustrate, let use data set 4 in Table 9.1: 20, 25, 25, 26, 28, 30, 32, 35, 180 (n = 9). We would like to indicate the percentile of the score 32.

When we calculate a percentile, we need to first order the data from lowest to highest. According to this data set, 32 is ranked as 7. The percentile rank of 32 is 0.70 (i.e. 7 ÷ 10). This means that 70 percent of the scores are below 32.

In another scenario, we can also figure out a student's percentile rank (e.g. Jack). For example, if his score was the fourth highest in a class of 20. Jack's score would be ranked as 16. The percentile rank for Jack was then 0.76 (i.e. 16 ÷ 21). This means that 76 percent of the scores were below Jack's.

The z-scores

The z-scores, on the contrary, are useful for a study as they allow us to see how an individual's score can be placed in relation to the rest of the partici-pants' scores. A z-score is basically a raw score that has been converted to a standard deviation format (see Figure 9.3 above). If a score is above the mean, the z-score is positive and if a score is below the mean, the z-score is negative. The z-score has the mean of 0 and a standard deviation of 1. A z-score can be easily calculated using a basic calculator as follows: [a raw score – the mean] ÷ SD. According to the data set 1 in Table 9.1, a z-score of the student whose score is 6 is 1.38 (i.e. [6 – 3.71] ÷ 1.66). This person's z-score is 1.38 standard deviations above the mean.

The t-scores

The z-score can be difficult for people to understand. For example, it is difficult to make sense of a student's (e.g. Jill) score of –1.3 with the mean score of 0. The t-score is thus an extension of the z-score, which allows us to avoid the use of negative values, while at the same time being more easily understood. The t-score is calculated as follows: *[10 × z-score] + 50*.

Note that a z-score has a mean of 0, which is at 50 percent. In the case of Jill's score, her t-score is 37 (i.e. [10 × –1.3] + 50 → –13 + 50 → 37).

Statistical package for social sciences (SPSS) program

Having discussed some of the basic concepts of descriptive statistics, let us now revisit them in relation to the use of the *IBM® SPSS® Program Version 22*. SPSS can help us conduct the statistical analysis required for experimental research. If you are a student and do not have this program, you can purchase the *student version*, which essentially works almost the same way as the fully licensed version, except some advanced analysis such as multivariate analysis and repeated-measures ANOVA). In order to learn and become familiar with SPSS, it is important that you have this SPSS program so that after each presentation of data analysis, you can try it out by yourself. Extensive practice and trials will result in success in using statistics via SPSS.

SPSS is a user-friendly program that allows us to manage and analyze quantitative data through dialog boxes. Many statistical analyses can be completed in a simple mouse click. Having said that, this book is not comprehensive enough to cover everything you need to know about SPSS. Further resources for SPSS will be included at the end of this chapter. This book will not focus on SPSS Syntax. Rather it will focus on the *point-and-click* method, which is more accessible to language researchers. It is recommended that you explore the tutorial section, which is located in the *Help* menu of SPSS.

SPSS data editor

Figure 9.4 shows the SPSS data editor, which you will see when you start the SPSS program. When the program starts, a small window 'What do you want to do?' with a list of several options appears, together with the screen shown in Figure 9.4. For the time being, you can simply close this window. An output file *(.spv)* will also be opened by default. If you are familiar with the Microsoft® Word® or Excel® programs, you will learn quite quickly about the content menus in this data editor. The data editor is a spreadsheet in which cases (e.g. participants) are in rows and variables are in columns. The best way to explore the main menus is by hovering your cursor over each menu. A drop-down menu appears, showing the content of that menu. On the bottom left in Figure 9.4, you will see that you can switch back and forth in this data editor by clicking "Data view" or "Variable view."

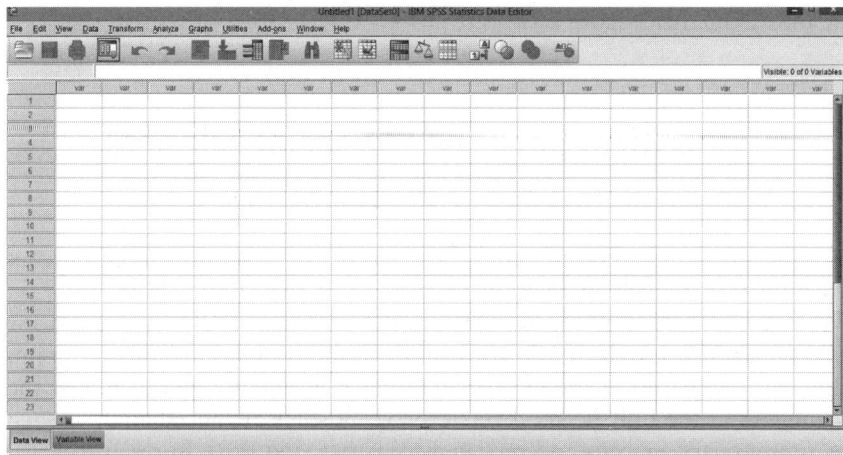

FIGURE 9.4   *SPSS data editor (data view)*

The figure here is in the data view mode. On an active screen, the *orange highlight* indicates the current mode.

Preparing a data file

In this section, we will explore some basic procedures that need to be followed when we create a new data file (*.sav*). When you prepare a data file, it is important to remind yourself of the functions of different scales as they are necessary when you define your variables. We need to assign numbers to represent nominal scales (e.g. 1 for males and 2 for females). In Figure 9.4, click *Variable view*, located in the bottom left of the data spreadsheet. Figure 9.5 is what you will see.

It is important to note that the *rows* in the variable view are the *columns* in the data view. You will see 11 columns in this window (Name, Type, Width, Decimals, Label, Values, Missing, Columns, Align, Measure, and Role). For the name and label columns, you simply type in the names and labels you wish to use. For the other columns, you can click on them for options. There are a few notes for some of these columns.

- *Name:* Be precise with the variable names you use. You cannot have a space in a variable name nor can a name end with a full stop. Special characters (e.g. ?, !, $, and @) cannot be used.

- *Type:* The options include numerical, comma, dot, date, string, etc. Usually you should choose numerical when you deal with your data. String can be letters, names and participants' IDs.

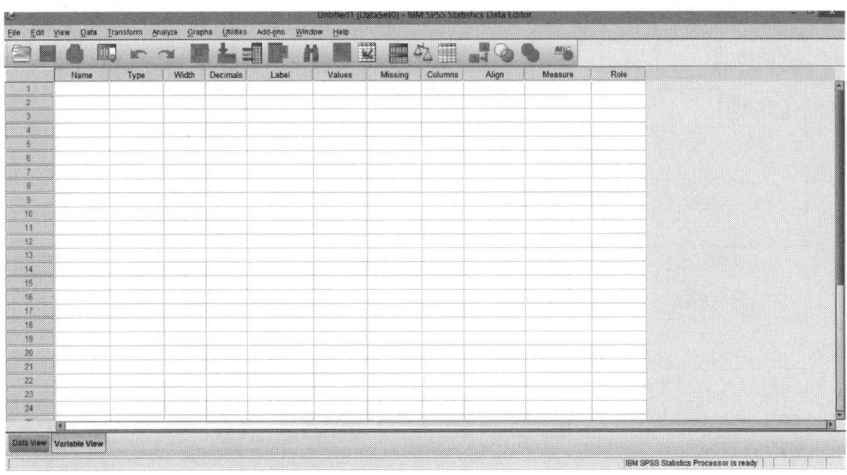

FIGURE 9.5 *SPSS data editor (variable view)*

- *Width:* This can be generated by default when you enter the data. The width is adjustable.

- *Decimals:* In some variables such as IDs and gender, you do not need a decimal, but in other variables, you may need to input data to two decimal points.

- *Label:* This is optional and where you can give a label to your variable name. Note that labels should be concise and precise.

- *Values:* This is where you assign numbers to nominal data that can be used to refer to independent variables (e.g. gender, first language, nationalities, proficiency levels, and experimental or control groups). You can simply assign a value to a label and add it (see Figure 9.6). For example, assign 1 to the label *male*, then click *Add*. Assign 2 to the label *female*, then click *Add*. Then, when you enter a gender variable, you can enter 1 or 2. SPSS does not accept letters as input. You can, however, view the values you have labeled in words by clicking the icon ![icon]. The value is

  where you can specify groups of participants. You can, for example, assign 1 for the experimental group and 2 for the control group. You can assign languages, nationalities and levels of language proficiency here.

- *Missing:* In some cases, we may have missing data. This is where we tell SPSS not to calculate some values in the data file. Typically,

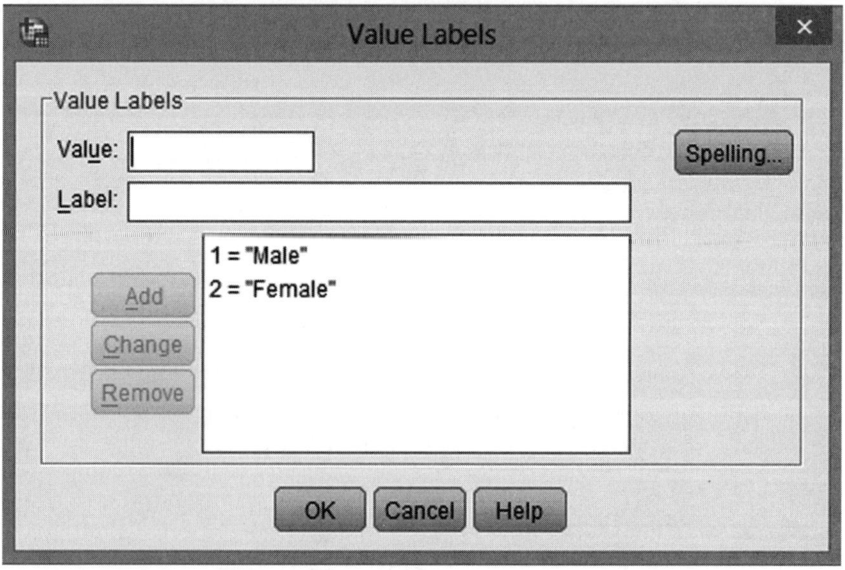

FIGURE 9.6 *Assigning gender codes*

use 99 for Likert scale data. For other data such as test scores, the value you should choose depends on the score range. You have to choose a missing value that does not belong to a possible value in your data set.

● *Columns:* This is set by default.

● *Align:* You can choose *Left*, *Right* or *Center*.

● *Measures:* This column is related to the value column. If your data are categorical or nominal, you should choose *Nominal*. Most data can be either *Scale* or *Ordinal*. *Scale* includes interval and ratio data.

● *Role:* This is the role of your data. The options include *Input*, *Target*, *Both*, etc. This function is more or less *optional*. Simply choose *Input*.

When you create a new data file, always create an *ID variable* that matches your participants' IDs (for the purpose of double-checking or deleting cases). The numbers of cases in the *Data View* windows cannot be used as your participants' IDs as you can insert or delete any case and the data will be re-ordered. Let us use Table 9.5, which is an extension of data set 4 in Table 9.1 for practice.

Table 9.5 Sample data for entry

ID	Gender	Test score
1	Male	20
2	Male	25
3	Female	30
4	Female	35
5	Female	28
6	Male	26
7	Male	25
8	Female	32
9	Female	180

Based on Table 9.5, we need to create three variables. We need to assign a value to *gender* in the label column (1 = male; 2 = female). Figure 9.7 presents what the variable view sheet looks like. When you click on the data

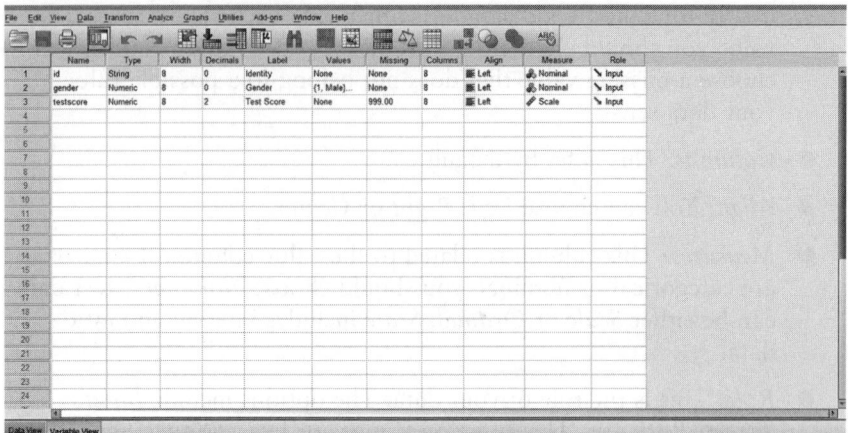

FIGURE 9.7   *SPSS variable view (based on Table 9.5)*

view, you can enter the data in Table 9.5 in the spreadsheet. You can also download this file (*Ch9 Data1.sav*) from the *companion website*.

Computing descriptive statistics

Let us use this file (*Ch9 Data1.sav*) to examine descriptive statistics as follows.

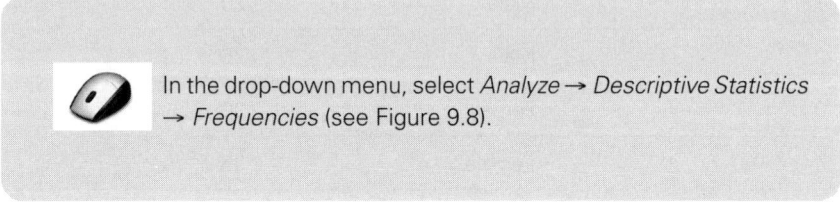

In the drop-down menu, select *Analyze → Descriptive Statistics → Frequencies* (see Figure 9.8).

This will lead to a pop-up dialog box where you can drag your variables into the variable box (see Figure 9.9). Note that you can do the same using *Descriptives*, which is below *Frequencies*. *Frequencies* allows us to examine nominal or dichotomous data through frequency tables. Let us drag gender and test score variables to the variable box.

The right part of this dialog contains three menu buttons (*Statistics*, *Charts* and *Formats*). Click the *Statistics* button and a new window dialog will pop up (see Figure 9.10).

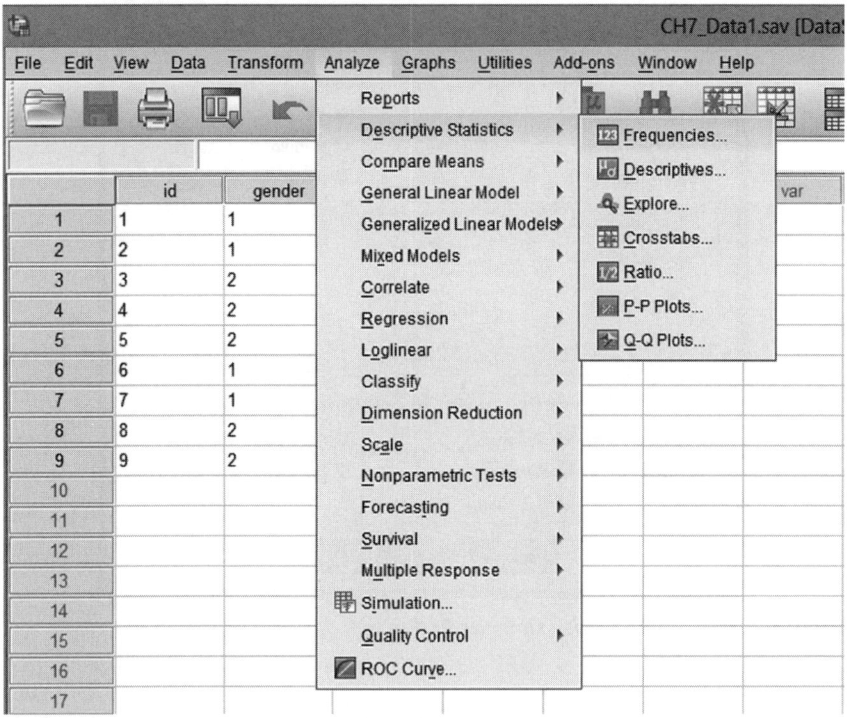

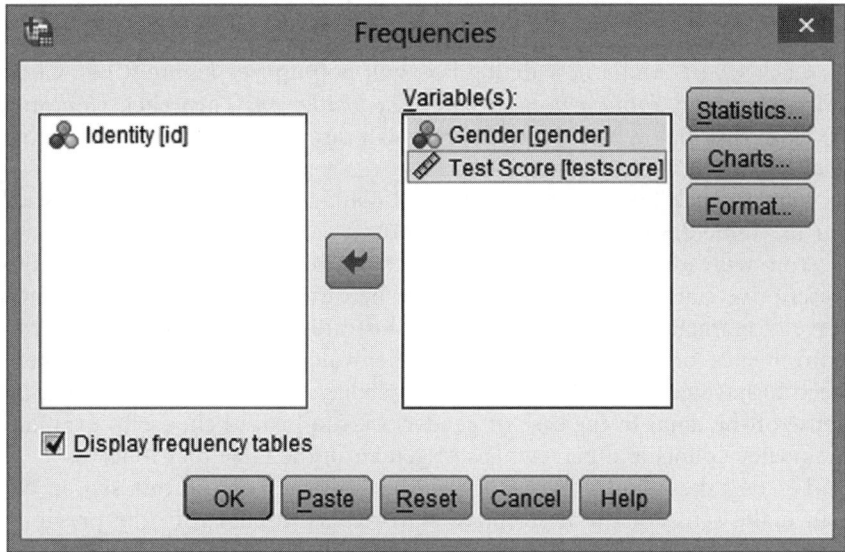

FIGURE 9.8 *Computing descriptive statistics*

FIGURE 9.9 *A frequencies dialog box*

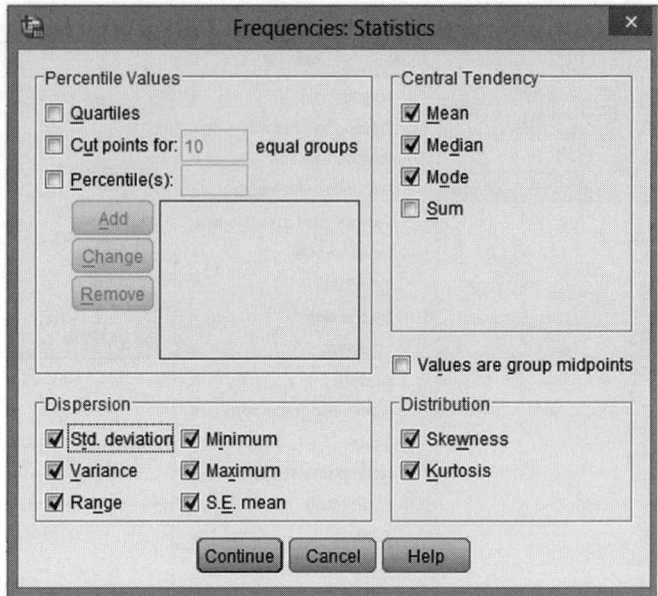

FIGURE 9.10 *Descriptive statistics dialog box*

This is exactly where we ask SPSS to compute descriptive statistics for us. For this section, click the following: Mean, Median, Mode, Std Deviation (i.e. measures of central tendency), Variance, Range, Minimum, Maximum, S. E. Mean (i.e. measures of dispersion), Skewness, and Kurtosis (i.e. measures of normal distribution). Then click *Continue* to close this dialog box and return to the previous dialog box.

Click *Charts* and a new dialog box will pop up (see Figure 9.11). Click *Histogram* and *Show a normal curve on histogram*. Then click *Continue* to close this dialog box. Note that we will discuss histograms later in this section.

Finally, click *OK*. An output file will contain several tables of statistics for us. Table 9.6 presents a partial output.

You will see that since the gender variable is a *nominal scale*, the descriptive statistics do not make sense because the gender values do not have a mathematical property. This illustrates the fact that despite the convenience of having SPSS to help them analyze the data, researchers need to have conceptual statistical knowledge as it assists them in making sense of the data. In the case of gender, we can instead choose to examine frequency counts and percentages of gender in the table that follows.

Let us take a look at the descriptive statistics of the test score. We can make sense of the descriptive statistics as discussed in the previous section. Note that the descriptive statistics are not representatives of the majority of the students due to an outlier (Participant id9). The data set is

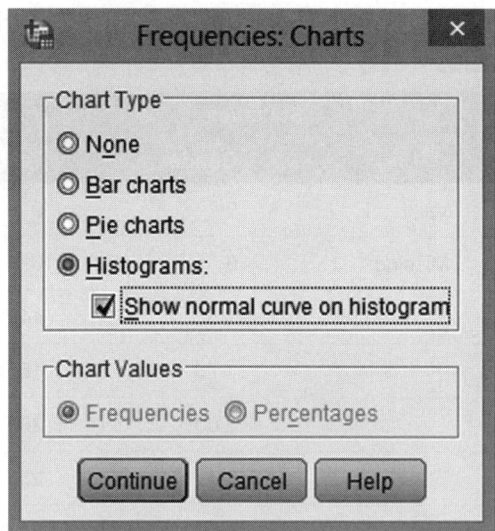

FIGURE 9.11   *Chart dialog box*

clearly not normally distributed (see the skewness and kurtosis statistics; also due to a small sample size). Now let us remove *id9* from this data file and re-calculate the descriptive statistics. When we work on a data file, apart from backing up the file, it is important to save a file using a new name when we plan to delete some variables or cases. For now, let us save this file as *Ch9 Data2.sav*. We can remove *id9* by clicking Row 9, right-clicking and choosing *cut*. Alternatively, we can click on Row 9 and go to *Edit* (on the top menu) and choose *Cut*. Table 9.7 presents the descriptive statistics of the test score after *id9* was removed.

You can see from Table 9.7 that the descriptive statistics provide better information about the participants. The mean, median and mode have similar values. The data set is normally distributed because the skewness and kurtosis statistics are close to 0 and within the ±1 acceptable range. Note that the standard errors of both skewness and kurtosis are quite high. Typically a *standard error* should be *close to zero*. The reliability of the research instrument and the sample size affect the standard error of measurement.

You will also notice that the *standard error of the mean* is quite high (i.e. 1.66). The standard error of the mean can be understood as the standard deviation of error of a sample mean, which should represent the mean of the larger population. That is, the larger the error, the more distant from the population mean the mean is. When we examine research reports and our own descriptive statistics, it is important that we pay attention to the *standard error statistics*.

According to this analysis through SPSS, we can use the descriptive statistics to understand the nature of the data. We can use the standard

Table 9.6 Sample SPSS outputs for the descriptive statistics and gender frequencies

Statistics		Gender	Test Score
N	Valid	9	9
	Missing	0	0
Mean		1.56	44.5556
Std. Error of Mean		.176	16.99355
Median		2.00	28.0000
Mode		2	25.00
Std. Deviation		.527	50.98066
Variance		.278	2599.028
Skewness		-.271	2.957
Std. Error of Skewness		.717	.717
Kurtosis		-2.571	8.811
Std. Error of Kurtosis		1.400	1.400
Range		1	160.00
Minimum		1	20.00
Maximum		2	180.00

Gender		Frequency	Percent	Valid Percent	Cumulative Percent
Valid	Male	4	44.4	44.4	44.4
	Female	5	55.6	55.6	100.0
	Total	9	100.0	100.0	

Table 9.7 SPSS Output for the descriptive statistics (after *id9* removed)

Statistics		
Test Score		
N	Valid	8
	Missing	0
Mean		27.6250
Std. Error of Mean		1.65764
Median		27.0000
Mode		25.00
Std. Deviation		4.68851
Variance		21.982
Skewness		.027
Std. Error of Skewness		.752
Kurtosis		-.048
Std. Error of Kurtosis		1.481
Range		15.00
Minimum		20.00
Maximum		35.00

deviation to examine the spread of the data. Basically, knowing that the highest score is 35 and the lowest score is 20, with the standard deviation of 4.69, we can say that the data set is quite homogenous (1SD = 32.31 and −1SD = 22.93). At least 68 percent of the scores fall within this ±1SD. The mean score is useful to represent the overall data.

Computing the percentile

Now let us examine the percentiles of individual scores using this data set. The percentile of the mean score (i.e. 27.63) is simply 50. We will follow the same step when we do the descriptive statistics above.

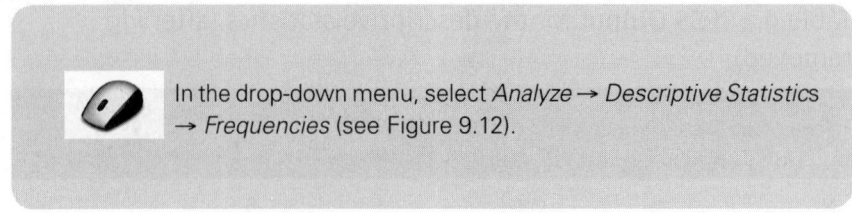

In the drop-down menu, select *Analyze → Descriptive Statistics → Frequencies* (see Figure 9.12).

For the purpose of this illustration, let us just calculate the percentiles. We can add a percentile value in the space and click *Add*. In this example, we only add 25, 50 and 75 because the data range we have is quite limited. We would like to also check the interquartile range discussed earlier.

Table 9.8 presents the output of the percentiles. We can see in this output that the score of 25 is at the 25th percentile, 27 is at the 50th percentile, and 31.5 is at the 75th percentile. We mentioned earlier the *interquartile range*. On the basis of the percentiles we have obtained, the interquartile range of this data set is 6.5 (i.e. 31.5 – 25).

The Z-score

A method to compute the z-score is also quite simple as discussed earlier. We need SPSS to create a variable called *ztestscore* for us first. This method can be used with any continuous variables.

FIGURE 9.12   *Computing percentiles*

Table 9.8 SPSS Output for the percentiles

Statistics		
Test Score		
N	Valid	8
	Missing	0
Percentiles	25	25.0000
	50	27.0000
	75	31.5000

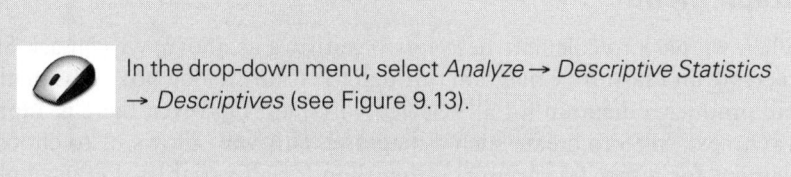

In the drop-down menu, select *Analyze → Descriptive Statistics → Descriptives* (see Figure 9.13).

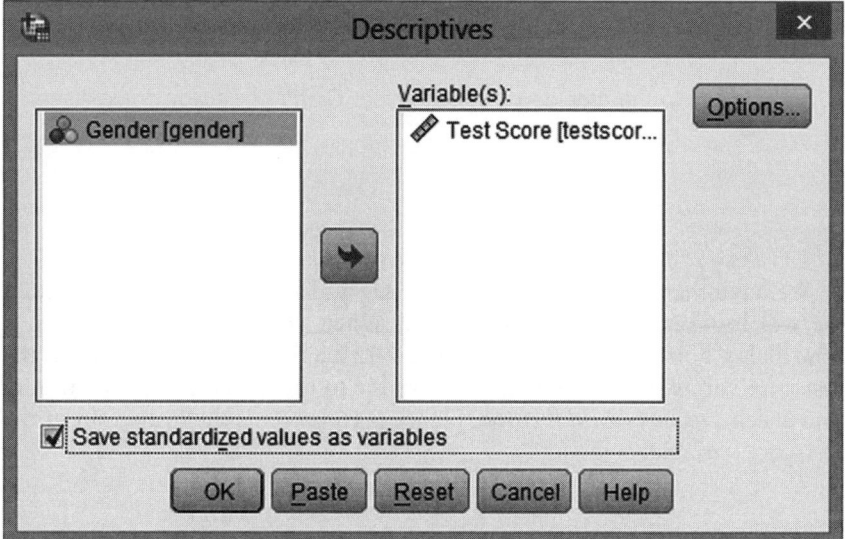

FIGURE 9.13 *Generating z-scores*

In Figure 9.13, make sure that you click *Save standardized values as variables* and click *OK*. In the output file, you will not yet see the z-score. In your data file (see the variable view), there is a new variable called *ztest-score*. In the data file, you can see each participant's z-score. If you would like to find out more on the descriptive statistics of the z-scores, you can do the same as we did above, either through the *Frequencies* or *Descriptives* options. In the *Frequencies* option, make sure you click *Display frequency tables* so that you can see frequency counts and accumulative percentages of the z-scores. You will find out that the maximum z-score is 1.57, the minimum z-score is −1.63 and the mean is 0.

Graphical representations

This section presents how to create graphs in SPSS programs.

Graph menu

When we wish to calculate descriptive statistics as above, we can ask SPSS to create an illustrative diagram through the *Chart* dialog box. This method will produce a diagram for all selected variables. However, there is another way to ask SPSS to create such a diagram. This way allows us to choose a diagram for a specific variable, rather than for all variables. Let us explore how we can display data through diagrams. This is useful when we would like to see the figure of data distributions.

 In the drop-down menu, select *Graph* → *Legacy dialogs* (see Figure 9.14).

We have the option to choose from *Bar* and *Histogram*. In this section, we will look at the *Histogram* option. When you click on *Histogram*, a new dialog box will appear (see Figure 9.15). Since we are interested in the testscore variable, we can drag this variable to the variable box. Make sure you check *Display normal curve*. Figure 6.16 presents the histogram of the testscore variable.

File Edit View Data Transform Analyze	Graphs	Utilities Add-ons Window Help

Chart Builder...
Graphboard Template Chooser...
Legacy Dialogs ▶

	id	gender	testscore	Ztestscore	var
1	1	1	20.00	-1.62632	
2	2	1	25.00	-.55988	
3	3	2	30.00	.50656	
4	4	2	35.00	1.57299	
5	5	2	28.00	.07998	
6	6	1	26.00	-.34659	
7	7	1	25.00	-.55988	
8	8	2	32.00	.93313	
9					
10					
11					
12					

Bar...
3-D Bar...
Line...
Area...
Pie...
High-Low...
Boxplot...
Error Bar...
Population Pyramid...
Scatter/Dot...
Histogram...

FIGURE 9.14   *SPSS graphs menu*

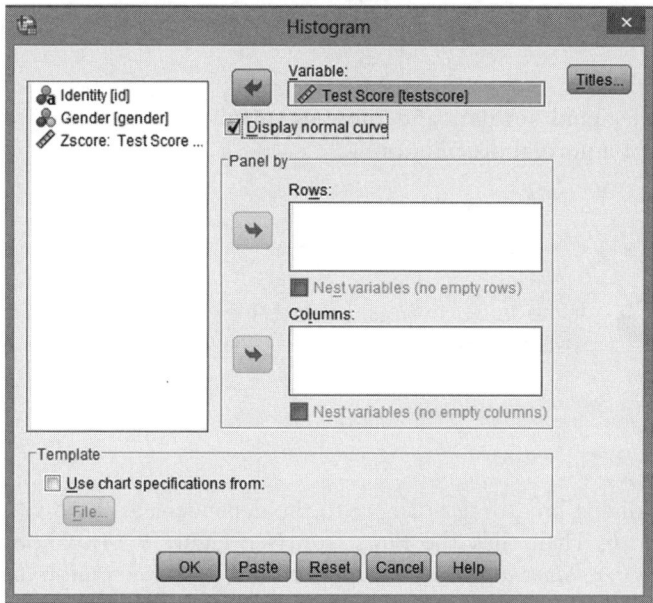

FIGURE 9.15   *Creating a histogram*

Explore menu in SPSS

One other useful way to explore the descriptive statistics of your data is by using the *Explore* menu of SPSS. In addition to the descriptive statistics discussed above, this Explore menu yields several useful data including *Kolmogorov–Smirnov* and *Shapiro–Wilk statistics*, stem-and-leaf diagrams, box plots and normal Q–Q plots of test scores. All this output will help us

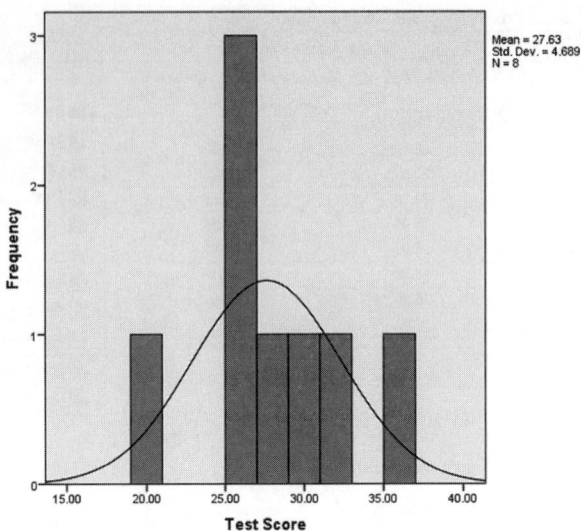

FIGURE 9.16   *A histogram of the test score*

better understand our data and allow us to collect further evidence for the presence of a normal distribution.

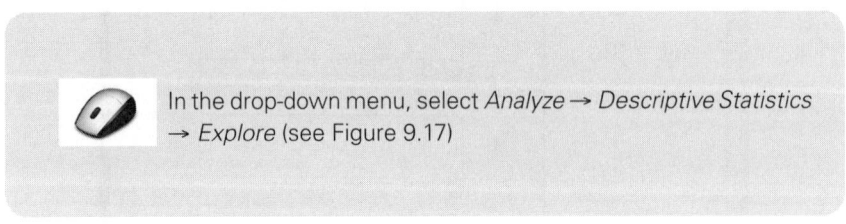

In the drop-down menu, select *Analyze → Descriptive Statistics → Explore* (see Figure 9.17)

In the dialog box, drag *testscore* to the dependent list box. Choose also *display both*. Then click the *Plots* icon (see Figure 9.18). Choose *Factor level together*, *Stem-and-leaf*, *Histogram* and *Normality plots with tests*. Then click *Continue* to return to Figure 9.17 and click *OK*. Several statistical outputs including diagrams will be produced.

Table 9.9 presents most of the discussed statistics in this chapter. However, there are two new statistics that you should learn: the *95 percent confidence interval (CI) for the mean* and the *5 percent trimmed mean*.

The 95 percent CI for the mean gives us the *upper bound* and *lower bound* of the mean that covers 95 percent of the statistics for estimating the population mean. According to Table 9.9, the mean is 27.63, the lower bound of the mean is 23.71 and the upper bound is 31.54. The values indicate that the 95 percent of the population mean score could fall between

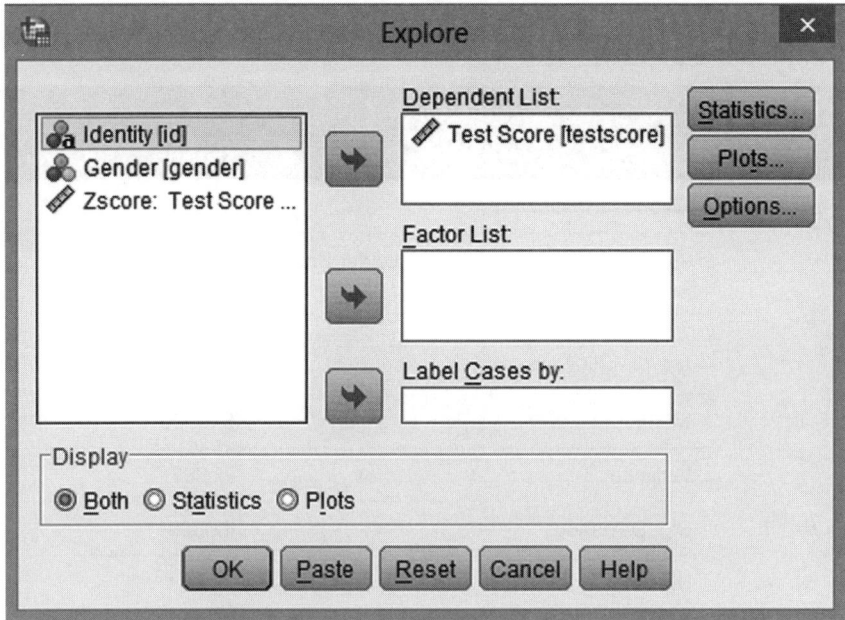

FIGURE 9.17   *SPSS data explore dialog box*

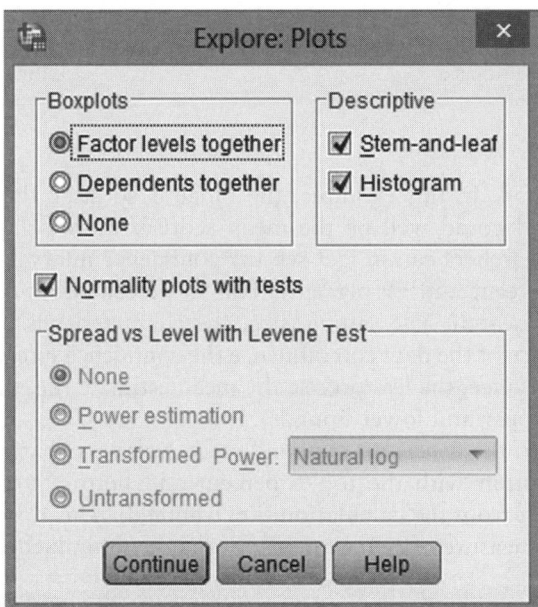

FIGURE 9.18   *SPSS data plot sub-dialog box*

Table 9.9 The 95% confidence interval (CI) for the mean and 5% trimmed mean

Descriptives			Statistic	Std. Error
Test Score	Mean		27.6250	1.65764
	95% Confidence Interval for Mean	Lower Bound	23.7053	
		Upper Bound	31.5447	
	5% Trimmed Mean		27.6389	
	Median		27.0000	
	Variance		21.982	
	Std. Deviation		4.68851	
	Minimum		20.00	
	Maximum		35.00	
	Range		15.00	
	Interquartile Range		6.50	
	Skewness		.027	.752
	Kurtosis		-.048	1.481

23.71 and 31.54. In this example, the range is so large that values from 23.71 to 31.54 could well be the mean score if more sample data were collected. Researchers can in fact set any confidence interval value (e.g. 50 percent, 90 percent and 99 percent). The 95 percent CI is *typical* in most quantitative research. The sample size, the characteristics of participants and the variance of the data can influence the confidence interval range. The greater the variance, the less precise the mean estimate (i.e. the broader the range of the upper and lower bounds).

In Table 9.9, the *5 percent trimmed mean statistic* is basically the mean of the distribution with the top 5 percent and bottom 5 percent of the scores *removed* from the calculation (i.e. trimmed). This method allows us to calculate a measure of *central tendency* that is not influenced by *extreme scores*.

Table 9.10 presents the Kolmogorov–Smirnov and Shapiro–Wilk statistics, which are also tests of normality. These statistics are easy to

Table 9.10 Kolmogorov–Smirnov and Shapiro–Wilk statistics

Tests of Normality					
Kolmogorov-Smirnov[a]			Shapiro-Wilk		
Statistic	df	Sig.	Statistic	df	Sig.
Test Score .163	8	.200[*]	.980	8	.962

*. This is a lower bound of the true significance.
a. Lilliefors Significance Correction

interpret. We examine the *significance level* of the statistics in the *Sig* column*. The data set can be considered normally distributed when the significance level is *larger than 0.05*. In Table 9.10, both tests are non-significant, implying that the data set can be normally distributed. Note that when the sample size is less than 100, the Shapiro–Wilk statistic is also computed.

Figure 9.19 presents the stem-and-leaf plot of the test scores. This plot gives the actual values in the distribution, unlike the histogram. In Figure 9.19, the stem is the left-hand column that contains the tens digits (e.g. 20 and 30). The leaf is the list in the right-hand column, showing the units digits for each of the 20s and 30s (i.e. 0 to 9). According to Figure 9.19, for example, the stem of the graph with the first digit of a score 3, the leaf includes 02. This means that the scores within this stem are 30 and 32.

Figure 9.20 presents the box plot of the test scores. The box plot indicates actual values and makes use of the median, 25th and 75th percentiles and extreme scores in the distribution. If the median line is placed toward the bottom, the data set is positively skewed and if it is located toward the top, the data set is negatively skewed.

Finally, Figure 9.21 presents the Q–Q Plot (quantile–quantile plot), which locates the observed scores along a 45° line. In a normal distribution, the scores should be in or close to the line. See Larson-Hall (2010, pp. 82–4) for a further discussion of this plot.

```
Test Score Stem-and-Leaf Plot

Frequency          Stem & Leaf

1.00               2 . 0
4.00               2 . 5568
2.00               3 . 02
1.00               3 . 5

Stem width:        10.00
Each leaf:         1 case(s)
```

FIGURE 9.19 *A stem-and-leaf plot*

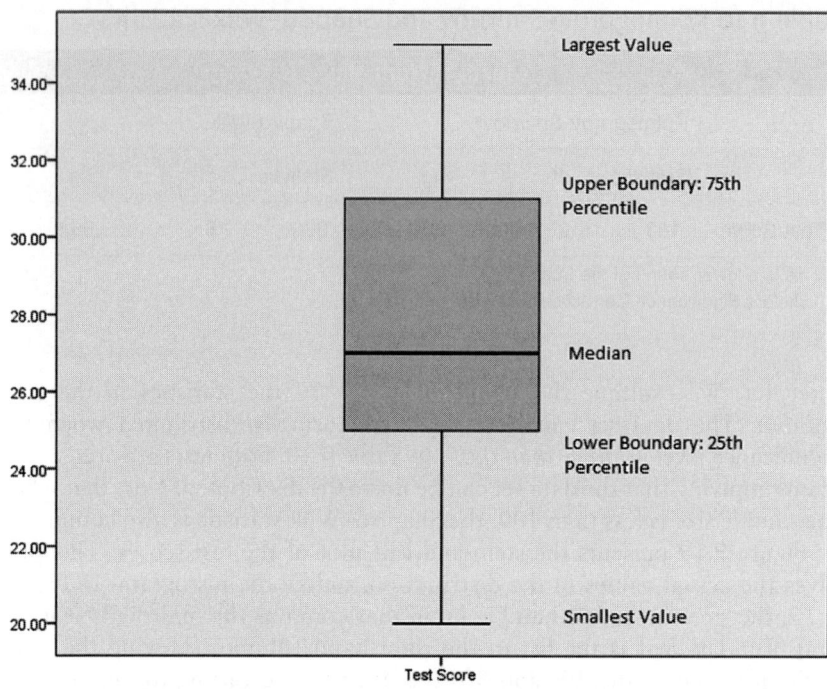

FIGURE 9.20   *A box plot*

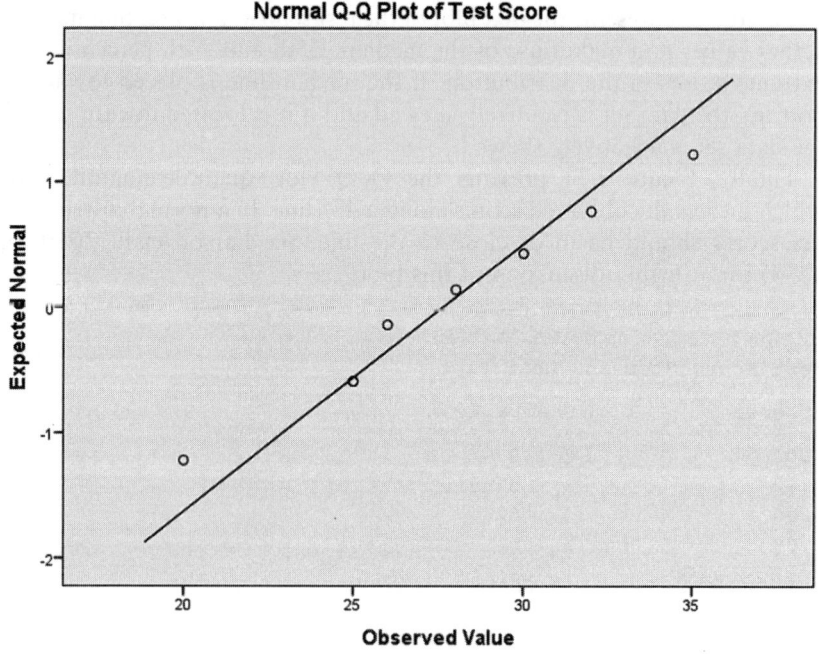

FIGURE 9.21   *The normal Q–Q plot of test scores*

Summary

This chapter has discussed the key stages involved in statistical analysis for experimental research. It is critical to be aware of these stages when we perform statistical analysis. We have started discussing the basic concepts of descriptive statistics. Some descriptive statistics are easy to learn (e.g. mean, median and mode). Others require further explanations (e.g. variance and standard deviation). In research reports, we should report the descriptive statistics of our data (whenever and wherever possible) so that readers can evaluate our data. It is important that researchers have a strong conceptual understanding of *what*, *how* and *why* a certain statistical method is to be used. At this stage of the exposition, statistical formulas have been avoided. Finally, we have introduced the IBM SPSS Program that can be used to perform statistical analysis. We have experienced how easy SPSS is to use. However, as we cannot cover everything that can be done with SPSS in this book, further resources for learning about SPSS are suggested. Remember that *SPSS practice makes perfect SPSS use*. The SPSS exercises as discussed in this and the next few chapters will be helpful to improve your statistical and SPSS skills. However, not until you work with real data for a real research project will you gain a complete grasp of both statistical concepts and SPSS. The next chapter will present issues and concepts in inferential statistics for experimental research.

Research exercise

To download exercises for this chapter visit: http://www.bloomsbury.com/experimental-research-methods-in-language-learning-9781441189110/

Discussion questions

1 What are the purposes of descriptive statistics for experimental research?
2 Can you think of an example of quantitative data that are normally distributed?
3 What are common types of measures of tendency? Can you explain what they are and how they are calculated?
4 What is the most difficult concept of descriptive statistics we have discussed in this chapter?
5 Reflection: What is the most important lesson you have learned from this chapter?

Further reading

Brown, JD 2000, 'Statistics as a foreign language: Part 1: what to look for in reading statistical language studies', *TESOL Quarterly*, vol. 25, no. 4, pp. 569–86.

This article presents how to make sense of statistics in research reports. The statistical explanations help readers develop a good conceptual understanding of statistical reasoning.

Larson-Hall, J 2010, *A guide to doing statistics in second language research using SPSS*, Routledge, New York.

This book is not only comprehensive in the treatment of statistics in second language research, but also in how to perform statistical analyses in SPSS. This book covers a range of topics (e.g. regression analysis and exploratory factor analysis) that the present book will not do due to its limited scope.

Lowie, W & Seton, B 2013, *Essential statistics for applied linguistics*, Palgrave Macmillan, Hampshire, UK.

This book clearly explains both descriptive and inferential statistics in applied linguistics. This book presents how to use SPSS for statistical analysis and examples of how a particular analysis can be done.

Urdan, TC 2005, *Statistics in plain English*, 2nd edn, Lawrence Erlbaum Associates, Mahwah, NJ.

This book explains the fundamental concepts of statistics effectively. Chapters 1 to 5 cover descriptive statistics. The rest of the chapters are related to inferential statistics. Some may find several statistical formulas daunting, but this is a good place to find out about some formulas when needed.

CHAPTER TEN

Inferential Statistics

Leading questions

1 What do you think are main differences between descriptive statistics and inferential statistics?
2 What is a population? What is a sample?
3 What is hypothesis testing?

Introduction

This chapter focuses on key concepts in inferential statistics (e.g. hypothesis testing, probability and significance values, and sample sizes). It will provide an overview of the common statistical tests used in language learning and experimental research.

The logics of inferential statistics

We use *inferential statistics* to gain a better understanding of the nature of the relationship between two or more variables (e.g. linear or causal-like relationships). Researchers need to make the distinction between a *population* (i.e. the totality of the people in which they are interested) and a *sample of that population (i.e. a selection of people from the population)*. A *parameter* is a characteristic of a population, whereas a *statistic* is a characteristic of a sample that will be used to infer a parameter. When we conduct research, we cannot always use all members of the population in our study for various reasons. We therefore perform a *parameter estimate* through inferential statistics. For example, Macaro and Erler (2008, pp. 98–9) discuss populations and samples in their study, which examined the effectiveness of reading strategy instruction for young beginner learners of French in England. Jarvis (2000, pp. 267–73), who examined the nature of L1 influence on L2 learning, discusses how participants were representative of the larger population. Accordingly, the inferential statistics these researchers employed aimed to estimate the parameter of the target population. We will now examine the key concepts of inferential statistics, including hypothesis testing, probability values, statistical significance and parametric and non-parametric tests, etc.

Hypothesis testing

In order for us to measure a potential relationship between two variables, we need to take three steps. First, we need to assume that *there is no relationship* between two variables. We always begin with *no relationship* in our assumption. Second, we need to determine (by collecting data or evidence) whether the no-relationship assumption is true. If it is not true, we can reject the no-relationship idea. In other words, we can now claim that a relationship does indeed exist. Third, we will find out whether the relationship is positive or negative (e.g. positive or negative linear relationship, or positive or negative causal-like relationship).

In statistical testing, we follow the same logic. For example, we want to provide a special treatment to a group of learners and we would like to find out whether our treatment is useful and does make a difference on their learning. First, what we need to do is to assume that our treatment *does not work* (i.e. there is no relationship between our treatment and their learning improvement). Second, we collect learners' performance before and after the treatment and we would like to compare whether there was a gain in their learning performance. Assuming that all threats to the internal validity were controlled and the treatment was the only independent variable that would be the cause, we would then perform a statistic that could compare the pretest and posttest mean scores. At this stage we would not know whether the posttest score mean was really higher than the pretest score mean. Therefore, taking the three steps presented above, first the pretest and posttest mean scores would be assumed to be equal (i.e. pretest = posttest). This would imply that there was no relationship between the treatment and the performance outcome.

Third, we would use a paired-samples *t*-test to determine whether they differed statistically. If they differed statistically, it would mean that one of the scores was higher than the other. This would in turn mean that our no-relationship assumption could not hold. Finally, we would be able to conclude that there was a relationship between the treatment and the learning performance. We then would need to find out which score was higher. If the posttest score was higher than the pretest score, we could argue that the treatment was useful. However, if the pretest score was higher than the posttest score, we might conclude that the treatment negatively affected their learning performance. In this latter case, we learned that the treatment had a negative causal-like relationship.

As discussed in Chapter 2, *hypothesis testing* is a statistical approach to investigating how well quantitative data support a hypothesis (known as the *null hypothesis*) that the researchers believe to be false. The *null hypothesis* (H_0) is basically the prediction that there is *no relationship* between two variables or *no difference* between two or more groups of learners. *This hypothesis testing approach directly tests the null hypothesis.* When the data do not support the null hypothesis, the researchers will accept the hypothesis called the *alternative hypothesis* (H_1), which is logically the opposite of the null hypothesis. The alternative hypothesis states that *there is a relationship* between two variables or that *there is a difference* between two or more groups of learners. Generally, researchers do not need to state their alternative hypothesis.

There are two types of alternative hypothesis: a *non-directional alternative hypothesis* (e.g. there is a relationship or a difference between the two variables) and a *directional alternative hypothesis* (e.g. there is a positive relationship between the two variables; Group A statistically outperforms Group B). See also the *one-tailed or two-tailed test* below. Usually, a directional hypothesis is *avoided* because there may be a relationship or difference as derived from the statistical analysis, but the relationship can be the opposite of that in the researcher's directional hypothesis (e.g. a negative relationship is found between the variables, i.e. Group B significantly outperforms Group A). According to the rule of hypothesis testing, the researchers cannot reject the null hypothesis. Such examples illustrate that researchers should formulate a non-directional alternative hypothesis.

Probability value

In order to reject the null hypothesis, researchers must set a *probability value* (i.e. *p*-value). The probability value is directly set for testing the null hypothesis, *not for the alternative hypothesis*. Statistically speaking, the null hypothesis can be rejected when the *probability* of the result assuming a true null hypothesis is very small. In language learning research, for example, researchers usually set a probability value to be less than 0.05 ($p < 0.05$). Some researchers may set a probability value to be less than or equal to 0.05 ($p \leq 0.05$). It is important to note that if we set a probability value to be less than 0.05 and we find that the test statistic has a *p*-value of 0.05, we need to reject the null hypothesis. What is meant by 0.05 is this: there is a 5 percent chance that the null hypothesis being tested is correct.

That is, a 5 percent margin for error is accounted for in rejecting the null hypothesis. In experimental research, a p-value of 0.05 is recommended. Frequently we see researchers set a probability value of 0.01. In the case of $p < 0.01$, there is less than a 1 percent chance that the null hypothesis is correct. A p-value of 0.001 means that there is one in a thousand chance that the null hypothesis is true.

When we analyze a data set in order to test a null hypothesis, we need to use a critical value to determine whether we can reject the null hypothesis at a particular probability level. Let us look at the following critical values for a chi-square (χ^2) test. In the case of a degree of freedom (df; see below) of 2, we will need a different χ^2 value to reject the null hypothesis. For example, according to Fisher and Yates's (1974) table of critical values: when $p \leq 0.05$, the required χ^2 value is 5.99; when $p \leq 0.01$, the required χ^2 value is 9.21; and when $p \leq 0.001$, the required χ^2 value is 13.82. If we set the p-value to be less than 0.05 and the test statistic produces a χ^2 value of 5.99 or larger, we can reject the null hypothesis. You can see from the example above that the smaller the p-value, the larger the required test statistic (e.g. χ^2 value) for us to be able to reject the null hypothesis. The p-value is related to the level of confidence that researchers are comfortable with when rejecting the null hypothesis.

This statistical procedure is related to the *statistical validity* discussed in Chapter 5. Traditionally, researchers will consult a significance value of a particular test, such as Pearson correlation, a t-test or an ANOVA. Tables of statistical significance are provided at the end of most statistics books (see also Urdan 2005). However, we are fortunate that we do not need to look for a critical value in tables because SPSS can produce a p-value for us, so we can evaluate whether it is less than 0.05.

Statistical significance

Students who are new to statistics are often confused about the difference between the probability value set and the *statistical significance*. To clarify the difference, remember that the significance value (i.e. alpha value) will be *fixed* (e.g. it must be less than or equal to 0.05 or 0.01). The *probability value*, on the other hand, is *data-driven* and produced by the test statistics. For example, when we set a p-value to be less than 0.05 to conclude that it is significant and when a p-value of 0.06 is obtained from the data, this data-driven p-value is not statistically significant at 0.05 because 0.06 is larger than 0.05. However, if we set a probability value at 0.10, the obtained p-value is considered statistically significant at 0.10 because 0.06 is smaller than 0.10. It is important to remember that the *level of significance* only says that there is a *high probability* that we are correct in rejecting the null hypothesis. It is essential to note that the word *significance* in statistics does not have the same meaning as *importance* in English. What it means is that researchers conclude that the null hypothesis is *highly likely* (Ary *et al.* 2006).

Type I and Type II errors

When we reject the null hypothesis, a possibility remains that we have made an error. There are countless reasons why such an error can be made. For example, we might not have a representative sample of the population. We might use unreliable research instruments and we might violate some statistical assumptions of the test we have used. When we reject a null hypothesis when it is true, we make a *Type I error*. There are many real-life examples of this kind of error. For example, Alex ordered a cup of coffee at a kiosk but unintentionally forgot to pay for it. The shop assistant asked Alex to pay for the coffee. Alex insisted that he had already paid for it. Clearly Alex had not paid for the coffee, but by denying it, Alex committed a Type I error. In research, the logic is the same. The significance level discussed so far is related to the possibility that researchers will have made a Type I error when they reject the null hypothesis. The significance value, therefore, is the level at which *researchers agree to take the risk of making the Type I error*. Technically, the probability of committing a Type I error is known as the *significance level* or *alpha* (α). In research reports, you will see some researchers use $\alpha < 0.05$.

On the other hand, there is a possibility that we accept the null hypothesis when we should reject it. This error is known as a *Type II error*. Let us revisit the scenario in which Alex ordered a cup of coffee. Today Alex ordered coffee again and paid for it, but he forgot that he had paid for it. When the shop assistant said that Alex had not paid for the coffee, Alex accepted the request and paid for it (again). In this case, Alex made a Type II error. He had accepted the claim when he should have rejected it. In statistics, the probability of making this type of error is known as *beta* (β). In order to avoid committing a Type II error, we need to have strong evidence that the null hypothesis should be accepted. In the case of Alex, if he had had a receipt for the payment or a credible eyewitness, he could have rejected the request from the shopkeeper. In statistical analysis, we therefore discuss the concept of *statistical power*, which is related to questions of, for example, the sample sizes required to be able to reject the null hypothesis, the appropriate use of a statistical test, and violations of a particular statistical assumption. We will discuss the practical significance of this after we have provided an overview of statistical tests.

One-tailed or two-tailed test

While Type I and II errors are associated with the testing of the null hypothesis, the one-tailed or two-tailed tests of significance are related to the alternative hypothesis. That is, they are concerned with whether researchers

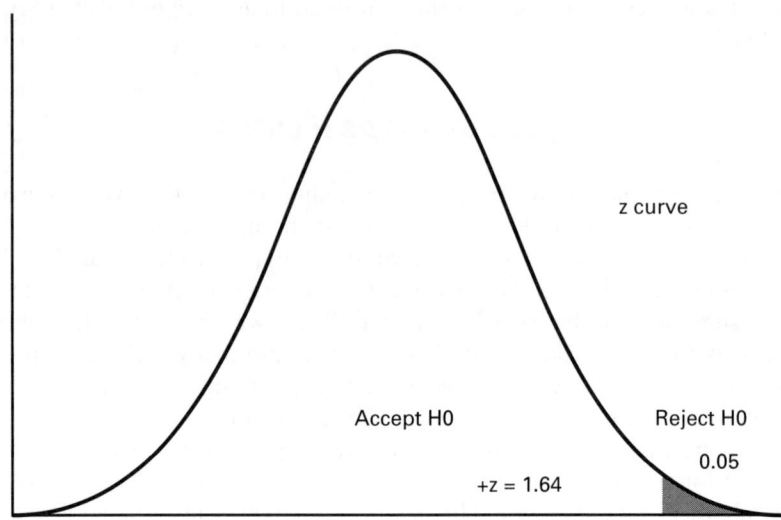

FIGURE 10.1   *The one-tailed test of significance*

specify the alternative hypothesis (i.e. one-tailed) or do not specify the alternative hypothesis (i.e. two-tailed). In experimental research, if we believe that teaching method A is more effective than teaching method B, we have specified an alternative hypothesis. This is a *directional alternative hypothesis*. For example, a study by Jensen and Vinther (2003, pp. 391–94) used a directional alternative hypothesis (e.g. Hypothesis 1: Students who listen to quasi-spontaneous input followed by an exact repetition of that input at the same or a slower rate of delivery will improve significantly *more in terms of* comprehension, phonological decoding and grammatical accuracy *than* the students who do not listen to this material.) However, if we are not sure whether one method is better than the other, we just need to say that the effectiveness of method A is different from that of method B. This is a *non-directional alternative hypothesis*. The concept of a one-tailed or two-tailed test of significance still seems more abstract than concrete. Let us explore this concept further by using Figure 10.1, which illustrates a one-tailed test of significance.

In a one-tailed test of significance, researchers expect that there is only one direction (i.e. one-tailed) that the *p*-value will fall in the shaded area (i.e. the region of rejection). Note that the tail can be on the left or right side. In Figure 10.1, the shaded area is called the 5 percent chance area where the null hypothesis could be true. This is also known as the 95 percent quantile of the normal distribution. The value at which the 5 percent chance area is cut off is called the *critical value*. In Figure 10.1, the critical value is the *z*-score of 1.64. Evidence for accepting or rejecting the null hypothesis is gathered by means of a *test statistic, calculated* on the basis of the data we use. If the test statistic

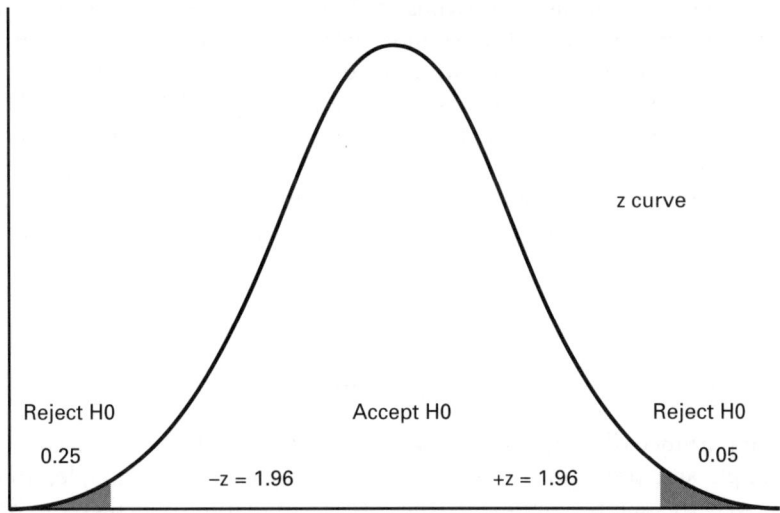

FIGURE 10.2   *The two-tailed test of significance*

produces a *z*-score of 1.73, we can reject the null hypothesis, because this value is larger than 1.64. Figure 10.2 presents a two-tailed test of significance.

As can be seen in Figure 10.2, the significance value for the two-tailed test of significance is calculated by dividing a *p*-value by 2 so that you can test whether there is a statistical significance on both sides of the tails. For example, if your *p*-value is 0.05, the significance value is 0.025. If the test statistic is within the top 2.5 percent (i.e. 97.5 quantile) or bottom 2.5 percent (i.e. 2.5 quantile) of its probability distribution, you can reject the null hypothesis. Let us use the same example about teaching methods A and B. If we obtain a *z*-score of 1.73, we cannot reject the null hypothesis because the value required to reject the null hypothesis is 1.96. As can be seen from both examples, the two-tailed test of significance provides a tougher, more significant condition to be satisfied for us to be able to reject the null hypothesis, compared to the one-tailed test.

Degree of freedom (df)

The concept of the degree of freedom (*df*) in statistical analysis can be difficult to make sense of without going into an actual analysis of a particular test. Let us first think of a *df* in a real-life situation. For example, we are on holiday at a beautiful beach resort for five days. We have brought with us one swimsuit. In this case, we have to wear the same swimsuit for the next five days. There can be no variation in what we wear to swim.

There is no *df* with just one swimsuit. However, if we have brought five different swimsuits, we will have more options of what to wear to swim. We have four *dfs* to vary our swimsuit (during the first four days). This is because on the fifth day, there is only one left to wear. There is no df on the fifth day. In this example, the df is the *total number of swimsuits less 1* (i.e. *N–1*).

Statistically speaking, when we aim to estimate a parameter of interest, we need to have a degree of freedom. A *df* is essentially the number of independent pieces of information that we use to estimate a parameter. We will explore this concept further in Chapter 11.

Sample size

The importance of sample size in experimental research cannot be ignored. A sample size provides us with general information, for example, about how well the sample represents the larger population, whether the data set is likely to be normally distributed, and whether we can use a parametric test (for normally distributed data) or a non-parametric test (for non-normal distribution). As noted earlier, we use inferential statistics as a means to generalize from a sample to a target population, so the larger the sample size, the better we can accurately estimate a parameter of interest. If we have a small sample size, we are at risk of making an error in statistical analysis, particularly in relation to hypothesis testing (discussed above) and estimates of effect sizes (discussed below). Hatch and Lazaraton (1991), and Ary *et al.* (2006) recommend a minimum sample size of 30 for parametric tests (e.g. Pearson correlations and a *t*-test). A large sample size is easily obtained in correlational or survey research as it often requires cross-sectional data collection. However, in experimental research, it can be difficult to obtain even a sample size of 30 per group.

Parametric versus non-parametric tests

Inferential statistics can be grouped into *parametric* and *non-parametric tests*. As pointed out earlier, we should aim to use parametric tests in statistical analysis because they are more robust than non-parametric tests in terms of the inferences we can make. There are statistical assumptions that determine whether we can use inferential statistics and whether we should use parametric or non-parametric tests. Statistical assumptions can be treated as regulated prerequisites that allow researchers to make appropriate applications of a statistical test. Statistical assumptions, such as the normality of the distribution and linearity, are obligatory, rather than optional. In other words, if a data set cannot meet the required statistical assumptions, a false inference about the target parameter is highly likely.

On the one hand, key assumptions for parametric tests include the normality of the distribution, interval or continuous data, and independence of data scores across instruments. On the other hand, a non-parametric test (known as a *distribution-free test*) can analyze frequency or rank-order data, as well as data that do not meet the parametric test assumptions. A non-parametric test can analyze discrete variables, frequencies or ranked-order data.

Although parametric tests are preferable, there are situations in experimental research where researchers need to use non-parametric tests because some data are frequency-based and are not interval-like. In addition, dichotomous data, such as pass or fail scores, are not inherently normally distributed. For example, this type of data occurs when we aim to examine whether learners in an experimental group (coded 1) and learners in a control group (coded 2) differ in terms of passing (coded 1) or failing (coded 2) a writing test. This kind of dichotomous data can be sorted using a contingency table. We can use a non-parametric test to investigate this. The next section provides an overview of statistical tests.

Overview of statistical tests

This section provides an outline of some statistical tests used in language learning research. A number of these tests are used in experimental research and are presented in greater detail in the next few chapters.

Correlation

Correlation is used to examine non-causal relationships between two variables. Through correlational analysis, researchers examine whether one variable can systematically decrease or increase together with another, rather than one variable causing the change in the other. Correlational tests include the *Pearson Product Moment correlation* or Pearson *r*, and *point-biserial correlation, Spearman's rho correlation, Kendall's tau-b correlation* and *phi correlation*. Given the properties of correlational analysis, experimental research *does not generally employ correlation* to test a group difference (see the study by Jarvis 2000 for an exception to this). We will discuss correlation further in the next chapter.

Regression analysis

Regression analysis is an extension of bivariate correlation analysis. It tests whether a dependent variable can be predicted from the values of one or more independent variables. *Simple regression* examines the effect of just one independent variable on the dependent variable. *Multiple regression* allows us to examine the effect of two or more independent variables on the dependent variable. The two independent variables need to be correlated with each other. In a multiple regression, researchers can evaluate which independent variable is the best prediction of a dependent variable. Although multiple regression can be used to analyze experimental data, most experimental research does not employ this test because researchers seek to determine where the difference between experimental and control groups lie. An ANOVA discussed below can tell them whether there is a statistically significant difference between two groups. We will not cover regression analysis further in this book (see Larson-Hall 2010 and Lowie & Seton 2013 for further details of how to conduct regression analysis in SPSS).

The t-test

There is a range of *t*-tests that can be used in experimental research (e.g. one-sample, paired-samples and independent-samples *t*-tests). A *t*-test is a statistical procedure that allows researchers to determine whether the difference in the means of the data in two groups is significant. This is essentially what a chi-square (χ^2) test does (discussed below), but a *t*-test is statistically more powerful because the data need to meet certain requirements such as being normally distributed before it can be used. There are two commonly used *t*-tests in experimental research. A *paired-samples t-test* examines whether two mean scores from the same group of participants differ significantly (e.g. pretest-posttest comparison). An *independent-samples t-test* investigates whether the mean scores between two groups of participants are significantly different (e.g. experimental and control group comparison).

Analysis of variance (ANOVA)

Analysis of variance (ANOVA) has a similar logic to the *t*-tests. There are also a range of ANOVAs (e.g. one-way ANOVA, factorial ANOVA) that can be used in experimental research. ANOVAs provide inferential statistics similar to the *t*-tests above. For example, a *within-group ANOVA* is similar to a *paired-samples t-test*, whereas a *between-groups ANOVA* is similar to an *independent-samples t-test*. The key difference between a *t*-test and an ANOVA is that an ANOVA can compare two or more mean scores of two or more groups, whereas a *t*-test can only compare the means of two groups. Given its more stringent set of statistical assumptions, an ANOVA test is more powerful than its homologous *t*-test. A repeated-measures ANOVA compares the mean scores among pretests, posttests and delayed posttests. A between-groups ANOVA compares two or more groups of participants (e.g. Group A, Group B and Group C) in terms of their language performance. Typically when more than two means are used for ANOVAs, a *post hoc test* needs to be further performed in order to identify where a significant difference lies exactly. A factorial ANOVA is related to the factorial design of an experimental study. It is used to examine the effects of more than one independent variable.

Analysis of covariance (ANCOVA)

As we have pointed out throughout, in experimental research, there are extraneous variables that can co-influence the dependent variable of interest. The analysis of covariance (ANCOVA) allows us to control an extraneous variable (treated as *covariate*) during the analysis. Extraneous variables include, for example, pre-existing language proficiency differences or a particular personal trait (e.g. age, anxiety, motivation, prior language exposure). This analysis allows us to understand to what extent the independent variable of interest accounts for changes in the dependent variable. ANCOVA is an extension of ANOVA. ANCOVA is suitable for between-groups comparisons.

Chi-square (χ^2) test

There are two kinds of *chi-square (χ^2) tests*, which are non-parametric: The χ^2 *test for goodness of fit* and χ^2 *test for relatedness or independence*. Generally speaking, a χ^2 test *for goodness of fit* helps researchers examine whether a difference between two groups of learners (e.g. males and female; group A and group B) exists using frequency scores. A χ^2 test for *relatedness or independence* uses categorical or nominal data to test whether paired variables are independent of each other. The analysis can be conducted by collecting frequency counts in a contingency table or a *cross-tabulation* (in which, for example, a row represents a categorical variable (e.g. Group A and Group B) and a column represents a dependent variable. A chi-square test will tell researchers whether an independent variable is more likely than another to have an effect on a dependent variable.

Wilcoxon signed ranks test

The Wilcoxon signed ranks test is a non-parametric test, parallel to a paired-samples *t*-test. This test can be used with ordinal, interval or ratio data. This test can be used even when the data are not normally distributed.

Mann–Whitney U test

The Mann-Whitney U test is a non-parametric test that can address a research question in a similar manner to that of the independent-samples *t*-test. The Mann-Whitney U test can be used with ordinal, interval or ratio data. The data do not need to be normally distributed for this test to be used. This test requires a ranking of data before analysis.

Kruskal–Wallis and Friedman tests

The Kruskal–Wallis test is a non-parametric test that has a function similar to that of the one-way ANOVA (between-group), whereas the Friedman test is parallel to the within-group ANOVA. The two tests are applicable to the analysis of the data associated with more than two groups. Again, the data need to be ranked in order to test whether differences among groups exist.

Practical significance and the effect size

Having discussed statistical significance and types of statistical tests, it is appropriate to discuss issues of practical significance to an empirical study. In the past few decades, there has been an increasing demand on researchers to report and discuss the effect sizes of their statistical analysis results. The statement in the Publication Manual of the American Psychological Association (APA, 2010) emphasizes that statistical significance p values are not acceptable indices of effect because they *depend on sample size*. In several situations, researchers may find a statistical significance, but the finding yields little meaning, leading to *no theoretical or pedagogical practicality*. That is, findings that are statistically significant are not always worthy in a practical sense. An effect size is a *magnitude-of-effect estimate* that is independent of sample size. A magnitude-of-effect estimate highlights the distinction between *statistical* and *practical significance*.

Use of an effect size estimate can assist researchers in establishing whether statistically significant findings are of practical or meaningful significance within the context of an empirical investigation. By examining an effect size, researchers can evaluate whether their significant findings are likely to be the result of an artifact of sample size. Good experimental research incorporates an effect size in interpretations and discussion of findings. By discussing an effect size, the practical relevance of the research outcomes can be evaluated. Effect sizes can be classified as *small, medium* or *large effect*. In an experimental study, researchers hope to find at least a medium effect size. Larson-Hall (2010, pp. 118–19) provides a table of effect sizes, their formulas and interpretations).

Different statistical tests require different effect size indices. For example, in a Pearson correctional analysis (Cohen 1988), Pearson r values of 0.10, 0.30 and 0.50 are considered to indicate small, medium and large effect sizes, respectively. When we examine correlations, the coefficient of determination, also known as a shared variance (i.e. r squared, R^2) can be used to determine this. R^2 indicates the extent to which two variables overlap in percentages. R^2 can further assist us in determining whether the finding is practically significant.

In a t-test, *Cohen's d* has been used as an effect size index: d-values of 0.2, 0.5 and 0.8 indicate small, medium and large effect sizes, respectively. Formulas to compute Cohen's d depend on the type of t-test being used (e.g. one-sample, paired-samples or independent-samples). According to Cohen (1988, pp. 21–3), the value of Cohen's d tells us about the percentage of non-overlap of the data associated with two groups of participants. For example, a Cohen's d value of 0 shows that the score distributions between the two groups entirely overlap, indicating that the distributions are not significantly different. A Cohen's d value of 0.2 is in the 58th percentile, which indicates the compared distributions have a non-overlap of 14.7 percent. A Cohen's d value of 0.8 is located in the 79th percentile, indicating a non-overlap of 47.4 percent in the two compared distributions. A Cohen's d of 1.0 indicates that the score distributions between two groups exhibit a 1 standard deviation difference. The larger a Cohen's d is, the larger the level of practical significant difference between the two compared groups.

When we perform a one-way ANOVA and some non-parametric tests such as the Friedman and Kruskall–Wallis tests, a partial eta-squared $(p\eta^2)$ can be obtained as an effect size. An eta-squared (η^2) tells us how much an independent variable accounts for the variability of a dependent variable. For example, an eta-squared (η^2) of 0.35 suggests that 35 percent of the variability of a dependent variable (e.g. learners' performance) is accounted for by the independent variable (e.g. feedback). Typically an eta-squared (η^2) can be converted into Cohen's f as follows (Cohen 1992): $f^2 = \eta^2 \div [1-\eta^2] \rightarrow$ Cohen's $f = \sqrt{f^2}$. According to Cohen (1992), f values of 0.10, 0.25 and 0.40 indicate small, medium and large effect sizes, respectively.

In a chi-square (χ^2) test, *Cohen's w* is used as effect size: $\sqrt{[\chi^2 \div N]}$, where N = total sample size (Cohen 1992). We can obtain a chi-square (χ^2) value from SPSS. According to Cohen (1992), w values of 0.10, 0.30 and 0.50 indicate small, medium and large effect sizes, respectively. The main point in this section is that it is not enough to obtain a statistical significance. We need to look into effect sizes and practical significance.

Summary

This chapter has introduced several essential concepts of inferential statistics in experimental research. Inferential statistics are analytical approaches to testing research hypotheses and inferring a causal-like relationship between an independent variable and a dependent variable. Although inferential statistics are complex and require a lot of effort to make sense of, it is critical that experimental researchers have a good understanding of the inferential statistics that are used to address their research questions.

Research exercise

To download exercises for this chapter visit: http://www.bloomsbury.com/experimental-research-methods-in-language-learning-9781441189110/

Discussion questions

1 What are key differences between a null hypothesis and an alternative hypothesis?
2 What does *statistically significant* mean?
3 What is *practical significance*?
4 How do you understand the concept of statistical effect size?
5 Reflection: What is the most important lesson you have learned from this chapter?

Further reading

Bachman, LF 2004, *Statistical analysis for language assessment*, Cambridge University Press, Cambridge.

This book is devoted to statistical analysis for language assessment. It covers several data analyses that are beyond the scope of the present book (e.g. Rasch item response theory, generalizability theory).

Brown, JD (2001a), Statistics as a foreign language: part 2: more things to consider in reading statistical language studies, *TESOL Quarterly*, vol. 26, no. 4, pp. 629–64.

This article explains the fundamental concepts of statistics in language studies. Although Brown focuses on how to make sense of statistical concepts in research articles, they are useful for a better understanding of the logic behind statistical analysis.

Larson-Hall, J 2010, *A guide to doing statistics in second language research using SPSS*, Routledge, New York.

This book comprehensively treats statistical analysis in second language research, focusing on applications of SPSS. It covers a range of statistical analysis techniques that the present book does not cover due to our focus on experimental research.

CHAPTER ELEVEN

Correlational Analysis

Leading questions

1 Can you think of real-life examples of correlations?
2 How do you express how much one thing is related to another thing?
3 What is a positive correlation? What is a negative one?

Introduction

This chapter illustrates how SPSS can be used to run a range of correlational analyses, which are the basis of many statistical tests including
reliability analysis of quantitative research instruments and qualitative data
coding. This chapter also aims to help you make more sense of the inferential statistics we discussed in the previous chapter.

Correlational analysis

It can be said that correlational analysis is one of the most widely used inferential
statistics in educational and language learning research. Correlation allows
us to explore a hypothetical relationship between variables. Correlational
analysis is typically used in non-experimental research, such as survey
research or correlational research, which aims to examine whether there is
an association between variables of interest and if such an association exists,
to what extent the variables are connected. Correlation is also fundamental
to other advanced statistical techniques, including factor analysis, reliability
analysis, regression analysis, path analysis and structural equation modelling.
In this section, we will only cover simple correlational analyses via SPSS.

The size and sign of a correlation coefficient

There are five types of correlations introduced in this chapter: Pearson Product Moment correlation, point-biserial correlation, Spearman's rho correlation, Kendall's tau-b correlation and phi correlation. A correlation coefficient is typically expressed on a scale from 0 (i.e. 0 percent, no relationship) to 1 (i.e. 100 percent, perfect relationship). If two variables are uncorrelated (i.e. 0), there is no systematic relationship between them and hence a prediction of one variable by the other is not possible. A positive (+) correlation indicates that two variables are associated and move in the same direction in a systematic way. That is, as one gets larger or smaller, so does the other. For example, as learners increase their vocabulary knowledge, their reading comprehension ability improves. A negative (−) correlation suggests that the two variables are associated with each other, but move systematically in the opposite direction. That is, as one gets larger, the other gets smaller, and vice versa. For example, the more learners are anxious about their language learning, the worse their language performance.

It should be noted that some variables can have a *curvilinear* relationship (e.g. the relationship between anxiety and test performance). A curvilinear relationship means that at some level, something can be positive, but when it exceeds a certain level, it can become negative. For example, we all know that some level of anxiety is good for test performance (because we will work harder and try to overcome it), but too much anxiety is bad for test performance because it takes control of our emotions.

Hypothesis testing in correlation

Researchers seek to test a hypothesis of whether two variables are related. The null hypothesis (H_0) states that there is *no* relationship between variable A and variable B (i.e. correlation coefficient = 0). Recall that researchers test the null hypothesis against the data. The *non-directional* alternative hypothesis (H_1) is when there is a relationship between variable A and variable B (i.e. correlation coefficient ≠ 0). A *directional* alternative hypothesis is when there is a *positive* relationship between variable A and variable B (i.e. one-tailed). The two-tailed test of significance is recommended. A typical *p*-value is taken to be 0.05. The degree of freedom (*df*) is determined by the total number of cases minus 1 (i.e. N−1).

In order to test the null hypothesis, a test statistic employing a *t* distribution is performed (see Urdan 2005). The process is just like doing a *t*-test to determine whether the *t*-score of a correlation is significant at a specific *p*-value. That is, in order to reject the null hypothesis, the *t*-score produced by the data needs to be larger than the critical *t*-score. For example, according to the *t*-distribution table (Fisher & Yates 1974), with a *df* of 120 and at the alpha level of 0.05 for the two-tailed test, a *t*-score of 1.98

is needed in order to reject the null hypothesis. At the alpha level of 0.01, a *t*-score of 2.62 is needed. Note that in the SPSS analysis (see below), a *t*-score is not produced, but SPSS will flag whether there is a statistical significance which is convenient for us.

Effect size and R-squared (R^2)

It is important to note that first, the sign of the correlation (i.e. + or −) is not related to the strength of the correlation. Second, a negative correlation does not mean that the finding is of no worth. Third, a correlation coefficient does not tell us how much one variable accounts for the other. Figure 11.1 presents an example of a correlation figure and how much variable A and variable B are shared. Table 11.1 presents the connection between *r* and R^2 and how the relationship can be interpreted. See Chapter 10 for the effect size interpretation of a correlation coefficient. It is important to note that in some research topics, fairly weak correlations can be very important (i.e. they can indicate theoretical or practical significance) and in some cases even a shared variance of 10 percent can be worth acting upon.

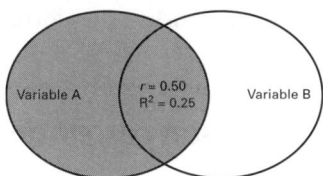

FIGURE 11.1 *Example of a shared variance (R^2) between variable A and variable B*

Table 11.1 Correlation coefficients, variances and interpretation

Value	Explained variance	Unexplained variance	Interpretation
0.90	81%	19%	Very strong
0.80	64%	46%	Strong
0.70	49%	51%	Fairly strong
0.50	25%	75%	Moderate
0.30	9%	91%	Fairly weak
0.20	4%	96%	Weak
0.10	1%	99%	Very weak

Correction for attenuation

If we know the reliability estimates of the research instruments used to collect data for two variables for a correlational analysis (especially in Pearson correlations), it is recommended that a correction for attenuation is computed and reported together with an uncorrected correlation. A correction for attenuation takes the reliability coefficients of the two measures into account in a Pearson correlation coefficient. According to Hatch and Lazaraton (1991, p. 444), a correction for attenuation can be computed as: $r_{AB} \div \sqrt{[\text{reliability of A} \times \text{reliability of B}]}$, where r_{AB} = correlation coefficient.

For example, a Pearson correlation between memory strategy use (MEM) and retrieval strategy use (RET) was found to be 0.53. Each strategy variable is made up of five Likert-scale questionnaire items. The Cronbach's alpha coefficients of MEM and RET were 0.65 and 0.70, respectively. The correction for attenuation for their correlation is: 0.79 (i.e. $0.53 \div \sqrt{[0.65 \times 0.70]} \rightarrow 0.53 \div \sqrt{0.455} \rightarrow 0.53 \div 0.675$). It is important to stress again that Pearson correlations and other standard correlational analyses assume that observed scores for variables are free of *error of measurement*. That is, if the reliability estimates for both variables are 1.0, the corrected correlation using the correction formula above is 0.53.

The Pearson correlation

The *Pearson Product Moment correlation* (Pearson's *r*) describes the relationship between two continuous variables. The Pearson correlation is known as a simple *bivariate* correlation—the most common measure of linear relationship. Pearson correlation can be used for numeric variables on *continuous scales* such as interval and ratio scales. Two variables must be from the same participants. A data set must be *normally distributed* or close to a normally distributed shape. The Pearson correlation is a parametric test.

There are five statistical assumptions that we need to check prior to doing a Pearson correlation: (1) Pairs of data are related (i.e. X and Y scores are from the same person); (2) continuous or interval-like data; (3) normal distribution; (4) linearity (i.e. the X–Y relationship can be represented as a straight line; see scatter plot below); and (5) a spread of score variability. Assumptions 1 and 2 are easy to check. Assumptions 3 and 5 can be addressed by computing descriptive statistics and creating a histogram. Assumption 4 is checked through a scatter plot. After we tick off these assumptions, we can perform a Pearson correlation analysis. The data *Ch11 Pearson.sav* (downloadable from the *companion website*) will be used to illustrate this analysis. These data examine the relationship between

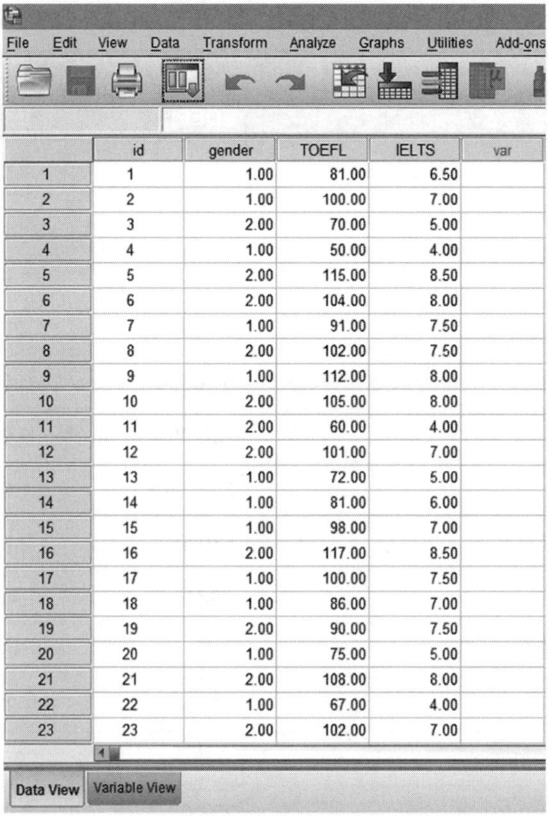

	id	gender	TOEFL	IELTS	var
1	1	1.00	81.00	6.50	
2	2	1.00	100.00	7.00	
3	3	2.00	70.00	5.00	
4	4	1.00	50.00	4.00	
5	5	2.00	115.00	8.50	
6	6	2.00	104.00	8.00	
7	7	1.00	91.00	7.50	
8	8	2.00	102.00	7.50	
9	9	1.00	112.00	8.00	
10	10	2.00	105.00	8.00	
11	11	2.00	60.00	4.00	
12	12	2.00	101.00	7.00	
13	13	1.00	72.00	5.00	
14	14	1.00	81.00	6.00	
15	15	1.00	98.00	7.00	
16	16	2.00	117.00	8.50	
17	17	1.00	100.00	7.50	
18	18	1.00	86.00	7.00	
19	19	2.00	90.00	7.50	
20	20	1.00	75.00	5.00	
21	21	2.00	108.00	8.00	
22	22	1.00	67.00	4.00	
23	23	2.00	102.00	7.00	

Data View Variable View

FIGURE 11.2   *Pearson correlation SPSS file*

TOEFL and IELTS test performance among 51 students (see Figure 11.2). Each student took both tests, which are measures of ESL or EFL academic English proficiency. Both scores are the overall scores.

Check the descriptive statistics

We will examine the descriptive statistics of both the TOEFL and IELTS variables and check if they are normally distributed. See Chapter 9 for how to perform descriptive statistics in SPSS. Check also the *Explore* options in the *Descriptive Statistics* menu, so you can check the 95 percent confidence interval of the mean. Table 11.2 presents the descriptive statistics. According to Table 11.2, the data set is normally distributed. Note that the standard error of the mean for the TOEFL scores is quite large.

Table 11.2 Descriptive statistics of the TOEFL and IELTS scores (N = 51)

Statistics		TOEFL	IELTS
N	Valid	51	51
	Missing	0	0
Mean		82.8039	6.0196
Std. Error of Mean		3.34359	.23679
Median		87.0000	6.5000
Mode		100.00[a]	7.00
Std. Deviation		23.87804	1.69104
Variance		570.161	2.860
Skewness		-.684	-.465
Std. Error of Skewness		.333	.333
Kurtosis		-.182	-.952
Std. Error of Kurtosis		.656	.656
Minimum		25.00	3.00
Maximum		118.00	8.50
Percentiles	25	67.0000	5.0000
	50	87.0000	6.5000
	75	102.0000	7.5000

a. Multiple modes exist. The smallest value is shown

Check the scatter plot

As illustrated in Chapter 9, the *Graph* menu has a *Legacy Dialogs* option. Choose *Scatter/Dot* option. Choose *Simple Scatter* and click *Define*. Figure 11.3 will appear. Move *TOEFL* to the Y-axis and *IELTS* to the X-axis. Then click *OK*. Figure 11.4 is the scatter plot obtained. It is important to note that SPSS does not produce a 45-degree line by default. To do this, you can double-click the figure. A new pop-up window will appear (see Figure 11.5). Then you have the option to choose to create the line. As you can see

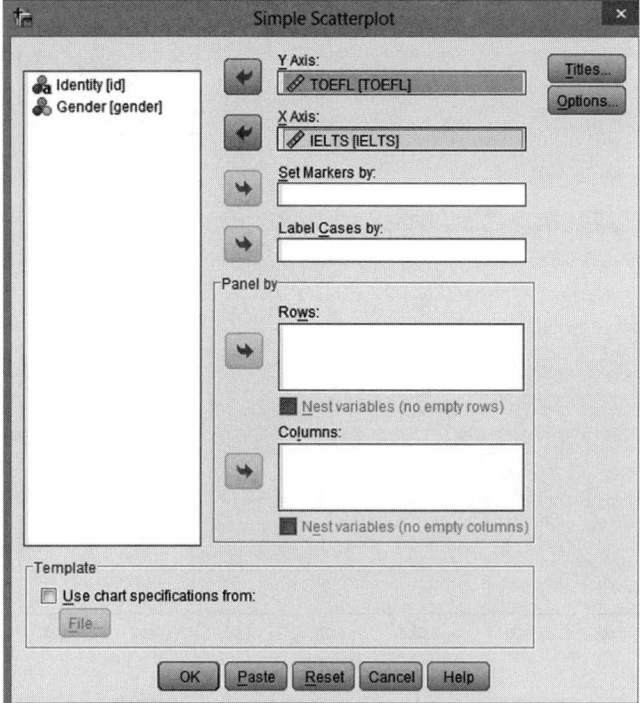

FIGURE 11.3 *SPSS dialog for creating a scatter plot*

in Figure 11.5, you can click on the icon *Add Fit Line at Total*. In Figure 11.5, two options were chosen. In the *Option* menu of Figure 11.5, you can choose the option called *Reference Line from Equation*, which will produce another line as shown in Figure 11.4. *Add Fit Line at Total* is sufficient to check whether the two variables are linear.

According to Figure 11.4, we can say that the variables have a linear relationship. This figure also indicates the R^2 to be 0.86. On the basis of this scatter plot, we have confidence that the linearity assumption has been met.

How to run the Pearson correlational analysis

 In the drop-down menu, select *Analyze → Correlate → Bivariate*. A dialog box will appear (see Figure 11.6)

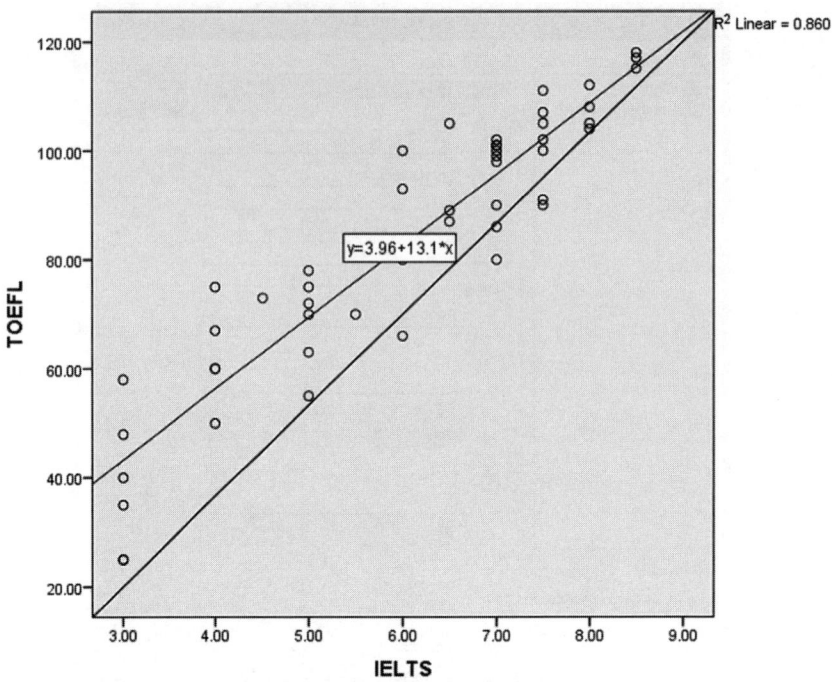

FIGURE 11.4   *SPSS Scatter plot between TOEFL and IELTS scores*

In Figure 11.6, move the TOEFL and IELTS variables to the variables box. Click *Pearson, Two-tailed, Flag Significant Correlations* and *OK*. Table 11.3 presents the SPSS output on the Pearson correlational analysis. Notice the redundancy in the table, so you need to focus on one half of the table. According to Table 11.3, the Pearson correlation coefficient was 0.93 (R^2 = 0.86, large effect size) and was significant at 0.01. Note that if we set the *p*-value to be 0.05, in our report we should indicate that this correlation was significant at 0.05 (despite the SPSS output). Note also that SPSS does not produce the *t*-score in the output. There is no need to try to obtain the *t*-score for this purpose.

The point-biserial correlation

The *point-biserial correlation* is a non-parametric test and a special case of the Pearson correlation. It can be used to examine the relationship between a *dichotomous variable* (e.g. male–female and yes–no) and a *continuous variable* (e.g. test scores).

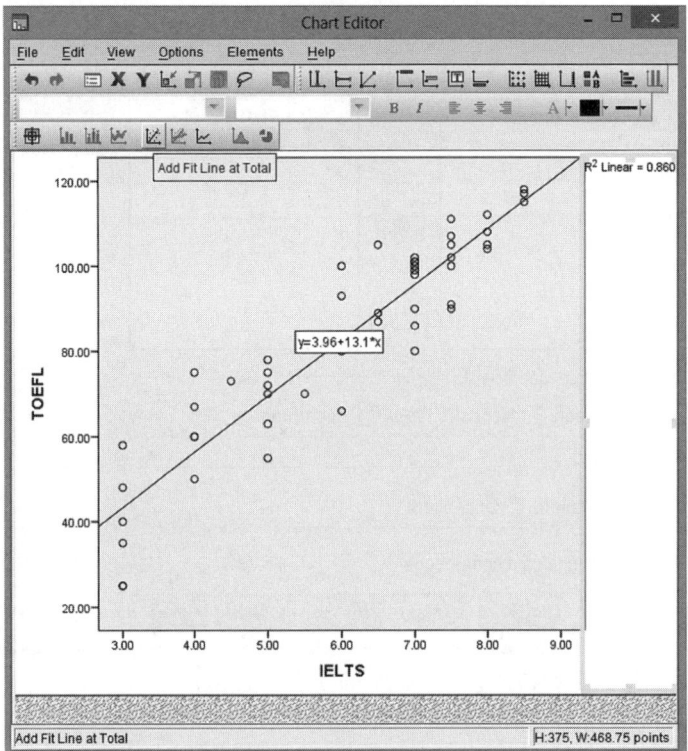

FIGURE 11.5 *Where to add the fit line in the chart editor*

How to run the point-biserial correlation

There is no special menu in SPSS to perform a point-biserial correlation, but we can do this analysis using Pearson since it is a special case of the Pearson correlation. The data *Ch11 Pointbiserial.sav* (downloadable from the *companion website*) will be used to illustrate this analysis (see Figure 11.7). In this file, we aim to examine the relationship between an ability-level variable (high and low) and an English reading test score (N = 17). Table 11.4 presents the point-biserial correlation. According to Table 11.4, there was a strong association between the two ability levels and the reading test scores ($r = 0.82$, $R^2 = 0.67$, large effect size). Note that we can also perform a *t*-test to examine the difference between the two groups (see Chapter 13). The *t*-test would imply that the ability level determined the differences in the reading test scores.

The Spearman's rho correlation

The *Spearman's rho correlation* (ρ) is a non-parametric test. The *Spearman correlation* is typically used for numeric variables on an ordinal or ranked

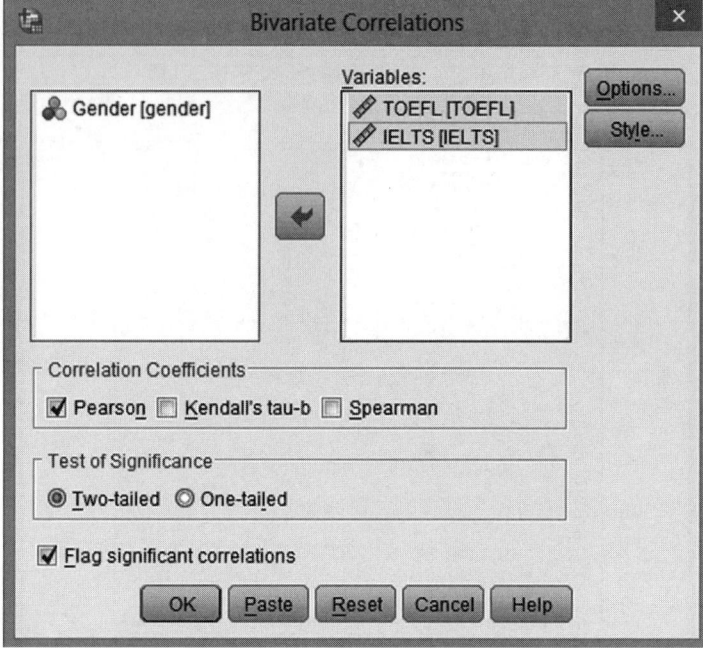

FIGURE 11.6 *SPSS dialog for the Pearson correlation*

Table 11.3 SPSS output for the Pearson correlation between the TOEFL and IELTS scores (N = 51)

Correlations		TOEFL	IELTS
TOEFL	Pearson Correlation	1	.928**
	Sig. (2-tailed)		.000
	N	51	51
IELTS	Pearson Correlation	.928**	1
	Sig. (2-tailed)	.000	
	N	51	51

**. Correlation is significant at the 0.01 level (2-tailed).

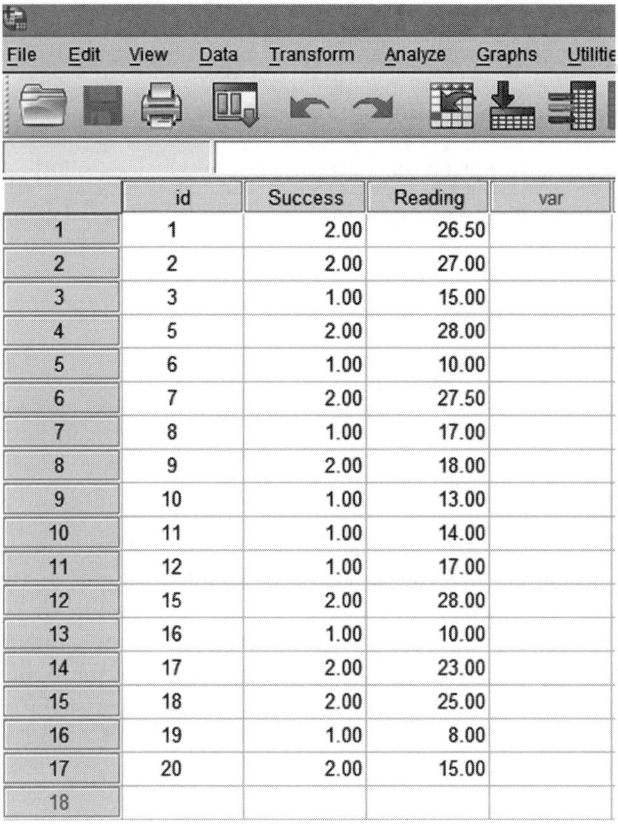

	id	Success	Reading	var
1	1	2.00	26.50	
2	2	2.00	27.00	
3	3	1.00	15.00	
4	5	2.00	28.00	
5	6	1.00	10.00	
6	7	2.00	27.50	
7	8	1.00	17.00	
8	9	2.00	18.00	
9	10	1.00	13.00	
10	11	1.00	14.00	
11	12	1.00	17.00	
12	15	2.00	28.00	
13	16	1.00	10.00	
14	17	2.00	23.00	
15	18	2.00	25.00	
16	19	1.00	8.00	
17	20	2.00	15.00	
18				

FIGURE 11.7   *Point-biserial correlation SPSS file*

scale (e.g. ranked list of test results, letter grades A–F and steps on a Likert scale). The Spearman can calculate the correlation of an ordinal score with an interval score. Since continuous variables will be ranked for the Spearman correlation analysis, some information may be lost. However, the Spearman correlation is not affected by extreme values or outliers because the data will be ranked.

How to run the Spearman correlation

The procedures involved in the Spearman correlational analysis in SPSS are the same as those used for the Pearson correlation (see Figure 11.6). We simply choose *Spearman* instead of *Pearson*. Note that we can run three correlational tests (including Kendall's tau-b discussed below) simultaneously in SPSS. Nonetheless, as we know the nature of our data, our choice of correlational tests is informed. The data *Ch11 Spearman.sav* (downloadable

Table 11.4 SPSS output for the point-biserial correlation (N =17)

Correlations			Success	Reading Test
Success	Pearson Correlation		1	.821**
	Sig. (2-tailed)			.000
	N		17	17
Reading Test	Pearson Correlation		.821**	1
	Sig. (2-tailed)		.000	
	N		17	17

**. Correlation is significant at the 0.01 level (2-tailed).

from the *companion website*) will be used to illustrate this analysis. Figure 11.8 presents the Spearman SPSS file. In this file, we aim to examine the relationship between an English grade of tenth grade students and an English vocabulary test score (N = 20). Table 11.5 presents the Spearman correlation. According to Table 11.5, there was a strong association between the English grade and the vocabulary test score ($\rho = 0.87$, $R^2 = 0.76$, large effect size).

Table 11.5 SPSS output for the Spearman correlation (N =20)

Correlations			English Grade	Vocabulary Test
Spearman's rho	English Grade	Correlation Coefficient	1.000	.870**
		Sig. (2-tailed)	.	.000
		N	20	20
	Vocabulary Test	Correlation Coefficient	.870**	1.000
		Sig. (2-tailed)	.000	.
		N	20	20

**. Correlation is significant at the 0.01 level (2-tailed).

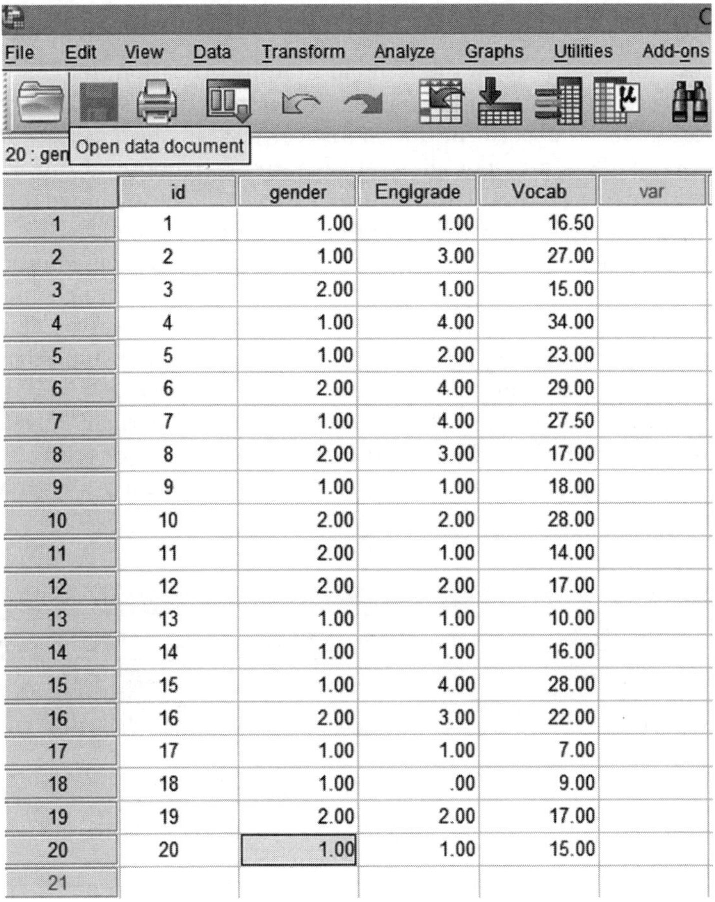

	id	gender	Englgrade	Vocab	var
File Edit View Data Transform Analyze Graphs Utilities Add-ons					
20 : ge| Open data document					
1	1	1.00	1.00	16.50	
2	2	1.00	3.00	27.00	
3	3	2.00	1.00	15.00	
4	4	1.00	4.00	34.00	
5	5	1.00	2.00	23.00	
6	6	2.00	4.00	29.00	
7	7	1.00	4.00	27.50	
8	8	2.00	3.00	17.00	
9	9	1.00	1.00	18.00	
10	10	2.00	2.00	28.00	
11	11	2.00	1.00	14.00	
12	12	2.00	2.00	17.00	
13	13	1.00	1.00	10.00	
14	14	1.00	1.00	16.00	
15	15	1.00	4.00	28.00	
16	16	2.00	3.00	22.00	
17	17	1.00	1.00	7.00	
18	18	1.00	.00	9.00	
19	19	2.00	2.00	17.00	
20	20	1.00	1.00	15.00	
21					

FIGURE 11.8   *Spearman SPSS file*

The Kendall's tau-b correlation

The *Kendall's tau-b* correlation is a non-parametric alternative to the Spearman correlation. It is, however, useful for examining the level of agreement and disagreement between two sources of data. For example, there are 20 students in the class and the two regular English teachers for the class are asked to rank them from highest (1) to lowest (20), according to their ability. We are interested to see if the two teachers see students' ability the same way. In another example, if a number of judges are used to score and rank candidates in order of performance outcomes, we would like to see the extent to which these judges agree with their ranking. The Kendall correlation subtracts the portion of the paired data that agree from that of the paired data that disagree.

How to run the Kendall's tau-b correlation in SPSS

The procedures involved in the Kendall's tau-b correlation in SPSS are the same as those used for the Pearson one. It is important to check descriptive statistics before you perform any statistical test. In the *bivariate dialog*, choose *Kendall's tau-b*. For illustrative purposes, choose also *Spearman* (explained further below). The data *Ch11 Kendall.sav* (downloadable from the *companion website*) will be used to illustrate this analysis (see Figure 11.9). In this file, three judges were asked to rate the writing ability of 15 teacher applicants. The judges included one experienced writing expert and two novice judges who received some training before the rating. It should be noted that Judges 1 and 2 ranked the candidates quite similarly, while Judge 3 had two extreme discrepancies in the ranking (i.e. Candidates 1 and 15). Table 11.6 presents the Kendall tau-b and Spearman correlations between the three judges. We should expect a correlation of 0.70 or above to show a strong agreement since 0.70 accounts for nearly 50 percent of the variances.

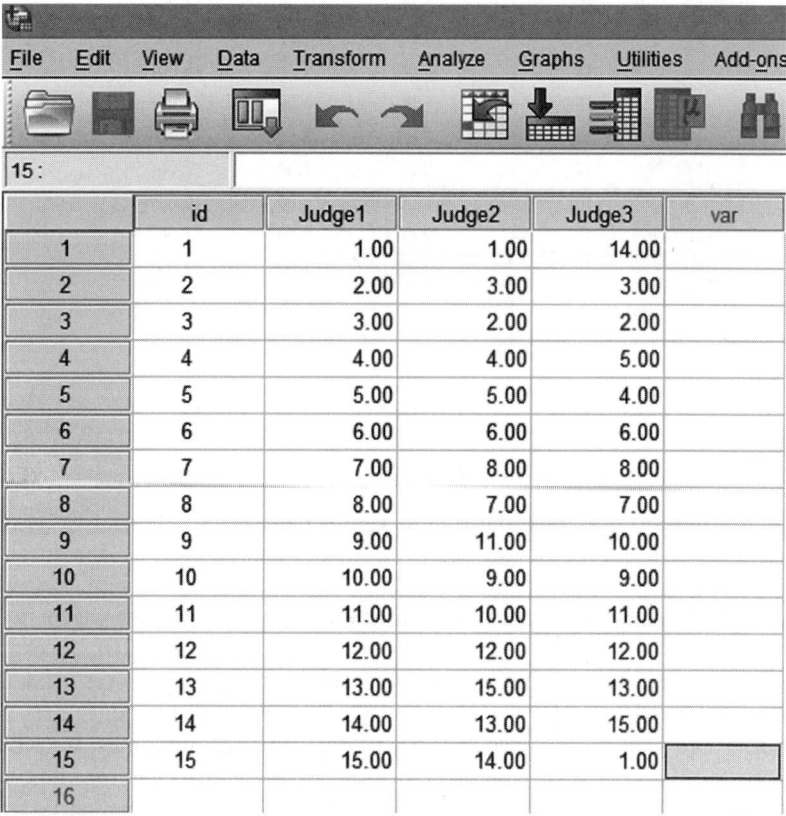

FIGURE 11.9   *Kendall SPSS file*

According to Table 11.6, the Kendall correlations indicate a strong association between the expert judge and the experienced judge (0.89, R^2 = 0.79, large effect size). However, the novice judge disagreed to a significant degree with the other two judges (0.43 (R^2 = 0.18) and 0.47 (R^2 = 0.22), respectively, medium effect size). When we look at the Spearman correlations, the expert and experienced judges' correlation was large. However, the Spearman correlation is better at detecting the large discrepancies in the rankings by Judge 3. The Spearman correlation produced non-significant correlations between Judge 3 and the other two judges. As we can see in these comparative analyses, both correlations can be used to complement each other to inform our decision.

The Phi correlation

The *Phi (ø) correlation* is a non-parametric test that is not used much in correlational studies. The Phi correlation is, however, useful for examining the relationship between *two dichotomous variables* (e.g. male or female, living or dead, pass or fail, agree or disagree, correct or wrong, homework or no homework, pair work or individual work). These variables can be assigned as 1 or 0, or 1 or 2, depending on how we code them in SPSS.

How to run the Phi correlation in SPSS

The data *Ch11 Phi.sav* (downloadable from the *companion website*) will be used to illustrate this analysis (see Figure 11.10). In this file, 30 male and female students were asked whether they preferred to be given homework. Males and females are coded 1 and 2, respectively. No homework and homework were coded as 1 and 2, respectively. We would like to see whether there is an association between gender and the preference for homework. The phi correlation does not have the same location in SPSS as the above correlational tests. It can be performed as follows.

 In the drop-down menu, select *Analyze → Descriptive Statistics → Crosstab*. A dialog box will appear (see Figure 11.11)

In Figure 11.11, move *Homework* into *Row* and *Gender* into *Column*. Then click *Statistics*. You will see several options of tests. Choose *Phi and*

Table 11.6 SPSS output for the Kendall's tau and Spearman correlations (N =15)

			Correlations		
			Expert Judge	**Experienced Judge**	**Novice Judge**
Kendall's tau_b	Expert Judge	Correlation Coefficient	1.000	.886**	.429*
		Sig. (2-tailed)	.	.000	.026
		N	15	15	15
	Experienced Judge	Correlation Coefficient	.886**	1.000	.467*
		Sig. (2-tailed)	.000	.	.015
		N	15	15	15
	Novice Judge	Correlation Coefficient	.429*	.467*	1.000
		Sig. (2-tailed)	.026	.015	.
		N	15	15	15
Spearman's rho	Expert Judge	Correlation Coefficient	1.000	.971**	.332
		Sig. (2-tailed)	.	.000	.226
		N	15	15	15
	Experienced Judge	Correlation Coefficient	.971**	1.000	.375
		Sig. (2-tailed)	.000	.	.168
		N	15	15	15
	Novice Judge	Correlation Coefficient	.332	.375	1.000
		Sig. (2-tailed)	.226	.168	.
		N	15	15	15

*. Correlation is significant at the 0.05 level (2-tailed).
**. Correlation is significant at the 0.01 level (2-tailed).

	id	Gender	Homework
1	1	1.00	1.00
2	2	2.00	2.00
3	3	2.00	1.00
4	4	2.00	2.00
5	5	1.00	1.00
6	6	1.00	2.00
7	7	1.00	1.00
8	8	2.00	2.00
9	9	2.00	1.00
10	10	2.00	2.00
11	11	1.00	1.00
12	12	1.00	2.00
13	13	2.00	2.00
14	14	1.00	2.00
15	15	2.00	2.00
16	16	2.00	1.00
17	17	1.00	1.00
18	18	2.00	2.00
19	18	2.00	1.00
20	20	1.00	1.00
21	21	1.00	1.00
22	22	1.00	2.00
23	23	2.00	2.00

FIGURE 11.10   *Phi SPSS file*

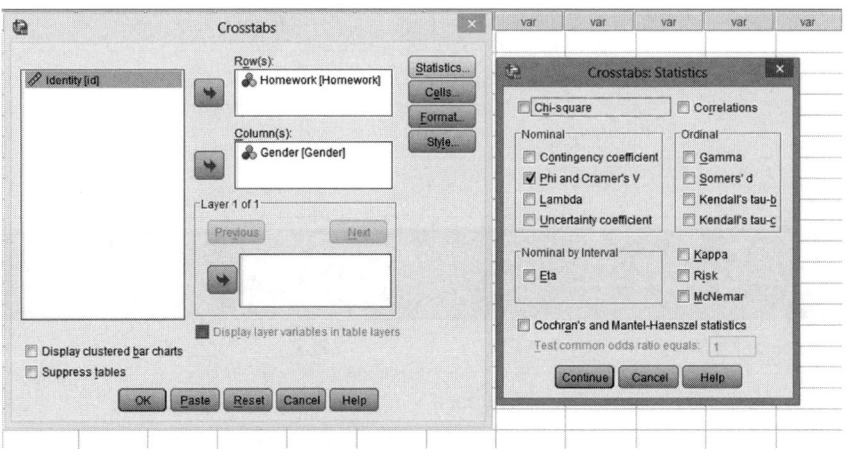

FIGURE 11.11   *SPSS dialog for the phi correlation*

Cramer's V. Click *Continue* and then *OK*. Table 11.7 presents the phi correlation outputs. The Phi correlation was 0.27 and it is not statistically significant at 0.05. This means that the gender variable does not have an association with students' preference for homework.

Factors affecting correlation coefficients

A correlation coefficient is affected by several factors, some known and some unknown. First, outliers can affect correlations. If we detect extreme scores, their removal may be necessary. Of course, this needs to be justified. Second, a correlation coefficient is affected by the reliability of the research instruments. Hence, we need to analyze all the instruments used to produce data for the computation of correlations. The higher the reliability, the more confidence we have in the correlational finding. If research instruments are not highly reliable, a correction for attenuation (discussed above) should be performed and accompany the uncorrected correlation. Third, like most standard statistics (e.g. *t*-tests, ANOVAs and chi-square test), correlational analysis assumes that the data are perfectly reliable (i.e. there is no error in the observed scores). Our empirical knowledge based on correlational analysis is limited to this matter. Fourth, the strength of a relationship can

Table 11.7 SPSS output for the phi correlation (N = 30)

Homework * Gender Crosstabulation				
Count				
		Gender		Total
		male	female	
Homework	No homework	9	5	14
	homework	6	10	16
Total		15	15	30

Symmetric Measures			
		Value	Approx. Sig.
Nominal by Nominal	Phi	.267	.143
	Cramer's V	.267	.143
N of Valid Cases		30	

be restricted by a data or score range. For example, if one variable has a very limited range (e.g. everybody gets between 6 and 8 on the IELTS test), the correlation will be lower and generally less interpretable. Data with a limited range of values are known as *truncated data*. It should be noted that the IELTS has a score from 1 to 9. Therefore, the broader the score range on both variables (i.e. variability of scores), the stronger and more meaningful the correlation. Finally, similar to the above, a correlation coefficient is affected by outliers. Unlike truncated data, a data set that has numerous high scores and numerous low scores, but few medium scores can result in a misleading correlation coefficient. In such a case, a parametric correlational analysis is not appropriate.

Summary

This chapter has illustrated how inferential statistics can be run in SPSS, focusing on correlational analyses. Studying correlation is one of the most efficient ways for new students of statistics to familiarize themselves with the abstract concepts associated with inferential statistics. Inferential statistics are by no means perfect in terms of their ability to address research questions, due to the nature of data and the context in which an experimental study takes place. Conclusions made on the basis of inferential statistics are based on probability. The next chapter will examine statistical procedures in examining the reliability of research instruments and data collection techniques.

Research exercise

To download exercises for this chapter visit: http://www.bloomsbury.com/experimental-research-methods-in-language-learning-9781441189110/

Discussion questions

1 Why do you think it is not suitable to use correlation to explain causation?
2 What is the difference between a correlation coefficient and a shared variance?
3 Do you think setting a probability value to be less than 0.05 is better or worse than setting it at 0.01? Why do you think so?
4 Can you think of a situation where truncated data (i.e. scores are clustered near the top or bottom of the score range) may affect a correlation

coefficient? That is, a correlation coefficient may not reflect the true relationship between two variables.

5 Reflection: What is the most important lesson you have learned from this chapter?

Further reading

Larson-Hall, J 2010, *A guide to doing statistics in second language research using SPSS*, Routledge, New York.

Chapter 6 presents several types of correlational analyses using SPSS.

Phakiti, A in press, 2015, 'Quantitative methods and analysis', in B Paltridge & A Phakiti (eds), *Research methods in applied linguistics*, Bloomsbury, London.

This chapter presents an approach to quantitative research and statistical analysis in applied linguistics.

Urdan, TC 2005, *Statistics in plain English*, Lawrence Erlbaum Associates, Mahwah, NJ.

Chapter 8 explains the conceptual principles of correlational analysis comprehensively with some statistical formulas so that the reader can see where a correlation coefficient is from.

CHAPTER TWELVE

Reliability and Reliability Analysis

Leading questions

1 What is reliability?
2 How do we know that a research instrument is reliable?
3 Why do you think reliability is important for experimental research?

Introduction

This chapter addresses the important issues of the reliability of research instruments and the data elicitation techniques. The first part of this chapter discusses several important conceptual issues related to reliability and reliability analysis (e.g. how reliability is related to validity, the classical true score theory, types of reliability estimates, standard error of measurement, and the factors affecting reliability estimates). The second part of this chapter presents how to calculate several reliability estimates through SPSS.

The reliability and validity of a measure

Norris and Ortega (2003), who discussed the importance of the reliability of SLA research instruments and measures, stressed that researchers must provide estimates of their research instruments in their reports. Researchers should not assume that their instruments are reliable merely because they have already piloted them or because they adopt them from trusted researchers in the field who originally reported high reliability estimates of the instruments. For example, Al-Homoud and Schmitt (2009) did not report the actual test reliability coefficient used in their reported experimental study. Instead, they reported that 'in the Schmitt *et al.* validation study, these tests had reliability figures of .920 (2000, Version 1), .922 (2000, Version 2), .929 (3000, 1), .927 (3000, 2), .958 (Academic Word List, 1), and .960 (Academic Word List, 2)' (p. 390).

While it might well be that these tests were also highly reliable, it is difficult to be certain that previously reported reliability estimates also applied to a particular study. If there is any particular reason why a reliability estimate could not be computed (e.g. due to a limited sample size), this should be mentioned in the report and acknowledged in the section dealing with limitations. A reliability estimate largely depends on the participants taking the tests, and the context in which they take them, and the test items or tasks that have been used. In other words, *a reliability estimate is based on, among other factors, the mean and standard deviation of the scores obtained by the participants in the tests, the number of test items or tasks, and the level of difficulty, and discrimination functions of the test items or tasks.* It is not an *inherent property* of an instrument, but rather, is context-dependent (i.e. it depends on where, when and by whom it is used).

Psychological and educational measurement theory (e.g. Cronbach 1988; Messick 1989) and language testing and assessment theory (e.g. McNamara 1996) have long emphasized the importance of measurement validity in educational research. Test validity was originally defined as *the degree to which a measure captures what it claims to measure.* It has long been known that test reliability is one type of validity evidence. Reliability is a necessary, but insufficient condition for measurement validity. Experimental researchers are required to evaluate both the reliability coefficient of their instruments and the validity of their measurements. Evidence of a high reliability coefficient, which implies a good level of precision and consistency of the instruments used, needs to be reported.

In several published experimental studies, even in high-ranking journals, researchers have not reported on the reliability of their research instruments or data analysis. Furthermore, numerous experimental studies that could not be published in peer-review journals suffer from poor instrument reliability analysis. As you are learning how to conduct an experimental study, it is important for you to understand what we mean by reliability and what experimental researchers need to do to check the reliability of their research instruments during the rating and scoring procedures.

Through various examples of experimental studies, we have learned that experimental researchers collect learners' language productions, such as in speaking and writing through various language tasks during the pretest and posttest stages of their studies. They also collect evidence of learners' psychological perceptions, such as motivation, self-regulation, learning strategies and anxiety. The reason they need such data is that they aim to examine whether there is a statistically significant difference between the pretest and posttest scores, as well as the posttest scores between experimental and control groups. They would like to know to what extent learners in different comparison groups differ.

Therefore, any claims about improvement or a causal-like relationship through an experimental exposure *cannot be valid* if research instruments *are not reliable*. The research instruments will be seen to be unreliable if, for example, the scoring of student performance on the basis of the pretest and posttest is inconsistent (e.g. sometimes high-ability students receive low scores when their performance is good or sometimes low-ability learners are awarded much higher scores when their performance is poor). If researchers use such scores, it would not accurately reflect the reality of the causal-like relationship or improvement of learning.

Estimating a reliability coefficient

Let us look at some examples of how experimental researchers reported on their research instruments or data coding procedures.

Takimoto (2007, p. 13) estimated interrater reliability through the use of the correlation of the two raters' scores. Both the discourse completion and role-play tests had a correlation of 0.99. The *Cronbach alpha* reliability estimates were also used for the four tests he used (0.85 for the listening test, 0.93 for the role-play, 0.89 for the acceptability judgment test and 0.92 for the discourse completion test).

Macaro and Erler (2008, p. 107) reported that 'interrater reliability was provided for by separate blind marking of 10 percent of each of the four tests by the two researchers. The correlations (Pearson's r) obtained between the two researchers were: Time 1 'translation' $r = .948$; Time 1 'idea units' $r = .930$; Time 2 'translation' $r = .960$; Time 2 'idea units' $r = .818$. All correlations were significant ($p < .01$). Disagreements were resolved via discussion.'

Adams *et al.* (2011) discussed their scoring and coding procedure as follows: 'The oral tests were scored by two of the researchers; the few discrepancies were discussed until 100 percent agreement was reached. The written tests were scored by an independent rater and then the scores were reviewed by two of the researchers. Interrater reliability was calculated to be 98 percent.'

Satar and Özdener (2008, pp. 601–2) used different methods to ensure reliability: 'Interrater reliability (Cronbach's alpha = .991, Pearson's corre-lation coefficient = .984); intrarater reliability (first rater: Cronbach's alpha = .988, Pearson's correlation coefficient = .977, second rater: Cronbach's alpha = .995, Pearson's correlation coefficient = .990).'

Ishida (2004) transcribed recorded utterances and two coders coded the transcriptions independently in regard to learners' morphology in an obligatory and non-obligatory context. After Ishida coded '831 utterances,

23 percent (187 utterances) were also coded by the other rater after a training session. The interrater reliability was .90 (kappa = 0.86)' (p. 340).

Sheen (2010) sought to understand whether there was any difference between the effects of oral and written corrective feedback on learners' accuracy in using English articles. In grading the speeded dictation test and writing test that he used, Sheen pointed out that a second researcher coded a sample of 25 percent of the total dictation and writing data. For the pretest, posttest, and delayed posttest dictation test, 'the percentage agreement scores were 87.1, 89.2, and 92.1, respectively' and for the pretest, posttest, and delayed posttest writing test, '84.4, 88.3, and 89.2, respectively' (p. 219).

The high reliability estimates of measures (e.g. 0.90) calculated in these examples are desirable. We will discuss further below what the estimates mean. Reliability is a *complex issue* because there are different aspects we need to take into account. Reliability needs to be understood together with *validity*. Researchers aim to collect information associated with the constructs of interest. Data (e.g. assigned scores or values) from tests, questionnaires, interviews and think-aloud protocols, for example, must be *accurate* and reflect the target construct. *Accuracy* is related to the standards or criteria researchers set to evaluate performance. Accuracy is therefore related to the *theoretical validity* of the research construct.

In experimental research, we consider instrument and data elicitation reliability estimates before the experiment takes place (e.g. by considering existing research instruments in terms of their reliability, considering whether we have adequate items or tasks to elicit performance, behaviors, or cognitive processes, and piloting instruments or data collection procedures to check whether they are reliable enough for use in the main study). We also consider them *after we have conducted the experiment and collected the data* (e.g. by analyzing the performance rating or data coding by two raters or coders). The results of both phases of analysis are critical to the validity of our experimental study.

What is discussed in this chapter is applicable and useful for analysis both before and after the data collection. Within the postpositivist paradigm, researchers are expected to report the *actual reliability estimates* of the instruments or data elicitation procedures to be used to answer the research questions or hypotheses. Researchers need to be *impartial* in their judgment so that they can get closer to the truth or what they aim to understand (see Chapter 3).

What does a reliability estimate tell us?

Reliability is typically described as the *consistency of scoring* (e.g. language tests or productive tasks), *coding* (e.g. coding think-aloud or interview data) or *rating* (e.g. Likert scale questionnaires and quantitative observations).

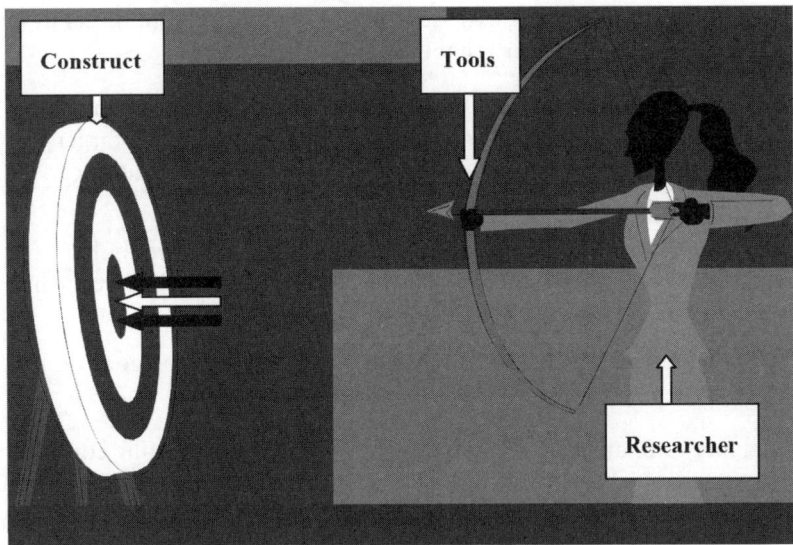

FIGURE 12.1 *Reliability as consistency in reaching the target*

Perhaps the best way to conceptualize what we mean by consistency is to use an analogy with archery. Suppose we aim at stationary circular targets at varying distances using different types of bow (see Figure 12.1).

In our case, as researchers we aim to measure a construct and suppose that our construct is the *center* of the circular targets. Here we know our target clearly, so we can aim at it. However, if we were blindfolded and tried to hit the target, what would happen? We would most likely miss and have wasted our arrows and time. This is similar to a situation in which we do not define a construct well enough. If we do not know what it is that we are looking for, it will be difficult to find it.

Our instruments would be the analog of the bow and arrows. Different researchers can make their own bow and arrows that can help them reach their targets as precisely as possible. The quality of the bow and arrows depends on how much we can invest and are willing to pay. This is analogous to how much we spend on developing our research instruments and what resources we have to help us develop them.

However, the bow and arrows alone are not enough. We need to *take an action* to shoot at the target. This is analogous to the fact that we have to be in a research setting to ask participants to answer a questionnaire or take a test. Furthermore, if we have never shot an arrow before, we are bound to miss the target several times. We need to practise. It would be good to have a coach (i.e. a research supervisor) to help us learn how to reach the target effectively and wisely. Practicing could also help us improve our skill (this is analogous to gaining experience in conducting research). Let us now consider the question of our reliability.

- *Unreliable and invalid*: Our archery results would be both unreliable and invalid if our arrows missed the circular target altogether and randomly hit the circular targets without once landing in the goal (the center).

- *Reliable but invalid*: In this case, our arrows repeatedly hit around or at the same spot in the circular targets, but never hit the goal.

- *Reliable and valid*: This was when our arrows hit the goal consistently.

A reliability estimate is therefore an estimate of scoring or rating consistency and as we can see above, it is not a sufficient condition. If scoring or rating is highly consistent, the reliability estimate should be at least 0.90 (i.e. 90 percent consistent). This value tells us that the majority of what we capture lands on target. When grading language performance and coding qualitative data, the reliability is derived from assessors, raters, coders or researchers who assign scores, make a judgment on learners' performance or quantify frequencies of behaviors. Researchers are *expected to* report on interrater or intercoder reliability estimates. When the method of scoring is *objective* (e.g. in multiple-choice or true–false techniques where answers are exact or absolute), researchers report an internal consistency estimate (or a test reliability estimate).

When learners complete Likert-scale questionnaires, the reliability derives from *the learners* since they need to read questionnaire items and evaluate the extent to which each item is true for them. A Cronbach's alpha (α) estimate is generally used. This is also the case when researchers use a quantitative observation scheme. Classroom observers are the source of reliability because the rating is given based on what is going on through their perceptions. Intra-observer reliability can be calculated using a Cronbach's alpha. However, when two observers are used, it is important to know *how much they agree* in their observations of the same aspect. In this case, a Pearson correlation coefficient between the two raters is typically used as an interrater reliability estimate, assuming that the data are normally distributed. Sometimes researchers report *intercoder* or interrater reliability estimates as *agreement percentages* (e.g. 95 percent agreement). We will discuss these reliability measures below.

As we can see from the reliability estimate values above, high reliability estimates are needed. They not only suggest that scoring or rating is highly consistent, but also imply that individuals will maintain a similar level of scores or ratings when repeated. For example, on the one hand, a reliability estimate of 0.90 of a language test indicates that students who score 60 out of 100 are 90 percent likely to obtain a similar test score when they take a similar test. This is *good news* because this likelihood is high. On the other hand, if a reliability estimate is 0.50, these same students are only 50 percent likely to obtain a similar score in a similar test. This is *not good news* because it is more difficult to be certain about their performance. It does not seem consistent. Experimental researchers who accept low reliability estimates for tests or measures in their data analysis to answer research questions are likely to produce misleading results and draw wrong conclusions, even though there is a statistical significance and a large effect size.

A reliability coefficient is built on the basis of a *correlation coefficient* (r). Generally speaking, a reliability coefficient is r^2, which ranges from 0 (0 percent reliable) to 1 (100 percent reliable). A reliability coefficient of 0.70 upwards (70 percent or above of the items consistently collects information about the target construct) is acceptable, but one of 0.90 or above is desirable for research (Dörnyei 2007). A reliability estimate is therefore the extent to which a research instrument, an observation or a coding system is *free from error of measurement.*

Classical true score theory

The idea behind the need to obtain test reliability estimates is derived from the classical true score theory (see Bachman 1990 and Brown 2014 for a detailed discussion on this topic). Theoretically speaking, an observed score (e.g. 5 out of 10, 70 out of 100) is composed of a *true score*, which is due to a learner's level of ability or traits, and an *error score*, which is due to factors other than a learner's level of ability or traits. These factors include the test methods or tasks being used, scoring rubrics, the raters' influence and a random error of measurement. Basically, we would like a score to be largely composed of the true score. According to classical true score theory, a calculation of a test reliability coefficient is essential because it tells us how much variance in a score is accounted for by the true score and how much by the error score. As discussed above, if a reliability estimate is 0.80, it suggests that the true score accounts for 80 percent of the score variance and the other 20 percent is accounted for by an error score.

Standard error of measurement

A reliability coefficient tells us about score consistency for a group of students. It tells us the precision of a test or a measure. It does not directly tell us whether an individual learner's score is within a reasonable range. To be able to identify this, we need to compute a *standard error of measurement (SEM) score.* We discussed the standard error of a mean in Chapter 9. The closer the standard error is to zero, the better the mean represents the group. In the same manner, the SEM score tells us a range of possible true scores for a learner. Before we move on to discussing how it can be calculated, let us think of a scenario where a reliability coefficient of a test is 1.0. We will know for sure that there is *no error score* in this test because it has perfect reliability. Given this, the standard error of measurement by default is *zero*. That is, whatever score an individual receives, it is their true score. However, a perfect reliability coefficient is an unattainable ideal because this coefficient is greatly affected by many factors (discussed below). In practice, SEMs are computed using the *reliability estimate* and the *standard deviation* of a test score. In a research report, it is therefore important to present the *standard deviation* of mean scores so that readers can compute the standard error of measurement.

An SEM statistic is used to determine a *68 percent confidence band* around a learner's score within which the learner's score would probably fall if the test were administered to them repeatedly. The purpose of the SEM is to estimate an average of the distribution of error deviation across all the test takers. The following is the formula that should be used to compute an SEM: *SD X √[1– a reliability coefficient*, where SD = a standard deviation on the test. For example, if a test has a reliability coefficient of 0.82 and SD is 5.29, we can compute the SEM as follows:

$$SEM = 5.29 \ X \ \sqrt{1-0.82} \quad \rightarrow 5.29 \ X \ \sqrt{0.18} \quad \rightarrow 5.29 \ X \ 0.42 \quad \rightarrow 2.24$$

So if a participant score was 28 out of 40, we simply use the SEM score to add and subtract the test score (i.e. 28 ± 2.24). Their true score would be within a range of 25.76 and 30.24. In this example, we see that a large SEM score will result in a large range of a score band. Now if the reliability coefficient is 1 and we use the SEM formula, we will find that the SEM score is *zero*.

Factors influencing a reliability coefficient

It is good to know that there is not one single factor that determines whether a test or measure is reliable. There are interrelated factors that influence the reliability coefficient of a test or a measure that need to be understood. As a researcher, once we realize potential factors, we can aim to control them. Sometimes we can have some control over these factors, but at other times, they are impossible to control.

1 The reliability coefficient of a test or measure is affected by whether or not it is scored *objectively*. If it is scored objectively (e.g. there is an answer key), the reliability coefficient is likely to be high as scoring will be consistent. If it is scored subjectively (e.g. in speaking and writing), the reliability coefficient is likely to be lower

than in the case of objective scoring. The reliability of performance assessment is affected by test tasks and rater characteristics, despite the raters' formal training.

2 The reliability is influenced by the *nature of the construct of interest*. Some constructs can be assessed more reliably than others because they are less complex (e.g. a grammar test versus an academic writing test). The more complex a construct, the less reliable an instrument or measure is.

3 The reliability is influenced by the *number of participants* or the *sample size*. With a large sample size, there will be access to students with a larger range of ability levels or the attributes we are interested in, than with a small sample size. A large sample size allows variability in a data set. A small sample size will result in a score restriction, which affects parameter estimates.

4 The reliability coefficient is influenced by *test length*. The longer the test, the more reliable it is. This principle is also true for *quantitative questionnaires*. The more items we include in a questionnaire, the more reliable it is. However, researchers need to consider the issue of the practicality of including many items, due to time and budget limitations. Researchers should also consider whether participants will be too tired to answer questions or items after a long period of time.

As mentioned above, in objective tests (e.g. multiple-choice vocabulary, grammar or reading tests) that contain many questions or tasks, we are likely to obtain a high reliability coefficient. The key reason for this is that we have more observations of the construct of interest, allowing us to observe the variability and stability of the learners' scores. Consequently, a number of performance assessments (e.g. essays and language production tests) exhibit a low reliability estimate.

The reliability coefficient is influenced by the *heterogeneity* of participants' abilities and attributes. The more variability in the scores obtained from participants, the more reliable a test or measure. Imagine a situation in which we give a TOEFL test to 100 beginner level students. Their scores would be all low and there would be little variability in their scores. If we calculated a reliability coefficient, we would obtain a low reliability coefficient. Now imagine we administered this same TOEFL test to 33 beginner, 34 intermediate and 33 advanced learners. The reliability coefficient would be high because the range of scores that the test could produce is much higher. The same principle applies to quantitative questionnaires. If we asked participants to report on the level of their motivation in language learning using a five-Likert scale questionnaire and if all participants were highly motivated, we would obtain similar reported scores across participants. There would be less variability in the scores obtained. The reliability estimate would be low, despite being *valid*.

Types and methods of calculation of reliability coefficients

We now explore a range of reliability coefficients that are used in quantitative and experimental research.

Language tests are used to measure learners' performance in some activity, be it a response to a test task or to some other elicitation technique. There are two types of reliability coefficient that need to be considered. The first is related to objective tests (e.g. multiple-choice tests, short-answer questions and true–false questions). This kind of test has a clear right or wrong answer, so marking is more or less objective. Anyone with the answer key can mark the test. With this type of test, we are interested in the nature of its *internal consistency*. In principle, we can understand a test's internal consistency using a *test-retest method* and a *parallel-test method*.

The *test-retest method* involves administering a test *twice* so that the stability of the test over time can be estimated. In other words, a learner taking the same test *yesterday*, *today* or *tomorrow* should get the same or similar score. Thus when we compute a correlation coefficient between two test scores based on the same test, it should be high. In many situations, this method is unrealistic as learners are likely to learn from their experience of taking the test the first time, and consequently get a higher score the second time they take it. The correlation between the two sets of scores is therefore likely to be unrealistically low.

A *parallel test method* follows a similar principle to the test-retest method, but administers two different but equivalent tests (e.g. forms A and B) to a single group of students. We discussed this method in Chapter 7 when we focused on the importance of test specifications. If two tests are parallel, the sets of student scores on the two tests should have a high correlation coefficient. In reality, it is nearly impossible to have identical parallel test forms. Nonetheless, for experimental research, a parallel-test method should be encouraged so that different pretests and posttests are used. It is important to note that the principles for the test-retest and parallel-test methods can be applied to other measures such as Likert scale questionnaires and rating scales. As you may have realized by now, both methods are often impractical and unrealistic to apply. Fortunately, research methodologists and statisticians have come up with a solution for some of their shortcomings. That is, we can compute a reliability coefficient from a one-time test administration.

Computing reliability coefficients in SPSS

In Chapter 11, we discussed how to compute different types of correlation coefficients. They are useful as indicators of a reliability coefficient of a measure as well. In this chapter, we will focus on the common reliability coefficients that are used in language tests including a *split-half reliability coefficient*, *Spearman–Brown prophecy coefficient* and *Cronbach's alpha coefficient*. We will discuss them in the context of SPSS. Each coefficient has a particular assumption that can be a limiting factor in accurately estimating a reliability coefficient as noted below.

The split-half reliability coefficient and Spearman–Brown prophecy coefficient in SPSS

The split-half reliability coefficient is suitable for objective tests with *dichotomous answers* (1 = correct; 0 = incorrect). The principle underlying the split-half reliability coefficient is simple. That is, it splits the test into two halves and calculates the correlation coefficient. It is argued that if learners are doing well in the first half, they should be doing well in the other half too. It is common to split the test items between the odd questions and the even questions. There are two limitations of this reliability coefficient. First, this method makes the assumption that all test questions are of the same level of difficulty. This is not always true because there are various constructs that a test may aim to measure. Some constructs are more difficult for students to demonstrate than others (e.g. identifying a main idea versus finding specific information in a text). This coefficient can be misleading. Second, the computed split-half coefficient only tells us half of the whole test reliability, so it needs to be adjusted. In other words, we need to transform the split-half coefficient to become a coefficient for the entire test.

We use the Spearman–Brown prophecy formula to produce the coefficient for the whole test for us. The Spearman–Brown prophecy formula is: *[2 × the split-half coefficient] ÷ [1 + the split-half coefficient]*. The Spearman–Brown prophecy calculation makes the statistical assumption that the two halves are parallel. In reality, this is not always true, particularly when a test has different sections that measure different language or psychological constructs. SPSS can calculate the split-half coefficient and the Spearman–Brown prophecy coefficient.

To illustrate how to calculate the split-half coefficient and Spearman–Brown prophecy coefficient, the data in *Ch12 Splithalf.sav* (downloadable from the *companion website*) will be used. This data set contains the comprehension reading test scores from 20 EFL students. There are 20 questions in this test. Figure 12.2 presents the split-half SPSS file. It is recommended that you compute the descriptive statistics of this data set

	ID	Q1	Q2	Q3	Q4	Q5	Q6
1	1.00	1.00	1.00	1.00	1.00	1.00	.00
2	2.00	1.00	1.00	.00	1.00	1.00	1.00
3	3.00	1.00	.00	1.00	.00	.00	.00
4	4.00	1.00	1.00	1.00	1.00	1.00	1.00
5	5.00	.00	.00	1.00	.00	.00	.00
6	6.00	1.00	1.00	.00	1.00	1.00	1.00
7	7.00	1.00	1.00	1.00	1.00	1.00	1.00
8	8.00	1.00	.00	1.00	.00	1.00	.00
9	9.00	1.00	.00	.00	.00	.00	.00
10	10.00	1.00	.00	.00	1.00	1.00	.00
11	11.00	.00	1.00	1.00	.00	1.00	1.00
12	12.00	1.00	1.00	1.00	1.00	1.00	.00
13	13.00	.00	1.00	.00	.00	.00	1.00
14	14.00	1.00	1.00	1.00	1.00	.00	.00
15	15.00	1.00	1.00	.00	1.00	1.00	1.00
16	16.00	.00	.00	1.00	.00	.00	1.00
17	17.00	.00	.00	1.00	.00	.00	.00
18	18.00	1.00	1.00	.00	1.00	1.00	.00
19	19.00	1.00	1.00	1.00	1.00	1.00	1.00
20	20.00	1.00	1.00	1.00	1.00	1.00	1.00
21							
22							
23							

Data View Variable View

FIGURE 12.2   *An outlook of the split-half SPSS file*

(follow the procedures in Chapter 9). Once you have completed examining
the descriptive statistics, you can begin to compute the split-half coefficient
following the instructions below.

 In the drop-down menu, select *Analyze → Scale → Reliability
Analysis*. A dialog box will appear (see Figure 12.3).

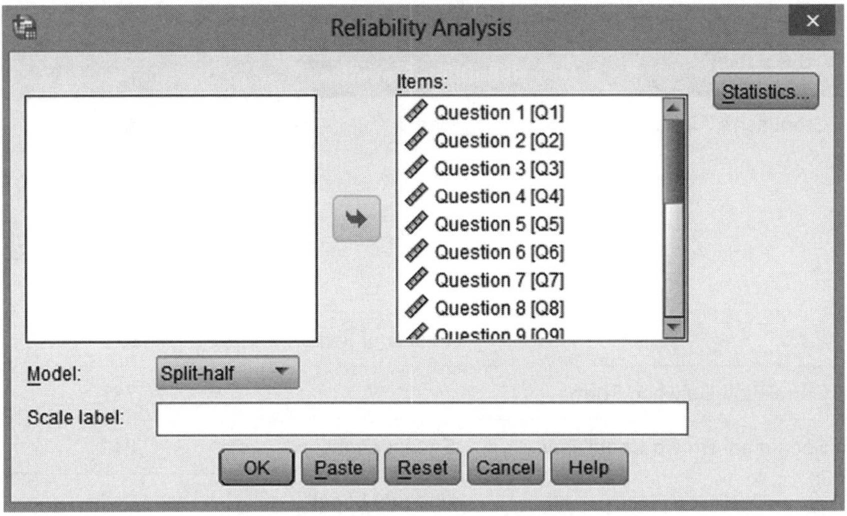

FIGURE 12.3 *The SPSS dialog to perform a reliability analysis*

In Figure 12.3, drag questions 1 to 20 into the item box. In the model option, select *Split-half*. Then click the *Statistics* icon. A new dialog box will appear (see Figure 12.4). For the time being, check *scale* which allows us to see the descriptive summary of each half of the test data. Then click *OK* to return to Figure 12.3 and then click *OK*. Table 12.1 presents the SPSS output on the split-half coefficient.

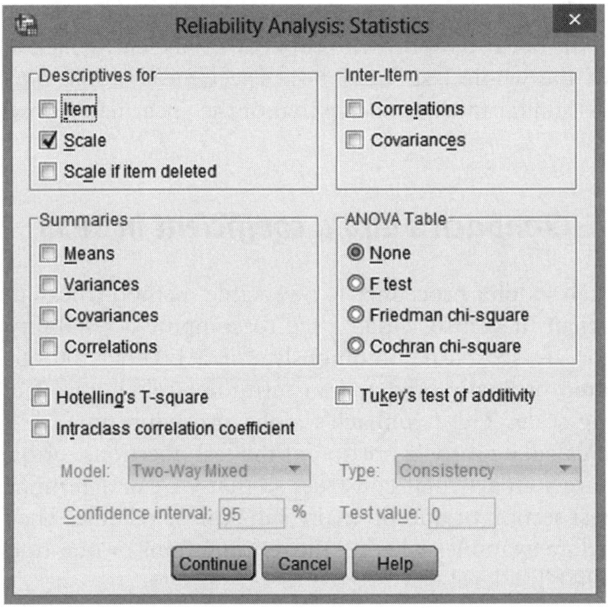

FIGURE 12.4 *The SPSS dialog of statistics in a reliability analysis*

Table 12.1 SPSS output on the split-half coefficient (N = 20)

Reliability Statistics			
Cronbach's Alpha	Part 1	Value	.632
		N of Items	10[a]
	Part 2	Value	.552
		N of Items	10[b]
	Total N of Items		20
Correlation Between Forms			.727
Spearman–Brown Coefficient	Equal Length		.842
	Unequal Length		.842
Guttman Split-Half Coefficient			.841

a. The items are: Question 1, Question 2, Question 3, Question 4, Question 5, Question 6, Question 7, Question 8, Question 9, Question 10.
b. The items are: Question 11, Question 12, Question 13, Question 14, Question 15, Question 16, Question 17, Question 18, Question 19, Question 20.

According to Table 12.1, the Cronbach's alpha for the first half is 0.63 and the second half is 0.55. These indices are what we have discussed as the split-half coefficients. The correlation between both parts is 0.73. This table also reports the Spearman–Brown prophecy coefficient, which indicates the reliability of the whole test (i.e. 0.84). The *Guttman split-half coefficient* also provides similar information to that of the Spearman–Brown prophecy coefficient.

Cronbach's alpha coefficient in SPSS

The Cronbach's alpha procedure is a versatile method to calculate a reliability coefficient. It is also widely used to compute a reliability coefficient for tests that are scored dichotomously, for a Likert scale questionnaire, which is rated ordinally, and for an intrarater reliability of a rater who uses a rating scale. The Cronbach's alpha procedure in SPSS is useful in that we can calculate it for a portion of the test questions, or questionnaire items that target a particular construct so that we can determine whether a particular test section or questionnaire sub-scale is reliable. The Cronbach's alpha procedure examines whether the test questions or questionnaire items affect the reliability level.

Cronbach's alpha for a language test in SPSS

To illustrate how to calculate a Cronbach's alpha of a language test, the data *Ch12 Alpha Grammar.sav* (downloadable from the *companion website*) will be used. This data set is from a grammar test section of a larger test completed by 48 EFL students. There are 20 questions in this test. Figure 12.5 presents the Alpha Grammar SPSS file. You can then begin to compute the Cronbach's alpha coefficient following the same procedure as you used in the calculation of the split-half coefficient.

File	Edit	View	Data	Transform	Analyze	Graphs	Utilities	Add-ons	Window	Help

	ID	gender	age	q21	q22	q23	q24
1	43110441	2.00	22.00	.00	.00	.00	1.00
2	43110450	2.00	22.00	.00	.00	.00	1.00
3	44907001	2.00	23.00	1.00	1.00	1.00	1.00
4	44907002	2.00	23.00	1.00	1.00	1.00	1.00
5	44907003	2.00	23.00	1.00	1.00	1.00	1.00
6	44907004	1.00	23.00	1.00	1.00	1.00	1.00
7	44907005	2.00	23.00	1.00	1.00	1.00	1.00
8	45210007	2.00	23.00	1.00	1.00	1.00	1.00
9	45210011	2.00	23.00	.00	.00	1.00	1.00
10	45210027	2.00	21.00	.00	1.00	1.00	.00
11	45210029	1.00	22.00	.00	1.00	1.00	1.00
12	45301405	1.00	20.00	1.00	1.00	.00	1.00
13	45301410	1.00	21.00	.00	1.00	.00	1.00
14	45301412	2.00	21.00	1.00	1.00	1.00	.00
15	45301414	1.00	19.00	1.00	1.00	.00	1.00
16	45301415	1.00	20.00	.00	1.00	1.00	.00
17	45301416	1.00	19.00	.00	1.00	1.00	.00
18	45301417	1.00	20.00	.00	1.00	1.00	.00
19	45301425	2.00	20.00	1.00	.00	.00	.00
20	45301427	2.00	20.00	1.00	1.00	.00	.00
21	45301433	2.00	19.00	1.00	.00	.00	1.00
22	45301435	2.00	20.00	.00	1.00	1.00	.00
23	45301436	1.00	20.00	1.00	1.00	.00	1.00

Data View | Variable View

FIGURE 12.5   *An outlook of the Alpha Grammar SPSS file*

Drag questions 21 to 40 into the item box. In the model option, select *Alpha*. Click on the statistics icon. Here, we will check *scale* and *scale if item deleted* (see Figure 12.6). Then click *OK* and *OK* again. Table 12.2 presents the SPSS output on the Cronbach's alpha coefficient.

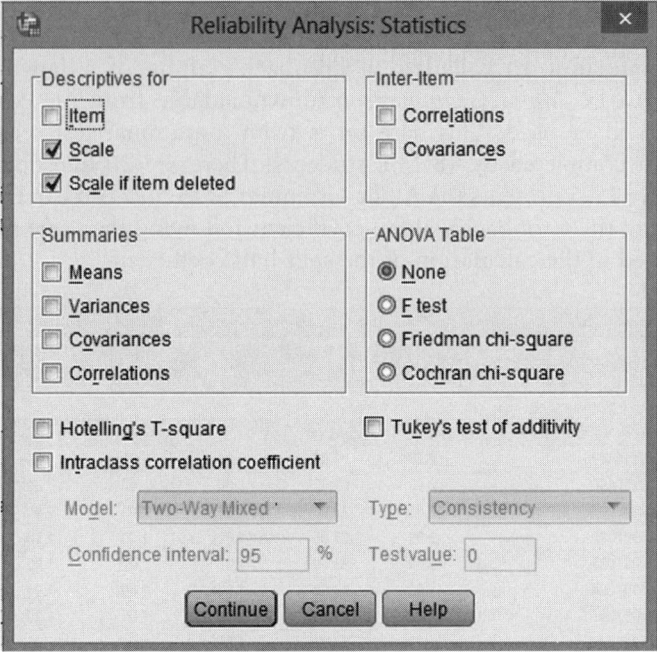

FIGURE 12.6   *The SPSS dialog of statistics in a reliability analysis*

The Cronbach's alpha coefficient for this test section is 0.80. We also see another table labeled as *Item-total statistics*. In this table, you will see many columns, but the most important column you need to look for is the *Cronbach's Alpha if item deleted*. This is where you can check if a particular question contributes positively or negatively to the entire Cronbach's alpha coefficient (i.e. 0.80). It is quite straightforward to examine this table. Basically, it tells us how much the overall Cronbach's alpha would be if a particular item were excluded from the analysis. For example, if we exclude Question 21, the Cronbach's alpha would be 0.79. This question is important for this test section and we should not exclude it for use because the Cronbach's alpha coefficient would be reduced. If we exclude Question 30, the reliability estimate would increase very little and it would not make a significant change. Let us imagine a scenario where this table indicated that if Question 40 were excluded, the Cronbach's alpha would be 0.93. On this basis, it would be a good decision to exclude this question as it reduced the Cronbach's alpha from 0.93 to 0.80. However, we do not need to exclude any questions from this analysis; we should be satisfied with the obtained Cronbach's alpha as it is *larger than 0.70*.

This *scale if item deleted* function in SPSS is very useful for experimental research because we can determine whether some test questions that are unreliable can be excluded from further statistical analysis to determine the

Table 12.2 SPSS output on the Cronbach's alpha coefficient (N = 48)

Reliability Statistics	
Cronbach's Alpha	N of Items
.801	20

Item-Total Statistics			
	Scale Mean if Item Deleted	Scale Variance if Item Deleted	Corrected Item-Total Correlation	Cronbach's Alpha if Item Deleted
q21	9.2083	18.594	.360	.793
q22	8.9167	19.014	.303	.796
q23	9.1667	18.823	.303	.797
q24	9.0833	18.887	.291	.797
q25	9.2917	18.594	.378	.792
q26	9.1458	18.425	.397	.791
q27	9.0833	18.418	.403	.791
q28	9.2917	18.977	.283	.798
q29	9.2292	18.393	.412	.790
q30	9.1250	19.601	.123	.807
q31	9.1458	18.553	.367	.793
q32	9.1042	19.585	.127	.807
q33	9.2083	18.041	.496	.785
q34	9.0833	18.333	.424	.790
q35	9.2917	17.573	.641	.777
q36	9.2708	17.946	.535	.783
q37	9.2292	19.457	.159	.805
q38	9.3333	17.887	.580	.781
q39	9.0625	17.890	.538	.783
q40	9.0000	19.149	.241	.800

effect of the treatment. This function is also useful for test validation in a pilot stage. It also prompts us to look into a particular item to see if there is something wrong in the question or the alternatives, providing us with some justification for revising or deleting it.

Cronbach's alpha for a Likert scale questionnaire in SPSS

To illustrate how to calculate a Cronbach's alpha of a Likert scale questionnaire, the data *Ch12 Alpha Questionnaire.sav* (downloadable from the *companion website*) will be used. This data set is from a cognitive and metacognitive questionnaire of a larger data set completed by 50 ESL students. There are 30 strategy items in this questionnaire. Figure 12.7 presents the Alpha Questionnaire SPSS file. Table 12.3 presents the questionnaire taxonomy.

Due to space limitations, the procedure of carrying out the Cronbach's alpha analysis for the entire questionnaire will not be illustrated here.

File	Edit	View	Data	Transform	Analyze	Graphs	Utilities	Add-ons	Window	Help

	id	gender	age	yrstudy	item1	item2	item3	item4
29	31.00	.00	21.00	9.00	2.00	4.00	4.00	3.00
30	32.00	1.00	21.00	10.00	1.00	3.00	2.00	5.00
31	33.00	.00	21.00	11.00	2.00	3.00	3.00	4.00
32	34.00	1.00	21.00	10.00	2.00	3.00	3.00	2.00
33	35.00	.00	20.00	12.00	3.00	3.00	2.00	4.00
34	36.00	.00	21.00	9.00	1.00	4.00	3.00	5.00
35	37.00	1.00	21.00	12.00	1.00	5.00	4.00	4.00
36	39.00	1.00	21.00	8.00	4.00	4.00	3.00	3.00
37	40.00	.00	21.00	10.00	1.00	2.00	2.00	3.00
38	41.00	1.00	21.00	10.00	2.00	4.00	4.00	4.00
39	42.00	.00	21.00	10.00	2.00	2.00	2.00	3.00
40	43.00	.00	21.00	10.00	3.00	4.00	4.00	4.00
41	44.00	.00	20.00	11.00	2.00	2.00	2.00	2.00
42	45.00	1.00	20.00	10.00	2.00	4.00	4.00	4.00
43	46.00	.00	20.00	12.00	4.00	4.00	4.00	3.00
44	48.00	1.00	20.00	13.00	1.00	3.00	2.00	3.00
45	49.00	.00	20.00	11.00	2.00	5.00	4.00	2.00
46	50.00	1.00	20.00	10.00	3.00	2.00	4.00	2.00
47	51.00	1.00	21.00	11.00	2.00	3.00	3.00	3.00
48	52.00	1.00	20.00	11.00	3.00	4.00	1.00	4.00
49	53.00	1.00	21.00	9.00	1.00	4.00	3.00	3.00
50	54.00	1.00	21.00	11.00	3.00	3.00	2.00	2.00
51								

Data View | Variable View

FIGURE 12.7 *An outlook of the alpha questionnaire SPSS file*

Table 12.3 The cognitive and metacognitive questionnaire structure

Processing	Subscale	No. of items	Items
Cognitive strategies	Comprehending	5	2, 3, 6, 7, 14
	Memory	4	1, 5, 8, 22
	Retrieval	4	4, 9, 26, 29
Metacognitive strategies	Planning	6	10, 11, 19, 20, 23, 27
	Monitoring	6	12, 16, 17, 21, 24, 25
	Evaluating	5	13, 15, 18, 28, 30
Total		30	

You can simply follow the instructions provided in the above section. You will see that SPSS would produce an overall Cronbach's alpha of 0.926 (≈ 0.93). The table *scale if item deleted* would also indicate that we should not exclude any items from this analysis.

Let us, nevertheless, examine the Cronbach's alpha at a *sub-scale* level using Table 12.3. According to Table 12.3, each sub-scale (e.g. comprehending and memory strategies) is made up of different questionnaire items. Let us examine the Cronbach's alpha of the memory strategy scale. Let us put Items 1, 5, 8, and 22 in the item box (see Figure 12.8) and in

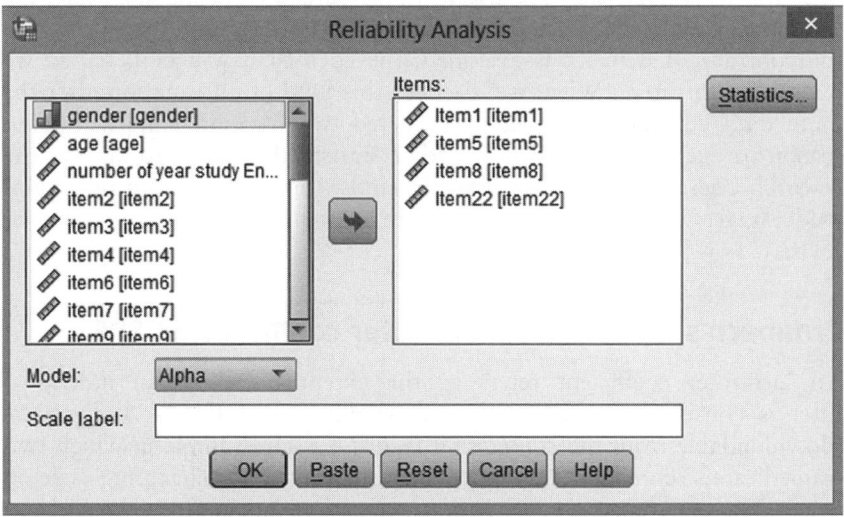

FIGURE 12.8   *The Cronbach's alpha analysis of the memory strategy scale*

the *Statistics* icon, check *scale* and *scale if item deleted*. Click *OK* and then *OK* again. Table 12.4 presents the SPSS output on the Cronbach's alpha coefficient of the memory strategy sub-scale.

Table 12.4 SPSS output on the Cronbach's alpha coefficient of the memory strategy sub-scale

Reliability Statistics	
Cronbach's Alpha	N of Items
.551	4

Item-Total Statistics				
	Scale Mean if Item Deleted	Scale Variance if Item Deleted	Corrected Item-Total Correlation	Cronbach's Alpha if Item Deleted
Item1	10.5000	4.786	-.031	.748
item5	9.0400	3.304	.574	.305
item8	9.1800	3.334	.345	.472
Item22	8.9000	2.745	.591	.229

According to Table 12.4, the overall Cronbach's alpha for this sub-scale is 0.55. However, as you can see from the Item-total Statistics, Item 1 does not fit in this scale because if it is excluded from the sub-scale, the Cronbach's alpha becomes 0.75, which is more desirable than 0.55. On the contrary, if Item 22 is excluded, the coefficient will be 0.23, so we must keep this item. When we discover this kind of information after the main data collection has been completed, we have an empirical-based reason to exclude Item 1 from further statistical analysis to answer the research question. If we discover this kind of information during a pilot study stage, we can look into the item and decide to either remove or revise it.

Cronbach's alpha for an intrarater coefficient in SPSS

An intrarater coefficient refers to the extent to which an individual rater is consistent in their ratings. The data *Ch12 Raters Analytic.sav* (downloadable from the *companion website*) is an example in which two trained raters scored an essay independently using a 5-point rating scale on five assessment criteria (i.e. content, organization, language use, vocabulary and mechanics). The data spreadsheet is presented in Figure 12.9.

	ID	ContentR1	OrgR1	LangR1	VocR1	MechR1	ContentR2	OrgR2
1	1	3.00	3.00	3.00	4.00	3.00	4.00	4.00
2	2	4.00	3.00	3.00	3.00	4.00	4.00	4.00
3	3	5.00	5.00	4.00	5.00	5.00	5.00	5.00
4	4	4.00	5.00	3.00	4.00	5.00	4.00	4.00
5	5	3.00	4.00	2.00	2.00	3.00	3.00	3.00
6	6	4.00	3.00	4.00	3.00	4.00	3.00	4.00
7	7	4.00	3.00	4.00	4.00	4.00	4.00	3.00
8	8	4.00	5.00	3.00	3.00	4.00	4.00	4.00
9	9	3.00	4.00	4.00	4.00	4.00	4.00	4.00
10	10	2.00	3.00	3.00	2.00	2.00	2.00	3.00
11	11	1.00	2.00	2.00	1.00	3.00	2.00	1.00
12	12	2.00	2.00	1.00	1.00	2.00	1.00	1.00
13	13	2.00	2.00	2.00	2.00	2.00	2.00	1.00
14	14	3.00	3.00	4.00	3.00	4.00	3.00	2.00
15	15	4.00	4.00	5.00	5.00	5.00	5.00	4.00
16	16	4.00	5.00	4.00	4.00	5.00	4.00	4.00
17	17	3.00	4.00	4.00	3.00	3.00	3.00	3.00
18	18	5.00	4.00	5.00	3.00	5.00	5.00	5.00
19	19	4.00	4.00	3.00	3.00	4.00	3.00	4.00
20	20	4.00	4.00	4.00	4.00	3.00	4.00	4.00
21	21	3.00	3.00	4.00	3.00	3.00	4.00	4.00
22	22	3.00	3.00	3.00	4.00	2.00	3.00	3.00
23	23	2.00	1.00	1.00	2.00	1.00	1.00	1.00

FIGURE 12.9   *An outlook of the raters' analytic file*

In a performance assessment such as essay writing, it is difficult to compute the internal consistency of a test task because performance is judged by an external person who is prone to variation due to, for example, bias, boredom or fatigue. What is common practice is to examine an intrarater reliability coefficient—the extent to which a rater is consistent in assigning a similar score to a similar performance. This concept is also applicable to coders of qualitative data. We can examine an intrarater reliability coefficient through a Cronbach's alpha procedure as above. We will compare the intrarater reliability coefficients of the two raters. You can follow similar steps to those outlined above. We only need to put the five scores of each rater in one at a time. Figure 12.10 illustrates an example. It was found that Raters 1 and 2 had Cronbach's alpha coefficients of 0.917 ($\approx$ 0.92) and 0.939 ($\approx$ 0.94), respectively. On this basis, we have good evidence to suggest that both raters are internally consistent in their rating of each essay criterion.

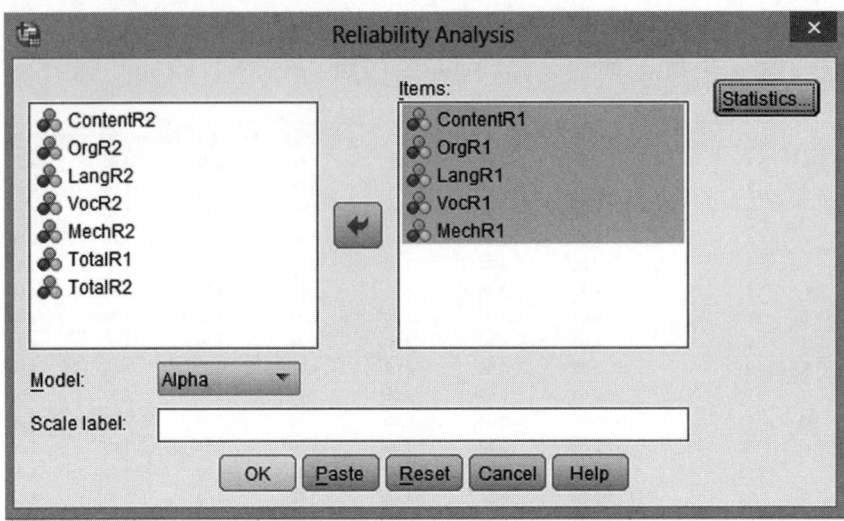

FIGURE 12.10   *The intrarater reliability analysis of rater 1*

Cronbach's alpha for an interrater coefficient in SPSS

An interrater reliability coefficient refers to the extent to which two raters agree with each other in their ratings. We can perform a similar Cronbach's alpha procedure to that illustrated above. For example, we can put the paired variables *ContentR1* and *ContentR2* and so on, in the item box, so that we can report the interrater coefficient for each scoring criterion. It was found that the Cronbach's alpha between *ContentR1* and *ContentR2* was 0.908 ($\approx$ 0.91).

We can compute the overall interrater reliability coefficient. This is also easy to do. We only need to create a new variable that combines the scores of each rater into one variable in the SPSS data file. To create a new variable, go to the *Transform* menu and then *Compute Variable* (see Figure 12.11). A new dialog box will appear (see Figure 12.12).

As can be seen in Figure 12.12, we need to type in a new variable name that will be inserted into the data sheet (Figure 12.9). In *Target Variable*, type *TotalR1* and in the *Numeric Expression*, move one scoring criterion in at a time and insert the plus sign (+) in between. When it is done, click *OK*. A new variable *TotalR1* has been added to the file. Do the same for *TotalR2*. Once you have done this, perform a Cronbach's alpha coefficient for these two variables. The Cronbach's alpha coefficient computed will indicate the interrater reliability coefficient. It was found that the Cronbach's alpha coefficient was 0.981 ($\approx$ 0.98). This was very high. A Pearson correlation coefficient was 0.967 ($\approx$ 0.97; see Chapter 7 for correlational analysis). As for the internal consistency of an instrument, we should obtain both an interrater coefficient and a correlation coefficient of at least 0.70.

File	Edit	View	Data	Transform	Analyze	Graphs	Utilities	Add-ons	Window

🖿 Compute Variable...

Programmability Transformation...

🔢 Count Values within Cases...

Shift Values...

	ID							MechR1

🔳 Recode into Same Variables...

🔳 Recode into Different Variables...

🔳 Automatic Recode...

Create Dummy Variables

🔳 Visual Binning...

🔳 Rank Cases...

🔳 Date and Time Wizard...

📈 Create Time Series...

🔳 Replace Missing Values...

🌐 Random Number Generators...

▶ Run Pending Transforms   Ctrl+G

	ID					MechR1
1	1				00	3.00
2	2				00	4.00
3	3				00	5.00
4	4				00	5.00
5	5				00	3.00
6	6				00	4.00
7	7				00	4.00
8	8				00	4.00
9	9				00	4.00
10	10				00	2.00
11	11				00	3.00
12	12				00	2.00
13	13				00	2.00
14	14	3.00	3.00	4.00	3.00	4.00
15	15	4.00	4.00	5.00	5.00	5.00
16	16	4.00	5.00	4.00	4.00	5.00

FIGURE 12.11   *An outlook of the SPSS menu for transforming variables*

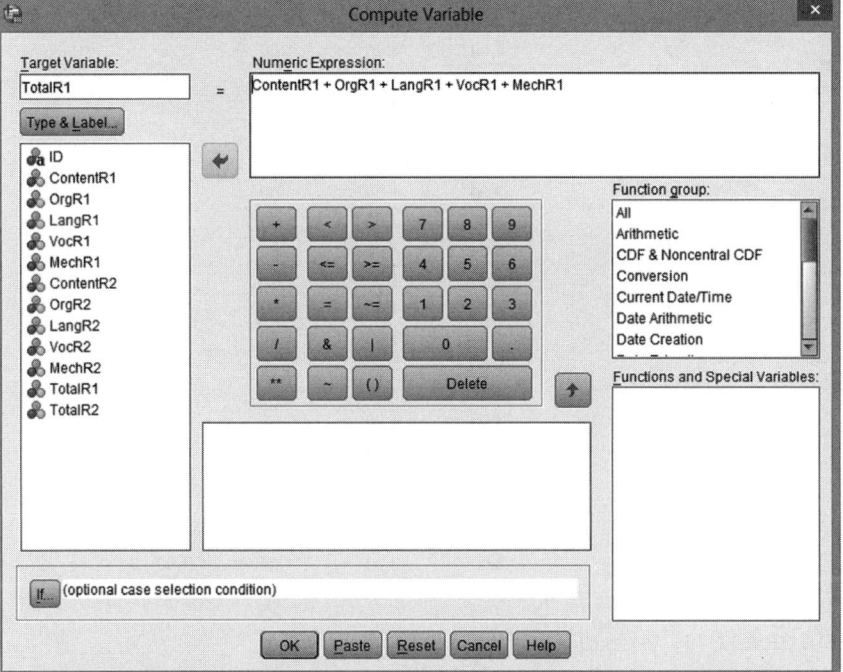

FIGURE 12.12   *A computing variable dialog in transform*

Rater agreements in percentages

Often we will see some experimental researchers report on a level of agreement between coders or raters (e.g. the coder agreement was 98 percent). Theoretically, agreements in scoring or coding are of two types: Exact and adjacent agreements. *Exact agreement* refers to an agreement in which two raters assign the same score to the same text (e.g. 4 versus 4 = 100 percent agree), whereas *adjacent agreement* refers to an agreement that 2 raters assign a score within one-scale point to the same text (e.g. 4 versus 5 = 100 percent agree). That is, an adjacent agreement covers both exact and adjacent agreements in counting. Let us examine the data in *Ch12 Raters Analytic.sav*. For the purpose of illustration, we will focus on the rater agreement in the "Content" criterion. A new data file was produced (*Ch12 Raters Content.sav*; downloadable from the *companion website*).

File Edit View Data Transform Analyze Direct Marketing Graphs Utilities Add-ons						
	ID	ContentR1	ContentR2	Exactagree	Adjacagree	var
1	1	3.00	4.00	.00	1.00	
2	2	4.00	4.00	1.00	1.00	
3	3	5.00	5.00	1.00	1.00	
4	4	4.00	4.00	1.00	1.00	
5	5	3.00	3.00	1.00	1.00	
6	6	4.00	3.00	.00	1.00	
7	7	4.00	4.00	1.00	1.00	
8	8	4.00	4.00	1.00	1.00	
9	9	3.00	4.00	.00	1.00	
10	10	2.00	2.00	1.00	1.00	
11	11	1.00	2.00	.00	1.00	
12	12	2.00	1.00	.00	1.00	
13	13	2.00	2.00	1.00	1.00	
14	14	3.00	3.00	1.00	1.00	
15	15	4.00	5.00	.00	1.00	
16	16	4.00	4.00	1.00	1.00	
17	17	3.00	3.00	1.00	1.00	
18	18	5.00	5.00	1.00	1.00	
19	19	4.00	3.00	.00	1.00	
20	20	4.00	4.00	1.00	1.00	
21	21	3.00	4.00	.00	1.00	
22	22	3.00	3.00	1.00	1.00	
23	23	2.00	1.00	.00	1.00	
24	24	4.00	4.00	1.00	1.00	
25	25	3.00	3.00	1.00	1.00	
26						

FIGURE 12.13 *An outlook of the raters contents file*

Figure 12.13 presents the *Raters Content* SPSS file. In the exact agreement, when the scores are the same, 1 is coded and when they are different, 0 is coded. In the adjacent agreement, when the score is within a 1-point range, 1 is coded. Otherwise, 0 is coded.

In this file, two additional columns have been added: *Exactagree* and *Adjacagree*. In order to compute the level of agreement, we can use SPSS to compute the frequencies in the *Descriptive* menu. Table 12.5 presents the SPSS output for the frequencies of the exact and adjacent agreement variables.

Table 12.5 The SPSS output for the frequencies of the exact and adjacent agreement variables

Exact Agreement		Frequency	Percent	Valid Percent	Cumulative Percent
Valid	.00	9	36.0	36.0	36.0
	1.00	16	64.0	64.0	100.0
	Total	25	100.0	100.0	

Adjacent Agreement		Frequency	Percent	Valid Percent	Cumulative Percent
Valid	1.00	25	100.0	100.0	100.0

On the basis of the frequencies in Table 12.5, we can see that the raters have just a 36 percent exact agreement rate, but a 100 percent adjacent agreement rate. We should note the large discrepancy in their exact agreement, which is problematic and can be a threat to the validity of the results. However, the Pearson correlation coefficient between this pair was quite high (see above). In language assessment, adjacent agreement is typically used because the two assigned scores are averaged.

It is important to note that we should *avoid* calculating an agreement in percentages between raters or coders of qualitative data. Instead, we should attempt to compute a reliability coefficient. The reasons for avoiding the use of a rater or coder agreement in percentages are that, first, the agreement rate can be affected by the rating scales or score points being used (Keith 2003). The larger the scale range, the less likely two or more people will agree on the score or code they assign. For example, people tend to have a higher level of agreement on a four-point scale than on a six-point scale in their ratings. Second, the agreement rate provides *inflated estimates* of the relationship between two scores because it depends on the total number of instances or examples being rated or coded (Yang, Buckendahl, Juszkewicz & Bhola 2002).

Cohen's kappa coefficient

Instead of computing agreement in percentages, Cohen's kappa should be used as a measure of agreement, particularly when coding qualitative data. This statistical method takes the chance level of agreement into account. As with other correlation coefficients, a kappa coefficient of 1 indicates perfect agreement and 0 indicates agreement due to chance. A moderate agreement ranges between 0.4 and 0.6. A kappa coefficient larger than 0.70 is considered substantial agreement (Viera & Garrett 2005).

We can compute a Cohen's kappa coefficient in SPSS. Let us use the data *Ch12 Raters Content.sav* so that we can illustrate how to compute the Cohen's kappa coefficient.

 In the drop-down menu, select *Analyze → Descriptive Statistics → Crosstabs*. A dialog box will appear (see Figure 12.14)

In the first dialog box, drag *ContentR1* to *Row(s)* and *ContentR2* to *Column(s)*. Then click on the icon *Statistics* and a new dialog box will appear. Check *Kappa* and then click *Continue* and *OK*. You can do the same for other pairs of the assessment criteria. Table 12.6 presents the SPSS output for the kappa coefficient.

The first table in Table 12.6 is what we call a cross-tabulation table, which considers the number of instances of agreement between Raters 1 and 2 across different scores (e.g. seven cases where Raters 1 and 2 agreed on the four-point rating). The second table reports on the kappa coefficient, which was found to be moderate (≈ 0.50, $p < 0.05$). A Cohen's kappa is more accurate when there are more rating observations. It should also be noted that the kappa is more appropriate and accurate for *categorical codes* (e.g. coded 1 for planning, coded 2 for monitoring and coded 3 for evaluating; coded 1 for correct suppliance of the morphology, coded 2 for nonsuppliance of the morphology and coded 3 for incorrect suppliance of the morphology) than the continuous data in this file. Rating scales for assessment are appropriate for Pearson correlations or Cronbach's alpha.

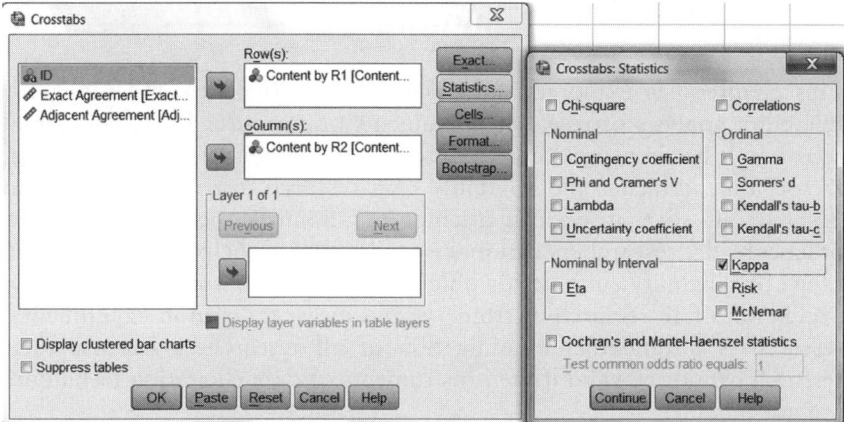

FIGURE 12.14 *The crosstabs in the descriptive statistics menu for kappa analysis*

Table 12.6 SPSS Output for the kappa coefficient between contentR1 and contentR2

ContentR1 * ContentR2 Crosstabulation							
Count							
		ContentR2					Total
		1.00	2.00	3.00	4.00	5.00	
ContentR1	1.00	0	1	0	0	0	1
	2.00	2	2	0	0	0	4
	3.00	0	0	5	3	0	8
	4.00	0	0	2	7	1	10
	5.00	0	0	0	0	2	2
Total		2	3	7	10	3	25

Symmetric Measures			Value	Asymp. Std. Error[a]	Approx. T[b]	Approx. Sig.
Measure of Agreement	Kappa		.499	.131	4.328	.000
N of Valid Cases			25			

a. Not assuming the null hypothesis.
b. Using the asymptotic standard error assuming the null hypothesis.

Summary

This chapter has explored and discussed the principles underlying the reliability analysis of research instruments or measures for experimental research. It has explained how to interpret a reliability coefficient. Several factors that influence the reliability of a research instrument have been pointed out so that we can attempt to minimize their impact. On a practical side, researchers can make use of SPSS to help them compute a range of reliability suitable for different kinds of measures. A systematic evaluation of all research instruments and measures used in experimental research is a fundamental obligation of all researchers because their research cannot be valid if their instruments or data elicitation techniques are not reliable.

Research exercise

To download exercises for this chapter visit: http://www.bloomsbury.com/experimental-research-methods-in-language-learning-9781441189110/

Discussion questions

1 What is the difference between a correlation coefficient and a reliability coefficient?
2 What is the meaning of a reliability coefficient to you?
3 What determines the kind of reliability coefficients we need to compute for a research instrument or method?
4 What do you think would be a problem in an experimental study when the researchers did not analyze their research instruments prior to inferential statistics?
5 Reflection: What is the most important lesson you have learned from this chapter?

Further reading

Bachman, LF 1990, *Fundamental considerations in language testing*, Oxford University Press, Oxford.

Chapter 6 provides a very thorough discussion about reliability in language tests, but can be useful for other measures. The chapter presents several relevant issues, including the classical true score measurement theory, factors affecting reliability and methods for computing reliability estimates.

Carr, NT 2011, *Designing and analyzing language tests*, Oxford University Press, Oxford.

Chapter 6 explains concepts of reliability and discusses approaches to reliability estimates and how to interpret reliability estimates.

Révész, A 2012, 'Coding second language data validly and reliably', in A Mackey & SM Gass (eds), *Research methods in second language acquisition: a practical guide*, Wiley-Blackwell, Malden, MA.

This chapter discusses the concepts of validity and reliability and reviews stages in a data coding procedure. This chapter is particularly useful for qualitative data coding.

CHAPTER THIRTEEN

Paired-samples and Independent-samples T-tests

Leading questions

1 If you were convinced that a particular type of instruction can help learners learn more effectively, how would you maintain objectivity while researching the effectiveness of that type of instruction?
2 Can you say that a mean score of 25 is significantly higher than a mean score of 22? Why or why not?
3 What do you know about *t*-tests?

Introduction

This chapter focuses on an application of *t*-tests for analyzing experimental research data. *T*-tests are *parametric* tests commonly used in experimental research to compare mean score differences. This chapter first presents the paired-samples *t*-test. The paired-samples *t*-test is used to compare scores of a pretest, which is administered prior to a special treatment, and a posttest, which is given either immediately after the treatment has finished or sometime later than that. The second part of this chapter presents the independent-samples *t*-test, which is used to compare the posttest scores between two comparison groups. The differences between the paired-samples and independent-samples *t*-tests are noted and discussed throughout. In the presentations of each type of *t*-tests, several published examples are used to illustrate how *t*-tests have been used. Most practically, this chapter illustrates how to conduct each *t*-test in SPSS, as well as how to interpret *t*-test results in light of a research aim.

Recall that if we would like to find out whether two mean scores differ due to an experimental treatment, we need to use inferential statistics to help us. Inferential statistics are probabilistic; they do not tell us absolute truths. There is still a chance that we can be wrong when we find that there is a significant difference between two means. Nevertheless, inferential statistics are much better for us to understand a causal-like relationship than descriptive statistics because inferential statistics make use of data distributions, sample sizes, and hypothesis testing to help us make a decision about a relationship.

The paired-samples *t*-tests

We saw in Chapter 10 that a paired-samples *t*-test or repeated-measures *t*-test can be used to examine whether there is a statistically significant difference between two sets of measures derived from the same participants. A paired-samples *t*-test is used in a *repeated-measures* or *within-group* experimental design in which researchers compare a *pretest* with a *posttest* after an experimental treatment. This statistical test uses the means score of the *pretest* and the *posttest* to statistically compare the two. Recall that an experimental design that relies on the use of a pretest and posttest without a comparison group is considered pre-experimental. In a true or quasi-experiment, researchers can examine the differences between the pretest and posttest scores in addition to making a group comparison.

When we use a paired-samples *t*-test, there will always be *two* mean scores that will be compared. Examples of experimental studies that employed a paired-samples *t*-test are Al-Homoud and Schmitt (2009), Baralt and Gurzynski-Weiss (2011), Rahimi (2013) and Satar and Özdener (2008). Satar and Özdener (2008) used *t*-tests to compare the pre- and post-anxiety levels within each group of participants in their study. They labeled this paired-samples *t*-test as 'related *t*-test' (p. 602). There was no statistically significant difference between the Voice Chat group and the control group (i.e. $t(29) = 1.26$, $p > .05$; and $t(29) = -0.29$, $p > .05$, respectively, p. 603).

The statistical assumptions of the paired-samples t-test

There are required key assumptions we need to check before we perform a paired-samples *t*-test:

- *Type of scale*: The data should be on a continuous scale such as an interval or ratio scale.

- *Random sampling*: Ideally, the participants should be randomly sampled from the population of interest. However, most of the time researchers may have to work with a small sample of the population of interest, so they may not be able to randomly sample participants.

- *Normal distribution*: The pretest and posttest scores should be normally distributed.

How to perform a paired-samples t-test in SPSS

The data *Ch13 Paired ttest.sav* (downloadable from the *companion website*) will be used to illustrate this analysis (see Figure 13.1). This data examines the effect of inductive instruction plus metacognitive evaluation

File Edit View Data Transform Analyze Graphs Utiliti				
	ID	Pretest	Posttest	var
1	1	15.00	17.00	
2	2	17.00	20.00	
3	3	18.00	16.00	
4	4	6.00	10.00	
5	5	12.00	13.00	
6	6	7.00	7.00	
7	7	14.00	17.00	
8	8	23.00	23.00	
9	9	5.00	8.00	
10	10	20.00	20.00	
11	11	15.00	14.00	
12	12	24.00	28.00	
13	13	11.00	16.00	
14	14	16.00	17.00	
15	15	19.00	16.00	
16	16	7.00	8.00	
17	17	10.00	13.00	
18	18	12.00	17.00	
19	19	7.00	15.00	
20	20	6.00	10.00	
21	21	9.00	5.00	
22	22	14.00	19.00	
23	23	22.00	24.00	

Data View   Variable View

FIGURE 13.1   *An outlook of the paired-samples t-test file*

on students' narrative essay writing performance. Twenty-five intermediate learners took part in the study. The students took a pretest consisting of two narrative essay writing tasks before the instruction. When the instruction was complete, they also took a posttest, also consisting of two narrative essay writing tasks—the pretest and posttest were parallel tests. The intrarater and interrater reliability coefficients were reasonably high ($r = 0.90$ and 0.85, respectively).

There are three steps to perform the paired-samples t-test.

- The first step is to check the descriptive statistics (e.g. the mean, median, mode, skewness and kurtosis statistics) of each test to make sure that the data are normally distributed. Make sure that all statistical assumptions for a paired-sample t-test are met for each data set. If the data do not follow a normal distribution, consider using the *Wilcoxon signed ranks test* (see Chapter 15).

- The second step is to perform a paired-samples t-test and to check whether there is a statistical significance ($p < 0.05$). The effect size should also be computed.

- The third step is to report and interpret the findings. In a research report, the findings should be discussed in relation to the existing literature and comparisons among studies may also prove to be useful.

The following are the steps in SPSS that should be followed to perform a paired-samples t-test.

 In the drop-down menu, select *Analyze → Compare Means → Paired-Samples T Test*. A dialog box will appear (see Figure 13.2). In this dialog box, drag *pretest* to *Variable1* and *posttest* to *Variable2* in the *Paired Variables*.

 Click on *Options*. You will see that the confidence interval of the means is set at 95 percent by default, which does not require you to make any changes.

 Click *OK*.

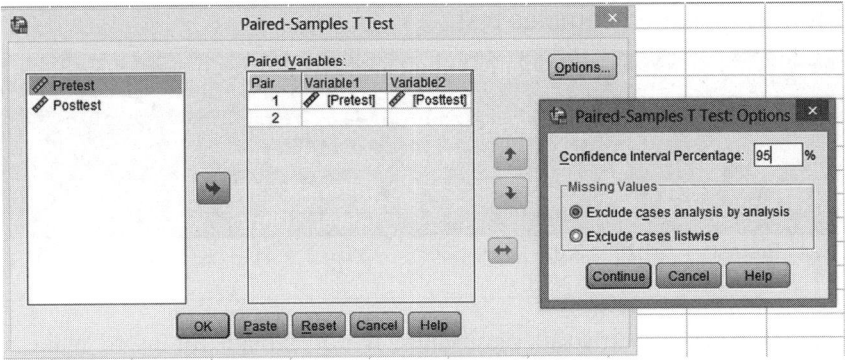

FIGURE 13.2   *SPSS dialog to run a paired-samples t-test*

Table 13.1 presents the SPSS outputs of the paired-samples *t*-test. Table 13.1.1 reports the descriptive statistics of each test. Table 13.1.2 reports the correlation coefficient between the two variables (i.e. *r* = 0.87). Table 13.1.3 is where we examine whether there is a statistical significance between the two test scores. Examine the *t*, *df* and *Sig* (2-tailed) columns in this output. Sig (2-tailed) will tell us whether there is a statistical significance between the two scores. It was found to be significant. Now if we set the significance level at 0.05, we can reject the null hypothesis, which hypothesized that there was no statistical difference between the two scores. You will also notice that in the paired-samples *t*-test, *df* is computed as *total N-1* (similar to Correlation). So in this analysis, *df* was 24 (i.e. 25 – 1).

Table 13.1 SPSS outputs of the paired-samples t-test (N = 25)

Table 13.1.1 Paired-samples statistics

		Mean	N	Std. Deviation	Std. Error Mean
Pair 1	Pretest	13.7600	25	5.76830	1.15366
	Posttest	15.5200	25	5.90988	1.18198

Table 13.1.2 Paired-samples correlations

		N	Correlation	Sig.
Pair 1	Pretest & Posttest	25	.867	.000

Table 13.1.3 Paired-samples test

		Paired Differences					t	df	Sig. (2-tailed)
		Mean	Std. Deviation	Std. Error Mean	95% Confidence Interval of the Difference				
					Lower	Upper			
Pair 1	Pretest – Posttest	-1.76	3.02	.60	-3.01	-.51	-2.92	24	.008

The existence of statistical significance is not enough for us to make a claim about the effect of an experimental treatment. We also need to provide details of the effect size such as Cohen's *d*. Cohen's *d* provides further evidence that will allow us to make a claim about the effect of the experimental treatment. In order to compute Cohen's *d* effect size for a paired-samples *t*-test, use the following URL by Melody Wiseheart: <http://www.cognitiveflexibility.org/effectsize/>, viewed March 7, 2014). To calculate Cohen's *d*, we need the mean scores of the pretest and posttest, their associated standard deviations (i.e. pretest = 13.76 [SD = 5.77]; posttest = 15.52 [SD = 5.91]), and the correlation coefficient (i.e. 0.867). It was found that Cohen's *d* was –0.58.

It is important to note that we *need to ignore the sign (positive or negative)* of Cohen's *d* because this will depend on which mean score was subtracted from the other. That is, *a negative Cohen's d does not imply a negative effect size.* As discussed in Chapter 10, a Cohen's *d* of 0.50 indicates a medium effect size. Note that: (1) the value was negative because the posttest mean score was subtracted from the pretest mean score; and (2) there is a different method to calculate Cohen's *d* of the independent *t*-test (this will be discussed in the next section).

How to report a paired-samples t-test result

It is strongly recommended that when space is available, all statistical outputs are presented because they will allow transparency of the findings and the conclusions reached, and other researchers can use these statistics for a meta-analysis in a future study. If you write a dissertation or a thesis, you will have plenty of space to report these tables such as those presented above. Make sure you explain what each table is purported to indicate. However, in some situations, when we are writing an article for a journal, there is a space limitation, so tables are often used strategically. The following is an example of how you would write up this finding in this situation:

According to the paired-samples t-test analysis, it was found that there was a statistically significant difference between the pretest and posttest scores ($t[24] = -1.76$, $p < 0.05$, $d = -0.58$, medium effect size). The finding indicates that the inductive instruction with metacognitive evaluation moderately helped increase the participants' narrative writing essay performance.

It has often been noted that even in top-ranking journals, not all authors provide or discuss Cohen's *d* effect size. For example, Rahimi (2013) reported that 'as for the first paragraphs, both groups have written better revisions; the mean for the first draft of the untrained groups is 68.25 and that of its revision, 70.72 ($t = 5.14$, $p < 0.001$)...' (p. 79). See also Satar and Özdener (2008) above. Eckerth and Tavakoli (2012), however, reported Cohen's effect sizes of their paired-samples *t*-tests for knowledge specific word gains on immediate and delayed posttests in a table (their Table 4, p. 241). In their study, Cohen's *d* ranged from medium to large. It is very important that experimental researchers report and discuss the Cohen's *d* effect size in their paired-samples *t*-test reports.

The independent-samples *t*-test

The logic behind the use of an independent-samples *t*-test is similar to that of the paired-samples *t*-test. That is, we would like to determine whether one mean is *significantly different* from another. Instead of comparing two means of scores from the same participants, we compare two means of scores from two different groups of participants (i.e. independent of each other—this is the reason it is called an independent-samples *t*-test). Examples of experimental studies that have employed an independent-samples *t*-test are Al-Homoud and Schmitt (2009), Henry, Culman and VanPatten (2009), Hirata-Edds (2011), Macaro and Erler (2008), and Rahimi (2013). Al-Homoud and Schmitt (2009) employed an independent-samples *t*-test to compare the posttest scores between extensive and intensive reading groups. The study found no statistical significance between the two groups for either preliminary TOEFL or PET (Cambridge Preliminary English Test) reading ($p > 0.05$). Rahimi (2013) found that the student reviewers in the trained group statistically gave more global comments than those in the untrained group ($t = 7.79$, $p < 0.05$, p. 77).

The statistical assumptions of the independent-samples t-test

The assumptions for the independent-samples *t*-test include those for the paired-samples *t*-test. However, there are *two* additional assumptions.

- *Group independence*: This assumption is that participants belong to *only one* group. For example, participants cannot be in an experimental group as well as the control group. Scores from participants who are in both groups need to be removed from the data set in order to perform this test.

● *Homogeneity of variance*: This assumption is that the variances for the two groups are equal. It is important to note that this assumption is not the same thing as equal sample sizes between two or more groups. The homogeneity of variance assumption is determined by statistics, not by the number of samples. This might sound complex to check, but in fact it is easy to do when we perform an independent-samples *t*-test. In SPSS, a test called the *Levene's test for equality of variances* can be run. We will need to examine the probability value (*p*-value) of this test, which is usually set at 0.05. We only need to remember that the *p*-value *must not be significant* (i.e. the *p*-value must be larger than 0.05). If it is significant (i.e. in the case when $p < 0.05$), it means that we *violate* the homogeneity of variance assumption because the Levene's test indicates that the variances for each group are *unequal*. We will discuss this further below.

How to run the independent-samples t-test in SPSS

The data *Ch13 Independent ttest.sav* (downloadable from the *companion website*) will be used to illustrate this analysis (see Figure 13.3). This *quasi-experimental* study examined the effect of explicit (with a provision of a rating scale and comments) and implicit feedback (with a provision of general comments) on students' picture description speaking tasks. There was *no control group* in this study.

There were two intact English-speaking classes. There were 18 students in the first class and 22 in the second. The researcher decided to toss a coin to assign the experimental conditions to the classes. The first class received the explicit feedback condition and the second class received the implicit feedback condition. Both classes had the same teacher, who was a native speaker of English (Australian) with five years' teaching experience and a Master of Education (TESOL). The teacher was trained on how to deliver lessons on picture description tasks with explicit and implicit feedback. The classes met twice a week each (1.5 hours each time). The first class had their sessions on Monday and Wednesday at 10 a.m., whereas the second class had their sessions on Tuesday and Thursday at the same time. The experiment lasted three weeks. It was not possible to have the two classes on the same day and at the same time due to the use of the same teacher. If one class had been held in the morning and the other in the afternoon, there would have been a concern that the hour of teaching and the teacher might prove to be confounding factors on the

	ID	Gender	Group	SpeakingPre	SpeakingP...	var
1	1	2.00	1.00	19.00	25.00	
2	2	2.00	1.00	16.00	26.00	
3	3	1.00	1.00	7.00	15.00	
4	4	1.00	1.00	19.00	24.00	
5	5	2.00	1.00	18.00	26.00	
6	6	2.00	1.00	10.00	20.00	
7	7	1.00	1.00	13.00	21.00	
8	8	2.00	1.00	9.00	18.00	
9	9	1.00	1.00	8.00	17.00	
10	10	1.00	1.00	9.00	16.00	
11	11	1.00	1.00	8.00	14.00	
12	12	1.00	1.00	6.00	12.00	
13	13	2.00	1.00	16.00	25.00	
14	14	2.00	1.00	18.00	28.00	
15	15	1.00	1.00	10.00	17.00	
16	16	2.00	1.00	16.00	18.00	
17	17	1.00	1.00	12.00	19.00	
18	18	2.00	1.00	13.00	20.00	
19	19	2.00	2.00	15.00	28.00	
20	20	1.00	2.00	12.00	16.00	
21	21	1.00	2.00	16.00	17.00	
22	22	1.00	2.00	12.00	15.00	
23	23	2.00	2.00	13.00	19.00	

Data View   Variable View

FIGURE 13.3   *An outlook of the independent-samples t-test file*

outcome. Both classes took a pretest and a posttest. Students' test performance was rated by the teacher and the researcher using a six-point rating
scale on: (1) accuracy of the picture description; (2) fluency in speaking;
(3) accuracy of the language structures used; (4) intelligibility of pronunciation; (5) range of vocabulary use; and (6) communication skills, such as
non-verbal communication (total of 30 points). The Cronbach's alpha for
the intrarater reliability coefficients were 0.96 (Rater 1) and 0.95 (Rater
2) for the pretest; and 0.97 (Rater 1) and 0.96 (Rater 2) for the posttest.

The interrater reliability coefficients (Cronbach's alpha) for the pretest and posttest were 0.97 and 0.98, respectively. Each score was an average of the two raters' scores.

After we have entered the data into SPSS and checked for data entry accuracy, there are *four* steps we need to take in order to examine the effect of the experimental conditions on students' speaking performance.

- The first step is to check the descriptive statistics (e.g. mean, median, mode, skewness and kurtosis statistics) of each test to make sure that the data were normally distributed. It is highly recommended that you use the *Explore* menu in the *Descriptive Statistics* in SPSS because it will allow you to examine the 95 percent confidence interval.

- The second step is to perform an independent-samples *t*-test to find out whether both groups differed significantly in their pretest scores. This is important because a pre-existing difference can covariate the posttest difference. If this is the case, ANCOVA should be used instead of an independent-samples *t*-test.

- The third step is to perform an independent-samples *t*-test on the posttest, check whether there is a statistical significance ($p < 0.05$), and compute an effect size.

- The fourth stage is to report and interpret the findings.

The following are the steps to follow to perform an independent-samples *t*-test in SPSS.

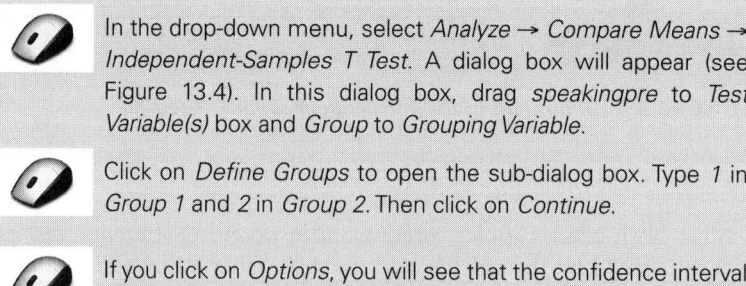 In the drop-down menu, select *Analyze → Compare Means → Independent-Samples T Test*. A dialog box will appear (see Figure 13.4). In this dialog box, drag *speakingpre* to *Test Variable(s)* box and *Group* to *Grouping Variable*.

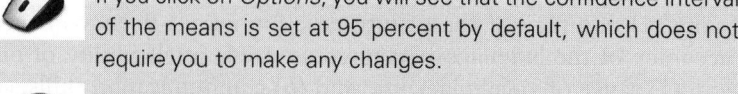 Click on *Define Groups* to open the sub-dialog box. Type *1* in *Group 1* and *2* in *Group 2*. Then click on *Continue*.

If you click on *Options*, you will see that the confidence interval of the means is set at 95 percent by default, which does not require you to make any changes.

 Click on *OK*.

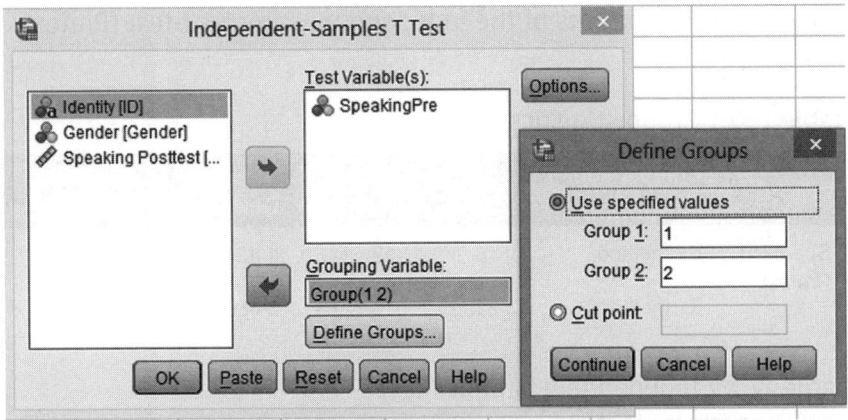

FIGURE 13.4   *SPSS dialog to run an independent-samples t-test*

Table 13.2 presents the SPSS outputs of the independent-samples *t*-test for the pretest speaking scores. Table 13.2.1 reports on the descriptive statistics (means, SD, and std error mean) between the two groups. Table 13.2.2 (which was split into two tables here due to the margin of the page) reports on the Levene's test for equality of variances. Remember that this variance must *not be statistically significant* in order to make sure that both groups are relatively equal. In Table 13.2.2, the Levene's test was non-significant ($p = 0.07$). In Table 13.2.3, examine the *t*, *df* and *Sig* (2-tailed) columns in this output. Sig (2-tailed) will tell us whether there was a statistical significance between the two groups. It is important to notice that *df* in the independent-samples *t*-test is different from that in the paired-samples *t*-test. In the independent-samples *t*-test, *df* is calculated as *total N–2* because there are two independent groups being compared.

We found that it was non-significant ($t[38] = -0.89$, $p = 0.38$, $d = -0.28$). We can use Melody Wiseheart's effect size website to compute a Cohen's *d* effect size. Note that for an independent-samples *t*-test, we do not need to compute a correlation coefficient. Because we set the significance value at 0.05, we *cannot reject* the null hypothesis (which hypothesized that there was no statistical difference between the two groups' scores) because the *p*-value was larger than 0.05. On the basis of this independent-samples *t*-test, we concluded that there was *no pre-existing difference* between the two groups prior to the experiment.

Table 13.2 SPSS outputs of the independent-samples t-test (Pretest, N = 40).

Table 13.2.1 Group statistics

	Comparison Groups	N	Mean	Std. Deviation	Std. Error Mean
Speaking Pretest	Ex method1	18	12.6111	4.42106	1.04205
	Ex method2	22	13.7273	3.48031	.74200

Table 13.2.2 Independent samples test

		Levene's Test for Equality of Variances	
		F	Sig.
Speaking Pretest	Equal variances assumed	3.448	.071
	Equal variances not assumed		

Table 13.2.3 Independent samples test

		t-test for Equality of Means					95% Confidence Interval of the Difference	
		t	df	Sig. (2-tailed)	Mean Difference	Std. Error Difference	Lower	Upper
Speaking Pretest	Equal variances assumed	-.894	38	.377	-1.11616	1.24875	-3.64413	1.4118
	Equal variances not assumed	-.873	31.958	.389	-1.11616	1.27924	-3.72201	1.4896

We will now follow the same steps to analyze the posttest scores. Table 13.3 presents the SPSS outputs of the independent-samples *t*-test for the posttest speaking scores. Note that Tables 13.3.1, 13.3.2 and 13.3.3 are interpreted the same way as discussed for Table 13.2.

Table 13.3 SPSS outputs of the independent-samples t-test (Posttest, N = 40).

Table 13.3.1 Group statistics

	Comparison Groups	N	Mean	Std. Deviation	Std. Error Mean
Speaking Posttest	Ex method1	18	20.0556	4.67122	1.10102
	Ex method2	22	16.1364	5.17591	1.10351

Table 13.3.2 Independent samples test

		Levene's Test for Equality of Variances	
		F	Sig.
Speaking Posttest	Equal variances assumed	.106	.747
	Equal variances not assumed		

Table 13.3.3 Independent samples test

		t-test for Equality of Means					95% Confidence Interval of the Difference	
		t	df	Sig. (2-tailed)	Mean Difference	Std. Error Difference	Lower	Upper
Speaking Posttest	Equal variances assumed	2.488	38	.017	3.91919	1.57527	.73022	7.10817
	Equal variances not assumed	2.514	37.597	.016	3.91919	1.55883	.76238	7.07600

How to report the independent-samples t-test results

As discussed in relation to the paired-samples *t*-test, all statistical outputs should be presented when space allows. The following is an example of how you would write up this finding:

It was found that all the statistical assumptions for the independent-samples *t*-test were not violated in the data set. The Levene's test for equality of variances was examined to ascertain that both experimental groups had equal variance. This test was not statistically significant (p = 0.75). It was found that there was a statistically significant difference between the two experimental groups (t[38] = 2.49, p = 0.05, d = 0.80, large effect size). The explicit feedback group (with a provision of a rating scale and comments) outperformed the implicit feedback group (with a provision of general comments) on students' picture description speaking performance (i.e. the mean difference was 3.92). According to Cohen (1992), as the Cohen's *d* effect size was large, the experimental condition was effective in improving students' oral performance in picture description tasks. On the basis of this independent-samples *t*-test, we concluded that there was a statistically significant difference between the two groups after the experiment.

There are many examples of published experimental research that reported on an independent-samples *t*-test. Note also that many research articles did not incorporate Cohen's effect size in their findings and discussion.

Cross (2009) examined the effect of listening strategy instruction on advanced-level, adult, Japanese EFL learners' listening comprehension by using BBC news videotexts and a quasi-experimental design. He first found that the paired-samples *t*-test indicated a significant gain between the pretest and posttest for both the control group and experimental groups (i.e. $t = -4.135$, $df = 7$, $p = .004$; $t = -4.436$, $df = 6$, $p = .004$, p. 161). An independent-samples *t*-test, however, suggests that Cross's study might have been limited in terms of the sample sizes (n = 8 for the control group and n = 7 for the experimental group) and ran the risk of committing a *Type II error*. Cross should not have used both types of *t*-tests in his study. Instead, the non-parametric version of the *t*-test should have been used (i.e. the Wilcoxon signed ranks test in place of the paired-samples *t*-test, and the Mann–Whitney U test in place of the independent-samples *t*-test). Furthermore, Cohen's *d* effect sizes should have been reported.

Summary

We have explored the paired-samples *t*-test and the independent-samples *t*-test for experimental research. We have examined the statistical proce-dures involved in *t*-test analysis using SPSS and discussed how to present *t*-test findings. We have seen examples of published experimental studies in language learning. We have learned that the two types of *t*-tests have two common features. The first is that they are both used to determine whether two mean scores are significantly different. The second is that they both rely on the use of the *t* distribution to determine whether there is a statistical significance ($p < 0.05$). Of course, as we use SPSS to analyze the data for us, we do not need to consult the critical t-value in a t-distribution table. Apart from these two common features, both t-tests are quite different. The independent-samples t-test has a similar function to repeated-measures ANOVA, which will be discussed in the next chapter. Finally, it has been noted that when a sample size is small, it may be more appropriate to employ the non-parametric version of t-tests, although an inference or claim made on the basis of the statistical findings is much weaker. We present non-parametric tests in Chapter 15.

Research exercise

To download exercises for this chapter visit: http://www.bloomsbury.com/experimental-research-methods-in-language-learning-9781441189110/

Discussion

1 What are the similarities between a paired-samples t-test and an independent-samples t-test?
2 What are the differences between a paired-samples t-test and an independent-samples t-test?
3 Why is statistical significance (e.g. $p < 0.05$) not enough to say about the effect of an independent variable on a dependent variable?
4 What does a Cohen's d effect size of 0.90 tell us about practical significance?
5 Reflection: What is the most important lesson you have learned from this chapter?

Further reading

Larson-Hall, J 2010, *A guide to doing statistics in second language research using SPSS*, New York: Routledge.

Chapter 9 explores more than the two t-tests presented in the current chapter. It includes, for example, the one-sample t-test. This chapter also illustrates how to use SPSS to run t-tests. There are several other examples of studies that this current chapter does not include.

Urdan, TC 2005, *Statistics in plain English*, Lawrence Erlbaum Associates, Mahwah, NJ.

Chapter 9 presents conceptual descriptions of both the paired- and independent-samples t-tests. It presents statistical formulas that this current chapter has avoided, but they may be useful if you would like to see exactly how each test is calculated.

CHAPTER FOURTEEN

Analyses of Variance (ANOVAs)

Leading questions

1 If there are three experimental groups and you would like to determine which group is more effective in terms of learning improvement, what would you do?
2 What do you know about analysis of variance (ANOVA) and analysis of covariance (ANCOVA)?
3 If you know something of these statistical tests, do you think they are difficult to learn? Why or why not?

Introduction

This chapter introduces three types of analyses of variance (ANOVAs) that can do similar jobs to the *t*-tests. ANOVAs are parametric tests that involve procedures that are more sophisticated than those of the *t*-tests. The first type is a one-way analysis of variance (ANOVA), which is similar to the independent-samples *t*-test. The second is an analysis of covariance (ANCOVA), which is an extension of an ANOVA obtained by including the covariates that play a significant role in influencing an experimental effect. Finally, we will consider a repeated-measures ANOVA, which has a similar logic to a paired-samples *t*-test, but can be used when we have several repeated measures of the same dependent variables. It can also be used to determine whether there is a group difference that indicates an experimental effect on the dependent variables.

The one-way analysis of variance (ANOVA)

A one-way (or one-factor) (independent-measures) ANOVA is a parametric test that is used to determine whether there is a statistical significance between scores obtained by two or more groups in an experimental study that examines the effects of one independent variable (i.e. one-factor which originates the term *one-way*). Generally speaking, a one-way ANOVA can perform the *same analysis* as the independent-samples *t*-test we discussed in the previous chapter. That is, if there are two groups of participants to compare, the statistical outcomes between an independent-samples *t*-test and a one-way ANOVA would be essentially the same, except that an independent-samples *t*-test reports a *t*-value, whereas a one-way ANOVA reports an *F*-value. You can use the data file for the independent-samples *t*-test analysis in the previous chapter to analyze a one-way ANOVA, after we have discussed how to conduct it in SPSS.

A one-way ANOVA has several advantages over a *t*-test. Its major advantage is that it can compare more than two groups (e.g. three, four, five, and so on) in one single analysis. Furthermore, ANOVA can minimize the possibility of a Type I error (i.e. rejecting the null hypothesis when it should not be rejected) more conservatively than a *t*-test. For example, if there are three groups of learners in our experiment, we need to compare two groups at a time using an independent-samples *t*-test and we would end up carrying out three separate *t*-tests (i.e. 1 versus 2, 2 versus 3, and 1 versus 3). This can not only be time-consuming, but it also means that we are more likely to make an error in judging a statistical significance each time we perform a *t*-test. When we compute three independent-samples *t*-tests from the three groups of participants, we typically set a *p*-value of 0.05 in each hypothesis testing. When we do one *t*-test, we allow a 5 percent chance to be wrong in rejecting the null hypothesis. That is, we are likely to be correct with a probability of 0.95. So if we perform two *t*-tests, this probability will be 0.95 × 0.95 (= 0.90) and for three *t*-tests, it will be 0.86 (i.e. 0.95 × 0.95 × 0.95). What it means is that our chance to be wrong in rejecting the null hypothesis has increased to 14 percent. The key problems when we use multiple *t*-tests within the same data set is that individual participants in a single group vary in their performance or reported thoughts or behavior not only within groups (i.e. within-group variation) but also between groups (i.e. between-group variation).

A one-way ANOVA therefore considers *errors* arising from within-group differences when it analyzes group differences. In other words, a one-way ANOVA separates the variance that is attributable to *between-group* differences from the variance that is attributable to *within-group* differences. When there are more than two groups to compare, a one-way ANOVA will be *more robust* in making a statistical inference as it takes a single analysis in testing a *p*-value at 0.05. It should be noted that in the previous chapter, we used an independent-samples *t*-test to check whether there is a statistical pre-existing difference between two groups prior to an experimental study. We can use a one-way ANOVA to do the same job when there are more than two groups (see e.g. Ammar & Spada 2006; Erdener & Burnham 2005).

It is crucial to note that since a one-way ANOVA performs comparisons among three or more groups all at once, when there is a statistical significance, *we will not know which groups differ* (unlike an independent-samples *t*-test, which has only two groups, making it easier to detect). In order to identify where a group difference exists, we need to perform a statistical test known as a *post hoc* analysis. SPSS can compute a *post hoc* test easily (this is illustrated below). There are more than ten *post hoc* tests for us to choose from in SPSS. We can use all of them, but it will mean there will be many statistical outputs. As several *post hoc* tests are likely to yield the same findings, in practice we only need *one post hoc* test to help us identify each group that significantly differs from the others. The following are examples of *post hoc tests*: *Bonferroni*, *Scheffe* and *Tukey*. Each of these *post hoc* tests functions similarly to an independent-sample *t*-test.

Numerous experimental studies in language learning have used a one-way ANOVA to answer research questions (e.g. Akakura 2012; Ahmadian 2012; Ahmadian & Tavakoli 2011; Morgan-Short & Bowden 2006; Sheen 2010; van Gelderen *et al.* 2011). We will discuss some of these studies below. These studies may have also used other types of ANOVAs to answer other research questions (e.g. ANCOVA and repeated-measures ANOVA, which will be discussed below).

The statistical assumptions of the one-way ANOVA

The statistical assumptions for the one-way ANOVA are the same as those for the independent-samples *t*-tests discussed in the previous chapter. It is essential that we check the relevant descriptive statistics prior to performing any statistical tests. For the one-way ANOVA, we need to make sure that the data for each group are normally distributed and that each comparison group has a homogeneous variance (so that it meets the homogeneity of variance assumption—checked by using the Levene statistic).

How to compute the one-way ANOVA with a post hoc test in SPSS

The data *Ch14 Oneway ANOVA.sav* (downloadable from the *companion website*) will be used to illustrate this analysis (see Figure 14.1). This study

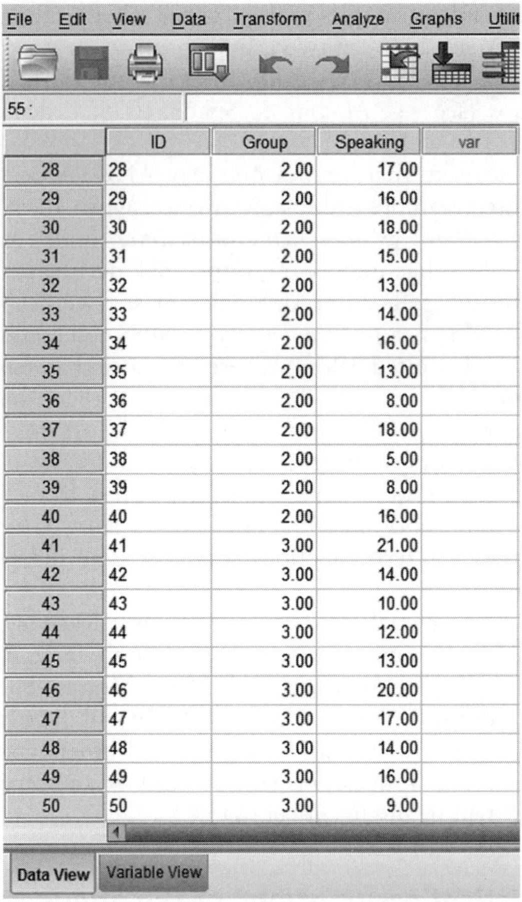

| File | Edit | View | Data | Transform | Analyze | Graphs | Utilit |

55:

	ID	Group	Speaking	var
28	28	2.00	17.00	
29	29	2.00	16.00	
30	30	2.00	18.00	
31	31	2.00	15.00	
32	32	2.00	13.00	
33	33	2.00	14.00	
34	34	2.00	16.00	
35	35	2.00	13.00	
36	36	2.00	8.00	
37	37	2.00	18.00	
38	38	2.00	5.00	
39	39	2.00	8.00	
40	40	2.00	16.00	
41	41	3.00	21.00	
42	42	3.00	14.00	
43	43	3.00	10.00	
44	44	3.00	12.00	
45	45	3.00	13.00	
46	46	3.00	20.00	
47	47	3.00	17.00	
48	48	3.00	14.00	
49	49	3.00	16.00	
50	50	3.00	9.00	

Data View | Variable View

FIGURE 14.1 *An SPSS outlook of the one-way ANOVA file*

was actually from the same *quasi-experimental* study that we examined in relation to the independent-samples *t*-test in the last chapter. The study examined the effect of explicit (with a provision of a rating scale and comments; Group 1, n = 18) and implicit feedback (with a provision of general comments; Group 2, n = 22) on students' picture description speaking tasks. There is one additional group in this data set—the *control group* (n = 22). This group was excluded in the previous discussion so that we could focus on illustrating the *t*-test analysis. In this data file, the pretest scores were removed. To perform a one-way ANOVA, we need to follow the same *four* steps we listed in our discussion of the independent-samples *t*-test.

One-way ANOVA or two-way ANOVA?

The one-way ANOVA in the *Compare Means* menu allows us to *compare several dependent variables simultaneously* (i.e. when we have more than one test), whereas the *General Linear Model for a univariate analysis* allows us to analyze one dependent variable at a time. However, in the univariate test, we can examine independent variables or factors that may interact with each other to affect the dependent variable of interest. This test is known as a *two-way ANOVA*. This book will not illustrate how to perform a two-way ANOVA due to the limited scope of the book, but in the ANCOVA analysis illustrated below, you can learn how to adapt it to performing a two-way ANOVA because the univariate function in SPSS is also what we use to perform an ANCOVA. The following are the steps to follow to perform a one-way ANOVA using the *Compare Means* menu in SPSS.

 In the drop-down menu, select *Analyze → Compare Means → One-Way ANOVA*. A dialog box will appear (see Figure 14.2). In this dialog box, drag *speakingpost* to the *Dependent List* box and *Comparison Group* to the *Factor* box.

 Click on *Post Hoc* to open the sub-dialog box. Check *Bonferroni*. Then click on *Continue*. Note that we do not need to perform a *post hoc* test if there is no statistical significance, but we will perform one now to illustrate how it is done.

 Click on *Options*, check *Descriptive, Homogeneity of variance test* and *Mean plot* (which is optional) (see Figure 14.3). Then click on *Continue* and finally *OK*.

Table 14.1 presents some of the SPSS outputs of the one-way ANOVA for the speaking posttest scores. Table 14.1.1 reports on descriptive statistics (e.g. means, SD and standard error mean) between the three groups. Table 14.1.2 reports the Levene's test for equality of variances. Remember that it must *not be statistically significant* in order to make sure that both groups were relatively equal. In this table, the Levene's test was non-significant (p = 0.73). Note that this table also reports the degrees of freedom for this analysis (df1 = 2 [i.e. 3 groups minus 1] and df2 = 59 [i.e. 62 minus 3 groups). We typically include these dfs in our report. Table 14.1.3 shows the ANOVA findings. We examine the F, *df* and *Sig* columns in this output.

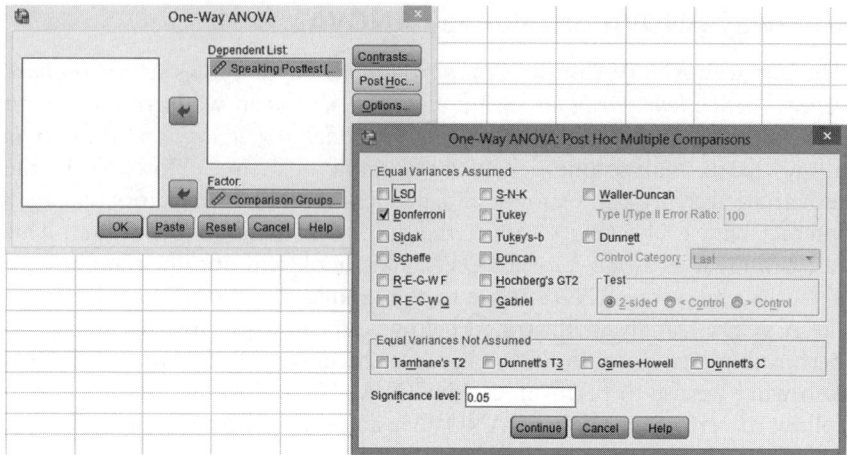

FIGURE 14.2 *SPSS dialog to run a one-way ANOVA*

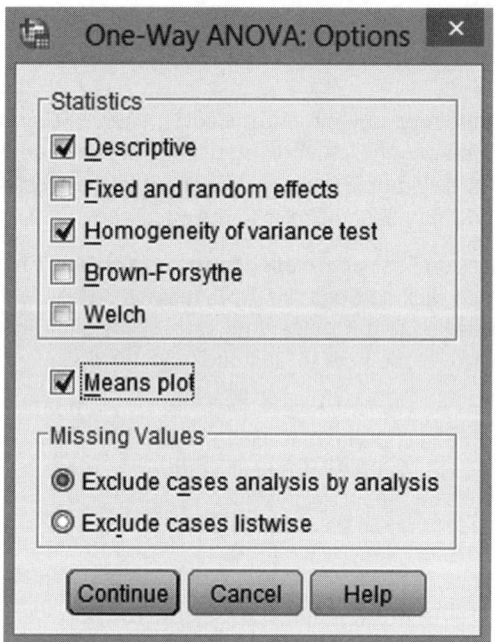

FIGURE 14.3 *The option sub-dialog in a paired-samples t-test*

Sig tells us whether there was a statistically significant difference between the three groups.

We found that such a difference did exist ($F[2, 59] = 7.97$, $p = 0.001$). Since there were three groups in this analysis, we could not tell which group differed from the others. By examining the mean scores of the three

Table 14.1 SPSS outputs of the one-way ANOVA (N = 62)

Table 14.1.1 Descriptive statistics

	N	Mean	Std. Deviation	Std. Error	95% Confidence Interval for Mean		Minimum	Maximum
Speaking Posttest								
					Lower Bound	Upper Bound		
Ex method1	18	20.0556	4.67122	1.10102	17.7326	22.3785	12.00	28.00
Ex method2	22	16.1364	5.17591	1.10351	13.8415	18.4312	5.00	28.00
Control Group	22	14.2727	3.90582	.83272	12.5410	16.0045	7.00	21.00
Total	62	16.6129	5.10979	.64894	15.3153	17.9105	5.00	28.00

Table 14.1.2 Test of homogeneity of variances

Speaking Posttest			
Levene Statistic	df1	df2	Sig.
.313	2	59	.732

Table 14.1.3 ANOVA

Speaking Posttest					
	Sum of Squares	df	Mean Square	F	Sig.
Between Groups	338.811	2	169.405	7.971	.001
Within Groups	1253.899	59	21.253		
Total	1592.710	61			

groups, we found that the experimental method 1 group had a higher score than the experimental method 2 group, which in turn was higher than the control group. However, we do not know whether these means were all significantly different. We need to perform a *post hoc* test to find out (which we have in this SPSS output). Table 14.1.4 presents the *Bonferroni post hoc* test outcome. It was found that there were statistically significant differences between the experimental methods 1 and 2 ($p = 0.029$), and the experimental method 1 and the control group ($p = 0.001$). However, the experimental method 2 and the control group did not differ statistically ($p = 0.55$).

Table 14.1.4 Multiple comparisons

Dependent Variable: Speaking Posttest						
Bonferroni						
(I) Comparison Groups	(J) Comparison Groups	Mean Difference (I-J)	Std. Error	Sig.	95% Confidence Interval	
					Lower Bound	Upper Bound
Ex method1	Ex method2	3.91919*	1.46517	.029	.3088	7.5296
	Control Group	5.78283*	1.46517	.001	2.1724	9.3932
Ex method2	Ex method1	−3.91919*	1.46517	.029	−7.5296	−.3088
	Control Group	1.86364	1.38998	.555	−1.5615	5.2888
Control Group	Ex method1	−5.78283*	1.46517	.001	−9.3932	−2.1724
	Ex method2	−1.86364	1.38998	.555	−5.2888	1.5615

*. The mean difference is significant at the 0.05 level.

Since SPSS did not report an effect size for us, we can use Melody Wiseheart's effect size website (<http://www.cognitiveflexibility.org/effectsize/>, viewed February 1, 2014) to compute a Cohen's *d* effect size for these two pairs. It was found that a Cohen's *d* for the difference between the experimental groups 1 and 2 was 0.796 (≈ 0.80), whereas a Cohen's *d* for the difference between the experimental group 1 and the control group was 1.35. Both effect sizes were large. Recall that a Cohen's *d* of 1.0 means that there is one standard deviation difference between the mean scores of the two comparison groups. In the case of 1.35, it means that there is a 1.35 standard deviation difference between the two groups.

How to report a one-way ANOVA with post hoc *tests*

As we discussed in the previous chapter, it is important to be specific and transparent in your report (e.g. all statistical outputs should be presented or made available upon request). Some of the tables in Table 14.1 (e.g. the Levene statistic and some *post hoc* outputs) may not be presented separately, but may be integrated into your writing. The following is an example of how you would write up the findings:

According to the one-way ANOVA, it was found that there was a statistically significant difference between the three groups ($F[2, 59] =$

7.97, $p < 0.05$). A Bonferroni post hoc test was performed to identify where the statistically significant differences occurred. It was found that there were statistically significant differences between the experimental methods 1 and 2 ($p < 0.05$, d = 0.80), and between the experimental method 1 and the control group ($p < 0.05$, d = 1.35). However, the experimental method 2 and the control group did not differ statistically ($p = 0.55$). The findings indicate that the explicit feedback group outperformed both the implicit feedback group and the control group on students' picture description speaking performance (the mean differences were 3.92 and 5.78, respectively). Figure 14.4 presents the mean plot between the three groups.

There are several examples of experimental studies using a one-way ANOVA to analyze the data. For example, Borodkin and Faust (2014) used a one-way ANOVA to examine the differences between high-proficiency L2 learners, low-proficiency L2 learners and individuals with dyslexia, and found statistical differences between the groups in all tasks (e.g. phonological awareness, Rapid Automatized Naming of Objects (RAN-O), and Rapid Automatized Naming of Letters (RAN-L) tasks. The researchers presented their findings in a table (their Table 2), which includes the mean scores, F values, dfs, p-values, and eta squared (η^2) as effect sizes. Note

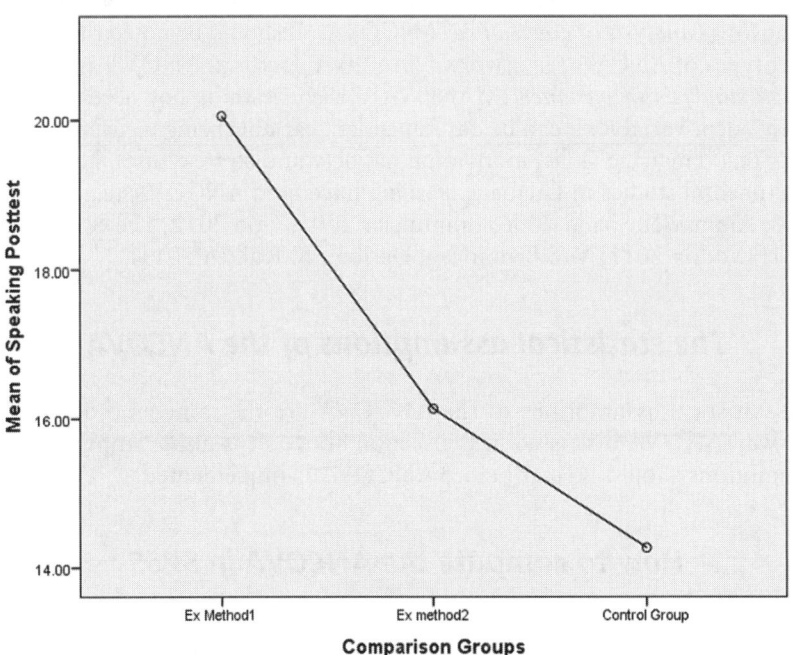

FIGURE 14.4 *Mean plot among the three groups*

that eta squared is interpreted in a similar way to a reliability coefficient. For example, an eta square of 0.30 means that 30 percent of the overall variance is due to the independent variable of interest.

Winke (2013) performed a one-way ANOVA to investigate whether visual enhancement affects noticing of the passive forms. Since the Levene's tests were significant at 0.05, Winke could not assume the equality of variances and used 'Welch's F-test, which accounts for unequal variance for each ANOVA' (p. 337). It was found that, for example, enhancement had a statistical effect on total fixation time ($F[1, 49] = 5.90$, $p < .05$, $r^2 = .31$), and on reading time ($F[1, 49] = 9.42$, $p < .001$, $r^2 = .38$, p. 337). It should be noted that r^2 *is interpreted the same way as the eta squared.*

The analysis of covariance (ANCOVA)

Experimental research in language learning often encounters a pre-existing difference in a dependent variable (e.g. a pretest score) before an experimental treatment begins. This situation is often a case for a quasi-experimental test because there is a lack of randomization to control confounding variables. In other words, a pre-existing difference in a dependent variable can be seen as a confounding factor that interferes with the main effect of the independent variable of interest in an experimental study. There is another type of ANOVA that has been designed to control such a pre-existing difference. This analysis is known as *analysis of covariance* (ANCOVA). It should be noted that unlike other types of ANOVA (e.g. two-way ANOVA, factorial ANOVA and *multivariate analysis of variance* [MANOVA]), a *covariate* is not necessarily an independent variable. It can be any dependent variable being measured in the study (e.g. language skills, motivation, anxiety and strategy use). Numerous experimental studies in language learning have used ANCOVA (e.g. Ammar 2008; Ammar & Spada 2006; Brantmeier 2005; Goo 2012; Lee & Kalyuga 2011; Lyddon 2011; Van Beuningen, De Jong & Kuiken 2011).

The statistical assumptions of the ANCOVA

The statistical assumptions of the ANCOVA are the same as those of the one-way ANOVA discussed in the section above. It is important that these assumptions should be met before ANCOVA is implemented.

How to compute the ANCOVA in SPSS

The data *Ch14 ANCOVA.sav* (downloadable from the *companion website*) will be used to illustrate this analysis (see Figure 14.5). This study examined

File   Edit   View   Data   Transform   Analyze   Graphs   Utilities   Add-ons

	id	Group	AnxietyPRE	IELTSPRE	IELTSPOST
16	16	1	3.00	5.00	6.50
17	17	1	3.00	6.50	7.50
18	18	1	4.00	6.00	7.00
19	19	1	2.00	5.00	7.50
20	20	1	5.00	4.00	5.00
21	21	1	1.00	6.50	8.00
22	22	1	5.00	4.00	5.00
23	23	1	2.00	6.00	7.00
24	24	1	3.00	6.00	7.00
25	25	1	5.00	5.00	5.50
26	26	2	5.00	4.50	5.00
27	27	2	5.00	5.00	6.00
28	28	2	5.00	6.00	6.00
29	29	2	4.00	7.00	7.00
30	30	2	4.00	7.00	7.00
31	31	2	5.00	7.00	7.50
32	32	2	5.00	6.00	6.00

FIGURE 14.5   *An SPSS outlook of the ANCOVA file*

the effect of test management strategy training on EFL students' listening comprehension IELTS performance. Fifty participants were randomly assigned into an experimental group who received the test management strategy training and the control group who received a general IELTS listening training. The experimental treatment and instructions lasted 10 weeks (three hours per week).

There were two pretests given to the participants prior to the experimental treatment (a general test-anxiety trait questionnaire and an IELTS listening pretest). Two independent-samples t-tests were performed on these two pretests. It was found that there was a statistically significant difference in the level of test-anxiety between the two groups ($t[48] = -2.47$, $p < 0.05$, $d = -0.70$). However, there was no statistical significance in their IELTS listening pretest scores ($t[48] = -0.88$, $p = 0.39$, $d = -0.25$). On the basis of the statistical analyses, it was decided that the level of their test anxiety would be used as a covariate when analyzing the posttest scores. It is important to note that when we conduct an ANCOVA, we need to follow the same *four* steps we discussed in the independent-samples *t*-test presented in the previous chapter.

The following are the steps to follow to perform a one-way ANCOVA using the *General Linear Model* menu in SPSS.

 In the drop-down menu, select Analyze → General Linear Model → Univariate. A dialog box will appear (see Figure 14.6). In this dialog box, drag *IELTS Listening Posttest* to the *Dependent Variable* box and *Comparison Group* to the *Fixed Factor(s)* box.

 Click on Options to open the sub-dialog box. Move *group* in the *Factor(s) and Factor Interactions* to the *Display Means for* box. Check *Compare main effects.* In the Display section, check *Descriptive statistics, Homogeneity of variance test, Estimates of effect size* and *Observed power* (see Figure 14.7). Then click on *Continue* and finally *OK.*

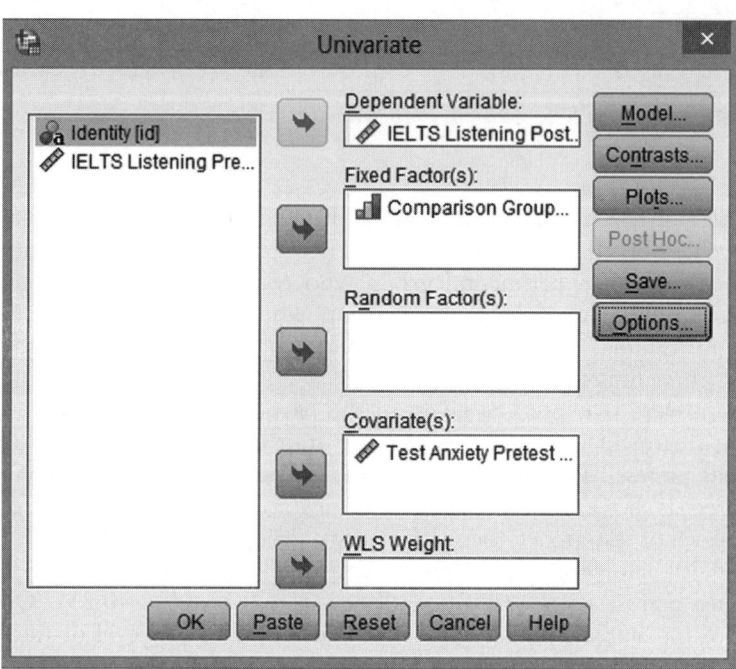

FIGURE 14.6 *SPSS dialog to run an ANCOVA*

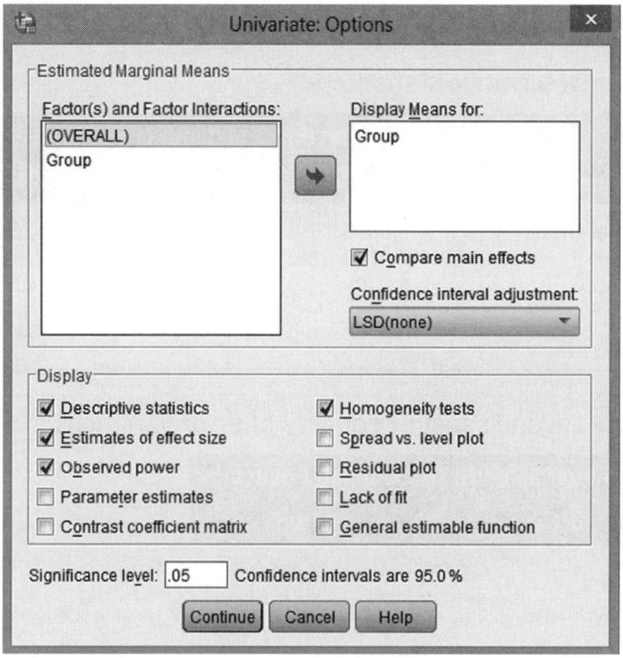

FIGURE 14.7   *The option sub-dialog in ANCOVA*

Table 14.2 presents some of the SPSS outputs of the ANCOVA for the IELTS listening posttest scores. Table 14.2.1 reports on the descriptive statistics (including means, SD and std error mean) between the two groups. Table 14.2.2 presents the Levene's test for equality of variances. This test was non-significant ($p = 0.26$). Note that this table also reports the degrees of freedom for this analysis (df1 = 1 [i.e. 2 groups minus 1] and df2 = 48 [i.e. 50 minus 2] groups). Table 14.2.3 presents the results of the Test of Between-subject Effect. We examine the F, df and Sig columns in this output. Sig tells us whether there was a statistically significant difference between the two groups. According to this table, it was found that the pre-existing test-anxiety trait was still the main factor affecting the posttest scores ($F[1, 48] = 14.96$, $p < 0.05$, partial eta squared $[\eta_p^2] = 0.24$).

There was also a statistically significant difference in the group effect ($F[1, 48] = 4.70$, $p < 0.05$, partial eta squared $[\eta_p^2] = 0.09$). The influence of a covariate must not be ignored. If we conduct a univariate ANOVA on the posttest without using the test-anxiety as a covariate (also see Table 14.2.6), we will find the following main effect of the experimental treatment: $F(1, 48) = 10.48$, $p < 0.05$, $\eta_p^2 = 0.19$. We can see that the effect size of the experimental treatment in the ANCOVA was reduced to half the size of that produced in a univariate ANOVA. ANCOVA therefore allows us to be more realistic in evaluating the effect of an experimental treatment.

Table 14.2 SPSS outputs of the ANCOVA (N = 50)

Table 14.2.1 Descriptive statistics

Dependent Variable: IELTS Listening Post			
Comparison Groups	Mean	Std. Deviation	N
Experimental Group	6.8600	1.05594	25
Control Group	5.9200	.99666	25
Total	6.3900	1.12163	50

Table 14.2.2 Levene's test of equality of error variances[a]

Dependent Variable: IELTS Listening Posttest			
F	df1	df2	Sig.
1.328	1	48	.255

Tests the null hypothesis that the error variance of the dependent variable is equal across groups.

a. Design: Intercept + AnxietyPRE + Group

Table 14.2.3 Tests of between-subjects effects

Source	Type III Sum of Squares	df	Mean Square	F	Sig.	Partial Eta Squared	Noncent. Parameter	Observ Power[b]
	Dependent Variable: IELTS Listening Posttest							
Corrected Model	23.262[a]	2	11.631	14.242	.000	.377	28.484	.998
Intercept	309.851	1	309.851	379.413	.000	.890	379.413	1.000
AnxietyPRE	12.217	1	12.217	14.960	.000	.241	14.960	.966
Group	3.837	1	3.837	4.698	.035	.091	4.698	.565
Error	38.383	47	.817					
Total	2103.250	50						
Corrected Total	61.645	49						

a. R Squared = .377 (Adjusted R Squared = .351)
b. Computed using alpha = .05

Table 14.2.4 Estimated marginal means

Estimates				
Dependent Variable: IELTS Listening Post				
Comparison Groups	**Mean**	**Std. Error**	**95% Confidence Interval**	
			Lower Bound	**Upper Bound**
Experimental Group	6.684[a]	.186	6.309	7.059
Control Group	6.096[a]	.186	5.721	6.471

a. Covariates appearing in the model are evaluated at the following values: TestAnxiety Pretest = 3.5400.

Table 14.2.5 Pairwise comparisons

Dependent Variable: IELTS Listening Posttest						
(I) Comparison Groups	**(J) Comparison Groups**	**Mean Difference (I-J)**	**Std. Error**	**Sig.[b]**	**95% Confidence Interval for Difference[b]**	
					Lower Bound	**Upper Bound**
Experimental Group	Control Group	.588*	.271	.035	.042	1.134
Control Group	Experimental Group	-.588*	.271	.035	-1.134	-.042

Based on estimated marginal means

*. The mean difference is significant at the .05 level.

b. Adjustment for multiple comparisons: Least Significant Difference (equivalent to no adjustments).

Table 14.2.6 Univariate tests

	Sum of Squares	**df**	**Mean Square**	**F**	**Sig.**	**Partial Eta Squared**	**Noncent. Parameter**	**Observed Power[a]**
Dependent Variable: IELTS Listening Post								
Contrast	11.045	1	11.045	10.477	.002	.179	10.477	.887
Error	50.600	48	1.054					

The F tests the effect of Comparison Groups. This test is based on the linearly independent pairwise comparisons among the estimated marginal means.

a. Computed using alpha = .05

How to report the ANCOVA

The following is an example of how you would write up the findings:

> According to the ANCOVA, it was found that there was a statistically significant main effect of the pre-existing test-anxiety trait (i.e. F[1, 48] = 14.96, p < 0.05, partial eta squared (η_p^2) = 0.24). There was also a statistically significant difference in the group effect (i.e. F[1, 48] = 4.70, p < 0.05, partial eta squared [η_p^2] = 0.09). In comparison with a univariate ANOVA that disregarded the existence of the test-anxiety trait among the participants, the main effect of the experimental treatment was found to be larger (F[1, 48] = 10.48, p < 0.05, η_p^2 = 0.19). The findings indicate that the test-anxiety trait had the potential to interact with the experimental treatment of test management strategies on IELTS listening improvement.

There are several examples of experimental studies in language learning research that have used a one-way ANCOVA. For example, using a quasi-experimental design, Ammar (2008) compared the effect of recasts to prompts and no corrective feedback on learners' acquisition of English third person possessive determiners. Using the pretest scores as the covariate in a posttest comparison between groups in an ANCOVA analysis, Ammar (2008, p. 198) found a statistically significant difference between the three groups (F[2, 37] = 6.20, $p < 0.001$). A *post hoc* comparison indicated that the prompt group was significantly faster than the recast group, which was also slower than the control group.

Lyddon (2012, p. 115) conducted 'a two-way ANCOVA using feedback type and target form enhancement as fixed factors, testing orders as a blocking variables, and pretest scores as a covariate.' Lyddon (2012, p. 115) found 'no effect for either feedback type, $F(3, 126) = 1.15$, $p = .334$, or textual enhancement, $F(1, 126) = .08$, $p = .774$, and no interaction, $F(3, 126) = 2.15$, $p = .097$.'

The repeated-measures analysis of variance (ANOVA)

In the last chapter, we discussed how to perform a paired-samples *t*-test to examine whether pretest scores differ statistically from posttest scores within a group of participants. The repeated-measures ANOVA can serve the same function. However, the repeated-measures ANOVA can measure changes at *more than two times points*. The repeated-measures ANOVA has broad applications for experimental data analysis. For example, it is useful for a pretest-, posttest-, and delayed-posttest design. It can examine the effects of one or more independent variables on repeated-dependent measures (a mixed ANOVA model). It can also be used to control the effects of covariates on the dependent variable of interest (a repeated-measures ANCOVA). This chapter only presents a one-way repeated-measures ANOVA.

The repeated-measures ANOVA follows the same principles as those of the other kinds of ANOVA. In particular, as we discussed in relation to the one-way ANOVA, the dependent variable of interest is affected by variations of participants' scores both within the same group and between groups. There is the need to consider such variations in estimating the effect of an experimental condition. Generally speaking, there are three sources of variation in the scores (Urdan 2005). The first source is variation associated with the average scores (i.e. mean scores) for each group each time participants' scores are measured. The second source is variation associated with the within-subject variance between Times 1, 2 and 3. The third source is the interaction between the first and the second sources. The repeated-measures ANOVA takes these sources of variation into account when evaluating whether there have been statistically significant changes across times points.

There are several experimental studies in language learning that have employed a repeated-measures ANOVA (e.g. Baralt & Gurzynski-Weiss 2011; Benati 2005; Folse 2006; Iwashita, McNamara & Elder 2001; Kissling 2013; Moskovsky, Alrabi, Paolini & Ratcheva 2012; Shintani 2011; Shintani *et al.* 2014; Strapp, Helmick, Tonkovich & Bleakney 2011; Takimoto 2008; Tian & Macaro 2012). In fact, it is one of the most commonly used statistical techniques in experimental research in language learning.

The statistical assumptions of the repeated-measures ANOVA

The statistical assumptions of the repeated-measures ANOVA are similar to those discussed previously in this chapter. However, there is one additional assumption that we need to consider. This assumption is known as the *sphericity* assumption. Sphericity refers to whether the variances of the differences between all possible pairs of comparison groups are equal. This assumption is assessed by using the *Mauchly's sphericity test*.

How to run a repeated-measures ANOVA in SPSS

The data found in *Ch14 Repeated ANOVA.sav* (downloadable from the *companion website*) will be used to illustrate a repeated-measures ANOVA (see Figure 14.8). The study for which the data was collected examined

| File | Edit | View | Data | Transform | Analyze | Graphs | Utilities | Add-ons | Window |

23 :

	ID	Gender	Group	Reading1	Reading2	Reading3
1	1	1.00	1.00	15.00	23.00	25.00
2	2	1.00	1.00	23.00	30.00	33.00
3	3	2.00	1.00	24.00	27.00	30.00
4	4	1.00	1.00	26.00	32.00	37.00
5	5	2.00	1.00	34.00	38.00	43.00
6	6	1.00	1.00	23.00	29.00	35.00
7	7	2.00	1.00	10.00	18.00	24.00
8	8	2.00	1.00	33.00	39.00	44.00
9	9	1.00	1.00	29.00	32.00	33.00
10	10	2.00	1.00	27.00	28.00	36.00
11	11	1.00	1.00	22.00	24.00	29.00
12	12	1.00	1.00	15.00	16.00	25.00
13	13	1.00	1.00	16.00	16.00	27.00
14	14	1.00	1.00	37.00	40.00	46.00
15	15	2.00	1.00	24.00	29.00	35.00
16	16	1.00	1.00	17.00	20.00	30.00
17	17	1.00	1.00	23.00	26.00	34.00
18	18	1.00	1.00	14.00	20.00	26.00
19	19	2.00	1.00	20.00	25.00	28.00
20	20	1.00	2.00	16.00	23.00	29.00
21	21	2.00	2.00	24.00	32.00	35.00
22	22	2.00	2.00	28.00	30.00	32.00
23	23	2.00	2.00	35.00	36.00	29.00

Data View | Variable View

FIGURE 14.8   *An SPSS outlook of the repeated-measures ANOVA file*

the effect of explicit feedback with a self-evaluation emphasis and implicit feedback with a topic knowledge emphasis on EFL students' reading comprehension. Sixty participants were randomly assigned into three groups: the explicit feedback group with a self-evaluation emphasis, the implicit feedback group with a topic knowledge emphasis and a control group. The instruction lasted eight weeks (two hours per week).

The participants took a reading comprehension pretest prior to the experiment and a posttest at the end of the experiment. Three weeks after the end of the experiment they took a delayed reading comprehension posttest. The tests were *parallel tests* and involved several reading test techniques, including short-answers, true-false, multiple-choice and cloze test techniques. There were 50 questions per test. The reliability coefficients for the pretest, posttest and delayed posttest were 0.91, 0.89, and 0.93, respectively.

The steps you need to take prior to a one-way repeated-measures ANOVA are similar to those discussed for the other ANOVAs.

The following are the steps to follow to perform a one-way repeated-measures ANOVA using the *General Linear Model* menu in SPSS. It should be noted that the *IBM SPSS students version* does not have this function,

 In the drop-down menu, select *Analyze → General Linear Model → Repeated Measures*. A dialog box will appear (see Figure 14.9). In the *Within-Subject Factor Name* box, type *Time* and *3* in the number of levels. We type *3* because we have three tests to be analyzed, so if you have five tests, you simply type *5*. Then click on *Define* and the *Within-Subjects variables (time)* dialog box will appear.

 In this *Within-Subjects variables (time)* dialog box (see Figure 14.10), drag *Reading1*, *Reading2* and *Reading3* to the *Within-Subjects Variables (time)* and *Group* to the *Between-Subjects Factor(s)*.

 Then click *Post Hoc* to open the sub-dialog box. In the *Factors*, drag *Group* to the *Post Hoc Tests for Group* box. Check *Bonferroni* and then click on *Continue*. Note that in this *Within-Subjects variables (time)* dialog box, you will see *Covariate* as we did when we discussed the ANCOVA above. This is where you can perform a repeated-measures ANCOVA.

 Click on *Options* to open the sub-dialog box (see Figure 14.11). In the *Factor(s) and Factor Interactions* box, drag *Group*, *Time* and *Group*Time* to *Display Means for*. In the Display section, check *Descriptive statistics, Estimates of effect size, Observed power* and *Homogeneity Test*. Then click on *Continue* and finally *OK*.

FIGURE 14.9 *SPSS dialog to run a repeated-measures ANOVA*

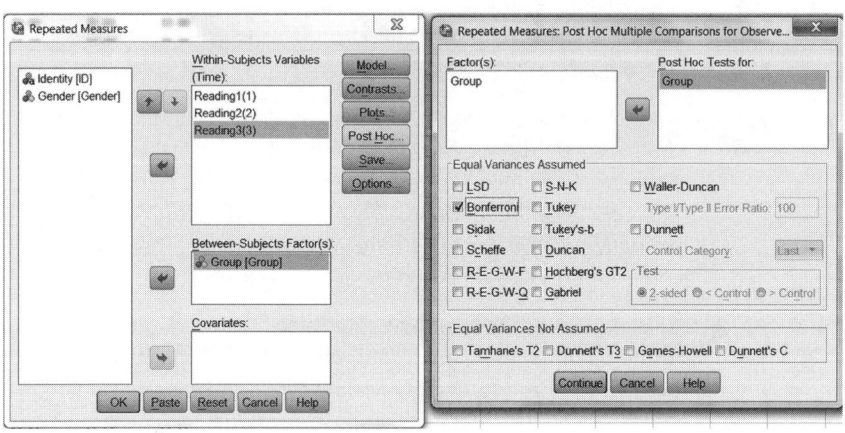

FIGURE 14.10 *SPSS sub-dialog for the within-subject variable*

nor multivariate analysis. Only the fully licensed SPSS program can perform this analysis.

Table 14.3 presents some of the SPSS outputs of the one-way repeated

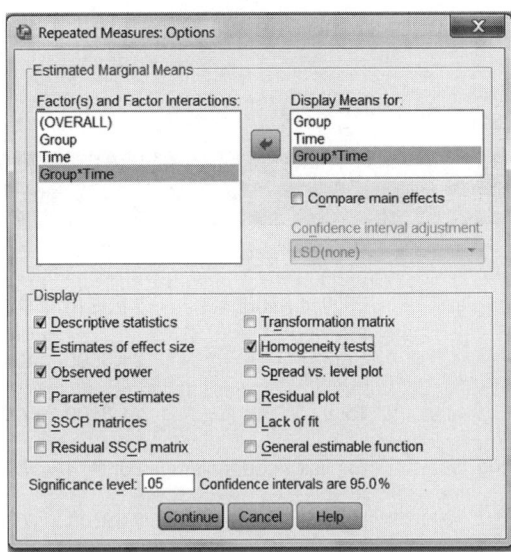

FIGURE 14.11   *SPSS option sub-dialog in a repeated-measures ANOVA*

ANOVA. It should be noted that SPSS produces many outputs in this analysis, but we discuss only some of the key results here. Table 14.3.1 is the output reports on the descriptive statistics (e.g. means, SD and std error mean) between the three groups. Table 14.3.2 is the Box's Test of Equality of Covariance Matrices. This test *must not* be significant at 0.001 ($p > 0.001$). This statistic tells us that we have homogeneity of variance. Table 14.3.3 presents the multivariate tests. This test is used to determine whether there are significant group differences for a linear combination of the dependent variables (i.e. the reading tests). This table contains four tests (i.e. Pillai's trace, Wilks' lambda, Hotelling's trace and Roy's largest root). However, we only need to consider *one* test. The Pillai's Trace is regarded as a powerful test to check whether there are group differences. This test must be statistically significant at 0.05. As you can see in this table, for both *time* and *time and factor*, the Pillai's Trace was significant ($p = 0.00$). This statistical significance means that we can now move on to examine the univariate/between-subjects effects that follow. If the Pillai's trace is *not significant, we stop our analysis here* because the rest of the outcome will not be meaningful because there are no group differences.

Table 14.3.4 presents the analysis for Mauchly's sphericity test. This test tells us whether our data violate the sphericity assumption. We need this test to be *non-significant* for this assumption to be met. In Table 14.3.4, we can see that this test was significant ($p < 0.05$). Fortunately, there is an alternative assessment to the sphericity assumption. In the same table, we can see three columns that include alternative tests (the Greenhouse–Geisser, the Huynh–Feldt, and the lower-bound). These tests indicate a

Table 14.3 SPSS outputs of the one-way repeated-measures ANOVA (N = 60)

Table 14.3.1 Descriptive statistics

	Group	Mean	Std. Deviation	N
Reading Pretest	Explicit Feedback	22.7368	7.27127	19
	Implicit Feedback	21.3810	7.69725	21
	Control	21.3500	6.45042	20
	Total	21.8000	7.07299	60
Immediate Reading Posttest	Explicit Feedback	26.9474	7.27609	19
	Implicit Feedback	24.8571	7.86311	21
	Control	22.2500	5.11834	20
	Total	24.6500	7.01530	60
Delayed Reading Posttest	Explicit Feedback	32.6316	6.55922	19
	Implicit Feedback	28.0476	6.75630	21
	Control	24.1000	4.89791	20
	Total	28.1833	6.95382	60

Table 14.3.2 Box's test of equality of covariance matrices[a]

Box's M	21.924
F	1.686
df1	12
df2	15493.572
Sig.	.063

Tests the null hypothesis that the observed covariance matrices of the dependent variables are equal across groups.

a. Design: Intercept + Group

Within Subjects Design: Time

Table 14.3.3 Multivariate tests[a]

Effect		Value	F	Hypothesis df	Error df	Sig.	Partial Eta Squared	Observed Power[d]
Time	Pillai's Trace	.788	104.024[b]	2.000	56.000	.000	.788	1.000
	Wilks' Lambda	.212	104.024[b]	2.000	56.000	.000	.788	1.000
	Hotelling's Trace	3.715	104.024[b]	2.000	56.000	.000	.788	1.000
	Roy's Largest Root	3.715	104.024[b]	2.000	56.000	.000	.788	1.000
Time * Group	Pillai's Trace	.466	8.666	4.000	114.000	.000	.233	.999
	Wilks' Lambda	.550	9.767[b]	4.000	112.000	.000	.259	1.000
	Hotelling's Trace	.790	10.865	4.000	110.000	.000	.283	1.000
	Roy's Largest Root	.751	21.416[c]	2.000	57.000	.000	.429	1.000

a. Design: Intercept + Group
Within Subjects Design: Time
b. Exact statistic
c. The statistic is an upper bound on F that yields a lower bound on the significance level.
d. Computed using alpha = .05

Table 14.3.4 Mauchly's test of sphericity[a]

Measure: MEASURE_1					Epsilon[b]		
Within Subjects Effect	Mauchly's W	Approx. Chi-Square	df	Sig.	Greenhouse-Geisser	Huynh-Feldt	Lower-bound
Time	.814	11.555	2	.003	.843	.896	.500

Tests the null hypothesis that the error covariance matrix of the orthonormalized transformed dependent variables is proportional to an identity matrix.
a. Design: Intercept + Group
Within Subjects Design: Time
b. May be used to adjust the degrees of freedom for the averaged tests of significance.
Corrected tests are displayed in the Tests of Within-Subjects Effects table.

Table 14.3.5 Tests of within-subjects effects

	Source	Type III Sum of Squares	df	Mean Square	F	Sig.	Partial Eta Squared	Observed Power[a]
	Measure: MEASURE_1							
Time	Sphericity Assumed	1246.098	2	623.049	150.877	.000	.726	1.000
	Greenhouse-Geisser	1246.098	1.686	739.208	150.877	.000	.726	1.000
	Huynh-Feldt	1246.098	1.792	695.227	150.877	.000	.726	1.000
	Lower-bound	1246.098	1.000	1246.098	150.877	.000	.726	1.000
Time * Group	Sphericity Assumed	255.490	4	63.873	15.467	.000	.352	1.000
	Greenhouse-Geisser	255.490	3.371	75.781	15.467	.000	.352	1.000
	Huynh-Feldt	255.490	3.585	71.272	15.467	.000	.352	1.000
	Lower-bound	255.490	2.000	127.745	15.467	.000	.352	.999
Error(Time)	Sphericity Assumed	470.765	114	4.130				
	Greenhouse-Geisser	470.765	96.086	4.899				
	Huynh-Feldt	470.765	102.165	4.608				
	Lower-bound	470.765	57.000	8.259				

a. Computed using alpha = .05

Table 14.3.6 Levene's test of equality of error variances[a]

	F	df1	df2	Sig.
Reading Pretest	1.061	2	57	.353
Immediate Reading Posttest	2.153	2	57	.125
Delayed Reading Posttest	1.196	2	57	.310

Tests the null hypothesis that the error variance of the dependent variable is equal across groups.
a. Design: Intercept + Group
Within Subjects Design: Time

Table 14.3.7 Tests of between-subjects effects

| Measure: MEASURE_1 | | | | | | | |
| Transformed Variable: Average | | | | | | | |
Source	Type III Sum of Squares	df	Mean Square	F	Sig.	Partial Eta Squared	Observed Power[a]
Intercept	111616.095	1	111616.095	873.094	.000	.939	1.000
Group	695.114	2	347.557	2.719	.075	.087	.517
Error	7286.864	57	127.840				

a. Computed using alpha = .05

non-statistical significance, which means that we can use these statistics to help us recalculate new degrees of freedom. Choose the Hyunh–Feldt test, which was significant at 0.896. That is, instead of having $df1$ and $df2$ as (2, 144), for example, the new dfs for Time: will be 1.79 (i.e. 2×0.896) and 102.14 (i.e. 114×0.896). Table 14.3.5 shows the results for the test within-subject effect in which we will consider whether the within-subjects effects are significant. This table contains information we do not require. Simply *focus on the Hyunh-Feldt* statistics for both *Time* and *Times*Group*.

In both sources, we find that there is a statistical significance of the F statistic ($p = 0.00$). In regard to the *Time* factor, it was found that there was a statistically significant difference between reading performances across the three reading tests ($F[1.79, 102.17] = 150.88$, $p < 0.05$, $\eta_p^2 = 0.73$). It was also found that there was a significant interaction between the time and group that contributed to the changes in the participants' reading scores across the three occasions ($F[3.59, 102.17] = 150.88$, $p < 0.05$, $\eta_p^2 = 0.35$).

Table 14.3.6 presents the Levene's Test of Equality of Error Variances. For all the three reading tests, the homogeneity assumption was not violated ($p > 0.05$). Table 14.3.7 reports the Tests of Between-subjects Effects, which will tell us whether there is a statistical group difference. According to this table, we found that the three groups did not significantly differ from one another ($F[2, 57] = 2.719$, $p = 0.08$, $\eta_p^2 = 0.09$).

It should be noted that when we conduct a one-way ANOVA on the immediate reading posttest, we will find that there is no statistical signifi-cance between the three groups ($F[2, 57] = 2.295$, $p = 0.11$). However, in the delayed reading posttest, there is a statistical significance difference detected ($F[2, 57] = 9.439$, $p = 0.00$, $d = 0.76$). The Bonferroni *post hoc* test indicates that the statistical significance lies in the difference between the experimental group 1 and the control group ($d = 1.49$). Since the repeated-measures ANOVA considers the three sources of variations of observed scores, but a one-way ANOVA does not consider the variation error arising from repeated measures, it can be misleading if we simply use a one-way ANOVA to determine the experimental effect.

How to report the repeated-measures ANOVA

The following is an example of how you would write up the findings:

> According to the one-way repeated-measures ANOVA, there was a statistically significant difference between participants' reading performances across the three reading tests ($F[1.79, 102.17 = 150.88$, p < 0.05, $\eta_p^2 = 0.73$). An interaction between the time and group was found to be significant across the three occasions ($F[3.59, 102.17] = 150.88$, p < 0.05, $\eta_p^2 = 0.35$). This finding in regard to the significant interaction suggests that the experiment might have contributed to the changes in the participants' reading scores across the three occasions. However, the tests of between-subjects effects were found to be non-significant ($F[2, 57] = 2.719$, p = 0.08, $\eta_p^2 = 0.09$). This suggests that on average, when we took the within-group variances into account, the three instructional conditions did not produce significantly different reading comprehension performance.

We now discuss how other experimental researchers report their repeated-measures ANOVA results. For example, to find out whether the adult participants involved in a word learning experiment understood the given task or were responding randomly, Strapp et al. (2011) used a repeated-measures ANOVA on the participants' production of three response types across negative and positive evidence conditions. The researchers found that there was a statistically significant difference ($F[2, 89] = 126.52$, $p = .01$, $\eta^2 = .62$; p. 518).

Another example is by Kissling (2013), who examined the pronunciation gains among first, second and third year learners of Spanish after they received either explicit instruction in Spanish phonetics (+PI) or a more implicit treatment with similar input (–PI). The researcher used a repeated-measures ANOVA to compare the effects and interaction of test time, instructional condition and course level. That is, the within-groups factor was the time of the test (i.e. pretest, immediate posttest and a delayed posttest = three levels) and the between-group factors were the instructional conditions (i.e. +PI and –PI = two levels) and the course level (i.e. first, second, and third year = three levels). According to this level of analysis, we can say that this was a *3 × 2 × 3 repeated-measures ANOVA*. Kissling found a main effect for time ($F[1.64, 125] = 4.34$, $p = .02$, $\eta_p^2 = .05$) and level ($F[2, 76] = 12.83$, $p < 0.001$, $\eta_p^2 = .25$; p. 731). However, there were no significant interaction effects for all aspects ($p > .05$).

Summary

This chapter has presented a complex statistical analysis for evaluating the effects of independent variables on dependent variables in experimental research. Analysis of variance (ANOVA) is a robust statistical technique that can help us achieve this research goal. We only have covered three common kinds of ANOVA that are often used in experimental research in language learning in this chapter. There are several other complex ANOVAs that we cannot cover in this book (e.g. factorial ANOVA and multivariate analysis of variance [MANOVA]). Perhaps the bases of ANOVAs discussed in this chapter will allow you to explore further how other ANOVA tests operate and can be applied to an experimental study you design.

Research exercise

To download exercises for this chapter visit: http://www.bloomsbury.com/ experimental-research-methods-in-language-learning-9781441189110/

Discussion questions

1 What are the principles underlying an ANOVA? How do they differ from an independent-samples *t*-test?
2 In what kind of experimental situations do we need to use an ANCOVA?
3 What experimental research designs (discussed in Chapter 4) is a repeated-measures ANOVA suitable for?
4 What is a *post hoc* test? When do we need to use a *post hoc* test?
5 Reflection: What is the most important lesson you have learned from this chapter?

Further reading

Larson-Hall, J 2010, *A guide to doing statistics in second language research using SPSS*, Routledge, New York.

Chapters 10, 11 and 12 in this book present several detailed concepts of various types of ANOVAs with SPSS applications. There are several other examples of studies that are useful to discuss in relation to each ANOVA type.

Urdan, TC 2005, *Statistics in plain English*, Lawrence Erlbaum Associates, Mahwah, NJ.

Chapters 10 to 12 in this book presents conceptual descriptions of the one-way ANOVA, factorial ANOVA (which is not covered in this chapter) and the repeated-measures ANOVA. Several statistical formulas are presented. These chapters are useful for a conceptual understanding of these statistical tests.

CHAPTER FIFTEEN

Non-parametric Versions of t-tests and ANOVAs

Leading questions

1 What is a non-normal data distribution? What does it look like?
2 How do we know whether a data set is normally distributed?
3 Do you know of a non-parametric test that can analyze non-normally distributed data? If so, what is it?

Introduction

Several chapters have discussed the inferential statistics that we can use to infer either a linear relationship (e.g. correlation and reliability analysis) or a causal-like relationship (e.g. *t*-tests and ANOVAs). Typically such statistical analyses require quantitative data to be *normally distributed* and *continuous-like*. The data we use are frequently language test scores. In general, we prefer parametric tests over non-parametric tests, given the power of statistical analysis. However, in language learning research, there can be circumstances that do not permit us to use parametric tests. For example, sometimes we need to examine aspects using qualitative methods such as interviews and observations. We need to use frequency counts of learners' language use or learning characteristics. This kind of data may not always be normally distributed. Furthermore, in several experimental research situations, we may have fewer participants than we would ideally like. Even though we have a small sample size, we still would like to find out whether a treatment has some effect on student learning. We need to use a non-parametric test that can allow us to explore an issue systematically.

This chapter presents four non-parametric tests, which are non-parametric versions of the *t*-tests and ANOVAs discussed in the last two chapters: (1) the Wilcoxon signed ranks test (the non-parametric version of the paired-samples *t*-test); (2) the Mann–Whitney U test (the non-parametric version of the independent-samples *t*-test); (3) the Kruskal–Wallis H test (the non-parametric version of the one-way ANOVA); and (4) the Friedman test (the non-parametric version of the repeated-measures ANOVA).

The Wilcoxon signed ranks test

When we use a pretest and posttest in an experimental study, there could be a situation in which participants are at the extremes (e.g. high- and low-ability students, highly motivated and highly unmotivated students). When this is the case, researchers often have extreme scores but scores in the middles of the distributions are scarce. This type of data set will not be normally distributed.

How to run a Wilcoxon signed ranks test in SPSS

We will discuss how to run non-parametric tests in SPSS. Figure 15.1 presents the SPSS menu where we can run a non-parametric test.

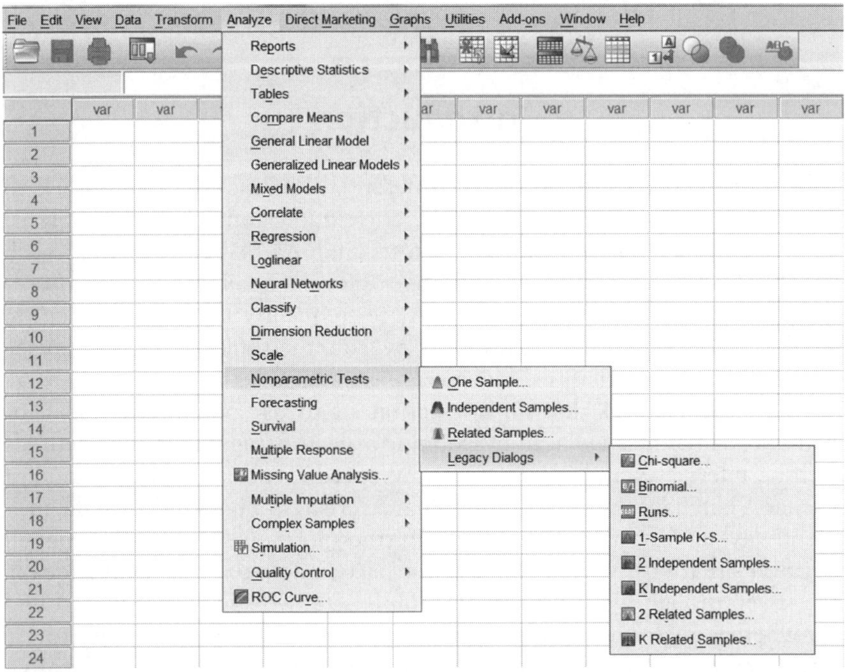

FIGURE 15.1   *SPSS menu for running a non-parametric test*

As we argue that the Wilcoxon signed ranks test is a non-parametric version of the paired-samples *t*-test, it is useful to use the same data that we used when we ran the paired-samples *t*-test because then we can check whether we reach the same conclusion. You can obtain the data file *Ch13 Paired ttest.sav* (downloadable from the *companion website*) to run the Wilcoxon signed ranks test.

The following are the steps in SPSS that should be followed to run a Wilcoxon signed ranks test.

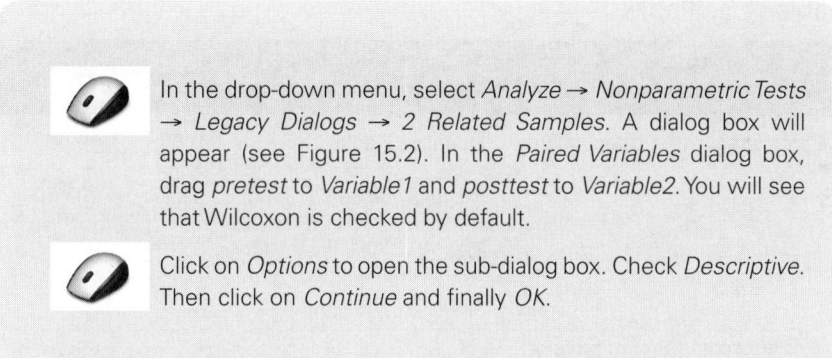

In the drop-down menu, select *Analyze → Nonparametric Tests → Legacy Dialogs → 2 Related Samples*. A dialog box will appear (see Figure 15.2). In the *Paired Variables* dialog box, drag *pretest* to *Variable1* and *posttest* to *Variable2*. You will see that Wilcoxon is checked by default.

Click on *Options* to open the sub-dialog box. Check *Descriptive*. Then click on *Continue* and finally *OK*.

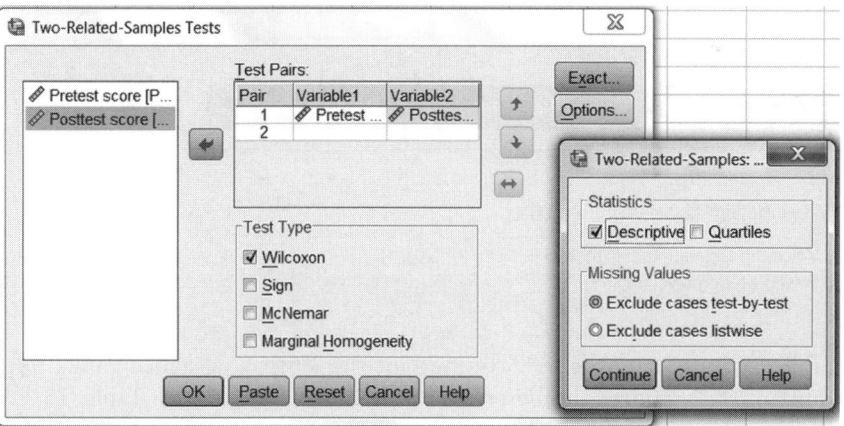

FIGURE 15.2   *SPSS dialog to run a Wilcoxon signed ranks test*

Table 15.1 SPSS outputs of the Wilcoxon signed ranks test (N = 25)

Table 15.1.1 Descriptive Statistics

	N	Mean	Std. Deviation	Minimum	Maximum
Pretest score	25	13.7600	5.76830	5.00	24.00
Posttest score	25	15.5200	5.90988	5.00	28.00

Table 15.1.2 Ranks

		N	Mean Rank	Sum of Ranks
Posttest score – Pretest score	Negative Ranks	5[a]	9.90	49.50
	Positive Ranks	17[b]	11.97	203.50
	Ties	3[c]		
	Total	25		

a. Posttest score < Pretest score
b. Posttest score > Pretest score
c. Posttest score = Pretest score

Table 15.1.3 Test statistics[a]

	Posttest score – Pretest score
Z	−2.512[b]
Asymp. Sig. (2-tailed)	.012

a. Wilcoxon Signed Ranks Test
b. Based on negative ranks

Table 15.1 presents the SPSS outputs of the Wilcoxon signed ranks test. Table 15.1.1 reports the descriptive statistics of each test. Table 15.1.2 presents the score ranks using the posttest and pretest scores. *Negative ranks* refers to the observation that an individual scored lower in the posttest than in the pretest, whereas *positive ranks* refers to the observation that an individual scored higher in the posttest than in the pretest. In this table, we can see that there were 5, 17 and 3 participants who scored lower, higher, and the same (i.e. ties) in the posttest than in the pretest, respectively. Table 15.1.2 also presents the mean rank and sum of ranks. Table 15.1.3 reports the Wilcoxon signed ranks test statistics. In order to determine whether the pretest and posttest scores differed significantly, we examine the Z score and the Asymp. Sig (2-tailed) value. We have found that there was a statistically significant difference between the pretest and posttest ($Z = -2.512$, $p < 0.05$).

Larson-Hall (2010, p. 378) presents a formula to compute the r effect size for both the Mann–Whitney U and Wilcoxon signed ranks tests. The formula is simple to calculate: $Z \div \sqrt{N}$. It is important not to confuse this r effect size with r correlation. However, I find the following statistical website practical to compute effect sizes: <http://www.ai-therapy.com/psychology-statistics/effect-size-calculator> [viewed March 1, 2014]. This statistics website provides precise descriptions of the statistical test being used. On this website, we can run some statistical tests without the need for SPSS. If you choose the Wilcoxon signed ranks test, you will be asked to enter your data. You can simply copy the column *pretest* and *posttest* from the SPSS file and paste them in the designated location. After you submit the information, an output similar to the example here will be produced. The r effect size was -0.36. According to Cohen (1992, p. 157), r effect sizes can be interpreted as small, medium and large when they are 0.1, 0.3 and 0.5, respectively.

How to report a Wilcoxon signed ranks test

As we have discussed in other chapters, we need to report the statistical findings as much as possible in tables, as well as explain what they mean to the reader. The following is an example of how you would write up this finding:

> According to the Wilcoxon signed ranks test analysis, it was found that there was a statistically significant difference between the pretest and posttest scores ($Z = -2.512$, $p < 0.05$, $r = -0.36$, medium effect size). The finding indicates that the inductive instruction with metacognitive evaluation marginally helped increase the participants' narrative writing essay performance.

Recall that when we performed the paired-samples *t*-test with the same data, we found a statistically significant difference between the pretest and posttest scores ($t[24] = -1.76$, $p < 0.05$, $d = -0.58$, medium effect size). The conclusions reached from the two analyses are similar.

There are many experimental studies in language learning that have employed the Wilcoxon signed ranks test (e.g. Gass, Svetics & Lemelin 2003; Kim & McDonough 2008; Marsden & Chen 2011; Yilmaz 2011; Yilmaz & Yuksel 2011). We can further examine how other researchers report their findings using a Wilcoxon signed ranks test. For example, Yilmaz and Yuksel (2011) examined the benefits of recasts through Face-to-Face Communication (F2FC) and text-based Synchronous-Mediated

Communication (SCMC) on the learning of two Turkish morphemes (the plural /-lAr/ and the locative case morpheme /-DA/. The researchers used a posttest-only, counterbalanced design to address their aim. The 24 participants were paired up with either one of the researchers to form a dyad to carry out the experimental treatment tasks. That is, each student received both experimental conditions. In this case, each student had two scores, one from each of the two treatment conditions. A Wilcoxon signed ranks test was performed to compare whether their morpheme scores differed. It was found that the participants' scores were 'significantly higher when they received SCMC recasts than their scores when they received F2FC recasts ($Z = -2.32$, $p = .02$, $r = -.34$, p. 467).'

The Mann–Whitney U test

The Mann–Whitney U test can serve a similar function to that of the independent-samples t-test for comparing two groups of participants.

How to run a Mann–Whitney U test in SPSS

To illustrate how to run a Mann–Whitney U test in SPSS, we will use the same data that we used to run the independent-samples t-test because then we will be able to check whether we reach the same conclusion. You can obtain the dataset *Ch13 Independent ttest.sav* (downloadable from the *companion website*) to run the Mann–Whitney U test.

The following are the steps in SPSS that should be followed to run a Mann–Whitney U test:

In the drop-down menu, select *Analyze → Nonparametric Tests → Legacy Dialogs → 2 Independent Samples*. A dialog box will appear (see Figure 15.3). Drag *Speakingpretest* and *Speakingposttest* into the *Test Variable List* dialog box.

Click *Define Groups* and open the sub-dialog box. Type *1* in *Group 1* and *2* in *Group 2*. Then click *Continue*.

Click on *Options* to open the sub-dialog box. Check *Descriptive* and click *Continue*. You will see that *Mann–Whitney U* is checked by default. Finally, click *OK*.

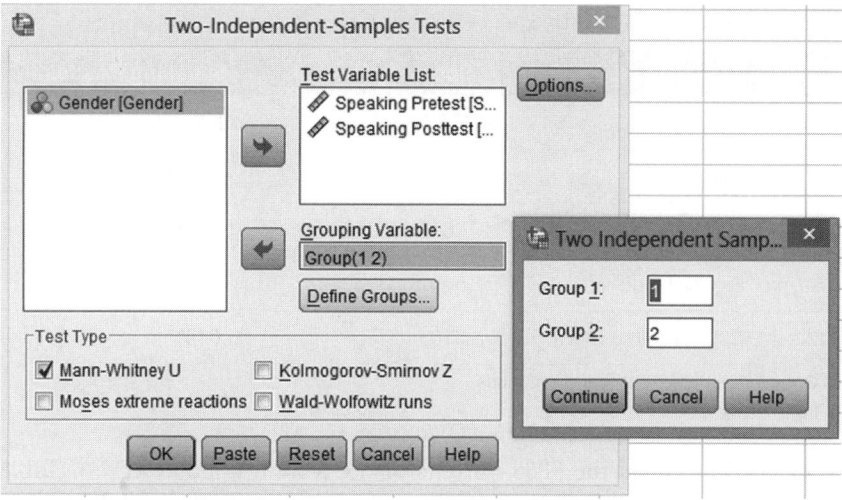

FIGURE 15.3   *SPSS dialog to run a Mann–Whitney U test*

Table 15.2 SPSS outputs of the Wilcoxon signed ranks test (N = 40)

Table 15.2.1 Descriptive statistics

	N	Mean	Std. Deviation	Minimum	Maximum
Speaking Pretest	40	13.2250	3.91897	6.00	20.00
Speaking Posttest	40	17.9000	5.27597	5.00	28.00
Comparison Groups	40	1.5500	.50383	1.00	2.00

Table 15.2.2 Mann–Whitney test

Ranks				
	Comparison Groups	N	Mean Rank	Sum of Ranks
Speaking Pretest	Ex Method1	18	19.14	344.50
	Ex method2	22	21.61	475.50
	Total	40		
Speaking Posttest	Ex Method1	18	25.28	455.00
	Ex method2	22	16.59	365.00
	Total	40		

Table 15.2.3 Test statistics[a]

	Speaking Pretest	Speaking Posttest
Mann-Whitney U	173.500	112.000
Wilcoxon W	344.500	365.000
Z	−.668	−2.346
Asymp. Sig. (2-tailed)	.504	.019
Exact Sig. [2*(1-tailed Sig.)]	.510[b]	.019[b]

a. Grouping Variable: Comparison Groups
b. Not corrected for ties.

Table 15.2 presents the SPSS outputs of the Mann–Whitney U test. Table 15.2.1 reports the descriptive statistics of each test. Table 15.2.2 presents the mean ranks using the speaking pretest and posttest scores. In this table, we can see the mean ranks and sum of ranks. The mean ranks for the experimental groups 1 and 2 in the speaking pretest were 19.14 and 21.61, respectively and in the speaking posttest were 25.28 and 16.59, respectively. Table 15.2.3 reports the Mann–Whitney U test statistics. In order to determine whether the two groups differed significantly, we examine the Z score and the Asymp. Sig (2-tailed) value. We have found that there was a non-statistically significant difference between the two groups in the pretest ($Z = -0.668$, $p = 0.50$, $r = -0.10$). However, in the posttest, the two groups significantly differed ($Z = -2.346$, $p = 0.02$, $r = -0.37$). The effect size formula for the Mann–Whitney U test is the same as that for the Wilcoxon signed ranks test.

How to report a Mann–Whitney U test result

The following is an example of how you would write up this finding:

According to the Mann–Whitney U test analysis, the two experimental groups did not differ significantly in their speaking pretest scores ($Z = -0.668$, $p = 0.50$, $r = -0.10$, small effect size). After the experimental treatments, it was found that the experimental group 1 (explicit feedback with a provision of a rating scale and comments) was found to significantly outperform the experimental group 2 (implicit feedback group with a provision of general comments; $Z = -2.346$, $p = 0.02$, $r = -0.37$, medium effect size). On the basis of this Mann–Whitney U test, it can be concluded that there was a statistically significant difference between the two groups after the experiment.

Recall that when we performed the independent-samples *t*-tests with the same data, we found the difference between the experimental groups 1 and 2 was non-significant in the pretest ($t[38] = -0.89$, $p = 0.38$, $d = -0.28$). We also found that there was a statistically significant difference between the two experimental groups ($t[38] = 2.49$, $p = 0.05$, $d = 0.80$, large effect size). The only difference is that we obtain a smaller effect size using the Mann–Whitney U test. However, the conclusions reached from both parametric and non-parametric analyses are similar.

Experimental studies in language learning that have used the Mann–Whitney U test include: Henry *et al.* (2009), Macaro and Masterman (2006), Marsden and Chen (2011) and Yilmaz and Yuksel (2011). Henry *et al.* (2009), who examined the role of explicit information (EI) on the learning of object pronouns and word order in Spanish, used a Mann–Whitney U test and found there was a statistically significant difference between the two groups (+EI and –EI; $Z = 12.50$, $p < 0.05$), indicating that the +EI group outperformed the –EI group (p. 570).

The Kruskal–Wallis H test

We discussed the characteristics of the one-way ANOVA in the previous chapter and how to run it in SPSS. The Kruskal–Wallis H test is a non-parametric test that can help us determine differences between two or more groups. We use the Kruskal–Wallis H test when our data are not normally distributed. The Kruskal–Wallis H test is an extended version of the Mann–Whitney U test (Larson-Hall 2010).

How to compute a Kruskal–Wallis H test in SPSS

As in the previous two non-parametric tests, we will use the same data that we used to run the one-way ANOVA. You can download the data file *Ch14 Oneway ANOVA.sav* from the *companion website*).

The following are the steps in SPSS that should be followed to run a Kruskal–Wallis H test.

In the drop-down menu, select *Analyze → Nonparametric Tests → Legacy Dialogs → K Independent Samples*. A dialog box will appear (see Figure 15.4). Drag *Speakingposttest* into the *Test Variable List* dialog box.

 Drag *Group* into *Grouping Variable*: and click *Define Range* to open the sub-dialog box. Type *1* in the *Minimum* and *3* in the *Maximum*. Note that if you have five groups, then the *Maximum* is 5. Then click *Continue*.

 Click on *Options* to open the sub-dialog box. Check *Descriptive* and click *Continue*. You will see that *Kruskal–Wallis H* is checked by default. Finally, click *OK*.

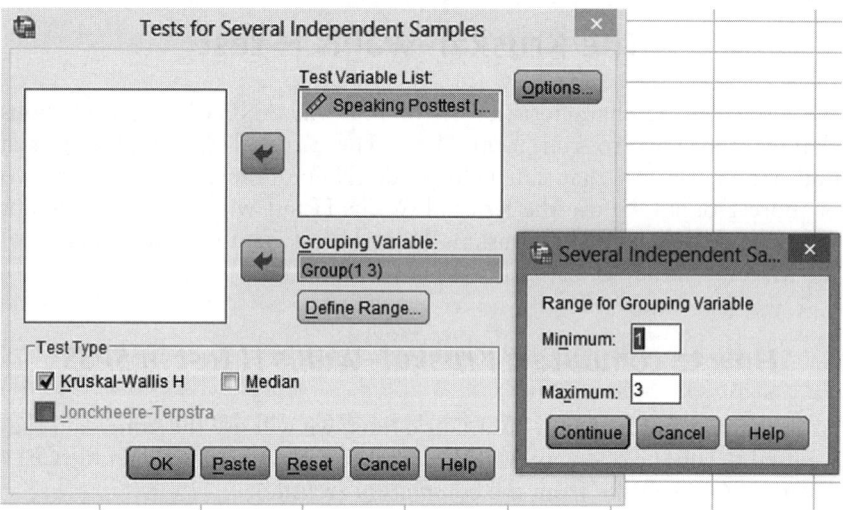

FIGURE 15.4 *SPSS dialog to run a Kruskal–Wallis H test*

Table 15.3 SPSS outputs of the Kruskal–Wallis H test (N = 62)

Table 15.3.1 Descriptive statistics

	N	Mean	Std. Deviation	Minimum	Maximum
Speaking Posttest	62	16.6129	5.10979	5.00	28.00
Comparison Groups	62	2.0645	.80716	1.00	3.00

Table 15.3.2 Kruskal–Wallis H test

Ranks			
	Comparison Groups	N	Mean Rank
Speaking Posttest	Ex Method1	18	43.31
	Ex method2	22	30.18
	Control Group	22	23.16
	Total	62	

Table 15.3.3 Test statistics[a]

	Speaking Posttest
Chi-Square	12.593
df	2
Asymp. Sig.	.002

a. Kruskal–Wallis Test
b. Grouping Variable: Comparison Groups

Table 15.3 presents the SPSS output of the Kruskal–Wallis H test. Table 15.3.1 reports the descriptive statistics of each test. Table 15.3.2 presents the mean ranks using the speaking posttest scores. In this table, we can see the experimental group 1 had the highest mean rank (43.31), followed by the experimental group 2 (30.18) and the control group (23.16). Table 15.3.3 reports the Kruskal–Wallis H test statistics. In order to determine whether the three groups differed significantly, we examine the chi-square (χ^2) statistic, df and the Asymp. Sig value. We have found that there was a statistically significant difference between the three groups in the posttest (χ^2 [2, N = 62] = 12.59, p = 0.002).

Unfortunately, unlike the one-way ANOVA, the Kruskal–Wallis H test does not produce a *post hoc* test for us when we detect a statistical significance. Larson-Hall (2010) discussed some methods to find out which groups differ from each other. Perhaps, the best scenario is to perform a Mann-Whitney U test in SPSS to compare pairs of groups. As noted in the Wilcoxon signed ranks test section above, you will find the following statistical website practical to compute a Mann-Whitney U test as well as the associated effect sizes: <http://www.ai-therapy.com/psychology-statistics/hypothesis-testing/two-samples?groups=0&parametric=1>, viewed March 1, 2014. You will be asked to enter your data. You can simply copy the column *Speakingposttest* from the SPSS file and paste it in the designated location. Make sure you only copy the posttest scores of each group (i.e. for groups 1, 2 or 3). Use the column *Group* next to the *Speakingposttest* to guide you. Then after you submit the data, it will produce the Mann-Whitney U test output and the *r* effect size.

How to Report a Kruskal–Wallis H Test Result

The following is an example of how you would write up this finding:

> According to the Kruskal–Wallis H test analysis, there was a statistically significant difference among the three groups (χ^2 [2, N = 62] = 12.59, $p < 0.05$). Post hoc tests from the Mann-Whitney U tests indicate that experimental group 1 significantly outperformed experimental group 2 and the control group (i.e. Z = –2.346, $p < 0.05$, r = –0.37, medium effect size; and in the posttest, both groups significantly differed (Z = –3.449, $p < 0.05$, r = –0.54, large effect size). The experimental group 2 did not significantly differ from the control group (i.e. Z = –1.342, $p > 0.05$, r = –0.22, small effect size).

It is important to recall that in the previous chapter, through the use of the one-way ANOVA, we found a statistically significant difference among the three groups (F[2, 59] = 7.97, $p < 0.05$). This finding is consistent with the result of the Kruskal–Wallis test. The Bonferroni *post hoc* test in the one-way ANOVA found that there were statistically significant differences between the experimental methods 1 and 2 ($p < 0.05$, d = 0.80) and between the experimental method 1 and the control group ($p < 0.05$, d = 1.35). The experimental method 2 and the control group did not differ statistically ($p = 0.55$). These findings are also consistent with the Mann-Whitney U tests.

There have been several studies in language learning that have employed Kruskal–Wallis tests (e.g. Chen and Truscott 2010; Li 2013; Marsden and Chen 2011). Marsden and Chen (2011, p. 1076) found 'no intergroup differences in their participants' pretest scores: GJT, $H(3)$ = .38, $p > $ .1; gapfill, $H(3)$ = 2.87, $p > $ .1; picture narration, $H(3)$ = 9.30, $p = $ .10; structured conversation, $H(3)$ = .91, $p > $ .1.' Note that H is from the Kruskal–Wallis

H test. Li (2011, p. 411) used a Kruskal–Wallis test to compare Chinese listening comprehension among three participant groups and found 'no significant difference among the groups (χ^2 [2, N = 30] = 2.65, p > .05).'

The Friedman test

We discussed the repeated-measures ANOVA in the previous chapter. The Friedman test can also do more than two levels of repeated measures. It is important to note that the Friedman test cannot test a group difference like the repeated-measures ANOVA, which uses only one independent variable. Therefore, we cannot argue that the Friedman test is a full parametric version of the repeated-measures ANOVA.

How to run a Friedman test in SPSS

We will use the same data that we use to run the repeated-measures ANOVA. You can download the data file *Ch14 Repeated ANOVA.sav* from the *companion website*).

The following are the steps in SPSS that should be followed to run a Friedman test.

 In the drop-down menu, select *Analyze* → *Nonparametric Tests* → *Legacy Dialogs* → *K Related Samples*. A dialog box will appear (see Figure 15.5). Drag *Reading1*, *Reading2* and *Reading3* to the *Test Variables* dialog box.

 Click on *Statistics* to open the sub-dialog box. Check *Descriptive* and click *Continue*. You will see that *Friedman* is checked by default. Finally, click *OK*.

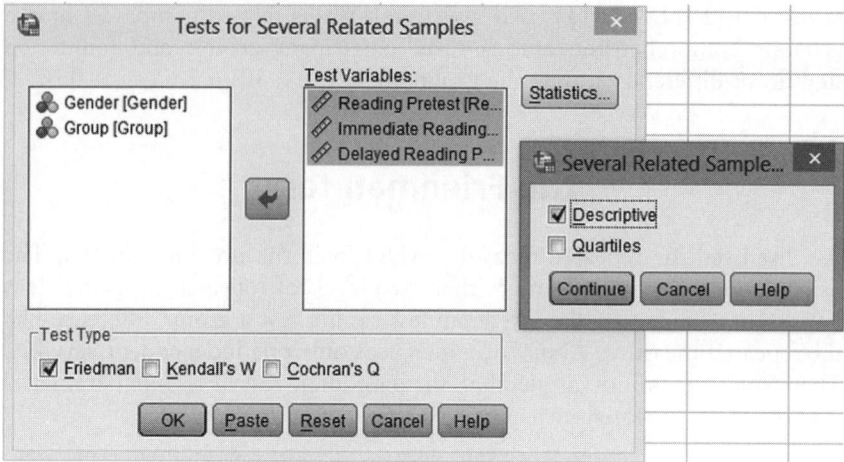

FIGURE 15.5   *SPSS dialog to run a Friedman test*

Table 15.4 SPSS outputs of the Friedman test (N = 62)

Table 15.4.1 Descriptive statistics

	N	Mean	Std. Deviation	Minimum	Maximum
Reading Pretest	60	21.8000	7.07299	7.00	37.00
Immediate Reading Posttest	60	24.6500	7.01530	12.00	40.00
Delayed Reading Posttest	60	28.1833	6.95382	14.00	46.00

Table 15.4.2 Friedman test

Ranks	
	Mean Rank
Reading Pretest	1.18
Immediate Reading Posttest	1.96
Delayed Reading Posttest	2.87

Table 15.4.3 Test statistics[a]

N	60
Chi-Square	87.838
df	2
Asymp. Sig.	.000

a. Friedman test

Table 15.4 presents the SPSS outputs of the Friedman test. Table 15.4.1 reports the descriptive statistics of each test. Table 15.4.2 presents the mean ranks of the three test scores. In this table, we can see the delayed reading posttest had the highest rank (i.e. 2.87). Table 15.4.3 reports the Friedman test statistics. In order to determine whether the three groups differed significantly, we examine the chi-square (χ^2) statistics, df and the Asymp. Sig value. According to Table 15.4.3, there was a statistically significant difference among the three reading tests (χ^2 [2, $N = 60$] = 87.838, $p = 0.000$).

A disadvantage of this non-parametric test is it does not produce a *post hoc* test for us, so we need to perform a Wilcoxon signed ranks test. It should be noted that this method increases our chance of making a Type I error as each time we perform a statistical test for each pair, the probability of a Type I error will be higher (see the previous chapter). We can perform Wilcoxon signed ranks tests in SPSS or through the following URL: <http://www.ai-therapy.com/psychology-statistics/hypothesis-testing/two-samples?groups=1&parametric=1>, viewed March 1, 2014.

How to report a Friedman test result

The following is an example of how you would write up this finding:

> According to the Friedman test analysis, there was a statistically significant difference among the three reading tests (χ^2 [2, $N = 60$] = 87.838, $p < 0.05$). *Post hoc* tests using the Wilcoxon signed ranks test indicate that the immediate reading posttest was significantly ranked higher than the reading pretest ($Z = 5.89$, $p < 0.05$, $r = 0.54$, medium effect size). The delayed reading posttest was significantly ranked higher than the immediate reading posttest ($Z = 5.99$, $p < 0.05$, $r = 0.55$, medium effect size). The delayed reading posttest was significantly ranked higher than the delayed reading pretest ($Z = 6.285$, $p < 0.05$, $r = 0.57$, medium effect size).

In the previous chapter, the repeated-measures ANOVA found a statistically significant difference among participants' reading performances across the three reading tests ($F[1.79, 102.17] = 150.88$, $p < 0.05$, $\eta_p^2 = 0.73$). So the findings from the two parametric and non-parametric analyses reached a similar conclusion. However, it should be noted that the *post hoc* results presented in this chapter were different from those in the repeated-measures ANOVA reported in the previous chapter. This is because in the previous chapter, we also examine the group effect, which could not be performed in this non-parametric test. In the previous chapter, we discovered the interaction effect between the time and group factors. The present analysis suggests that compared to the Friedman test, the repeated-measures ANOVA is much more robust in reducing the chance of a Type I error.

Other experimental studies that have used the Friedman tests are: Li (2013), and Marsden and Chen (2011). Li (2013) used a Friedman test to examine whether three groups had a significant gain in pragmatic listening judgment task accuracy over time. It was found that the statistic was non-significant (χ^2 [2, N = 10] = 4.32, $p = 0.11$) for the RT [Regular Training] group; χ^2 [2, N = 10] = 0.74, $p = 0.73$) for the IT [Intensive Training] group; χ^2 [2, N = 10 = 3.5, $p = 0.19$) for the control group.

Summary

This chapter has presented the four non-parametric tests for experimental research: Wilcoxon signed ranks test, Mann-Whitney U test, Kruskal–Wallis H test and Friedman test. These tests are useful alternatives to the parametric tests when our data are not normally distributed. They yield similar conclusions to their parametric homologues as illustrated in this chapter. We have not discussed a chi-square test in this chapter because this chapter aims to illustrate the parallel concepts of the parametric and non-parametric tests. Recommendations for further reading on chi-square tests are provided below.

Research exercise

To download exercises for this chapter visit: http://www.bloomsbury.com/experimental-research-methods-in-language-learning-9781441189110/

Discussion questions

1 What do you think the analytical limitations are when raw scores are ranked before being analyzed?
2 An independent-samples *t*-test is sensitive to outliers in a data set. Do you think the Mann–Whitney U test can better cope with the effect of outliers?
3 Do you find it useful to know the logic of these non-parametric tests? Does it help you understand experimental studies using these statistical tests?
4 What are the benefits of knowing an alternative statistics when our data are not normally distributed?
5 Reflection: What is the most important lesson you have learned from this chapter?

Further reading

Larson-Hall, J 2010, *A guide to doing statistics in second language research using SPSS*, Routledge, New York.

Chapter 8 presents some foundations for chi-square tests and how to run a chi-square in SPSS. Chapter 14 presents the non-parametric tests that we cover in this chapter in detail. There are several other examples of studies that are useful to discuss in relation to non-parametric tests.

Lowie, W & Seton, B 2013, *Essential statistics for applied linguistics*, Palgrave Macmillan, Hampshire, UK.

This book provides clear instructions on how to perform statistical analysis using SPSS. It presents how to perform a chi-square test for frequency data.

CHAPTER SIXTEEN

Experimental Research Proposals

Leading questions

1 What is a research proposal?
2 What do you think should be included in a research proposal?
3 Why do you think it is important to develop a research proposal prior to an experimental study?

Introduction

This chapter concludes this book by presenting some guidelines for developing a research proposal for an experimental study. It discusses the importance of having a well-developed research proposal and the key considerations that should be taken into account when designing a research proposal for an experimental study. Several examples are presented for the purpose of illustration.

Developing a research proposal for an experimental study

In Chapter 3, we discussed the stages involved in completing an experimental study. We discussed what is involved in each stage. Knowledge of the complete research process allows the researcher to see what will need to be accomplished for the study to fulfill the objectives of the research proposal.

Any highly regarded researchers in applied linguistics and language learning research would agree that a good research proposal is a prerequisite for a successful experimental study. Developing a research proposal is therefore *significant* for a research project because it allows researchers to establish a plan to complete the study. Moreover, research students have to write research proposals for their dissertations or theses, which will be read by a *departmental dissertation* or *thesis committee* before they can be officially approved. The committee also provides comments or feedback on their proposals.

What is a research proposal?

Generally speaking, a research proposal is a carefully crafted, written document that describes what the proposed research is trying to achieve, how it will go about achieving the aim, what it will add to existing knowledge and why it will be worthwhile conducting. According to Paltridge and Starfield (2007), a good research proposal should be *original*, *significant to advance knowledge, feasible* and *manageable* by the researcher within a given time frame and resources, and *of interest* to people in the field of research. A research proposal presents the following information:

- the objectives of the proposed study
- a summary of the previous research, which the researcher has drawn upon in terms of the theoretical and methodological implications for the proposed study
- a set of research questions or hypotheses
- a proposed research methodology for the study (e.g. a proposed experimental design, setting, participants, research instruments and data analysis)
- ethical considerations associated with the study
- a statement of the significance of the proposed study (e.g. theoretical, methodological and pedagogical)
- the limitations and delimitations of the proposed study
- the proposed timeline and required budget to complete the proposed study.

How long is a research proposal?

The length of a research proposal varies. It depends on the context in which we write it. For example, in the Faculty of Education and Social Work at the

University of Sydney, the length of a research proposal varies according to the research degree being taken. In this faculty, once students are admitted into the program, their research proposal needs to be approved by an academic committee before they can submit an ethical application to collect the necessary data for the research project. For a master of education (by research) degree, students are asked to write about 2,000–3,000 words, whereas a PhD research proposal is expected to be about 10,000 words. Furthermore, when we apply for a research grant, the length of the proposal will also vary, depending on the organization that will fund the project.

Some funding agents may specify that the research proposal should be no longer than a certain length (e.g. ten pages). Therefore, to be sure that we meet this requirement and use our time wisely to develop the proposal, we should always find out about the funding agent's expectations of its length. It is important to note that it is the ideas and considerations we put into a proposal that count, and not the number of words used. Given a restriction on the length of a proposal, we should aim to use words efficiently in the proposal. Sometimes less is more.

The structure of a research proposal

Different institutes may have their own preferred structure, so there is no one standard structure of a research proposal. However, there are common components across research proposals that we can use to guide our writing. These components may be altered or excluded to suit a particular purpose. Figure 16.1 presents an example of the key components or headings of an experimental research proposal.

Since this proposal structure is comprehensive, it may not be suitable for a short proposal (e.g. 500 to 1,000 words) that is used for an admission application into a study program. Based on my experience of teaching research methods courses and writing several research proposals, a *minimum* required length for this suggested structure is about 3,500 words. It is important to consider the length of different sections in a research proposal. For example, some people have a tendency to write a lot about the literature and say little about the method they propose to use. Remember that the proposal committee makes a decision on: (a) how well you review the relevant literature that your study draws upon; and (b) how your proposed research methodology is logical, sound and suitable to address the research problem and to answer the research questions. Let us discuss what should be included in each component.

Common Components of a Research Proposal

1   Title of a Proposed Study
2   Summary of the Proposed Study
3   Introduction
    • The Research Problems
    • The Aim(s) of the Proposed Study
    • Definitions of the Key Terms
4   Review of the Relevant Literature
5   Implications of the Literature on the Proposed Study
6   Research Questions or Hypotheses
7   Proposed Research Methodology
8   Research Method
    • Proposed Setting
    • Prospective Participants
    • Experimental Conditions
    • Research Instruments or Data Elicitation Techniques
    • Data Collection Procedure
    • Ethical Considerations
    • Data Analysis
9   Significance of the Proposed Study
10 Anticipated Limitations of the Proposed Study
11 Proposed Timeline of Completion
12 Required Resources and Budget
13 References
14 Appendices (if any)

FIGURE 16.1   *An example of the key components of an experimental research proposal*

The title of a proposed study

The title of your proposed study tells the reader about the topic of your research. Often the title tells a lot about a proposed study (e.g. its constructs, purpose, the type of research to be conducted, its context and who the study participants will be). It is important to craft the title of your proposal carefully. You may need to revise your title several times before it captures the key elements of your proposed study. A good proposal title may only emerge when you have completed a first draft of the proposal because it is only then that you may have developed a clear idea of what your proposed study seeks to achieve. Seek advice from various people once you are happy with your title. There are a few potential issues that should be pointed out. First, you should not make your title too long because it can confuse the reader. Remember that the reader will soon be reading the details of your proposal, so you do not need to include too much information in the title. Try to keep your title down to 15 words.

Second, a good title should contain *what* will be investigated (i.e. the independent and dependent variables) and *how* it will be investigated (i.e. will it be a causal-like investigation or an experimental design?). The context of the proposed study should also be indicated (i.e. which learners will be the subject of the study and possibly where it will take place). As we noted in Chapter 1, researchers often use words such as *the effects of*, *the effectiveness of*, *the roles of* and *the comparison of*. These words often imply an experimental design. Some people may prefer to use their key research question as their title, but often this restricts the scope of your proposed study because you may have more than one central research question to address. The following are examples of good experimental titles that tell the reader *what*, *how*, *where* and/or *who*:

- Effectiveness of different Pinyin presentation formats in learning Chinese characters: A cognitive load perspective (Lee & Kalyuga 2011)

- The effect of pleasure reading on Japanese university EFL learners' reading rates (Beglar, Hunt & Kite 2011)

- Evaluating the effectiveness of explicit instruction on implicit and explicit L2 knowledge (Akakura 2012)

These titles are from published research articles. It is good practice to imagine what these experimental researchers included in the titles of their research proposals.

Summary of the proposed study

This section provides an overview of your proposal. Typically, it presents the constructs, research problem, the purpose of the study, research method (including the proposed design, setting, participants, research instruments and data collection) and the significance of the proposed study. This section may be similar to an abstract of a research article, but it does not have actual data analysis, findings and discussion. This section is useful at the beginning of a proposal because it allows the reader to gain an overview of your research proposal.

Introduction

This section is *critical* to the success of a proposed study because it is where you can capture the reader's attention and interest in your proposed study. That is, it must convince the reader to see the *importance* of your proposed topic and the *problem* you have chosen to investigate. Avoid beginning your introduction with strong criticism of a research area or other researchers. You do not have enough space to justify such criticisms. You can do this later during or at the end of your literature review. Start your introduction broadly enough to cover the area of your research and narrow it down to your research problem soon after. Do not spend too much time discussing the general background of your proposal. A comprehensive discussion of the background to your study could be very lengthy, so stick to the main points. The research problem should be stated explicitly and clearly. You should briefly link your research problem to the research field and provide a signpost that it will be further elaborated in the literature review section below. The introduction section is important because it introduces the framework of your proposed study.

The research problem

The research problem needs to be explicitly stated early in the introduction. A research problem is not necessarily a problem per se. It can be about the *lack of understanding of the effects of the independent variable on the dependent variable of interest*. In other words, a limited body of knowledge or conflicts in previous research findings can be considered a research problem. The research problem is closely associated with *gaps in the literature* that you have identified in the literature review section. It is important to note that since this is the introduction section, you should not assume that the reader has significant background knowledge of your topic. However, care should be taken not to devote too many words to the background of your topic. Any theoretical background that is complex should be avoided at this stage because it can overwhelm the reader, but also shift the reader's attention away from your research problem. The following are three examples of descriptions of research problems:

> Despite the apparent importance of nonverbal communication in L2 production (e.g. McCafferty, 2002), little research has been conducted on the effects of visual cues on ESL learners' listening comprehension (Sueyoshi & Hardison 2005, p. 666).

> In light of the undeniable importance that motivation has for learning outcomes, the need to find effective means of reinforcing and sustaining learners' motivation does not seem to require justification. The amount of research on practical applications designed to enhance learner motivation however has been extremely limited (Moskovsky *et al.* 2012, p. 35).

> Much of the recent research has focused on the indefinite and definite English articles or verb forms but it is important to know whether written feedback is effective for complex subordinate constructions. To date, no study of written feedback has investigated this (Shintani *et al.* 2014, p. 104).

The aim(s) of the proposed study

The aim(s) of the proposed study should be well connected with the research problem you have presented. In this section you may present the aims of your study in more detail. This section is also critical to your proposal since it tells the reader the extent to which you have considered the existing literature in the topic area and whether you are being too ambitious in undertaking this project. The more aims you set to achieve, the more ambitious your proposed study will be. Experimental researchers often use infinite verbs such as to *investigate, examine, evaluate* and *compare* to indicate the aim(s) of their study. A good proposal states the aim clearly and precisely. For example:

> The first aim of the proposed study is to examine the effects of cognitive feedback types on metacognitive strategy use in advanced ESL learners' academic writing. The second aim is to compare the effectiveness of *immediate cognitive feedback* with *delayed cognitive feedback* on students' academic writing improvement.

Definitions of key terms

Depending on the length of your proposal, this section may or may not be required. Theoretical or specific terms are often explained in the literature review. However, if space permits, this section will be an opportunity for you to demonstrate your ability to explain complex theoretical constructs in plain language. This section prepares the reader for what they will read in the literature. Therefore, present only important theoretical constructs (e.g. focused independent and dependent variables) or methodological terms that will be used in the proposal. Make sure that all the terms you include are necessary for an understanding of your proposal. Too many terms may serve only as a distraction. Ensure also that terms requiring lengthy elaboration are not discussed in this section, but in your literature review. As a rule of thumb, consider five key terms to be a reasonable number to explain in this section. The following is an example of an inadequate definition of a key term. It does not help the reader who is unfamiliar with the topic to understand the construct:

> *Metacognition*: thinking about thinking

Some students are not clear about the function of the key term section. Instead they present abbreviations or acronyms in this section. For example, *L1* = First language, *L2* = Second language and *EFL* = English as a foreign language.

The following explanation of a key term, however, is quite sufficient.

> *Collaborative writing*: A writing activity where multiple learners create a piece of writing together, rather than individually. It is usually carried

out as a group project. Some projects are overseen by an editor or editorial team, but many can be successful without any oversight. In a true collaborative environment, each writer has an almost equal ability to add, edit and remove text. The writing process in collaborative writing can be recursive because one change can prompt others to make more changes.

Review of the relevant literature

According to Wolery and Lane (2010), a literature review has three main functions. First, it articulates what is known and not known about your research topic. Second, it builds a foundation and rationale for your proposed study. Third, it identifies successful designs, instruments or measures, and data analysis methods used by other previous researchers that can be applied in future research. Further, it can be organized chronologically (e.g. from the oldest to the newest studies), according to theoretical viewpoints or aspects, or methods (e.g. correlational, quasi-experimental and experimental).

It is important to remember that a review of the relevant literature in a research proposal *cannot be as lengthy, comprehensive* or *critical* as one written in a thesis, dissertation or journal article (because in these cases the study has already been completed). The literature review will expand and become more mature once you are committed to your approved project. At this stage, the purpose of a review of the literature is to help the reader understand your research perspective and evaluate whether there are any flaws in your proposal that can be prevented, as well as to determine whether you are ready to begin your study. That is, the reader does not necessarily expect a comprehensive and critical review of the literature. However, they expect to understand your logical thinking and how you see your research topic as *timely*, and thereby significant and worthwhile pursuing. You can use various resources for your literature reviews (e.g. academic books, journal articles, theses, dissertations and databases). At this stage of the proposal, focusing on research within the last ten years is more than sufficient. Avoid a complete replication of a single study because you will not be able to illustrate how you understand the nature of research and research methodology in a comprehensive fashion, as you will not have much to say from your own perspective.

Generally speaking, a review of the literature should provide some connectedness between the theoretical framework, previous relevant research, the proposed research problem and aims, and the proposed research methodology. In other words, you should attempt to relate and reorient the literature to your research problem. A discussion of similar studies in other contexts is essential. The review of the literature (which will include a list of previous studies, by whom they were written, their aims, the context in which the underlying studies were conducted, their findings and implications, and the conclusions they reached) should lead logically to your identified research gap, your research aims and the research questions you are asking. In this way, you can identify and build on an understanding of the current research issues in the field. It will allow you to critique the current literature and identify the limitations of previous studies, thereby leading to the rationale of what you would be focusing on in your proposed research and why it will be important work. In so doing, you will be able to highlight the significance of your study (i.e. how your study will contribute to the existing body of knowledge and how it will address the limitations of the research already carried out.

For a more detailed discussion of how to effectively review relevant literature, see, for example, Creswell (2014), Johnson and Christensen (2008), and Paltridge and Starfield (2007), who present how to conduct and write a literature review successfully.

Implications of the literature on the proposed study

This section is significant for your proposal because your *voice* can be heard more pronouncedly than in the preceding section. This is where you explicitly state the gap(s) in the literature you have identified and consolidate your account of the research problems you presented at the beginning of your proposal. It should be noted that the gap(s) you identify should derive from your critical synthesis of what is missing from previous studies. Often we can find out about important gaps in existing knowledge, the limitations of previous studies, and recommendations for further research in journal articles.

This literature review section should also include a discussion of the *theoretical implications* and *methodological implications of your proposal*. Theoretical implications are related to the research problems you have identified and propose to address through your research method. This section is linked to the research questions or hypotheses you address in detail in the next section. The methodological implications of your literature review are related to a discussion of the methodological limitations of previous studies, on which you may seek to improve, as well as the advances in methodology that some previous studies have made. This discussion allows you to connect your proposed study to methodologies used in previous studies, as well as to future research methodologies. An excerpt from Stafford, Bowden and Sanz (2011, pp. 746–7) can help illustrate how to draw implications from the literature review:

> In summary, results of the foregoing studies by and large reveal minimal benefits of preemptive instruction for L2 outcomes when L2 exposure involves task-essential practice. … with regard to the role of metalinguistic feedback provided during L2 practice, whereas Rosa and Leow's (2004) results indicated a facilitative role for some L2 outcomes, Sanz's

(2004) and Sanz and Morgan-Short's (2004) did not. ... A factor that may have influenced the results of the preceding studies is previous L2 exposure. ... To control for effects of previous instruction, the current study ...

Research questions or hypotheses

Research questions are used to help you focus on your research problem and proposed aim. In other words, they provide a boundary for your decisions to focus on what, how and where to research. Experimental research questions should include variables such as participants, key independent variable(s) and dependent variable(s). For example:

- Does IE [interaction enhancement], in which a teacher provides implicit negative feedback during an interactive problem-solving task, affect EFL learners' restructuring of their interlanguage article systems? (Muranoi 2000, p. 624).

- What are the effects of explicit instruction on the acquisition of generic and non-generic article usages in L2 English, as measured by (a) tests of implicit knowledge, and (b) tests of explicit knowledge? (Akakura 2012, p. 16)

In experimental research, research questions should be written using neutral language. Predictive or one-directional questions should be avoided, despite the fact that researchers often ask them. For example:

Is explicit instruction more effective than implicit instruction in developing learners' use of epistemic stance forms in writing: (a) in the short-term; (b) in the long-term? (Fordyce 2014, p. 13).

Usually researchers ask a question broadly and narrow it down in the following question(s). The best way to learn how to form a research question is by examining how well-regarded researchers in the field or areas of your study form their research questions. The number of research questions that is appropriate depends on the scope of the proposed study and therefore should be manageable. For a master's dissertation, a set of two to three research questions may be sufficient. Many students make the mistake of asking too many research questions because they think this will impress the reader on account of the amount of work they intend to do. It is important that research questions are not *interview questions because research questions aim to address a research problem or a theoretical question.* Some students new to research mistakenly include *interview questions* as their research questions. If this is the case, it is easy for the reader to decide whether your proposed study is to be approved or not.

Proposed research methodology

Research methodology refers to the framework that your proposed study will be based on. Of course, the methodological framework for an experimental study is an experimental research framework discussed throughout this book. In this section, you need to define what *kind* of experimental research design you propose to use to address your research problems and questions. You need to state explicitly whether it will be a *true experimental* or *quasi-experimental design*, what particular design you propose to use and why it will be suitable for your proposed study (see Chapter 4).

In case you propose to use a mixed-methods design, the rationale for your decision to do so needs to be discussed. This discussion should justify your decision to combine qualitative and quantitative research methods in your experimental research (i.e. your decision to adopt a hybrid approach). This section signifies how well you know and have considered the research methodology you plan to adopt, so study wisely the assumptions underlying a particular experimental design, including how validity and threats to the internal validity are to be considered. The following example is adapted from Ammar (2008) to illustrate a particular methodological framework:

> A pre-test-treatment-immediate post-test-delayed post-test design [will] be used to identify the effects of prompts and recasts. ... the recaster [will] be assigned to the first experimental groups (i.e. recasts [approximate n = 20]), the prompter to the second (i.e. prompts [approximate n = 20]), and the no corrector to the control group condition ([approximate n = 20]) (p. 190).

The methodological section is closely linked in content to the research method section, so the two may be presented at the same time (see below).

Research method

Unlike your research methodology, your proposed research method is related to your proposed research instruments, materials and data collection procedures. This section is one of the two most important sections that will determine the success of your proposal. The other is your literature review section.

Proposed setting and prospective participants

Usually it is difficult to separate a setting from its participants, so researchers normally include a description of both in the same section. In this section, describe and explain the setting (including its characteristics and environment) where you will conduct your experimental study. This section should explain how you will set up the experimental conditions under which you will manipulate the independent variables and control confounding variables. If the proposed experiment takes place in intact classes, describe the setting and justify why the random assignment of students cannot be achieved.

It is important to note that in a research proposal, you do not yet know who your research participants will be. However, you will need to have a general idea of *who* they will be and *how many* you will need for your proposed study to succeed. If you know where your study will take place, it is a good idea to do some research on prospective participants, so you can identify their characteristics (e.g. age, gender and levels of proficiency). It is essential to consider your prospective participants in relation to your research design (e.g. how many treatment and control groups will be needed, issues in pretest and posttest designs, and the length of your experiment). The following example is adapted from Marsden and Chen (2011, p. 1072):

> Participants [will] be taken from four classes that each [will] contain, according to the school's data, an equivalent mix of academic abilities and socioeconomic backgrounds. One of these classes [will be] selected at random as an intact control group and [will do] all the pretests, posttests, and delayed posttests. From the remaining three classes, participants [will be] assigned using matched randomization to the three conditions.

Another example is:

> Participants will be approximately 100 EFL, first year English major students at a Thai university. They are between the age of 18 and 19 years. Their English proficiency level is at an intermediate level. They will have been studying English prior to the proposed study for approximately 8 years. Participating students will be randomly assigned into four groups (i.e. 3 experimental groups and 1 control group).

In some cases, you need to explain your sampling method and specify any inclusion and exclusion criteria for selecting your research participants so that you can control several potential confounding variables. Furthermore, you should discuss who will carry out the experimental instruction for you. How will you choose the instructor(s) for your proposed study? The following example is adapted from Yang and Lyster (2010, pp. 242–3):

> The control group teacher [will be] the regular classroom teacher, ... with a master's degree in English literature and 1 year of teaching experience. ... The teacher [to be] assigned to the recast condition [will have] a master's degree in English linguistics and [have] been teaching for three years ... The teacher [to be] assigned to the prompt condition [will be] the first [researcher], a doctoral candidate with 2 years of prior teaching experience ...

Experimental conditions

Provide enough information about your experimental design and the conditions under which you aim to undertake your study. Provide a citation or reference of your design. How long do you plan to take to complete your experiment? Will it be a pretest-posttest control-group design? Will you be able to have a random assignment procedure? A diagram to illustrate your experimental design is useful in this section. It should be noted that your design will not be perfect at this proposal stage. The reader would like to know how much you have thought about your proposed study and how well you understand the strengths and weaknesses of your proposed design. To illustrate a proposed experimental condition, van Gelderen *et al.* (2011) is adapted. Perhaps you should begin this section with something like this:

> Although more considerations are needed to tackle the research problem and answer the research questions this proposed study seeks to address, the following are some of the preliminary ideas of how to design the proposed study.
>
> A posttest only (between-subjects) experimental design [will] be used with randomized assignment to the two experimental groups. Students within each classroom [will be] randomly assigned to one of these conditions [fluency training and topic knowledge training groups]. The baseline control group [will] consist of two intact classes from one of the schools that [have] participated in the experimental lessons. ... The two experimental groups [will] receive a series of writing lessons. In addition, the lexical group [will] receive training in the productive use of English words and collocations related to the writing topics. To compensate for the extra time for this lexical training, the other experimental group [will] receive extra topic knowledge, hence the name "knowledge group." ... The baseline control group [will] not receive the experimental lesson. These students [will] only participate in the administration of the covariate tests and the posttest writing assignments (van Gelderen *et al.* 2011, p. 290).

See Chapter 3 for options of experimental designs.

Research instruments

This section discusses your proposed research instruments or data collection techniques (including qualitative data, if appropriate). Describe how you will develop and make use of a pretest and a posttest in your study. Will they be language tests, questionnaires, interviews or observations? It is important to explain what they are and how you will develop them. You should note some of the key strengths and limitations of your research instruments. If you plan to include a pilot study, it is important to state this here so that you can justify how you will refine your research instruments and data collection procedures in the main study. You should mention how you will address the issues of reliability of your measures.

Data collection procedures

This section outlines the steps and procedures required to collect your data using the research instruments and experimental procedures discussed above. This section relates how you will implement your proposed study. In other words, how you will carry out your treatment and collect data during your experimental study. A diagram to illustrate your data collection procedure can be effective in this section. It is useful for the reader to see the overall flow of your proposed study. Figure 16.2 presents an example of a diagram explaining a data collection procedure.

Week 1
- **Pretest Data Collection**
- Listening comprehension test; a perceived listening difficulty questionnaire; a listening anxiety questionnaire; and a listening strategy use questionnaire.

Weeks 2-7
- **Experiment starts (a randomized, pretest-posttest, control-group design)**
- **Experimental Group 1** will receive a strategy training focusing on cognitive listening strategy use, plus corrective feedback.
- **Experimental Group 2** will receive a strategy training focusing on metacognitive monitoring and evaluating, plus corrective feedback.
- **Experimental Group 3** will receive a strategy training focusing on metacognitive monitoring and evaluating, plus corrective and cognitive feedback.
- **Control Group** will not receive any strategy training but will be placed in a regular class.

Week 8
- **Posttest Data Collection**
- Listening comprehension test; a perceived listening difficulty questionnaire; a listening anxiety questionnaire; and a listening strategy use questionnaire.
- Focus group interviews.

FIGURE 16.2   *A flowchart for the proposed experimental data collection and treatments*

Ethical considerations

This section describes how you value the importance of dealing with and treating human participants in your proposed study. With reference to the research ethics guidelines discussed in Chapter 6, you should discuss the important issues of consent, anonymity and confidentiality.

Data analysis
In this section, explain your approach to analyzing your data. Depending on the experimental research design you adopt, you should discuss the particular statistical test that you will use to answer a particular research question. Include a discussion of all the statistical tests you plan to use. If you plan to collect qualitative data in your study, explain the steps you plan to follow to analyze your data and how you will present the findings. In this section, it is useful to imagine what the findings will be like so that you can consider if the proposed data analysis is logical and achievable. Some students can be too vague in this section and write something like: 'The data will be analyzed statistically using SPSS' or 'The data will be analyzed qualitatively using a qualitative software program (e.g. NVivo).' The following example is an excerpt adapted from Shintani *et al.* (2014):

> When a learner [attempts] a sentence including an if clause corresponding to one of the hypothetical conditional sentences in the dictogloss passage, one point [will be] scored irrespective of whether the sentence [is] correct … (pp. 114–15) … The scores for the writing tasks [will be] subjected to a series of statistical analyses. After confirming the assumption of normality and homogeneity, repeated measures analyses of variance (ANOVAs) [will be used to test] the comparative effects of the treatments for the writing task's scores. A post hoc Bonferroni adjustment test [will be] used to investigate differences between pairs of groups when there [is] a significant time x group effect (p.117).

The significance of the proposed study

This section highlights the prospective contributions of your proposed study to the field. It is concerned with how your proposed methodology and method can successfully address your research problems, answer your research questions and shed light on the topic being investigated. It is important to distinguish significance from implications here. You can discuss the implications of your study after you have completed it, but at the time of the proposal, you will not have determined any implications to the field of research. You can discuss three kinds of significance of your study: theoretical significance (i.e. in what way your study can advance the relevant theory or improve existing knowledge), methodological significance (i.e. in what way your study can advance the research methodology in this area of research) and/or pedagogical significance (i.e. in what way your study can improve teaching practice). It will be useful for you to read what other researchers have discussed in their conclusion sections. Remember that you need to project what would be the key yields (i.e. significance) of your proposed study.

Anticipated limitations of the proposed study

This section presents how you anticipate the possible limitations of your proposed study. Limitations are related to claims about the research validity. Will there be potential threats in your study that do not allow you to draw firm conclusions? For example, is it likely that there will be a high participant dropout rate during the course of your proposed study?

Proposed timeline of completion

This section presents the steps required to complete your proposed study and an estimate of the time that will be needed to complete each step. It is important to be realistic in terms of the amount of time that will be required to complete each stage. It is useful to assign a date of completion for each stage. Some students may state that they will need about one week to write their review of the literature and another week to write the research method. This would be seen as unreasonable.

Required resources and budget

This section states what resources are required for your proposed study. It should include a discussion of how much you will need to spend to complete your proposed study. Costs may include electrical equipment, such as a digital audio-recorder or video recorder, photocopying, stationery and travel expenses.

References

This section provides all the references you have cited in your proposal. It is important to check if there is a requested reference style. The American Psychological Association (APA) reference style (6th edn) is normally used in educational, social sciences and applied linguistics research. It is important to study formats of different references (e.g. books, book chapters, journal articles, theses, etc.). It should be noted that the Harvard Referencing Style is used in this book. Although this section seems less important than the rest, the reader can gain a sense of your worthiness as an academic by observing the *consistency* and *accuracy* of your references. Therefore, it is important for all students to learn how to write a reference properly. Based on my personal experience, some students simply copy existing references from different journal articles that they cite in their proposal, without being aware that journals adopt different reference styles. This practice consequently creates inconsistency and messiness in the reference list.

Appendices (if any)

This section is more or less optional. Any additional documents (e.g. proposed research instruments and treatment procedures) can be included here. You should state in the main proposal text (where appropriate) that additional information is provided in an appendix.

Summary and conclusion

This chapter has presented a research proposal structure that you can use to develop your own research proposal. Several issues related to each component or heading have been discussed in order to prevent novice mistakes. It is important to note that you will need to write several drafts of your research proposal before you are likely to be satisfied with its content and clarity. Make sure to write notes on what you have read as you go along. It is easy to spend a lot of time searching for previous studies and to read them without making an adequate record of what insights you have gained from them. If you do not record your reflections as you proceed, you will find yourself overwhelmed by the task of recollection.

There are other issues that you need to be aware of, especially during the period in which you are writing up your proposal. These include the following: *academic writing style* (e.g. you need to write objectively, support any claims with references and beware of unintended plagiarism), the correct *use of tenses in writing* (e.g. you should use the future tenses to describe your proposal and the present simple to describe general theory or facts) and the accepted *use of acronyms* (e.g. avoid complicated acronyms because they negatively affect readers' comprehension). Most importantly, do not rush to finish off your proposal in the final days before the deadline. You will not have time to evaluate what you have written and you will not be able to appraise your proposal critically.

Finally, as stated in the preface, this book aims to make experimental research methods in language learning *accessible* and *meaningful* to readers. However, to improve our research skills, of course, we also have to actually do research. It is my hope that this book can provide valuable guidelines for putting theory into practice.

Research exercise

To download exercises for this chapter visit: http://www.bloomsbury.com/experimental-research-methods-in-language-learning-9781441189110/

Discussion questions

1 What are the research topics you would like to investigate using an experimental research designs?
2 What are your current research questions or problems? In what way can you refine them?
3 Paltridge and Starfield (2007) point out that a good research proposal should be *original, significant to advance knowledge, feasible* and *manageable* by the researcher within a given time frame and resources, and *of interest* to people in the field of research. What are these characteristics?
4 Why do you think the sections on the review of the literature and proposed method are the most important components of a research proposal?
5 Reflection: What is the most important lesson you have learned from this chapter?

Further reading

American Psychological Association (APA) 2010, *Publication manual of the American Psychological Association*, 6th edn, American Psychological Association, Washington, DC.

This book provides comprehensive guidance on issues related to writing a research report, including academic writing styles, citations and referencing. It also addresses ethical considerations in research.

Bourke, S & Holbrook AP 2013, 'Examining PhD and research masters theses', *Assessment and Evaluation in Higher Education*, vol. 38, no. 4, pp. 407–16.

This article presents an analysis of what examiners look for (i.e. evaluation criteria such as literature review, methodology, contribution and presentation) when they evaluate PhD and master's theses or dissertations.

Chapelle, CA & Duff, PA 2003, 'Some guidelines for conducting quantitative and qualitative research in TESOL', *TESOL Quarterly*, vol. 37, no. 1, pp. 157–78.

This article provides guidelines for good research writing practice for both qualitative and quantitative research.

Creswell, JW 2014, *Research design: qualitative, quantitative, and mixed methods approaches*, 4th edn, Sage, Thousand Oaks.

This book presents approaches to designing qualitative, quantitative or mixed-methods research. In this edition, Creswell has updated and covered more of the mixed-methods approach. This book is useful for both developing a research proposal and writing up a research report.

Evans, D, Gruba, P & Zobel, J 2011, *How to write a better thesis*, 3rd edn, Melbourne University Press, Melbourne.

This book introduces the nature of theses. It covers various issues involved in thesis writing (e.g. thesis structure, academic writing and content). Several examples are used to illustrate particular issues.

McIntosh, K & Ginther A (2014), 'Writing research reports', in AJ Kunnan (ed.), *The companion to language assessment*, John Wiley & Sons, London.

This chapter presents useful discussion about what is involved in writing a research report and provides tips and strategies for successful research reports.

Nastasi, BK, Hitchcock, J, Sarkar, S, Burkholder, G, Varjes, K & Jayasena, A 2007, 'Mixed methods in intervention research: theory to adaptation', *Journal of Mixed Methods Research*, vol. 1, no. 2, pp. 164–82.

This article demonstrates how mixed-methods research designs can be applied to an intervention study such as an experimental study.

Paltridge, B & Starfield, S 2007, *Thesis and dissertation writing in a second language: a handbook for supervisors*, Routledge, London and New York.

This book provides a comprehensive treatment of and resources for thesis and dissertation writing. It discusses numerous strategies for success in writing a research proposal.

Porte, GK 2010, *Appraising research in second language learning: a practical approach to critical analysis of quantitative research*, 2nd edn, John Benjamins, Amsterdam.

This book is a recommended resource for people new to quantitative research. As the title of the book suggests, this book discusses how to critically make sense of a quantitative report, so that readers can draw implications from their reading for their further use (e.g. for a literature review purpose). There are various exercises and activities to help readers learn about quantitative research.

Ramos-Álvarez, MM, Moreno-Fernández, MM, Valdés-Conroy, B & Catena, A 2008, 'Criteria of the peer review process for publication of experimental and quasi-experimental research in psychology: a guide for creating research papers', *International Journal of Clinical and Health Psychology*, vol. 8, no. 3, pp. 751–64.

This article provides a comprehensive list of scientific criteria for assessing the quality of an experimental research report submitted to a peer-review journal. The authors present essential, obligatory, complementary and methodological criteria. They also suggest some guidelines for manuscript reviewers.

GLOSSARY OF KEY TERMS IN LANGUAGE LEARNING RESEARCH

Academic research systematic work undertaken with the intention of discovering new facts or knowledge.

Achievement test a test that is associated with the language curriculum or syllabus for a course that students are undertaking.

Adjacent agreement an agreement that two raters assign a score within one-scale point to the same text (for example, 4 versus 5 = 100 percent agree). An adjacent agreement covers both exact and adjacent agreements in counting.

Alternative hypothesis the statistical hypothesis that is contrary to the null hypothesis. It states that there is a relationship between two variables, or there is a difference between two or more groups of learners.

Attrition effect the mortality effect due to an imbalance in the loss of participants across comparison groups.

Block randomization a random assignment procedure that guarantees that an equal number of participants are assigned to different groups.

Ceiling effect a situation in which some learners are at the advanced level and may not have much room for improvement.

Chi-square (χ^2) test a statistical test for examining whether a difference exists between two groups of learners (e.g. males and female; group A and group B) on the basis of frequency scores.

Classical true score theory a measurement theory that separates a true score from an error score.

Cohen's kappa coefficient a statistical measure of agreement, particularly when coding qualitative data. This method takes a chance level of agreement into account. Like other correlation coefficients, a kappa coefficient of 1 indicates perfect agreement and 0 indicates zero agreement.

Coin-toss technique a method for random assignment in which coin tossing is used to randomly assign participants into different groups in an experimental study.

Comparison groups groups of participants exposed to different conditions for an experimental comparison.

Conflict of interest an unfair gain of a person or group of people when their particular role can favor an outcome.

Confounding variable an unwanted variable that may interfere with the primary independent variable.

Construct   an abstract concept or general idea or the focused topic of a study.

Construct validity   the degree to which the construct of interest is validly defined, measured and inferred. It concerns the extent to which an instrument measures what it is intended to measure (e.g. language tests, questionnaires and observation schemes).

Constructivist paradigm   unlike the positivist and postpositivist paradigms, the constructivist paradigm does not share the realist or critical realist perspective. On the contrary, it takes the relativist stance that realities are multiple and exist in people's minds.

Content validity   the extent to which sample behaviors or abilities are relevant to, and representative of, the construct being defined.

Control group   the group that did not receive an experimental treatment in experimental research. This group is used for comparison purposes with the experimental group.

Correlation   a statistical procedure of examining non-causal relationships between two variables.

Criterion-related validity   the extent to which a research instrument has a relationship with other instruments that measure the same or similar construct.

Cross-sectional research   research in which researchers collect data from one or more cohorts at a single point in time. This contrasts with longitudinal research.

Curvilinear relationship   a relationship between two or more variables, which is not represented graphically by a straight line.

Data   information collected through observation by researchers to respond to a research question or hypothesis.

Data analysis   the analytical approach to analyzing data with the goal of addressing research questions.

Data coding   the process of classifying or grouping data sets. In some sense, coding data is closely related to organizing data so that we know how to statistically analyze them meaningfully.

Debriefing session   a session at which researchers meet participants or their guardians to explain the research project, including the aims of the study and the research procedures to be used. They also answer any questions related to the study.

Deductive reasoning   a process in which researchers make use of pre-existing theories to guide their observations or to direct their attention to what to observe.

Degree of freedom   the number of independent pieces of information that we use to estimate a parameter.

Demoralized effect   an effect arising from students in the control group who feel that they are not being treated fairly because an experimental treatment could have helped improve their learning, had they been placed in the experimental group. Consequently, they feel demoralized and unenthusiastic, and do not invest any effort in their learning.

Dependent variable   a factor that changes as the independent variable being examined changes.

Dichotomous variable   the simplest type of categorical variable, which has only two classes.

Diffusion effect   a threat to the internal validity of an experimental study that is resulted from the fact that participants in an experimental group share what they do with those in the control group.

Direct observation   a data collection technique that can help researchers to observe learners' patterns of behavior in a specific context.

Dispersion   the extent to which the data set is spread out. Measures of dispersion are interchangeably known as measures of variability.

Effect size   an effect size is a magnitude-of-effect estimate that is independent of sample size. It highlights the distinction between statistical and practical significance.

Empiricism   a term used to describe the discovery of knowledge through the collection of data or evidence in a real context or environment.

Ethical considerations   the importance of dealing with and treating human participants. In general, researchers are required to discuss the important issues of consent, anonymity and confidentiality to remain within acceptable ethical bounds.

Ethics   norms of research conduct that distinguish the acceptable and unacceptable behavior of researchers. Ethics require researchers to act in a socially and ethically responsible manner, and to follow the various codes of conduct for research.

Exact agreement   an agreement in which two raters assign the same score to the same text (for example, 4 versus 4 = 100 percent agree).

Experimental group   the group that receives an experimental treatment (e.g. interaction activity) in experimental research.

Experimental research   research that aims to address a causal-like relationship by controlling influences of factors that are not of interest. Experimental researchers usually aim to test whether their hypothesis is supported by empirical data, under a strictly controlled environment.

Experimenter/researcher effect   the unintentional influence of the experimenters on the research outcome. This could be due, for example, to a personal bias toward a particular treatment or an expectation that the research outcome may be transmitted to the research participants.

Exploratory factor analysis (EFA)   a statistical method of determining the correlations among a large set of variables in a data set.

External validity   a generalization of the study to other participants and settings.

Face validity   the degree to which a research instrument or a research design appears to measure or study something in the eyes of a non-expert.

Floor effect   the extent to which lower ability students' performance cannot be captured adequately, simply because the test is too difficult for them.

Friedman test   a non-parametric test that has a function similar to that of the within-group ANOVA.

Hawthorne effect   the influence of experimental participants' change of behaviors due to the mere fact of the experiment taking place, rather than the specific treatment of the experiment, leading to results that favor the treatment.

History effect   a specific situation or event that takes place during an experimental study. This can result in changes in the experimental outcome (i.e. in target dependent variables).

Homogeneity of variance   a statistical assumption that the variance for each group has equal variance. This assumption is needed for analysis of variance (ANOVA).

Hypothesis   a statement about the nature of something that may predict some forms of behavior or thinking.

Hypothesis testing   a statistical approach by which researchers investigate how well the quantitative data support a hypothesis (known as the null hypothesis) that the researchers believe to be false.

IBM SPSS   a statistical software package that can be used to help researchers compute descriptive statistics.

Independent-samples t-test   a statistical test for investigating whether the mean scores between two groups of participants are significantly different (e.g. experimental and control-group comparison).

Independent variable   a variable that influences certain behaviors or psychological processes. It exists freely and is hypothesized to have an effect on other variables that are described as dependent variables.

Inductive reasoning   a process in which researchers first observe language learners' behaviors or a particular phenomenon, and then draw conclusions on the basis of those behaviors.

Inferential statistics   key statistical analyses that go beyond raw data and can yield answers to research questions.

Instrumentation effect   a threat that relates to the testing effect. While researchers may attempt to avoid the testing effect by using different instruments for the pretest and posttest, the change of the instrument for measuring the dependent variable can influence the research outcome.

Internal validity   the extent to which confounding variables do not influence the research outcomes. It is the most fundamental type of research validity because it is concerned with the logic of the causal-like relationship between the independent and dependent variables under examination.

Interrater reliability   the extent to which two raters agree with each other in their rating.

Interval scale   a type of measurement scale that has both the feature of ordinal scales and equal distances or intervals (e.g. language test scores, personality scores and language aptitude scores).

Intrarater reliability   the extent to which an individual rater is consistent with their ratings.

John Henry effect   this phenomenon occurs when participants in the control group invest more effort in their learning to compete with those in the experimental group.

Kendall's tau-b correlation   a non-parametric alternative to the Spearman correlation that is useful for examining the level of agreement and disagreement between two sources of data.

Kruskal–Wallis test   a non-parametric test that has a function similar to that of the one-way ANOVA (between-group).

Kurtosis statistic   a statistic that shows the extent to which the shape of the distribution is pointy. A normally distributed data set has a kurtosis value of zero.

Language proficiency test   a test that is based on a theoretical model of language proficiency. It can assess students' knowledge of, and ability to use, a language in general without reference to a curriculum or syllabus.

Levene's test for equality of variances   an inferential statistic used to examine whether two experimental groups have equal variance.

Likert scale   a discrete response scale from which research participants choose a single response (e.g. 1 [never], 2 [rarely], 3 [often], 4 [usually] or 5 [always]). It is named after Rensis Likert who was the first to develop it to quantify a construct of interest.

Longitudinal research   research in which researchers collect the same aspects of information from the same participant(s) over a period of time. This contrasts with cross-sectional research.

Manipulation   researchers' control of independent variables by holding several conditions for two or more groups of comparisons constant. Manipulation of variables helps experimental researchers to avoid the potential confounding effects on the experimental factor being examined.

Mann–Whitney U test   a non-parametric test that has a function similar to that of the independent-samples t-test.

Matching technique   a technique that ensures participant groups are equivalent in terms of personal characteristics or traits.

Maturation effect   a threat to the internal validity of an experimental study associated with biological, cognitive or psychological developments that occur naturally. It interferes with the effect of an experiment on the dependent variable of interest.

Mean   the average of the data/scores.

Measurement   the act of assigning values to something.

Measurement instrument   an instrument that is used to measure and show the extent or the quantity of a certain feature or characteristic of variables (e.g. motivation, language proficiency or beliefs).

Median   the value that divides the data set exactly into two sets: half the scores are smaller than the median and half the scores are larger.

Mixed-methods research   research that integrates quantitative and qualitative methods in a single study.

Mode   the value that occurs most frequently in the data.

Naturalistic data   data that occurs naturally without researchers' intervention or act of gathering.

Nominal scale   a type of data measurement scale that uses numbers to label or classify variables into categories.

Normal distribution   the shape of the data distribution that is unimodal (one mode), symmetrical about the mean, and bell-shaped.

Novelty effect   a threat that involves the innovative look of a treatment or method that may excite learners, thereby causing them to be enthusiastic about the treatment.

Null hypothesis   the statistical prediction that there is no relationship between two variables, or there is no difference between two or more groups of learners.

Objective test   a test that can be marked without the need to rely on personal judgments.

Ordinal scale   a type of data measurement scale that is used for ranking some quality or ability. For example, students may be ranked based on their grade point average (GPA).

Paired-samples t-test   a statistical procedure that examines whether two mean scores from the same group of participants differ significantly (e.g. pretest-posttest comparison).

Parallel test forms   tests that measure the same constructs with similar test questions or tasks, but based on new texts or questions.

Parallel test method   a technique that administers two different but equivalent tests (for example, Forms A and B) to a single group of students. If two tests are highly parallel, the student scores on the two tests should have a high correlation coefficient.

Parameter   a characteristic of a population.

Participants   people who take part in a study by providing data related to a particular study.

Pearson Product Moment correlation (Pearson's r)   a measure that describes the relationship between two continuous variables.

Percentile rank   a statistic that tells us the percentage of scores in the distribution that are below a given score.

Performance assessment   a form of assessment that aims to measure what students can do (e.g. to speak and write), rather than what they know (e.g. grammatical, vocabulary and pragmatic knowledge).

Phi (ø) correlation   a non-parametric test that is not used much in correlational studies. The phi correlation is, however, useful for examining the relationship between two dichotomous variables.

Placebo effect   a threat to the internal validity of an experimental study that occurs when experimental participants believe that they are receiving a special treatment that can help them improve their current condition when, in fact, they are not receiving any special treatment.

Point-biserial correlation   a non-parametric test and a special case of the Pearson correlation that can be used to examine a relationship between a dichotomous variable (for example, male-female and yes-no) and a continuous variable (for example, test scores).

Population   the number of people we are interested in in a study.

Portfolio assessment   a form of assessment that is related to a collection of language performance samples of students over time.

Positivist paradigm   a paradigm that believes that the object of an inquiry really exists *out there* in the world. In language learning, for example, the positivists would assert that there are things such as language learning motivation, self-regulation and interlanguage inside each language learner's mind.

Postpositivist paradigm   a modified positivism that takes similar stances to the positivists. The modifications are designed to distinguish ideology from reality when conducting research.

Predictive validity   the degree to which the measurement instrument successfully predicts results on some criterion measure.

Pre-experimental design   a preliminary form of a more complex experimental design, such as a randomized design. This design is labeled as pre-experimental because it is not robust enough for conclusions to be drawn about a causal-like relationship or a treatment effect.

Prestige bias   a form of bias related to a situation when participants provide answers that make them look good or feel better.

Primary research research that uses first-hand data collected from research participants or documents to answer research questions.

Probability value a probability point for rejecting the null hypothesis. In language learning research, for example, researchers usually set a probability value to be less than 0.05 ($p < 0.05$).

Qualitative data data that can be described in words, rather than numbers.

Qualitative research research that aims to explore and describe the language learning and language use of an individual or a group of individuals in a natural environment, as well as in classroom settings.

Quantitative data data to which we can assign values or numbers.

Quantitative research research that seeks to determine a relationship between two or more variables using numerical data and statistical analysis.

Quasi-experimental research a weaker version of experimental research in which researchers cannot randomly assign participants into different conditions. They cannot achieve complete control over potential confounding variables that can be threats to the internal validity of the study.

Random assignment a technique to place research participants into groups in experimental research on the basis of chance (e.g. experimental or control groups).

Random selection a typical procedure in survey research that aims to generate a representative sample of a population group.

Range the difference between the highest and lowest scores in the data set.

Ratio scale a type of measurement scale with all the properties of nominal, ordinal and interval scales, and also possessing a true zero.

Reasoning the act of drawing conclusions about a topic under study.

Regression analysis a statistical process used to test whether a one-dependent variable can be predicted from the values of one or more independent variables.

Reliability estimate the extent to which a research instrument, an observation or a coding system is free from error of measurement.

Reliability of instruments the degree to which the results of a questionnaire, test or other measuring instrument are consistent.

Reliability of the research result the degree to which the research result (for example, the difference between experiment and control groups) is likely to reappear if the study could be replicated under the same conditions.

Research instruments tools used by researchers to collect data (e.g. a survey, questionnaire, interview, observation and test).

Research methodology this refers to the theoretical framework on which the proposed study will be based.

Research paradigm a set of related beliefs (or assumptions) that underlie an approach to research and its relationship to the world.

Research proposal a carefully crafted, academic written document that describes what the proposed research is about, what it is trying to achieve, how it will go about achieving the aim, what it will yield and why it will be worthwhile doing.

Researcher-made test a test that a researcher develops for a particular purpose.

Retrospection a post-event verbal report that aims to access language learners' cognitive activities or processes.

Science an approach to discovery of knowledge through the use of empirical evidence.

Scientific knowledge   accumulative knowledge derived from empirical data through the use of an appropriate research method, systematic data analysis and empirical reasoning.

Selection bias   bias that occurs in the process of choosing participants for research. It is particularly influential to the internal validity of an experimental study when there are major pre-existing differences between the treatment and control groups.

Self-deception bias   a form of participants' perception by which they think they can do something, but they cannot.

Significance value   the level in which researchers agree to take the risk of rejecting the null hypothesis when it could be true.

Simple-factorial design   an experimental research design that takes into account different levels of two or more independent variables that may together play a role to affect the dependent variable of interest.

Single-case experimental design   an experiment that has a sample size of one participant. It aims to examine whether an intervention is effective for a particular individual in terms of improvement in learning or behavior.

Skewness statistic   a statistic that shows the extent to which the data set is symmetrical. A data set is symmetrical if the skewness statistic is zero.

Solomon three-group design   an extension of an experimental design that aims to address the problem of having the same test for the pretest and posttest. In the Solomon three-group design, one treatment group that does not take a pretest is added.

Spearman's rho correlation (ρ)   a non-parametric test that typically uses numerical variables on an ordinal or ranked scale (e.g. ranked list of test results, letter grades A–F and steps on a Likert scale).

Spearman–Brown prophecy formula   a formula used to transform the split-half coefficient to a coefficient for the entire test.

Split-half reliability   a coefficient obtained by splitting a test into two halves and correlating the scores on each half. It is suitable for objective tests with dichotomous answers (1 = correct; 0 = incorrect).

Standard deviation   a statistical term that indicates how much, on average, the individual values differ from the mean.

Standard error of measurement (SEM)   a measure of error gives a range of possible true scores for each learner. If we know a reliability estimate and the standard deviation of a test score, we can compute an SEM.

Statistic   a characteristic of a sample that will be used to infer a parameter.

Statistical regression effect   a threat that is often observed when participants with extreme scores (e.g. the highest or lowest) in the pretest achieve scores in the posttest that are closer to the mean score (e.g. the average group score).

Statistical validity   the extent to which an observed causal-like relationship between the independent and dependent variables is likely to be true.

Subjective test   a test that requires a human scorer to make a judgment on students' performance.

Testing effect   an effect that typically occurs when researchers use the same test for a pretest and posttest.

Test-retest method   a technique that can be used to estimate the reliability of a test over time by administering the test twice.

Think-aloud protocol   an introspective technique that allows researchers to have access to participants' online cognitive processing or thinking, particularly higher-level thinking.

Time-series design   a quasi-experimental research design that is used in intact classes in which participants are periodically measured on a dependent variable multiple times before and after an experimental treatment is introduced.

Truncated data   data with a limited range of values, especially with only highest and lowest possible scores.

T-score   a transformation of raw scores into a standard form, in which the transformation is made without knowing the mean and standard deviation in a set of scores.

T-test   a statistical procedure that allows researchers to determine whether the difference in the means between two groups is significant.

Type I error   an error related to the mistake of rejecting the null hypothesis when it is true.

Type II error   an error related to the mistake of accepting the null hypothesis when it is false.

Validation   the steps taken by the researcher to make sure that a measure to be used will likely be valid and that proper inferences can be made about the construct of interest based on the data.

Validity   the extent to which research findings, inferences and interpretations are accurate, reasonable and supported by empirical data.

Variable   an aspect or characteristic of something that can take different values or scores.

Variance   the average of the squared deviations from the mean.

Wilcoxon signed ranks test   a non-parametric test that is parallel to a paired-samples *t*-test.

Z-score   a standard score that indicates the relationship between a particular score and the mean. It allows us to see how an individual's score can be placed in relation to the rest of the participants' scores.

BIBLIOGRAPHY

Abbuhl, R 2012, 'Why, when, and how to replicate research, in A Mackey & SM Gass (eds), *Research methods in second language acquisition: a practical guide*, Blackwell Publishing, West Sussex, UK.

Adams, R, Nuevo, AM & Egi T 2011, 'Explicit and implicit feedback, modified output, and SLA: Does explicit and implicit feedback promote learning and learner-learner interactions?', *The Modern Language Journal*, vol. 95, supplementary, pp. 42–63.

Ahmadian, MJ 2012, 'The effects of guided careful online planning on complexity, accuracy and fluency in intermediate EFL learners' oral production: the case of English articles', *Language Teaching Research*, vol. 16, no. 1, pp. 129–49.

Ahmadian, J & Tavakoli, M 2011, 'The effects of simultaneous use of careful online planning and task repetition on accuracy, complexity, and fluency in EFL learners' oral production', *Language Teaching Research*, vol. 15, no., 1, pp. 35–59.

Akakura, M 2012, 'Evaluating the effectiveness of explicit instruction on implicit and explicit L2 knowledge'. *Language Teaching Research*, vol. 16, no. 1, pp. 9–37.

Alderson, JC 2000, *Assessing reading*, Cambridge University Press, Cambridge.

Al-Homoud, F & Schmitt, N 2009, 'Extensive reading in a challenging environment: a comparison of extensive and intensive reading approaches in Saudi Arabia', *Language Teaching Research*, vol. 13, no. 4, pp. 383–401.

Allison, D 2002, *Approaching English language research*, Singapore University Press, Singapore.

American Psychological Association (APA) 2010, *Publication manual of the American Psychological Association*, 6th edn, American Psychological Association, Washington, DC.

Ammar, A 2008, 'Prompts and recasts: differential effects on second language morphosyntax', *Language Teaching Research*, vol. 12, no. 2, pp. 183–210.

Ammar, A & Spada, N 2006, 'One size fits all?: recasts, prompts, and L2 learning.' *Studies in Second Language Acquisition*, vol. 28, no. 4, 543–74.

Ary, D, Jacobs, L, Razavieh, A & Sorensen, C 2006. *Introduction to research in education*, 7th edn, Thomson Wadsworth, Belmont, CA.

Bachman, LF 1990, *Fundamental considerations in language testing*, Oxford University Press, Oxford.

—2004, *Statistical analysis for language assessment*, Cambridge University Press, Cambridge.

Bachman, LF & Palmer, AS 2010, *Language assessment in practice*, Oxford University Press, Oxford.

Baralt, M & Gurzynski-Weiss, L 2011, 'Comparing learners' state anxiety during task-cased interaction in computer-mediated and face-to-face communication', *Language Teaching Research*, vol. 15, no. 2, pp. 201–29.

Beglar, D, Hunt, A & Kite, Y 2011, 'The effect of pleasure reading on Japanese university EFL learners' reading rates', *Language Learning*, vol. 62, no. 3, pp. 665–703.

Benati, A 2005, 'The effects of processing instruction, traditional instruction and meaning – output instruction on the acquisition of the English past simple tense', *Language Teaching Research*, vol. 9, no.1, pp. 67–93.

Berge, BL 2007, *Qualitative research methods for the social sciences*, Pearson Education, Boston, MA.

Bitchener, J & Knoch, U 2008, 'The value of written corrective feedback for migrant and international students', *Language Teaching Research*, vol. 12, no. 3, pp. 409–30.

Block, D 2000, Problematizing interview data: voices in the mind's machine? *TESOL Quarterly*, vol. 34, no. 4, pp. 757–63.

Blom, E & Unsworth, S (eds) 2010, *Experimental methods in language acquisition*, John Benjamins, Amsterdam.

Borodkin, K & Faust, M 2014, 'Native language phonological skills in low-proficiency second language learners', *Language Learning*, vol. 64, no. 1, pp. 132–59.

Bowles, MA 2010, *The think-aloud controversy in second language research*, Routledge, New York and London.

Brantmeier, C 2005, 'Effects of readers' knowledge, text type, and test type on L1 and L2 reading comprehension in Spanish', *The Modern Language Journal*, vol. 89, no. 1, pp. 37–53.

Brown, JD 1988, *Understanding research in second language learning*, Cambridge University Press, Cambridge.

—2001a, 'Statistics as a foreign language: part 2: more things to consider in reading statistical language studies', *TESOL Quarterly*, vol. 26, no. 4, pp. 629–64.

—2001b, *Using surveys in language programs*, Cambridge University Press, Cambridge.

—(ed.) 2012, *Developing, using, and analyzing rubrics in language assessment with case studies in Asian and Pacific languages*, National Foreign Language Resource Center, the University of Hawai'i at Mānoa, Honalulu.

—2014, 'Classical theory reliability, in AJ Kunnan (ed.), *The companion to language assessment*, John-Wiley & Sons, London.

Brown, JD & Rogers, T 2002, *Doing applied linguistic research*, Oxford University Press, Oxford.

Buck, G 2000. *Assessing listening*, Cambridge University Press, Cambridge.

Burns, A 2010, 'Action research', in B Paltridge & A Phakiti (eds), *Continuum companion to research methods in applied linguistics*, Continuum, London.

Carr, NT 2011, *Designing and analyzing language tests*, Oxford University Press, Oxford.

Carroll, J & Sapon, S 1959, *Modern language aptitude test (MLAT)*, Psychological Cooperation, SanAntonio, CA.

Casanave, CP 2010, 'Case studies', in B Paltridge & A Phakiti (eds), *Continuum companion to research methods in applied linguistics*, Continuum, London.

Chaudron, C 1988, *Second language classrooms: research on teaching and learning*, Cambridge University Press, Cambridge.

Chen, C & Truscott, J 2010, 'The effects of repetition and L2 lexicalization on incidental vocabulary acquisition', *Applied Linguistics*, vol. 31, no. 5, pp. 693–713.

Cohen, J 1988, *Statistical power analysis for the behavioral sciences*, Sage, Newbury Park, CA.

—1992, 'A power primer', *Psychological Bulletin*, vol. 112, no. 1, pp. 155–9.

Cook, TD & Shadish, WR 1994, 'Social experiments: some developments over the past fifteen years', *Annual Review of Psychology*, vol. 45, pp. 545–80.

Creswell, JW 2014, *Research design: qualitative, quantitative, and mixed methods approaches*, 4th edn, Sage, Thousand Oaks.

Cronbach, L 1988, 'Five perspectives on validity argument', in H Wainer & H Braun (eds), *Test validity*, Lawrence Erlbaum, Hillsdale, NJ.

Cross, J 2009, 'Effects of listening strategy instruction on news videotext comprehension', *Language Teaching Research*, vol. 13, no. 2, pp. 151–76.

Davidson, F & Lynch, BK 2002, *Testcraft: A teacher's guide to writing and using language test specifications*, Yale University Press, New Haven and London.

Davies, A & Elder, C (eds) 2004, *Handbook of applied linguistics*, Blackwell, London.

Dörnyei, Z 2005, *The psychology of the language learner: individual differences in second language acquisition*, Routledge, New York.

—2007, *Research methods in applied linguistics: quantitative, qualitative, and mixed methodologies*, Oxford University Press, Oxford.

Dörnyei, Z with Taguchi, T (2010). *Questionnaires in second language research: Construction, administration, and processing*, 2nd edn, New York and London: Routledge.

Doughty, CJ 2014, 'Assessing aptitude', in AJ Kunnan (ed.), *The companion to language assessment*, John-Wiley & Sons, London.

Doughty, C, Campbell, S, Bunting, M, Mislevy, M, Bowles, A & Koeth J 2010, 'Predicting near-native L2 ability: The factor structure and reliability of Hi-LAB', in MT Prior, Y Watanabe & S-K Lee (eds), *Selected proceedings of the 2008 Second Language Research Forum: Exploring SLA perspectives, positions, and practice*, Cascadilla Press, Somerville, MA.

Doughty, CJ & Long, MH (eds) 2003, *The handbook of second language acquisition*, Blackwell Publishing, Malden, MA.

Duff, P 2008, *Case study research in applied linguistics*, Routledge, New York.

Eckerth, J & Tavakoli, P 2012, 'The effects of word exposure frequency and elaboration of word processing on incidental L2 vocabulary acquisition through reading', *Language Teaching Research*, vol. 16, no. 2, pp. 227–52.

Ellis, R 2008, *The study of second language acquisition*, 2nd edn, Oxford University Press, Oxford.

Erdener, VD & Burnham, DK 2005, 'The role of audiovisual speech and orthographic information in nonnative speech production', *Language Learning*, vol. 55, no. 2, pp. 191–228.

Ericsson, KA & Simon, HA 1993, *Protocol analysis: verbal reports as data*, 2nd edn, MIT, Cambridge, MA.

Fernández, AP 2008, 'Reexamining the role of explicit information in processing instruction', *Studies in Second Language Acquisition*, vol. 30, no. 3, pp. 277–305.

Field, A & Hole, G 2003, *How to design and report experiments*, Sage, Los Angeles.

Fisher, RA & Yates, F 1974, *Statistical tables for biological, agricultural, and medical research*, 6th edn, Long Group, London

Folse, KS 2006, 'The effect of type of written exercise on L2 vocabulary retention', *TESOL Quarterly*, vol. 40, no. 2, pp. 273–93.

Fordyce, K 2014, 'The differential effects of explicit and implicit instruction on EFL learners' use of epistemic stance', *Applied Linguistics*, vol. 35, no. 1, pp. 6–28.

Foster, P, Tonkyn, A & Wigglesworth, G 2000, 'Measuring spoken language: A unit for all reasons', *Applied Linguistics*, vol. 21, no. 3, pp. 354–75.

Friedman, DA 2012, 'How to collect and analyze qualitative data', in A Mackey & SM Gass (eds), *Research methods in second language acquisition: a practical guide*, Wiley-Blackwell, Malden, MA.

Galaczi, ED 2014, 'Content analysis', in A Kunnan (ed.), *The companion to language assessment*, John-Wiley & Sons, London.

Gass, S 2010, 'Experimental research', in B Paltridge & A Phakiti (eds), *Continuum companion to research methods in applied linguistics*, Continuum, London.

Gass, SM with Behney, J & Plonsky, L 2013, *Second language acquisition: an introductory course*, Routledge, New York.

Gass, S & Mackey, A 2000, *Stimulated recall methodology in second language research*, Lawrence Erlbaum Associates, Mahwah, NJ.

—2007, *Data elicitation for second and foreign language research*, 2nd edn, Lawrence Erlbaum Associates, Mahwah, NJ.

—(eds) 2012, *The Routledge handbook of second language acquisition*, London and New York, Routledge.

Gass, S, Mackey, A, Alverez-Torres, MJ & Fernández-Garcia, M 1999, 'The effects of task repetition on linguistic output', *Language Learning*, vol. 49, no. 4, pp. 549–611.

Gass, S, Svetics, I & Lemelin, S 2003, 'Differential effects of attention', *Language Learning*, vol. 53, no. 3, pp. 497–545.

Gast, DL 2010, *Single subject research methodology in behavioral sciences*, Routledge, New York and London.

Gilham, B 2007, *Developing a questionnaire*, 2nd edn, Continuum, London.

Goo, J 2012, 'Corrective feedback and working memory capacity in interaction-driven L2 learning', *Studies in Second Language Acquisition*, vol. 34, no. 3, pp. 445–74.

Goodwin, CJ 2010, *Research in psychology: methods and design*, 6th edn, Wiley, Hoboken, NJ.

Grigorenko, EL, Sternberg, RJ & Ehrman, ME 2000, 'A theory-based approach to the measurement of foreign language learning ability: the Canal-F theory and test'. *The Modern Language Journal*, vol. 84, no. 3, pp. 390–405.

Guba, EG & Lincoln, YS 2005, 'Paradigmatic controversies, contradictions, and emerging confluences', in NK Denzin & YS Lincoln (eds), *The Sage handbook of qualitative research*, 3rd edn, Sage, Thousand Oaks.

Guilloteaux, MJ & Dörnyei, Z 2008, 'Motivating language learners: A classroom-oriented investigation of the effects of motivational strategies on student motivation', *TESOL Quarterly*, vol. 42, no. 1, pp. 55–77.

Hammersley, M & Atkinson, P 2007, *Ethnography: principles in practice*, 3rd edn, Routledge, London.

Hatch, E & Farhady, H 1982, *Research design and statistics for applied linguistics*, Newbury House, Rowley, MA.

Hatch, E & Lazaraton, A 1991, *The research manual: design and statistics for applied linguistics*, Newbury House, Rowley, MA.

Henry, N, Culman, H & VanPatten, B 2009, 'More on the effects of explicit information in instructed SLA: A partial replication and a response to Fernández (2008)', *Studies in Second Language Acquisition*, vol. 31, no. 4, pp. 559–75.

Hirata-Edds, T 2011, 'Influence of second language Cherokee immersion on children's development of past tense in their first language, English', *Language Learning*, vol. 61, no. 3, pp. 700–33.

Holliday A 2007, *Doing and writing qualitative research*, 2nd edn, Sage, London.

—2010, 'Analysing qualitative data', in B Paltridge & A Phakiti (eds), *Continuum companion to research methods in applied linguistics*, Continuum, London.

Hulstijn, JH & Laufer, B 2001, 'Some empirical evidence for involvement load hypothesis in vocabulary acquisition', *Language Learning*, vol. 51, no. 3, pp. 539–58.

Hunt, K 1966, 'Recent measures in syntactic development', *Elementary English*, vol.43, pp.732–739.

Ishida, M 2004, 'Effects of recasts on the acquisition of the aspectual form *te i-(ru)* by learners of Japanese as a foreign language', *Language Learning*, vol. 54, no. 2, pp. 311–95.

Iwashita, N, McNamara, T & Elder, C 2001, 'Can we predict task difficulty in an oral proficiency test? Exploring the potential of an information-processing approach to task design', *Language Learning*, vol. 51, no. 3, pp. 401–36.

Jarvis, S 2000, 'Methodological rigor in the study of transfer: Identifying L1 influence in the interlanguage lexicon', *Language Learning*, vol. 50, no. 2, pp. 245–309.

Jensen, ED & Vinther, T 2003, 'Exact repetition as input enhancement in second language acquisition, *Language Learning*, vol. 53, no. 3, pp. 373–426.

Johnson, B & Christensen, L 2008, *Educational research: quantitative, qualitative, and mixed approaches*, 3rd edn, Sage, Los Angeles.

Kazdin, AE 2011, *Single-case research designs: methods for clinical and applied settings*, 2nd edn, Oxford University Press, New York.

Keith, ZK 2003, 'Validity of automated essay scoring systems' in MD Shermis & J Burstein (eds), *Automated essay scoring: A cross-disciplinary perspective*, Lawrence Erlbaum Associates, Hillsdale, NJ.

Kelle, U (ed.) 1995, *Computer-aided qualitative data analysis: theory, methods, and practice*, Sage, London.

Kim, Y 2008, 'The effect of integrated language-based instruction in elementary ESL learning', *The Modern Language Journal*, vol. 92, no. 3, pp. 433–51.

Kim, Y & McDonough, K 2008, 'The effect of interlocutor proficiency on the collaborative dialogue between Korean as a second language learners', *Language Teaching Research*, vol. 12, no. 2, pp. 211–34.

Kissling, EM 2013, 'Teaching pronunciation: Is explicit phonetics instruction beneficial for FL learners?', *The Modern Language Journal*, vol. 97, no. 3, pp. 720–44.

Larson-Hall, J 2010, *A guide to doing statistics in second language research using SPSS*, Routledge, New York.

Laufer, B & Rozovski-Roitblat, B 2011, 'Incidental vocabulary acquisition: the effects of task type, word occurrence and their combination', *Language Teaching Research*, vol. 15, no. 4, pp. 391–411.

LeCompte, MD, Preissle, J & Tesch, R 1993, *Ethnography and qualitative design in educational research*, 2nd edn, Academic Press, San Diego, CA.

LeCompte, MD & Schensul, J 2010, *Designing and conducting ethnographic research: an Introduction*, AltaMira Press, Plymouth, UK.

Lee, CH & Kalyuga, S 2011, 'Effectiveness of different Pinyin presentation formats in learning Chinese characters: A cognitive load perspective,' *Language Learning*, vol. 61, no. 4, 1099–118.

Li, S 2013, 'The interactions between the effects of implicit and explicit feedback and individual differences in language analytic ability and working memory', *The Modern Language Journal*, vol. 97, no. 3, pp. 634–54.

Lightbown, PM & Spada, N 2013, *How languages are learned*, 4th edn, Oxford University Press, Oxford.

Linck, JA, Hughes, MM, Campbell, SG, Silbert, NH, Tare, M, Jackson, SR, Smith, BK, Bunting, MF & Doughty, CJ 2013, 'Hi-LAB: a new measure of aptitude for high-level language proficiency, *Language Learning*, vol. 63, no. 3, pp. 530–66.

Liu, Y, Wang, M, Perfetti, CA, Brubaker, B, Wu, S & MacWhinney B 2011, 'Learning a tonal language by attending to the tone: an in vivo experiment', *Language Learning*, vol. 61, no. 4, pp. 119–1141.

Lowie, W & Seton, B 2013, *Essential statistics for applied linguistics*, Palgrave Macmilan, Hampshire, UK.

Luoma, S 2004, *Assessing speaking*, Cambridge University Press, Cambridge.

Lyddon, PA 2011, 'The efficacy of corrective feedback and textual enhancement in promoting the acquisition of grammatical redundancies', *The Modern Language Journal*, vol. 95, no. 1, pp. 104–29.

Lynch, BK 2003, *Language assessment and program evaluation*, Edinburgh University Press, Edinburgh.

Macaro, E (ed.) 2010, *Continuum companion to second language acquisition*, Continuum, London.

Macaro, E & Erler, L 2008, 'Raising the achievement of young-beginner readers of French through strategy instruction', *Applied Linguistics*, vol. 29, no. 1, pp. 90–119.

Macaro, E & Masterman, L 2006, 'Does intensive explicit grammar instruction make all the difference?, *Language Teaching Research*, vol. 10, no. 3, pp. 297–327.

Mackey, A & Gass, SM 2005, *Second language research: methodology and design*, Lawrence Erlbaum Associates, Mahwah, NJ.

—(eds) 2012, *Research methods in second language acquisition: a pratical guide*, Wiley-Blackwell, Malden, MA.

Mackey, A, Oliver, R, & Leeman, J 2003, 'Interactional input and the incorporation of feedback: an exploration of NS-NNS and NNS-NNS adult and child dyads', *Language Learning*, vol. 53, no. 1, pp. 35–66.

Marsden, E & Chen, H-Y 2011, 'The roles of structured input activities in processing instruction and the kinds of knowledge they promote', *Language Learning*, vol. 61, no. 4, pp. 1058–98.

McDonough, J & McDonough, S 1997, *Research methods for English language teachers*, Arnold, London.

McKay, SL 2006, *Researching second language classrooms*, Lawrence Erlbaum, Mahwah, NJ.

McNamara, T 1996, *Measuring second language performance*, Longman, London and New York.

Messick, S 1989, 'Validity', In RL Linn (ed.), *Educational measurement*, 3rd edn, Macmillan, New York.

Miles, MB & Huberman, AM 1994, *Qualitative data analysis: an expanded sourcebook*, Sage, Thousand Oakes.

Mizumoto, A & Takeuchi, O 2009, 'Examining the effectiveness of explicit instruction of vocabulary learning strategies with Japanese EFL university students', *Language Teaching Research*, vol. 13, no. 4, pp. 425–49.

Morgan, DL & Morgan, RK 2009, *Single-case research methods for the behavioral and health sciences*, Sage, Los Angeles.

Morgan-Short, K & Bowden, HW 2006, 'Processing instruction and meaningful output-based instruction: effects on second language development', *Studies in Second Language Acquisition*, vol. 28, no. 1, pp. 31–65.

Moskovsky, C, Alrabi, F, Paolini, S & Ratcheva, S 2012, 'The effects of teachers' motivational strategies on learners' motivation: A controlled investigation of second language acquisition', *Language Learning*, vol. 63, no. 1, pp. 34–62.

Muranoi, H 2000, 'Focus on form through interaction enhancement: integrating formal instruction into a communicative task in EFL classrooms', *Language Learning*, vol. 50, no. 4, pp. 617–73.

Nastasi, BK, Hitchcock, J, Sarkar, S, Burkholder, G, Varjes, K & Jayasena, A 2007, 'Mixed methods in intervention research: theory to adaptation', *Journal of Mixed Methods Research*, vol. 1, no. 2, pp. 164–82.

Norris, J & Ortega, L 2003, 'Defining and measuring SLA', in CJ Doughty & MH. Long (eds), *The handbook of second language acquisition*, Blackwell Publishing, Malden, MA.

Nunan, D 1992, *Research methods in language learning*, Cambridge University Press, Cambridge.

Nunan, D & Bailey, K 2009, *Exploring second language classroom research: a comprehensive guide*, Heinle Cengage Learning, Boston.

Ortega, L 2009, *Understanding second language acquisition*, Hodder, London.

—2010, 'Research synthesis' in B Paltridge and A Phakiti (eds), *Continuum companion to research methods in applied linguistics*, Continuum, London.

Ortega, L & Iberri-Shea, G 2005, 'Longitudinal research in second language acquisition: recent trends and future directions', *Annual Review of Applied Linguistics*, vol. 25, pp. 26–45.

Oscarson, M 2014, 'Self-assessment in the classroom', in AJ Kunnan (ed.), *The companion to language assessment*, John-Wiley & Sons, London.

Oswald, FL & Plonsky, L (2010), 'Meta-analysis in second language research: choices and challenges' *Annual Review of Applied Linguistics*, vol. 30, pp. 85–110.

Oxford, RL 2011, *Teaching and researching language learning strategies*, Longman, Harlow, England.

Paltridge, B 2006. *Discourse analysis*, Continuum, London.

—2012, *Discourse Analysis*, 2nd edn, Bloombury, London.

Paltridge, B & Phakiti, A (eds) 2010, *Continuum companion to research methods in applied linguistics*, Continuum, London.

Paltridge, B & Starfield, S 2007, *Thesis and dissertation writing in a second language: a handbook for supervisors*, Routledge, London and New York.

Park, S 2010, 'The influence of pretask instructions and pretask planning on focus on form during Korean EFL task-based interaction', *Language Teaching Research*, vol. 14, no. 1, pp. 9–26.

Perry, FL 2005, *Research in applied linguistics: becoming a discerning consumer*, Lawrence Erlbaum, Mahwah, NJ.

Peters, E 2014, 'The effects of repetition and time of post-test administration on EFL learners' form recall of single words and collocations', *Language Teaching Research*, vol. 18, no. 1, pp. 75–94.

Peterson, CR & Al-Haik, AR 1976, 'The development of the Defense Language Aptitude Battery (DLAB), *Educational and Psychological Measurement*, vol. 36, no. 2, pp. 369–80.

Phakiti, A 2010, 'Analysing quantitative data', in B Paltridge & A Phakiti (eds), *Continuum companion to research methods in applied linguistics*, Continuum, London.

—2014, 'Questionnaire development and analysis', in AJ Kunnan (ed), *The Companion to Language Assessment*. Wiley & Sons, London.

Pimsleur, P 1966, *Pimsleur language aptitude battery*, Harcourt Brace Jovanovich, New York.

Plano Clark, VL & Creswell, J 2011, *Designing and cConducting mixed methods research*, Sage, Thousand Oaks.

Porte, GK 2002, *Appraising research in second language learning: A practical approach to critical analysis of quantitative research*, John Benjamins, Amsterdam.

—2010, *Appraising research in second language learning: a practical approach to critical analysis of quantitative research*, 2nd edn, John Benjamins, Amsterdam.

Punch, KF 2005, *Introduction to social research: quantitative and qualitative Approaches*, Sage, London.

Purpura, JE 2004, *Assessing grammar*, Cambridge University Press, Cambridge.

Rahimi, M 2013, 'Is training student reviewers worth its while?: a study of how training influences the quality of students' feedback and writing', *Language Teaching Research*, vol. 17, no. 1, pp. 67–89.

Read, J 2000, *Assessing vocabulary*, Cambridge University Press, Cambridge.

Reinders, H 2009, 'Learner uptake and acquisition in three grammar-oriented production activities', *Language Teaching Research*, vol. 13, no. 2, pp. 201–22.

Riazi, M & Candlin, CN 2014, 'Mixed-methods research in language teaching and learning: Opportunities, issues and challenges, *Language Teaching*, vol. 47, no. 2, pp. 135–73.

Richards, K 2003, *Qualitative inquiry in TESOL*, Palgrave Macmillan, New York, NY.

Ross, S 1998, 'Self-assessment in second language testing: A meta-analysis and analysis of experiential factors', *Language Testing*, vol. 15, no. 1, pp. 1–20.

Sagarra, N & Abbuhl, R 2013, 'Optimizing the noticing of recasts via computer-delivered feedback: Evidence that oral input enhancement and working memory help second language learning', *The Modern Language Journal*, vol. 97, no. 1, pp. 196–216.

Sasaki, M 2014, 'Introspective methods', in AJ Kunnan (ed.), *The companion to language assessment*, John Wiley & Sons, London.

Satar, HM & Özdener, N 2008, 'The effects of synchronous CMC on speaking proficiency and anxiety: text versus voice chat', *The Modern Language Journal*, vol. 92, no. 4, pp. 595–613.

Seliger, HW & Shohamy, E 1989, *Second language research methods*, Oxford University Press, Oxford.

Serrano, R 2010, 'The time factor in EFL classroom practice', *Language Learning*, vol. 61, no. 1, pp. 117–45.

Sheen, Y 2010, 'Differential effects of oral and written corrective feedback in the ESL classroom', *Studies in Second Language Acquisition*, vol. 32, no. 2, pp. 203–34.

Shintani, N 2011, 'A comparative study of the effects of input-based and production-based instruction on vocabulary acquisition by young EFL learners', *Language Teaching Research*, vol. 15, no. 2, pp. 137–58.

Shintani, N, Ellis, N & Suzuki W 2014, 'Effects of written feedback and revision on learners' accuracy in using two English grammatical structures, *Language Learning*, vol. 64, no. 1, pp. 103–31.

Solomon, RL 1949, 'On extension of control group design', Pschological Bulletin, vol. 46, no. 2, pp. 137–50.

Spada, N & Fröhlich, M 1995, *The communicative orientation of language teaching observation scheme: coding convention and applications*, National Centre for English Language Teaching and Research, Macquarie, Sydney.

Spada, N & Lyster, R 1997, 'Macroscopic and microscopic views of L2 classrooms, *TESOL Quarterly*, vol. 31, no. 4, pp. 787–95.

Stafford, CA, Bowden, HW & Sanz, C 2011, 'Optimizing language instruction: matters of explicitness, practice, and cue learning', *Language Learning*, vol. 62, no. 3, 741–68.

Starfield, S 2010, 'Ethnographies' in B Paltridge and A Phakiti (eds), *Continuum companion to research methods in applied linguistics*, Continuum, London:

Stevens, SS 1946, 'On the theory of scales of measurement', Science, vol. 103, no. 2684, pp. 677–80.

Strapp, CM, Helmick, AL, Tonkovich, HM & Bleakney, DM 2011, 'Effects of negative and positive evidence on adult word learning', *Language Learning*, vol. 61, no. 2, pp. 506–32.

Sueyoshi, A & Hardison, DM 2005, 'The role of gestures and facial cues in second language listening comprehension', *Language Learning*, vol. 55, no. 4, pp. 661–99.

Takimoto, M 2006, 'The effects of explicit feedback on the development of pragmatic proficiency', *Language Teaching Research*, vol. 10, no. 4, pp. 393–417.

—2007, 'The effects of input-based tasks on the development of learners' pragmatic proficiency', *Applied Linguistics*, vol. 30, no. 1, pp. 1–25.

—2008, 'The effects of deductive and inductive instruction on the development of language learners' pragmatic competence', *The Modern Language Journal*, vol. 92, no. 3, pp. 369–86.

Talmy, S 2010, 'Qualitative interviews in applied linguistics: From research instruments to social practice', *Annual Review of Applied Linguistics*, vol. 30, pp. 128–48.

Tashakkori, A 2009, Foundations of mixed methods research: integrating quantitative and qualitative approaches in the social and behavioral sciences, Sage, Thousand Oaks, CA.

Tian, L & Macaro, E 2012, 'Comparing the effect of teacher codeswitching with English-only explanations on the vocabulary acquisition of Chinese university students: A lexical focus-on-form study.' Language Teaching Research, vol. 16, no. 3, pp. 367–90.

Urbaniak, GC & Plous, S 1997–2014, viewed 1 January 2014, <http://www.randomizer.org/>.

Urdan, TC 2005, Statistics in plain English, 2nd edn, Lawrence Erlbaum Associates, Mahwah, NJ.

Vainio, S, Pajunen, A & Hyönä, J 2014, 'L1 and L2 word recognition in Finnish: examining L1 effects on L2 processing of morphological complexity and morphophonological transparency', Studies in Second Language Acquisition, vol. 36, no. 1, pp. 133–62.

Van Beuningen, C, De Jong, NH, Kuiken, F 2011, 'Evidence on the effectiveness of comprehensive error correction in second language writing', Language Learning, vol.62, no.1, pp.1–41.

Van Gelderen, A, Oostdam, R & van Schooten, E 2011, 'Does foreign language writing benefit from increased lexical fluency? Evidence from a classroom experiment', Language Learning, vol. 61, no. 1, pp. 281–321.

Vandergrift, L & Tafaghodtari, MH 2010, 'Teaching L2 learners how to listen does make a difference: an empirical study, Language Learning, vol. 60, no. 2, pp. 470–97.

Viera, AJ & Garrett, JM 2005, 'Understanding interobserver agreement: the Kappa statistics', Family Medicine, vol. 37, no. 5, pp. 360–3.

Walters, J & Bozkurt, N 2009, 'The effect of keeping vocabulary notebooks on vocabulary acquisition', Language Teaching Research, vol. 13, no. 4, pp. 403–22.

Weigle, SC 2004. Assessing writing, Cambridge University Press, Cambridge.

Winke, PM 2013, 'The effects of input enhancement on grammar learning and comprehension', Studies in Second Language Acquisition, vol.35, no. 2, pp. 323–352.

Wolery, M & Lane, KL 2010, 'Writing tasks: literature reviews, research proposals, and final reports', in DL Gast, Single-subject research methodology in behavioral science, Routledge, New York and London.

Woodrow, L 2010, 'Researching motivation', in B Paltridge & A Phakiti (eds.), Continuum companion to second language research methods, Continuum, London.

Yang, Y, Buckendahl, CW, Juszkewicz, PJ & Bhola, DS 2002, 'A review of strategies for validating computer-automated scoring', Applied Measurement in Education, vol. 15, no. 4, pp. 391–412.

Yang, Y & Lyster, R 2010, 'Effects of form-focused practice and feedback on Chinese EFL learners' acquisition of regular and irregular past tense forms', Studies in Second Language Acquisition, vol. 32, no. 2, pp. 235–63.

Yilmaz, Y 2011, 'Task effects on focus on form in synchronous computer-mediated communication', The Modern Language Journal, vol. 95, no. 1, 115–32.

Yilmaz, Y & Yuksel, D 2011, 'Effects of communication mode and salience on recasts: a first exposure study, *Language Teaching Research*, vol. 15, no. 4, pp. 457–77.

Zyzik, E 2011, 'Second language idiom learning: the effects of lexical knowledge and pedagogical sequencing', *Language Teaching Research*, vol. 15, no. 5, pp. 413–33.

INDEX